25.00
25

The Socialist
Workers Party
in World War II

James P. Cannon
WRITINGS AND SPEECHES, 1940-43

The Socialist Workers Party in World War II

PATHFINDER PRESS, NEW YORK

Edited by Les Evans

Library of Congress Catalog Card Number 75-20719
ISBN: 0-87348-456-8 (cloth); 0-87348-457-6 (paper)
Manufactured in the United States of America

First Edition, 1975

Pathfinder Press, Inc.
410 West Street
New York, N.Y. 10014

CONTENTS

James P. Cannon at Trotsky Memorial Meeting, August 1940.

About the Author

James Patrick Cannon was born in Rosedale, Kansas, on February 11, 1890, into a working-class Irish family. Won to socialist ideas by his father, he joined the Socialist Party in 1908 and the Industrial Workers of the World in 1911 when he was twenty-one. In the IWW Cannon worked with Vincent St. John, "Big Bill" Haywood, and Frank Little as a strike organizer and journalist. As a leader of the Socialist Party left wing after the Russian Revolution, he joined the Communist Party in September 1919 and was elected to its Central Committee in 1920. One of the key leaders of the CP in its first decade, he served on the Presidium of the Communist International in Moscow (1922-23) and headed the International Labor Defense (1925-28). Won over to Trotsky's Left Opposition at the Sixth World Congress of the Comintern in Moscow in 1928, he was expelled from the CP later that year for Trotskyism. With Max Shachtman and Martin Abern he was a founding leader of the Communist League of America, the first American Trotskyist organization, and served as editor of its newspaper, *The Militant.*

Cannon was a founder of the Socialist Workers Party in January 1938 and a participant in the founding conference of the Fourth International held in France later that year, where he was elected to the International Executive Committee. Convicted with seventeen other leaders of the SWP and of the Minneapolis Teamsters union in 1941 for opposing the war policy of the American government, Cannon served thirteen months of a sixteen-month sentence at Sandstone penitentiary in 1944-45. Cannon was the national secretary of the SWP until 1953. Thereafter he was the party's national chairman, and later national chairman emeritus until his death on August 21, 1974.

James P. Cannon's more than sixty years of active struggle in the cause of socialism are recorded in his many books. Published in his lifetime were *Socialism on Trial* (1942), *The Struggle for a Proletarian Party* (1943), *The History of American Trotskyism* (1944), *America's Road to Socialism* (1953), *Notebook of an Agitator* (1958), *The First Ten Years of American Communism* (1962), *Letters from Prison* (1968), *Speeches for Socialism* (1971), and *Speeches to the Party* (1973). This volume is one of a posthumous series of his writings and speeches.

INTRODUCTION

The great radical labor upsurge of the 1930s in Western Europe and the United States ended in 1939, engulfed in the abyss of the Second World War. The war, as James P. Cannon would remark, was the price paid by the working class for the failure of its official leaders to lead in seizing the opportunity of the 1930s at its flood and wresting power from the capitalist ruling class in one or more of the advanced industrial nations of the world.

James P. Cannon was fifty years old in 1940. He had spent thirty-two of those years in the socialist movement. It was as though his whole political life had prepared him for the part he would be called on to play now. He had been a participant in the antiwar wing of the American socialist movement in World War I, and he recognized the Second World War as a continuation of the First. It too was the result of a ruthless struggle for markets and areas for capital investment under conditions of generalized overproduction and intensified interimperialist competition. He had seen proved in life in the First World War what the Marxists had postulated in theory: That the expansion of capitalist production had outgrown national boundaries. It had created a world division of labor through trade and colonial empires, but the vast growth of the productive forces remained ultimately trapped within the borders of competing capitalist nation states. Wars were the inevitable outcome of national economies dependent on foreign markets but excluded from them by more efficient rivals. Cannon was won to the Bolshevik Revolution of 1917 when it showed the way out of this deadly impasse.

The imperialist victors of World War I solved nothing. They won for themselves a breathing spell while condemning the vanquished to an unviable corner of the world market that could breed only new crises and wars. The German invasion of Poland on September 1, 1939, came just ten years after the beginning of the depression that had plunged the capitalist world order into the deepest crisis in its history. The facade of slow, peaceful progress under the benign auspices of a blind, self-regulating market, shaken in the First World War, had been shattered in the economic collapse.

The formative years of American Trotskyism were years of massive unemployment and catastrophic declines in national production as paying markets evaporated. Cannon had observed how ephemeral were the roots of a parliamentary democracy that cloaked the rule of the propertied few. Fascism was no morbid aberration; it was the logical consequence of an economic breakdown that compelled the entrenched plutocracy to abandon democratic pretense and confront the working class directly. Those ruling classes hardest hit were the first to dispense with electoral sanction and seek to impose a fascist dictatorship. Cannon was convinced that their more prosperous competitors, whatever their hypocritical moralizing about the evils of Nazi Germany, were prepared to follow the same path if it should prove necessary. The economic and social crisis had awakened raw class forces that would struggle for mastery over the machinery of society.

Cannon understood very early that it was not enough to proclaim the need for socialism in the abstract. The working class must be organized to fight and win, independently of all the agencies of capitalist rule. This conviction led him to break with the Socialist Party in 1919 in reaction to the proven incapacity of the Social Democrats of the Second International to lead such a fight for the revolutionary reorganization of society. They staked all on the corrupted and illusory institutions of bourgeois democracy. He had seen a qualitatively superior form of working-class organization in the mass Communist parties, brought into being by the shock waves of the victorious Russian Revolution. And he had led a fight within the top leadership of the American CP against the diversion of the party from its revolutionary goals under the influence of Stalin in the few years of prosperity and working-class retreat bought by world capitalism at the price of World War I. Convinced that without a correct program even the most imposing organizational structure would prove incapable of affecting historical events, Cannon was won to Trotsky's side by the exiled Russian revolutionist's lucid explanation of why the isolation of backward Russia had turned the revolution in on itself. A momentous struggle, little understood by the mass of Communist workers in other lands, had pitted the rising, narrowly nationalistic, and privileged bureaucracy of Stalin against the Marxist and internationalist wing of the ruling party led by Trotsky and the Left Opposition.

Cannon was confirmed in his decision to fight against Stalinism when it became evident that Stalin's victory in the Soviet Union had paved the way for the defeat of socialist revolution in Europe. In 1933, despite the warnings of Trotsky, Cannon, and others, directed at the Communist workers, Hitler walked to power without serious opposition from a Communist Party numbering 600,000 and commanding six million votes. The even larger German Social Democracy played, if anything, a more abject role. In Spain in 1936, when Franco's fascist troops rebelled, the revolutionary mobilization of the Spanish working class was hamstrung by Stalin's pledge to preserve capitalism in Spain at any cost, as a bid to hoped-for alliances with democratic France and England against Germany.

The pact for which Stalin sacrificed the Spanish revolution never materialized. At Munich the Western democracies, understanding their class affinities far better than Stalin, opted for appeasement of Hitler. Stalin, still looking for salvation in governmental agreements with this or that imperialist power, then turned to Hitler and in August 1939 signed the nonaggression pact with Nazi Germany that freed Hitler's hands for the invasion of Western Europe.

For Cannon, the crucial task which must be accomplished if socialism were to become a reality was the building of a revolutionary Leninist party that could head off the destructive capitulation to the status quo by the existing mass workers' organizations. It was not enough to recognize that capitalism, as a system of unplanned, anarchic production for private profit, was heir to depressions and wars. Socialism would not arise from those depths automatically. No matter how costly the crisis, if the working class failed to act to establish its own social order, capitalism would blunder on through dictatorship and a new bloodletting.

Cannon and the Socialist Workers Party opposed all theories that the United States was somehow exempt from this process. They viewed the rise of the industrial union movement of the 1930s as confirmation of the perspective of a coming socialist revolution in America, with the proviso that the union ranks must be won to the support of a revolutionary leadership that could supply conscious anticapitalist direction to the workers' struggles. The Trotskyists proved to be too small and isolated to provide such leadership on a mass scale before time ran out and the war began. The majority of the union movement was commanded by leaders who viewed its role in narrowly trade union terms completely inappropriate to the issues that faced the American workers. The traditional union officialdom did not deviate from the paralyzing strategy of rewarding friends and punishing enemies within the framework of the two dominant capitalist parties.

The Communist Party, which won considerable influence in the CIO after 1936, uncritically pursued Stalin's policy of seeking allies among the liberal imperialists who might be expected to bloc with the Soviet Union against Hitler. In practical terms this meant promoting the political fortunes of Franklin Delano Roosevelt with the votes of the union members influenced by the CP. This left the American working class without any political expression of its own, either a mass socialist or communist party, or even a labor party based on the trade unions, that could steer an independent course in time of war. By the default of the entrenched workers' leaderships, Roosevelt, the commander in chief of American imperialism, became the de facto leader of the union movement.

In certain basic political respects the situation at the onset of hostilities in Europe paralleled that in the First World War. Cannon returns to this theme many times in his writings and speeches during the war years and for good reason. From the time of Marx the most elementary premise of the socialist movement was its character as an international movement of the workers of every country whose aim was to unite the whole of the proletariat in the struggle for a socialist world. Of what use was opposition to capitalism in time of peace if during a war, the most destructive and indefensible of all capitalism's evils, the workers' parties abandoned their internationalism and became patriotic supporters of capitalist governments against the workers of other lands?

Cannon's writings are distinguished by their Bolshevik realism. He never deviated from the long-term goals of Marxism, but neither did he delude himself as to what could be actually accomplished at a given moment in the class struggle. He did not see the measure of a revolutionary Marxist party in its success or failure in making a revolution in the course of an imperialist war. That outcome is a result not only of a correct program and determination but of complex objective factors and the organized relationship of forces between the working class and the capitalists, and, within the workers' movement, between the revolutionists and the reformists. But the minimum that Cannon expected from a revolutionary party, however small, was that it teach the working class to place no confidence in its capitalist rulers and that it seek by all means at its command to strengthen the class independence of the proletariat. On a world scale, only the Fourth International, founded by Trotsky in 1938, and in the United States its American section, the Socialist Workers Party, carried out such a program.

The Social Democrats, respectful of the power and authority of the democratic imperialist governments and contemptuous of the capacities of the workers, acted as they had in World War I and began an orgy of jingoistic support for their own governments.

Cannon's opposition to the war policy of the Communist parties was based on the essential similarity of their course and that of the Social Democracy, although it operated from a somewhat different center. The CPs acted in defense of the interests of the conservative bureaucratic caste in Moscow. They did not fragment along national lines as did the Social Democrats. But inasmuch as Stalin had long since abandoned any interest in socialist revolution and was concerned only with military blocs with existing governments, the CPs were led in turn to the support of Britain and America, from 1935 to 1939; then to a shamefaced defense of Nazi Germany for the duration of the Stalin-Hitler pact, from August 1939 until the Nazi invasion of the Soviet Union in June 1941; and finally to an uncritical backing of the imperialist democracies for the rest of the war.

With the outbreak of hostilities in Europe the American government began to prepare public opinion for eventual entry into the war. The propaganda of the Roosevelt administration was both simple and effective. It capitalized on the instinctive revulsion among the masses at the barbaric cruelties of German fascism. A quarter century later this same American democracy in whose name and for whose interests the war against fascism was to be fought would pour down on the peoples of Indochina a rain of bombs exceeding everything it used against its German rival. But in 1939 and 1940 when Cannon and the SWP sought to explain the real war aims of American imperialism, the altruistic pretensions of Washington were accepted at face value to a considerable extent.

The American ruling class skillfully used its pose as an opponent of fascism in seeking to line up the workers from whose ranks most of the conscripts would come for the European and Pacific wars. The Stalin-Hitler pact provided an additional boost to this effort, permitting the ideologists of capitalism to portray communism as an ally and twin of fascism and to discredit the very idea of socialism as a totalitarian monstrosity.

The radical American intelligentsia were among the first to sense the change marked by the beginning of the war. The large periphery of literary fellow travelers amassed by the CP during the 1930s quickly dwindled after September 1939.

Cannon, after decades of experience in watching the effect of alien class forces on the communist and socialist movements wear away the determination of many early adherents, was not taken unawares when a similar desertion began in the ranks of the Trotskyists too. Members and supporters whose social ties bound them to liberal democratic public opinion found themselves suddenly unpopular among their nonparty friends. The reasons for this were more complicated than simply the flight from internationalism in wartime. They hinged on the attitude adopted by the Trotskyists toward the Soviet Union.

After the consolidation of Stalin's power, no tendency within the Communist movement with the exception of the Trotskyist Left Opposition proved capable of adequately explaining or grappling with the reasons for the bureaucratic degeneration of the first workers' state. Trotsky provided an explanation resting on the material privileges of the administrative hierarchy in a planned economy created in a backward and isolated country. Wishful thinking, routinism, or corruption by the privileges at the disposal of the Stalinist bureaucracy led a majority in the Communist movement to go with Stalin, only to become themselves pawns or agents of the Stalinist machine. Others, disillusioned by the police-state methods of Moscow, wrote off the Russian Revolution entirely, ending either as capitulators to bourgeois society or as sectarian abstentionists from the real life of the working class of their countries.

Trotsky made a dialectical distinction between the bureaucratic apparatus that had usurped power from the working class at the governmental level and the continued existence of patently noncapitalist property forms in the Soviet economy. These last he defended. For such a defense to be meaningful, Trotsky insisted that in time of war it was the duty of socialists to take the side of the Soviet Union if it were attacked by an imperialist power. This did not imply any reconciliation with the Stalin regime: Trotsky continued to call for its overthrow by the Russian workers and replacement by a regime based on proletarian democracy.

Among those within the Trotskyist movement influenced by middle-class public opinion such an attitude was easily proclaimed as long as it appeared that when war came the USSR would be in the same camp as Washington in a common fight against Germany. It was quite a different matter after the Stalin-Hitler pact when it now appeared that the war would be fought between a Soviet-German axis on one side and the imperialist democracies on the other. The call for defense of the Soviet Union against imperialist attack had suddenly become a very unpopular proposition.

In the SWP this mood led rapidly to the formation of an opposition within the central leadership. James Burnham gave the most finished theoretical expression to this tendency, declaring flatly that nothing progressive remained of the postcapitalist property relations established by the Russian Revolution. He branded the Soviet invasions of Poland in September 1939 and of Finland in November as "imperialist." The party majority rejected this view. Trotsky and Cannon insisted that in the midst of a global war that would inevitably lead to an invasion of the Soviet Union by one imperialist camp or the other, right and wrong could not be judged by who fired the first shot in some local engagement. While criticizing Stalin's policy, they sided with the Soviet Union in the Polish and Finnish campaigns. Burnham was supported organizationally, though not always from the same theoretical considerations, by Max Shachtman and Martin Abern, two of Cannon's oldest collaborators in the party leadership, who had been expelled with him from the CP in 1928.

The fight broke out within the SWP immediately after the Stalin-Hitler pact and culminated just after the party's April 1940 convention in a split of some 40 percent of the membership. In the course of a written and oral debate lasting more than six months the minority broadened the range of issues to include a repudiation of virtually the whole body of Marxist theory, from its philosophical method, dialectical materialism, to the theory of the state and of classes, to a rejection of democratic centralism as a principle of party organization.

Cannon rallied the party majority in a decisive rebuff to this challenge to the SWP's program and principles, not hesitating to break with even his oldest associates in the struggle to protect the integrity of the movement he had helped to found. Trotsky, in exile in Mexico City, energetically supported Cannon and the SWP majority in the fight with the petty-bourgeois minority. The record of this debate and a discussion of the issues it raised can be found in Trotsky's book *In Defense of Marxism* and in Cannon's *Struggle for a Proletarian Party*.

This collection of Cannon's writings begins where *The Struggle for a Proletarian Party* leaves off, in April 1940. Having settled accounts with the internal opposition, the party now turned its attention to the external tasks that lay before it: to proletarianize the membership, to extend its influence within the trade unions, to seek opportunities to explain to workers the underlying imperialist war aims of the Roosevelt government.

The party faced not only a mounting patriotic hysteria, but a government witch-hunt against radicals as well. During the period of the Stalin-Hitler pact this was directed first of all against the Communist Party and its fellow travelers in the trade unions. Both Earl Browder, the CP's general secretary, and Harry Bridges, the head of the International Longshoremen's and Warehousemen's Union and a supporter of the CP's line at that time, were under indictment. With the German invasion of the Soviet Union in June 1941, however, the CP would make an overnight flipflop and become superpatriotic. From that point forward the SWP would bear the brunt of the government attack.

In the meantime the war in Europe was spreading as the seemingly invincible Nazi legions resumed the march that had been temporarily halted by the "sitzkrieg" on the borders of France in the winter of 1939–40. In April Hitler's forces invaded Norway and Denmark by sea. On May 10 German Panzer divisions swept into the Low Countries and outflanked the French Maginot Line. By June 22 France had fallen and the aged Marshal Pétain had become the head of a German satellite regime at Vichy.

Cannon was now called on to play an increasingly central role in the leadership of the SWP as the party was dealt a series of severe blows by its capitalist and Stalinist opponents. In the

Communist Party in the 1920s he had led one faction among three. In the founding of the Trotskyist movement in America he had been able to rely on the capacities of Shachtman and Abern. And while the political collaboration of Cannon and Shachtman had been marked by crises and disputes, it had been an effective one while it lasted. Now an important part of that leadership team had deserted. And with the split, the party was reduced from a thousand members to six hundred and lost a majority of its youth organization and of its writers.

The greatest blow was yet to come. War is the cauldron of revolution, and the greatest living symbol of revolution was the Russian exile Leon Trotsky. Though he was the leader of a small and persecuted movement, none of the world's governments doubted that Trotsky and the Fourth International remained a force to contend with. They knew that the Bolsheviks under Lenin had also been a numerically insignificant group in 1914. The French ambassador to Germany, Coulondre, in his last interview with Hitler, on August 25, 1939, told the German dictator, "I would also have the fear that as a result of the war, there would be only one real victor—Mr. Trotsky." Hitler shouted in reply, "Why do you then give Poland a blank check?"— accepting as though self-evident the ambassador's statement.

In Moscow also the name of Trotsky still embodied not only the revolutionary past that Stalin had betrayed but the threat of new revolutions to come. The Kremlin's murder machine was set in operation to snuff out the life of this man before his ideas took root in a mass movement. In May 1940, a machine-gun assault was made on Trotsky's home at Coyoacan in the outskirts of Mexico City. Failing in this first attempt, in August a Stalinist assassin gained access to Trotsky's study where he drove a pickax into Trotsky's brain.

Many of its enemies predicted that the Trotskyist movement would not survive the death of its founder. Had the Fourth International been, as they alleged, a cult of Trotsky, they would have been right. Such groups revolve around the personal charisma of a single individual. Trotsky's movement was bound by different ties: by the theoretical heritage of Marx and Lenin, by the common organizational experience of years of struggle under difficult conditions in a score of countries.

Trotsky's death came at a time of the deepest difficulties for the Fourth International. The fascist tide in Europe had engulfed France, and the European Trotskyists were driven underground, facing death for their political activities if captured by the Nazi occupiers.

Trotsky had never tried to substitute himself for the construction of strong national parties of the Fourth International making their own decisions in their own leading committees. But unquestionably Trotsky was the principal day-to-day leader of the world movement. He carried on a voluminous correspondence with every corner of the globe on questions of revolutionary strategy and tactics. He met with delegations from the leadership of the various sections of the International and drew on his vast experience, in and out of power, in a ceaseless round of discussions that helped to orient revolutionists of diverse backgrounds and capabilities. This collaboration was the closest with the leaders of the SWP, who were in constant correspondence with the "Old Man," and who visited Mexico frequently for advice on difficult tactical problems.

That collaboration was now at an end. This blow would most deeply affect the newer and weaker sections of the International, which lacked sizable and experienced leadership groups. The SWP was more fortunate in this regard, but it was still a staggering loss. All the more in that the SWP must now assume direct responsibility for the functioning of an international center for the movement: In response to the war, the Fourth International had transferred its headquarters to New York after the war began in Europe.

Cannon did not pretend to be another Trotsky. He did not aspire to the personal authority that had accrued to Trotsky from his great accomplishments in the founding of the Russian workers' state, his forging of the Red Army in the Russian civil war, or his role in leading the opposition to the Stalinist degeneration of the Russian Revolution. Cannon sought to construct a leadership team that could fill the breach and apply the program inherited from the Marxist tradition.

Measured against the grandiose aspirations of the socialist program, Cannon's accomplishments in the war might seem modest. Such a view greatly underestimates the difficult and demanding task of building a revolutionary party. Measured against the performance of every other tendency on the American left, the SWP's successes in holding together a trained cadre of revolutionary Marxists and standing up to the imperialist war makers are unmatched.

The other radical tendencies without exception fell into two basic categories: those, the great majority, who capitulated to the war and gave uncritical support to the war aims of American imperialism. These included the Socialist Party of Norman Thomas, which was reduced to a hopeless sect; the followers of Jay Lovestone, who dissolved outright and are now long forgotten; and the Communist Party, which after June 1941 built on a foundation of American patriotism that was ripped away in the cold war that began in 1946.

At the other extreme were the isolated ultraleft sects who spoke a language of their own, alien from the American working class and incapable of bridging the gap between revolutionary slogans and the real life of the proletariat. These groups have almost without exception disappeared utterly—who now remembers the Oehlerites, Fieldites, Marlenites, etc.? They have not left a trace.

Under Cannon's leadership, the SWP alone took a principled stand of opposition to the imperialist war and for the class independence of the American workers. Above all this meant avoiding the pitfall of sloganeering from the sidelines. What was required was for SWP members in the unions to fight to protect the strength of the unions, to preserve and defend the right to strike, to convince the workers that the declaration of war did not give the capitalist class a license to roll back the organizational gains made by the workers in the union drives of the 1930s. It meant opposing those forces that sought to subordinate the rights of Blacks and other national minorities to the war effort. It meant opposing the campaigns to dragoon workers behind Roosevelt and the capitalist government.

Another question that faced the party was what attitude to take toward the draft. The patriotic socialists sold war bonds and advocated enlistment into the army. The pacifists and the ultraleft sects called on individuals to refuse to serve. The SWP held a two-month discussion on its military policy and this volume contains Cannon's report on that question at the party's September 1940 Plenum-Conference in Chicago, the first national gathering after the death of Trotsky. Individual draft refusal, Cannon said, would be a futile gesture of moral opposition that would succeed only in cutting the revolutionists off from contact with the mass of young worker-conscripts. The fight must be made not on the question of conscription but on the question of workers' democratic rights within the army. This would ultimately raise the possibility for a struggle for workers' control over the armed forces. The Shachtmanite Workers Party, then passing through a flurry of ultraleftism before its ultimate drift to the right, denounced this idea as a backhanded way of supporting the war. Later events showed that the fight for democratic rights and rank-and-file GI control in the seemingly monolithic army became a profound reality at the end of the war, when the "Bring Us Home" movement deprived American imperialism of the military instrument it needed in the Pacific to prop up the tottering Chiang Kai-shek government, thus contributing to the success of the Chinese Revolution.

Roosevelt's perspective required a docile labor movement and could brook no threat of opposition within the country. Measures to ensure such a condition began to be implemented in the spring and summer of 1941. The biggest potential threat was the Communist Party, with tens of thousands of members and a powerful foothold in a number of key industrial unions. But with the Nazi attack on the Soviet Union the CP's antiwar opposition was instantly reversed and its members became progovernment strikebreakers in the name of national defense.

That left the Trotskyists. While the SWP was much smaller than the CP, it had built a strategic position for revolutionary trade unionism in Teamsters Local 544 in Minneapolis, which had influence among truck drivers throughout the Middle West. Local 544 had long been embroiled in a fight with Daniel J. Tobin, president of the International Brotherhood of Teamsters, who was deeply involved in Democratic Party politics.

In June 1941, after Local 544 had sought to escape Tobin's dictatorial threats by disaffiliating from the AFL Teamsters and joining the CIO, he appealed directly to Roosevelt for intervention. In response to Tobin's request, the FBI raided the headquarters of the SWP and of Local 544 in the Twin Cities. On July 15, twenty-nine men and women were indicted by a federal grand jury in St. Paul on charges of "seditious conspiracy" under the antilabor Smith Act of 1940. Brought to trial in October in the most famous labor trial of the war years, eighteen of the twenty-nine, including Cannon, were convicted and sentenced to prison for up to sixteen months.

Much of Cannon's writings in this book deal with the Minneapolis trial: with the SWP's response to the government's attempt to declare the party illegal, with the course to be taken by the defense in the courtroom, with the need to reject ultraleft tactics in defending against government attacks. These are issues that are as alive today as they were three decades ago, and many a radical group has come to grief in recent years by not knowing how to respond to a federal frame-up prosecution.

The SWP succeeded in turning back Roosevelt's effort to silence it. It used the trial to expose the ruling class's underlying hostility to democracy. An important part of the work of SWP members after the indictments was the rallying of nationwide support for the defendants. The party met the assault in a calm and determined way. Its leaders and members refused to panic or take ill-considered actions. It sought out support from labor unions, prominent intellectuals, and civil libertarians, wherever such could be found who would stand up in wartime and protest an injustice. The Civil Rights Defense Committee (CRDC) organized the legal and political defense and raised funds to publicize the case. It won endorsement from almost 250 international unions, labor councils, and union locals representing 1.5 million workers. This included national endorsement from the Textile Workers and the International Ladies Garment Workers Union, and the backing of fifty locals of the United Auto Workers and twenty locals of the Steelworkers. A large number of Black organizations, including the NAACP, supported the demand to free the eighteen, and a wide range of academic and intellectual figures joined the CRDC.

A year after the Minneapolis convictions, while the defendants were still out on bail during their appeals, the government made a second attempt to silence the SWP. In November 1942 the post office, acting at the instigation of U.S. Attorney General Francis Biddle, seized and burned two issues of *The Militant*, the weekly newspaper reflecting the party's antiwar views. In March 1943 *The Militant*'s second-class mailing permit was revoked, under the wartime Espionage Act, for criticizing the government. It took a year-long fight to have it restored. In the meantime the paper was sent by slower and more expensive classes of mail and was frequently delayed or destroyed by post office officials.

The party's ability to survive repression and even to grow under such conditions depended on the most clear-eyed assessment of the realities of the situation. It could not afford to make the mistake of exaggerating the depth of the antiwar sentiment within the American working class and calling, on the basis of a false estimate, for actions that would not only fail but lead to further victimization. The SWP, which during the Vietnam war in the 1960s and 1970s would demonstrate its capacity to lead masses in antiwar action when such sentiment existed, concluded at the very beginning of World War II that it would have to swim against the stream. One of the most instructive discussions of this problem is the stenographic transcript of Cannon's report to the SWP Political Committee on December 10, 1941, immediately after Congress had declared war against Germany and Japan.

An important factor in the initially prowar attitude of the working class was the jingoistic leadership of the unions. Of the major union leaders, only John L. Lewis defended the right to strike in wartime. The Stalinists supported him in this—until June 1941. The AFL and the wing of the CIO led by Sidney Hillman supported Roosevelt from the outset.

The Communist Party's jingoism after 1941 went so far that the CP publicly applauded the government's prosecution of the Trotskyists in the Minneapolis case, criticizing the prosecution only for being too lenient and not adding "treason" to the list of charges. It likewise defended the effort to exclude *The Militant* from the mails.

The Minneapolis trial succeeded in one of its aims. It destroyed the militant Teamsters movement of that city and replaced it with a hand-picked gang appointed by Tobin. It did not succeed in intimidating or seriously damaging the SWP. In the first year after the split with Shachtman the party had become deeply rooted in the unions throughout the country. After the trial it began to grow numerically, growth that had been almost halted by the prowar hysteria of the early months of the war. In the year after the convictions a hundred new members joined, and another hundred and fifty the year after.

Throughout, the party leadership sought to involve the ranks in a full and complete discussion of every major turn of events. There were no less than three party conventions, two plenary meetings of the National Committee combined with conferences of the membership, and two NC plenums between 1940 and 1943.

In April 1940 there was the convention that defeated the Shachtman opposition in a democratic discussion and vote. In September a plenum of the NC combined with a nondelegated conference of the membership was held in Chicago to take stock after the death of Trotsky and to discuss the party's military policy. In December 1940, after Congress had passed the anticommunist Voorhis Act, which prohibits affiliation to international political organizations, a special convention was held in New York at which the SWP voted to comply under protest with this reactionary legislation by disaffiliating from the Fourth International. In October 1941 a second plenum-conference was held in Chicago to outline the party's answer to the government prosecution in the Minneapolis trial. In February and March 1942 a plenum in New York assessed the tactics to be employed following the formal entry into the war. This was followed in October by a full convention in New York where one of the SWP's major antiwar declarations was adopted. And finally, in October-November 1943, when it appeared that the final appeal would be lost and the eighteen, including the top leaders of the party, would go to prison, the National Committee met to select a replacement leadership that could guide the party in the absence of its most authoritative representatives. That this task was successfully accomplished also testifies to the efficacy of Bolshevik methods of organization and to Cannon's skill in applying them on American soil.

Nor were any of these gatherings mere formalities, of the kind staged by other so-called workers' parties or by the Democrats and Republicans, where decisions are rubber-stamped by the delegates. There is an ample record in these pages of the many disagreements that of necessity arise in any living movement. One of the sharpest appears in Cannon's remarks to the October 29-November 1, 1943, plenum in New York. It was there that in the course of the discussion on the replacement leadership the first sharp exchanges of opinion took place before the party ranks between Cannon and a minority tendency taking shape around Albert Goldman, the party's attorney, and Felix Morrow, then editor of the party's theoretical magazine, *Fourth International*. These differences over Leninist organization methods were to deepen during the time the eighteen spent in jail, and can be followed in Cannon's *Letters from Prison*, which begins where this volume leaves off: When the eighteen, their appeals rejected, entered prison on December 31, 1943.

The party had remained intact through the war, and had begun to grow. It would grow more rapidly while the eighteen were in prison. As the end of the European war came in sight after the Nazi tide had been turned at Stalingrad in January 1943, workers began to look more closely at the war profits of the big defense contractors and the antilabor moves of a government seeking to extend the power of American monopoly capitalism throughout the world in the name of defending democracy against fascism. In 1944 the log-jam broke and the first tremors of the great postwar labor strike-wave began to be felt. The SWP had prepared itself for this through its response to the tests of wartime and would begin to reap the results of this preparatory work in the further growth of its size and influence in the postwar period. But that is the subject of the next volume in this series.

*   *   *

The materials collected in this volume are taken from several sources. Some 45 percent is taken from Cannon's published articles and speeches, all long out of print, as they appeared in *Socialist Appeal, The Militant,* and *Fourth International.* Almost half of the collection comes from Cannon's private papers, which are on deposit at the Library of Social History in New York, and from the files of the Socialist Workers Party national office. This material is published here for the first time. A few items are reprinted from Cannon's other books to round out this collection. A source note precedes each selection indicating whether it has previously been published, and if so, where it first appeared.

The selection printed here is inclusive but does not pretend to be complete. It constitutes approximately two-thirds of Cannon's known writings for the years 1940–43, not counting his books *The Struggle for a Proletarian Party* and *Socialism on Trial,* or *The History of American Trotskyism,* which was completed before he went to prison though published in 1944. The basis for including or excluding material was the general interest in the questions discussed, and the light shed on the history of the SWP by a particular document.

Most of the material left out of this collection consists of resolutions presented to conventions or plenums of the party, which were often edited by many hands and published in the SWP press without signature. In each case we have included Cannon's report on the resolution under discussion, which generally summarizes the points made by the document and which we felt would be of greater interest in a collection of this kind. Also omitted are the many letters of a routine character that make up part of the correspondence of any party administrator, as well as Cannon's purely personal letters to his family. A final category that was excluded were the outline notes for Cannon's many public speeches which would make difficult reading in the form in which they now exist.

A special problem occurs with the previously unpublished

stenographic transcripts of reports and speeches. The source notes indicate which these are. These were taken down in shorthand by a stenographer, invariably with omissions and gaps in the transcript. We have carefully compared the known instances where we have in our possession both such a stenographic record and a published version of the same speech edited by Cannon himself. We did not feel at liberty to edit as freely as Cannon did in such circumstances, but we have made certain small changes that the reader should be aware of. First of all, the original typescripts of the stenograms indicate lapses by ellipses (. . .). Following Cannon's practice, if the sentence reads on logically without the words that have been lost, we have omitted such marks from the text. If an important thought was contained ih a sentence that broke off in the middle, or if the ellipses were followed by an abrupt change of subject, we have left them intact. Lastly, there occasionally appeared a sentence or paragraph that was hopelessly garbled in transcription. Where no meaning could be derived from such a fragment that would add to understanding the train of thought of the speaker, we have deleted it. To distinguish our deletions from the lapses of the stenographer's pencil we have placed all of our deletions in square brackets [. . .]. (This method applies only to the stenographic transcripts, where elisions in the original appear. In a few cases elsewhere in the book, letters or circulars have been abridged; in these cases ordinary ellipses are used by the editors and the source note indicates that the item has been excerpted.)

The reader should keep in mind several things in reading this collection. While he wrote a good deal, Cannon was primarily a speaker and organizer and much of that record by its very nature has not been preserved. Nor is this a rounded history of the Socialist Workers Party in the war. In the division of labor within the party leadership, others took primary responsibility for areas of work or subjects covered in the party press such as the struggle for Black liberation, specific trade union policies, the developments within the Soviet Union in wartime, the defense of Marxist philosophical theory, etc.

Cannon spoke and wrote for different audiences. Some of his writings, such as "The Pathology of Renegacy" (published June 1940), are addressed to the general public or to radicals outside the SWP as well as to party members. Others of his speeches and articles are addressed primarily to the members and close sympathizers of the party. As is the case with Lenin, whom he took as a model in this, many of Cannon's writings are addressed to the party leadership. Each category assumes a different interest and level of understanding and a different set of agreed upon assumptions that did not need to be debated.

Another difficulty is the practice, under threat of arrest and government prosecution for holding unpopular views, of using pseudonyms in many of the letters and internal meetings. Such a necessity has been imposed on all revolutionary organizations at one time or another by the conditions under which they function. Marx used many names in his correspondence, and such famous figures as Lenin and Trotsky have passed into history under names assumed in the course of their revolutionary activity, leaving behind the names with which they were christened, Ulyanov and Bronstein. This usage was also common among American revolutionists such as Sam Adams and Mercy Otis Warren. We have left such pseudonyms as they appeared in the letters and transcripts, trying where possible to place in brackets the person's real name following the first usage of a pseudonym. To help the reader through a multitude of unfamiliar names and references we have provided extensive notes and a glossary of names, including pseudonyms, organizations, and periodicals.

LES EVANS
May 1975

THE CONVENTION OF THE
SOCIALIST WORKERS PARTY

April 1940

This appraisal of the Burnham-Shachtman factional fight and split was published in the May 1940 Fourth International.

The special convention of the Socialist Workers Party, held in New York April 5-8, summed up the internal discussion which has been in progress ever since the outbreak of the war in Europe. The task of the convention was to determine whether the party shall maintain its allegiance to the program of the Fourth International*; that is, whether it shall continue to exist as a revolutionary organization or begin to degenerate along the lines of reconciliation with democratic imperialism. The convention accomplished its task in a revolutionary fashion. By the decisive vote of fifty-five to thirty-one, the delegates from the branches reaffirmed their allegiance to the program and rejected the revisionist improvisations of the opposition.

The victory of the proletarian revolutionary tendency was in reality far more decisive than these figures indicate. More than half of the delegates of the opposition came from New York branches which are predominantly petty bourgeois in composition. Outside New York the delegates stood three to one behind the majority of the National Committee in its defense of the program. But even these figures do not adequately portray the weakness of the opposition in the proletarian ranks of the party. Among the genuine worker elements of the party, those members connected with the mass movement and directly engaged in the class struggle, the position of the majority of the National Committee prevailed by not less than ten to one. The opposition

---

*Glossary of names, organizations, and periodicals begins on page 397.

started and finished as a purely literary tendency, making big pretensions, but without any serious base of support in the proletarian ranks of the party.

The decision of the party came at the end of a thoroughgoing, democratic party discussion which left not a single question unclarified. The discussion was formally opened early in October and continued uninterruptedly for six months. It is highly doubtful that any party discussion anywhere was ever so extensive, so complete, and so democratically conducted as this one. Thirteen big internal bulletins were published by the National Committee during the discussion, with the space about equally divided between the factions; and there was an unrestricted distribution of factional documents, besides those published in the official bulletins. In addition, there were innumerable debates and speeches in party membership meetings. Such an extensive and drawn-out discussion may appear to be abnormal, even for a democratic organization such as ours which settles all disputed questions by free and democratic discussion. So it was. But the controversy which preoccupied our members in this instance went far beyond the usual differences of opinion as to the best methods of applying the program. The revisionist opposition attacked the program itself.

Their position at bottom represented a fundamental break with the programmatic concepts, traditions, and methods embodied in the Fourth International. Consequently it was necessary to carry the fight out to a definitive conclusion. The result justified the extraordinary amount of time and attention devoted to the dispute. The internal fight was imposed upon the party by the war. Disoriented by the war, or rather by the approach of war, a section of the leadership turned their backs on the program, which had been elaborated in years of struggle in preparation for the war. Overnight, they forgot the principles which they had defended jointly with us up to the very day of the signing of the Stalin-Hitler pact.[1]* These soldiers of peace had evidently assimilated the ideas of Bolshevism only as a set of literary formulas. They wrote endlessly, and sometimes cleverly, in favor of them. But the moment the formulas were put to the test of life—or rather the threat of such a test, for America has not yet entered into the war—the literary exponents crumpled miserably and shamefully. And with amazing speed.

---

*Explanatory notes begin on page 412.

Even a revolutionary party is not free from the pressure of its bourgeois environment. In the case of Burnham and Shachtman this pressure was reflected in its crudest form. Stalin in alliance with the brigands of French imperialism, and prospectively with the United States, was acceptable to democratic public opinion; his frame-up trials and purges and his bloody work in Spain were passed over as the peccadillos of an eccentric "democrat." During all this time—the time of the Franco-Soviet pact[2]—all the leaders of the opposition fully agreed with us that the defense of the Soviet Union is the elementary duty of every workers' organization. When the same Stalin "betrayed" the imperialist democracies by making an alliance with Hitler Germany, he became anathema to the bourgeois democrats. Immediately, as if by reflex action, our heroic Burnham, and after him Shachtman and the others, disavowed the defense of the Soviet Union by the world proletariat as an "outmoded" idea. This is the essence of the dispute they started in the party, and its immediate causes. All the rest of their explanations are literary trimming.

Fortunately the proletarian militants of the party took their program more seriously, and showed they are capable of adhering to it without regard to external pressure. Our eleven years' struggle for a proletarian party—which has also been an unceasing struggle against alien tendencies within our own ranks—was recapitulated in our six months' discussion. The convention drew a balance from this whole experience, and put an end to all speculation about the course of the party. It recorded the determined will of the proletarian majority to face the war with the same program that had been worked out in years of international collaboration in anticipation of the inevitable war. It showed clearly that, in spite of all obstacles and difficulties, the party has become predominantly proletarian in composition. Thereby it has reenforced its proletarian program.

Our convention had more than national significance. The Fourth International, as a whole, like all other organizations in the labor movement, was put to a decisive test by the outbreak of the war. Fortuitous political circumstances have delayed the entry of U.S. imperialism into the war. This provided our party with a more favorable opportunity for a free and democratic discussion of the issues posed by the war crisis than was enjoyed by any other section of our International. Our party was also the best equipped by past experience and training to carry out this discussion in all its implications, from all sides, and to the very end. In addition, outstanding representatives of several other important sections of our International were able to participate directly in the literary discussion in our party. The discussion in the SWP became in effect a discussion for the entire Fourth International and was followed with passionate interest by the members of all sections.

It was clear from the beginning that the issues at stake were international in character and that our decisions would have fateful consequences for our movement on a worldwide scale. Thus our convention, formally and nominally a convention of the Socialist Workers Party, was in its political import a veritable congress of the Fourth International. Under war conditions, and the consequent illegality of many of the sections, a formally organized world congress, composed of representative delegations, could not be held. Our convention had to serve as temporary surrogate for the world congress. Politically, there can be no doubt that it had this meaning for all the other sections.

The discussion initiated in our party was transferred into the other sections; and one after the other, they began to take positions on the dispute. In every case where we have been able to establish communication under war conditions, and have direct knowledge of their position, the sections have supported the majority of our party. The international report at our convention disclosed that the Canadian, Mexican, Belgian, German, Argentine, Chinese, Australian, and Russian sections have all declared categorically in support of the position of the majority of our party. The other sections, with whom communication is faulty or who have not formally recorded their position, indicate the same tendency. After our convention there can no longer be the slightest doubt that the overwhelming majority of the members and sections of the Fourth International remain true to their banner—to the doctrine and program of revolutionary Marxism. The decision is made. The revisionist movement of Burnham and Co. can no longer hope for success in our movement, nationally or internationally. The Fourth International remains, after the first test of the war, firm in its programmatic position—the only revolutionary organization of the workers' vanguard in the entire world.

From the beginning to the end, and in all respects, the two factions in the SWP confronted each other in a classic struggle of the proletarian against the petty-bourgeois tendency. This line of demarcation was unmistakably evident in the class composition of the factions and in their general orientation, as well as in the programs they defended.

Despite the extraordinary preoccupation of the entire party with the theoretical dispute, the convention, on the initiative of the majority, devoted two whole sessions and part of a third to discussion of the trade union question and mass work in general. Led by the informed and inspiring report of Farrell Dobbs, the discussion of the delegates on this point revealed that our party in many localities and industries is already deeply integrated in the mass movement of the workers, and that its whole orientation is in this direction. The reports of the delegates showed that even during the six months' discussion, when the literary panic-mongers were crying havoc and discovering nothing but weaknesses and failures, the proletarian supporters of the majority were busy in many sections with their trade union work, burrowing deeply into the mass movement and establishing firm bases of support for the party there. The opposition at the convention was greatly compromised and discredited by the fact that it virtually abstained from participation in this extensive discussion. They had nothing to say and nothing to report. Here again the petty-bourgeois composition of the opposition, and its lack of serious interest in mass work, were flagrantly manifest.

The report and discussion on the trade union question and mass work dealt a knockout blow to the calamity howlers, pessimists, and quitters who have been attributing to the movement their own weaknesses, cowardice, and futility. The convention resounded with proletarian optimism and confidence in the party. The trade union report and discussion, following the decisive reaffirmation of the proletarian program, engendered a remarkable enthusiasm. It was clear from this discussion that the turn of the party toward mass work is already well under way and that the proceedings of the convention could not fail to give it a powerful acceleration.

If any came to the convention with the usual discouragement over a heated factional fight and the prospect of a split, there was no evidence of it. In the camp of the proletarian majority there was not a trace of pessimism, or discouragement, or doubt that the party is going forward to the accomplishment of its historic goal, and that the period ahead of us will be one of expansion and growth and integration in the mass movement. They approached the factional situation in the convention with the calm assurance of people who have made up their minds and know precisely what they want. When the leaders of the petty-bourgeois opposition, defeated in the convention, hurled the threat of split, it was received without a ripple of agitation. The demand of Burnham and Shachtman for the "right" to publish a press of their own in opposition to the press of the party—that is, to make a split in the hypocritical guise of unity; to attack the party in the name of the party—was rejected out of hand by the majority of the convention. The minority was confronted with a clear alternative: either to accept the decision of the majority under the rules of democratic centralism or go their own way and unfurl their own banner.

The majority did everything possible to preserve unity, and even made extraordinary concessions to induce the minority to turn back from their splitting course before it was too late. Their party rights as a minority were guaranteed by a special resolution at the convention. This resolution went to the extreme length of sanctioning a continuation of discussion of the decided questions in the internal bulletin, and a discussion of the theoretical aspects of the question in the *New International*. At the same time, the convention resolution decreed that discussion in the branches must cease, and that all attention and energy of the party membership be concentrated on practical mass work in the next period.

The minority was given proportional representation on the National Committee and a period of time to make up their minds whether to remain in the party or not under the terms and conditions laid down. The minority leaders rejected the convention decision, launched their own publication, and began a public attack on the program of the party and the Fourth International. Thus, by their own decision and actions, they placed themselves outside the ranks of the party and the Fourth International. Their political degeneration is inevitable; nobody has ever yet found a revolutionary road outside the Fourth International. But that is their own affair. Our discussion with them, which was fully adequate, is now concluded.

We are looking forward, not backward. Our task is a deeper penetration of the workers' mass movement on the basis of the convention decisions. That is our way to prepare for the war. In this course we are assured of the support of the overwhelming majority of the sections of the Fourth International. With a correct program, and the assurance of international collaboration and support, we have every reason to be confident of our future.

WE ARE GOING AHEAD EVERYWHERE

April 25, 1940

This letter about the final stage of the SWP split was sent to Charles Curtiss, then the SWP organizer in Los Angeles. It was mimeographed and sent to the party branches for their information.

New York

Charles Curtiss, Organizer
Los Angeles

Dear Charlie,

I was glad to get your letter of April 23 with the information about your windup with the minority. This just about completes the business all over the country.

The attitude you express is universal among our comrades. We are going ahead everywhere without the slightest concern about those who have left our ranks.

The split is definitive in all respects. It is different from any other we have had in this sense. The more we think about it the more we are beginning to realize that this fight was the most fundamental of all. In my pamphlet[3] I spoke of it as a recapitulation of our eleven-and-one-half-year struggle to found a Bolshevik party in this country. In reality it was even more than that. It was a concentrated reenactment of the whole struggle of Marxism against petty-bourgeois influences since the beginning of the movement of scientific socialism.[4]

A few months from now we will all wonder why this showdown fight didn't come sooner and how we survived so long with these alien tendencies in our ranks. The true explanation of course is that it took the pressure of the approaching crisis to develop the latent tendencies. Nevertheless, it is pretty clear now that even in their dormant state these tendencies were slowing us down and hampering our revolutionary progress towards genuine Bolshevism.

We all here have an undiluted feeling of satisfaction and relief and also of optimism. It is clear already that the spirit engendered and the steps taken since the convention were possible only because we finished the business with the petty-bourgeois opposition.

The only place we are hit hard organizationally is in New York—but that is only from a numerical point of view. Even here there is 100 percent satisfaction with the outcome of the struggle and not a single voice of opposition or criticism of the way we handled the fight and the way we concluded it.

The whole experience of eleven and one-half years is a great lesson in the contradictory process by means of which a Bolshevik party evolves and takes shape and the various kinds of lame ducks who are utilized in the process. It would be interesting and valuable now, I think, if one had the time to elaborate on this theme which I touched briefly in my pamphlet. I never came out of a fight feeling as *clean,* and as free from regrets, as in this case. All the other comrades here express the same sentiments.

Proportionately, the Oehlerite split[5]—which was also necessary and unavoidable at the time—cost us much more blood. They were more serious people and for the most part motivated by revolutionary considerations, badly understood.

What we lose with the split of the opposition combination is mostly pus. As far as I know, a good 50 percent of the Oehlerite rank and file eventually returned to our ranks. We must not expect such an outcome of the present split. If we appraise the question soberly we will most probably have to say that we don't want the return of more than 10 percent of the present membership of the split group, and will most likely not get more than 5 percent.

There are a few individuals in whose case it is still worthwhile to have a patient attitude and to keep the door open. I think you have a few such in Los Angeles. But it would be folly for us to continue to live in the atmosphere of faction struggle, or even to waste time in speculating about the further evolution of any of those who have left us.

I hear that you have succeeded in recruiting three or four

important workers in the aircraft plants since the convention. That is more important by itself than your total losses in the split.

You have received the special circular about the theft of the *New International*. I think nearly all the comrades will agree with our action in deciding not to divert our energies in a squabble over the name, but to strike out with the new magazine. *Fourth International* is now on the press. I think it is the best, and the best balanced, issue we have ever published. The myth that the revisionist opposition has all the journalists and writers will be quickly exploded when it is seen what kind of theoretical magazine we can publish without their assistance.

I am absolutely confident that the *Socialist Appeal* will also show some radical improvements in proletarian content and appeal.

I am sending along some extracts from letters from the field which give a picture of the situation since the split. In your next letters be sure to include brief reports of new recruitment and activities started or contemplated. It is our intention to work up a good column for the paper on the party at work and we need informative items for it.

With warmest greetings to all the comrades,

Fraternally yours,
J.P. Cannon
National Secretary

THE PATHOLOGY OF RENEGACY

Published June 1940

This article about the mass flight of the refugees from Marxism that occurred after the Stalin-Hitler pact was first published in the June 1940 Fourth International.

Recently I have been reading some popular accounts of the scientific work of the pioneer microbe hunters. It is extremely interesting to follow their patient and unrelenting pursuit of the tiny agents of human disease, the obscure germs working in the dark, unknown to the victims. They finally tracked them down and brought them to view wriggling on a glass slide under the microscope. Thus, one after another, the microbes of tuberculosis, syphilis, diphtheria, and other devastating sicknesses were identified and their life habits exposed. Only after this could the cures be prescribed.

In my weekend reading I alternated some of the chapters of *The Microbe Hunters* [Paul De Kruif, 1932], which I read for pleasure and instruction, with an examination of some of the latest effusions of numerous fugitives from Marxism, which I read without pleasure in the line of duty. Both readings, however, could properly be classified under the same head: the study of harmful bacteria. Like the human organism, the revolutionary labor movement, a social organism, must be guarded against infections. A fighter in the cause of socialism is obliged to take notice of what is said and done by its enemies, especially those enemies who pretend to be its friends. Such are those deserters who invite the revolutionary workers to pass over with them into the camp of democratic imperialism under guise of "reconsidering" socialism and Marxism. Such are those who, in the name of morality and truth, serve the social system founded on lies. The operations of these hypocritical morality-fakers, who seek to spread pessimism and demoralization in the workers' movement, are of interest to us in the same way that malignant disease germs are of interest to people who want to safeguard the public health.

The death agony of capitalism not only repels some enlightened individuals of the bourgeois class who foresee its inevitable downfall and identify themselves with the proletarian struggle for socialism; it also attracts to its side a peculiar species of supporters, ex-socialists and ex-radicals—deserters from the workers' movement—who have become converted to a fanatical belief in the indestructibility of the capitalist world order and who do everything they can to shield it from the revolutionary blows of the proletariat. In recent years, parallel with the feverish advance of capitalist decay, these anomalous conversions have increased and multiplied, particularly among the camp followers of the workers' movement. Overwhelmed by the violent social convulsions which characterize our epoch, not a few intellectuals who once sympathized with the workers' movement, and even some of its former representatives, have been seized with capitulatory panic and insist upon communicating it to others. Mistaking their visceral disturbances for the processes of profound thought, they seek to translate their own personal demoralization into a "way of life" for the masses.

They have discovered, on the eve of the explosion of bankrupt capitalism in a new world war, that the revolutionary struggle for socialism is not worthwhile. Boiled down to its essentials, and stripped of its hypocritical pretensions and moralistic vaporings, this is the message of all of them, including the uncouth and not very intellectual rookie in the legion of renegacy, the repentant ex-communist, Benjamin Gitlow.

The fight for socialism is a hard fight, and they are not the first to desert it. Nor are they able, despite their frantic search for novelty, to discover or say anything new. As for their theories, they are nothing but a warmed-over hash of the old revisionism and standardized bourgeois criticism, mixed with the conceptions of the pre-Marxian utopians, who deduced their socialistic schemes from moral considerations divorced from the real process of historical development. As for their actions, the neo-renegades follow in the footsteps of their masters, the Social Democrats of 1914.[6] Their psychological motivation is the same: an inexplicable confidence in the durability of capitalism when it is cracking at every seam, and a disbelief in the power of the masses when they are gathering their forces for colossal efforts.

But the American would-be saviors of democratic capitalism are different from the Social Democrats of 1914 in two respects. First, the latter were more decent; they waited for the entry of their governments into the war before they rushed to their support. The traitors of 1940 are deliberately preparing in advance to summon the submerged and cruelly exploited millions in the mass-production hells, the unemployed, the sharecroppers, and the Negroes to pour out their blood on the battlefields in defense of American democracy. That is the political meaning of all their moralistic fulminations against "totalitarianism." Secondly, the social patriots of 1914 represented great mass organizations of the workers which they in part had helped to build. Their little brothers of 1940 represent nothing and nobody but themselves. The measure of their seriousness and their social value is indicated by the fact that they could not create even a small organization under conditions of the free democracy which they recommend so highly.

They are all isolated individuals, yet each one of them considers his disillusionment with the proletarian revolution an important public event and continually makes all kinds of elaborate explanations of how it came to pass. On the eve of the real beginning of capitalism's second world war, which will crush out the lives of millions and tens of millions of human beings, they write about themselves, their disappointments and reactions, as though these were the most interesting and important subjects in the world. Well aware of their own shabbiness, they feel the need of self-justification and public approval. They are uneasy of conscience and seek to stifle it by shouting imprecations at those who have remained faithful to the banner they have deserted. They give every explanation of their motivation but the real one—the fact that they have no confidence in the socialist future of humanity and no stomach for the struggle to achieve it.

Isolated from the workers' movement and only conditionally accepted by the real masters of bourgeois society, they constitute a little coterie of their own, a sort of apostates' fraternity, engaged in log-rolling and back-scratching for each other, and foregathering in that house of ill-fame known as the *New Leader*. Conscious of the fact that they are practicing fraud, they insist on their "morality," as every confidence man wants to be known as "Honest John." Each of them, separately, is "reconsidering," revaluating, and revising Marxism, and collectively they hold discussions and symposia on the various individual revelations— only to discover that they all add up to the same zero.

After each discussion the fact remains that there is no way out for humanity on the capitalist road. The continued private ownership of socially operated industry and the artificial national barriers between competitive states can yield not progress any more, but only stagnation and decay, ever more devastating economic crises and civilization-devouring wars. In one country after another rotting capitalism turns to its last reserve—fascism. Wars have become totalitarian, and the so-called democratic countries at war are transformed into military camps under dictatorial rule. Capitalism in its death crisis is incompatible with peace, or security, or—if the democratic gentlemen will permit me—democracy. The revolutionary over-throw of capitalism is a burning historic necessity. This prognosis of Marx remains unassailable, asserting itself ever stronger after each new experience.

Capitalism had landed in a blind alley already thirty years ago. The First World War gave violent notice of this fact at the cost of more than ten million dead and twenty million wounded. Capitalism, after the war, could not save itself. It is incontestable that the social patriots at the head of the German labor movement, who believed in the viability of capitalism after its authentic representatives had lost all faith and all authority, saved the tottering structure of German capitalism. They prolonged its life artificially until it slipped into fascism and then plunged into the Second World War. The revisionists and reformists of all shades never tire of repeating that the world revolution envisaged by Lenin and Trotsky after the war did not materialize on schedule, and imagine that this refutes the Marxist thesis. They conveniently overlook the services which the reformist leaders of the German socialist and labor movement rendered to German capitalism. And they never think of mentioning the fact that these worthy German democrats utilized the most reactionary military forces to drown the developing workers' revolution in the blood of thousands of its best sons.

The First World War and its aftermath produced revolutions in Russia and Hungary, revolutionary situations in Germany and Italy, and a mighty upsurge of the labor movement throughout the entire world. In the two decades since the defeat of the German revolution there was the grandiose revolutionary upheaval in China, the British general strike, the revolution in Spain and the great wave of sit-down strikes which signalized a revolutionary situation in France. There has been no lack of revolutionary situations in the past twenty-five years. The thesis of Lenin and the early Comintern proved to be infinitely more realistic than that of the skeptics, pessimists, and traitors who are ready to believe in anything except the power of the masses to take their destiny into their own hands and reshape the world on socialist lines. Capitalism long ago lost all capacity to survive by its own resources. Its firmest bases of support are provided by the reformists and revisionists in the labor movement, who do not understand that capitalism is historically doomed and do not believe in the capacity of the workers to accomplish their historic mission.

Stalinism, which is not Marxist but revisionist, not communism but its mortal enemy, plays fundamentally the same role in the international labor movement as the Social Democracy. The Stalinist betrayal brought even more devastating results because it was able to exploit the tremendous authority of the Russian Revolution with the advanced workers who had broken with Social Democracy and its perfidious twin, anarcho-syndicalism.[7] The deceptiveness of Stalinism was a mighty power for the demoralization of the vanguard labor movement of the whole world. The phenomenon of a degenerated and traitorous bureaucracy, operating in the name of a workers' state which symbolized the Russian Revolution in the minds of millions of militant workers throughout the world, was unique in history. It worked all the more destructively because it was not understood; and in part because it did not understand itself, working blindly in the service of alien class forces.

In politics and theory Stalinism introduced nothing new; it simply took over the baggage of the reformists and revisionists of Social Democracy. Even in methods it invented nothing. Stalin only borrowed, adapted, and intensified enormously the methods of the bourgeois world and its reformist agents in the struggle against the proletariat. Misrepresentation and falsification? These are the stock in trade of the ruling class and its agents; a society founded on class exploitation could not live without them. Stalin did not originate the newspaper lie or any other lie. He simply took over the art of lying and adapted it to his purposes. Frame-ups against revolutionary opponents? Kerensky and his gang, the Mensheviks and Social Revolutionaries, set the pattern in their characterization of Lenin and Trotsky as the mercenary agents of the Kaiser.[8] The murder of revolutionists in the name of socialism? Noske and Scheidemann and similar champions of democracy began this ghastly business. Stalin originated nothing. He only copied and developed the arts of deception, violence, and perfidy to an unprecedented degree.

The social basis of the renegacy of Stalinism is fundamentally the same as that of Social Democracy—a privileged stratum which seeks to serve its interests against the interests of the great mass. The psychological source of the politics of Stalinism is likewise identical with that of all the other renegades—a terribly exaggerated estimate of the strength and durability of world capitalism and a lack of confidence in the world revolution. Acting on this falsely motivated and at bottom unrealistic premise, Stalinism dealt its heaviest blows against the world proletariat just at the time when the bankruptcy of capitalism was engendering revolutionary situations in one country after another.

It is an ironical circumstance that revulsion against Stalinism has been instrumental in leading a whole school of its opponents to a position which, from a class point of view, is on the same level as that of the Stalinists. Seeing in Stalinism the incarnation of all things evil and fighting it to the point of phobia, they arrive at a prescription for the proletariat which is no better and not fundamentally different from that of Stalinism. Stalin recommends to the workers of the world a reconciliation with their exploiters at home in behalf of a fictitious socialism in the Soviet Union. The professional anti-Stalinists recommend an alliance against Communism with the masters of America in the name of a fictitious democracy which can't even tell a hungry worker where he can get a job or show a dispossessed sharecropper where he can find a roof to shelter his family from the elements.

All opportunists and renegades—Stalinist and anti-Stalinist—have common traits. They see only the power of the present day and bow down before it. The fact that rich American capitalism is caught in the insoluble crisis of the world system and cannot escape from it; that it is already past the peak of its development and has also entered into decline and decay; that the all-powerful American proletariat must and will take the road of social revolution in order to save itself—these pitiful skeptics don't believe in that. They don't believe in anything but defeat.

Renegacy is not a doctrine, not a new idea; it is a disease. The reconsiderers and revisers of Marxism cannot teach the advanced workers anything and do not seriously try. They have no program to substitute for the scientific program of Marxism. Farthest from their minds is any plan to organize a movement to lead an attack on capitalism. Their function, insofar as they have one, is simply to spread skepticism in the ranks of the workers' movement and undermine its morale.

In order to save themselves and all humanity from the chaos breaking over the world with the death agony of capitalism, the advanced workers must know the road to the socialist future and take it resolutely. The richest gift of the scientific socialism of Marx and Engels to the proletarian vanguard is the knowledge that the downfall of the capitalist order and the victory of the proletariat are alike historically necessary and inevitable. It is the assurance that the historic process works unceasingly on the side of the proletarian revolution which gives to the conscious movement of the workers' vanguard its confidence, its morale. The disciples of Marx who fight for socialism, not as a utopian scheme but as the realization of a historic necessity—it is they alone, as experience has already shown, who never doubt the future, who keep their heads and persevere in the face of temporary setbacks and defeats. The Marxist doctrine is the greatest treasure of the proletariat precisely because it shows the way. Marxism is for the workers' movement what military theory, maps, superior equipment, and realistic confidence are to an army. The struggle against Marxism, now more than ever, serves only to undermine the confidence and paralyze the striking power of the proletariat. The defense of Marxism against any and all opponents and critics remains the most progressive and revolutionary of all tasks.

To be sure, the latest American crop of revisionists and traitors to socialism don't amount to much at the present time. They are only disillusioned individuals who are trying to spread their demoralization to others. But they talk a lot; and later, speaking with the authority of former socialists, they might get a hearing and help to disorient some workers from the path of resolute struggle. It is that possibility, rather than their present importance, that justifies and necessitates a brutal struggle against them. The smallest infection should be treated with antiseptic. So taught the pioneers of scientific medicine who discovered disease germs and the way to fight them. The revolutionary labor movement must guard its health by the same method.

AFTER THE MAY 24 ASSAULT
ON TROTSKY[9]

June 14, 1940

This letter to Albert Goldman, a party leader in New York, was sent by Cannon at the end of a visit with Leon Trotsky shortly after the May 24, 1940, Stalinist machine-gun attack on Trotsky's home at Coyoacan, Mexico.

Coyoacan, Mexico

Dear Al:

We are finished here, and after a holiday tomorrow with L.D. [Trotsky] will start home Sunday morning. We should be back in New York within a week.

The situation here is very serious, and it is necessary to anticipate and prepare for another attack. We have decided to really *fortify* the house against *bombing* as well as against shooting. Complete plans have been drawn up by a military architect and work has already begun. The money you sent is already being spent for materials and labor to construct the fortifications. It will cost about $2,500 and should be completed without delay. The time of the elections will be the most critical time. We think every effort should be made to collect the funds without delay. We will help all we can as soon as we return.

Naturally, we cannot write in detail about the plans, etc. When we return we can explain things in meetings of party members and sympathizers.

It was a real attack—the escape was a miracle. It is obvious the assailants thought they had finished the job. It is difficult to explain the escape in writing, but I think we can do so orally.

We are all of the opinion that the twice-a-week *Appeal* must be subordinated to the task of fortifying the house here and providing the necessary equipment.

We have had a number of the most fruitful political discussions which we will report on after our return.[10] As I am explaining by wire, the $100 you wired was not received. As fast as funds are collected they should be sent here to Joe [Hansen].

Fraternally,
JPC

FUNDS NEEDED TO DEFEND TROTSKY

Published July 20, 1940

This appeal by Cannon and Farrell Dobbs was printed in the
Socialist Appeal.

To All Party Members and Sympathizers:

Stalin's latest and most serious attempt to murder Trotsky was
meticulously planned and carried out in a workmanlike manner.
There is abundant evidence of the experienced hands of the GPU
assassins. Feminine agents of the GPU were assigned to seduce
the members of the regular police guard for the purpose of
obtaining detailed descriptions of the inside of the house and the
defense mechanism. Others were assigned to take residence in the
neighborhood and watch the house for months carefully to study
the movements of the household.

The attackers were well supplied with necessary equipment for
all possible emergencies—machine guns, incendiary and high-
explosive bombs, scaling ladders, portable electric saw, etc., etc.
The thirty members of the murder band were dressed in military
and police uniforms. Tremendous resources were necessary for
such large-scale preparations.

After brutally murdering Robert Sheldon Harte, the secretary-
guard who was on watch, the attackers proceeded toward the
main objective in their gruesome task, the assassination of
Comrade Trotsky. Hundreds of rounds were fired from the
machine guns into the patio and the house. An incendiary bomb
was exploded in the house in an unsuccessful attempt to burn
Comrade Trotsky's archives.

Scores of bullets were found embedded in the floor and walls of
Comrade Trotsky's bedroom. Slugs ripped huge gashes in the
bedding and mattresses of the beds of both Comrade Trotsky and

Comrade Natalia. Powder burns in the mattress gave mute testimony of the assassins standing at the foot of the bed to fire what was to have been the *coup de grace*.

Confident that they had accomplished their objective, the attackers fired a final volley and departed. But they had failed. The intended victims were not in their beds; they had quietly concealed themselves in a protected corner of the dark bedroom. Comrade Trotsky remains alive to hound Stalin with his merciless exposures of every step taken by this hangman of the October Revolution and the world proletariat.

Intensive investigations by the Mexican police have resulted in the arrest of a large number of suspects. Confessions have been obtained from eight GPU agents who were actual participants in the assault. Stalin now has world discredit for the attempt on Trotsky's life. But more intolerable to him than the brand of murderer is the stigma of failure in an attempted murder. He will try again, no doubt soon. And the next time on an even larger scale and in a more desperate manner.

Events during the Mexican national elections on Sunday, July 7, and the turmoil which has arisen over the counting of the ballots, indicate plainly the dangers of the period ahead. The outbreak of an insurrection is not excluded. There are certain to be periodic flare-ups of open conflict between the contending parties. In either case a good cover will have been provided for a new attack on Trotsky's life by Stalin and his GPU.

Efforts of the Socialist Workers Party and its friends and sympathizers played an important role in saving the life of Comrade Trotsky. Had he been without any special defense it would have been an easy matter for the GPU to invade his home and take ample time to make sure that they had accomplished their task. But the very existence of a special defense made it necessary for the GPU to organize on a large scale for the attack and to hurry through with the job.

This experience demonstrates that the defense must be entirely revamped and made much more intricate and complete. It is necessary to build fire-towers for the guard, redoubts, bomb-proof shelters, and antibomb screening. Provisions must be made for more efficient lighting, additional alarm protection, automatic defense mechanisms, and numerous other measures. The services of military architects, recommended by the Mexican government, have been engaged to assure technical precision in this work. Considerable quantities of material are needed. Skilled workmen must be employed. And above all else, the job must be done quickly.

Thanks to the prompt response of the branches to our first appeal, funds were provided to begin construction and keep it in progress. But substantial additional funds are required to complete the job. It will take approximately $2,500.

Bob Harte has forfeited his young life for the workers' cause. He accepted his assignment like a soldier and made the supreme sacrifice with the courage, devotion, and selflessness of a revolutionary fighter. He joins the ranks of our honored dead, but his name lives on as an inspiration to all. Others have come forward to fill the gap left by his tragic loss, others who know that the reward for their services may be death. But, just as Bob did, they serve loyally and without thought of self.

We have no doubt that all members of the party and all sympathizers will recognize the importance of doing everything possible to reinforce the defense of Comrade Trotsky. Under the present world conditions we alone are in a position to provide this defense. It depends on us alone and we must do it on top of our other obligations to maintain the party press and organization.

Make all checks and money orders for the defense of Leon Trotsky payable to Coyoacan Fund, and mail them to Rose Karsner, 116 University Place, New York City.

> Fraternally,
> James P. Cannon
> Farrell Dobbs

WE ACCUSE STALIN
BEFORE THE WORLD[11]

August 21, 1940

This press release was issued the morning after Leon Trotsky was struck down by a Stalinist assassin at his home in Mexico City. He died during the early evening of August 21.

I have just talked again by long distance phone with Joseph Hansen, secretary to Trotsky in Mexico City. He told me that he was with Trotsky continuously after the assault up until the time he lost consciousness. Trotsky said to him:

"I will not survive this attack. Stalin has finally accomplished the task he attempted unsuccessfully before."

With his last conscious words before lapsing into a coma, he repeated his accusation that the assailant who struck him down was a direct agent of the monster in the Kremlin.

This man, pleading for his life with the guards immediately after the attack, cried again and again: "They made me do it. They threatened to kill my mother."

No one the least familiar with the murderous methods of Stalin can have any doubt as to the identity of "they." Stalin's own agents, members of the Mexican Communist Party, confessed that they carried out the attack on Trotsky in May which failed. No one can doubt that Stalin is equally guilty of this new attempted murder.

We accuse Stalin before the world as the real organizer of this crime.

Stalin, whose regime has enmeshed the Soviet Union in the perils of the capitalist war, thinks that in this way he can silence the voice of Trotsky, which has been the steadfast and eloquent voice of working-class internationalism throughout these decades of Stalinist reaction and degeneration in the Soviet Union and in the Communist parties throughout the world.

He shall fail of his purpose. The fight for Trotsky's life will be fought while there is still breath in his body. We have already announced that Dr. Walter Dandy, director of neural surgery of Johns Hopkins University, is flying tonight to Trotsky's bedside.

The fight for Trotsky's ideas will go on whatever the fate that awaits this titanic figure in the history of man's struggle for liberation. This we of the Fourth International pledge to Stalin and to the rulers of the capitalist world, who have shared their violent hatred of the man who, with Lenin, stood as the living symbol of the world workers' revolution.

TO THE MEMORY OF THE OLD MAN

August 28, 1940

This speech to the Leon Trotsky Memorial Meeting, held at the Hotel Diplomat in New York City, was first published in Socialist Appeal, *September 7, 1940.*

Comrade Trotsky's entire conscious life, from the time he entered the workers' movement in the provincial Russian town of Nikolayev at the age of eighteen up till the moment of his death in Mexico City forty-two years later, was completely dedicated to work and struggle for one central idea. He stood for the emancipation of the workers and all the oppressed people of the world, and the transformation of society from capitalism to socialism by means of a social revolution. In his conception, this liberating social revolution requires for success the leadership of a revolutionary political party of the workers' vanguard.

In his entire conscious life Comrade Trotsky never once diverged from that idea. He never doubted it, and never ceased to struggle for its realization. On his deathbed, in his last message to us, his disciples—his last testament—he proclaimed his confidence in his life-idea: "Tell our friends I am sure of the victory of the Fourth International—go forward!"

The whole world knows about his work and his testament. The cables of the press of the world have carried his last testament and made it known to the world's millions. And in the minds and hearts of all those throughout the world who grieve with us tonight one thought—one question—is uppermost: Will the movement which he created and inspired survive his death? Will his disciples be able to hold their ranks together, will they be able to carry out his testament and realize the emancipation of the oppressed through the victory of the Fourth International?

Without the slightest hesitation we give an affirmative answer to this question. Those enemies who predict a collapse of Trotsky's movement without Trotsky, and those weak-willed friends who fear it, only show that they do not understand Trotsky, what he was, what he signified, and what he left behind. Never has a bereaved family been left such a rich heritage as that which Comrade Trotsky, like a provident father, has left to the family of the Fourth International as trustees for all progressive humanity. A great heritage of ideas he has left to us; ideas which shall chart the struggle toward the great free future of all mankind. The mighty ideas of Trotsky are our program and our banner. They are a clear guide to action in all the complexities of our epoch, and a constant reassurance that we are right and that our victory is inevitable.

Trotsky himself believed that ideas are the greatest power in the world. Their authors may be killed, but ideas, once promulgated, live their own life. If they are correct ideas, they make their way through all obstacles. This was the central, dominating concept of Comrade Trotsky's philosophy. He explained it to us many, many times. He once wrote: "It is not the party that makes the program [the idea]; it is the program that makes the party." In a personal letter to me, he once wrote: "We work with the most correct and powerful ideas in the world, with inadequate numerical forces and material means. But correct ideas, in the long run, always conquer and make available for themselves the necessary material means and forces."

Trotsky, a disciple of Marx, believed with Marx that "an idea, when it permeates the mass, becomes a material force." Believing that, Comrade Trotsky never doubted that his work would live after him. Believing that, he could proclaim on his deathbed his confidence in the future victory of the Fourth International which embodies his ideas. Those who doubt it do not know Trotsky.

Trotsky himself believed that his greatest significance, his greatest value, consisted not in his physical life, not in his epic deeds, which overshadow those of all heroic figures in history in their sweep and their grandeur—but in what he would leave behind him after the assassins had done their work. He knew that his doom was sealed, and he worked against time in order to leave everything possible to us, and through us to mankind. Throughout the eleven years of his last exile he chained himself to his desk like a galley slave and labored, as none of us knows how to labor, with such energy, such persistence and self-discipline, as only men of genius can labor. He worked against time to pour out through his pen the whole rich content of his mighty brain and preserve it in permanent written form for us, and for those who will come after us.

The whole Trotsky, like the whole Marx, is preserved in his books, his articles, and his letters. His voluminous correspondence, which contains some of his brightest thoughts and his most intimate personal feelings and sentiments, must now be collected and published. When that is done, when his letters are published alongside his books, his pamphlets, and his articles, we, and all those who join us in the liberation struggle of humanity, will still have our Old Man to help us.

He knew that the super-Borgia in the Kremlin, Cain-Stalin, who has destroyed the whole generation of the October Revolution, had marked him for assassination and would succeed sooner or later. That is why he worked so urgently. That is why he hastened to write out everything that was in his mind and get it down on paper in permanent form where nobody could destroy it.

Just the other night, I talked at the dinner table with one of the Old Man's faithful secretaries—a young comrade who had served him a long time and knew his personal life, as he lived it in his last years of exile, most intimately. I urged him to write his reminiscences without delay. I said: "We must all write everything we know about Trotsky. Everyone must record his recollections and his impressions. We must not forget that we moved in the orbit of the greatest figure of our time. Millions of people, generations yet to come, will be hungry for every scrap of information, every word, every impression that throws light on him, his ideas, his aims, and his personal life."

He answered: "I can write only about his personal qualities as I observed them; his methods of work, his humaneness, his generosity. But I can't write anything new about his ideas. They are already written. Everything he had to say, everything he had in his brain, is down on paper. He seemed to be determined to scoop down to the bottom of his mind, and take out everything and give it to the world in his writings. Very often, I remember, casual conversation on some subject would come up at the dinner table; an informal discussion would take place, and the Old Man would express some opinions new and fresh. Almost invariably the contributions of the dinner-table conversation would find expression a little later in a book, an article, or a letter."

They killed Trotsky not by one blow; not when this murderer, the agent of Stalin, drove the pickax through the back of his skull. That was only the final blow. They killed him by inches. They killed him many times. They killed him seven times when they killed his seven secretaries. They killed him four times when they killed his four children. They killed him when his old coworkers of the Russian Revolution were killed.[12]

Yet he stood up to his tasks in spite of all that. Growing old and sick, he staggered through all these moral, emotional, and physical blows to complete his testament to humanity while he still had time. He gathered it all together—every thought, every idea, every lesson from his past experience—to lay up a literary treasure for us, a treasure that the moths and the rust cannot eat.

There was a profound difference between Trotsky and other great men of action and transitory political leaders who influenced great masses in their lifetime. The power of such people, almost all of them, was something personal, something incommunicable to others. Their influence did not survive their deaths. Just recall for a moment the great men of our generation or the generation just passed: Clemenceau, Hindenburg, Wilson, Theodore Roosevelt, Bryan. They had great masses following them and leaning upon them. But now they are dead; and all their influence died with them. Nothing remains but monuments and funeral eulogies. Nothing was distinctive about them but their personalities. They were opportunists, leaders for a day. They left no ideas to guide and inspire men when their bodies became dust, and their personalities became a memory.

Not so with Trotsky. Not so with him. He was different. He was also a great man of action, to be sure. His deeds are incorporated in the greatest revolution in the history of mankind. But, unlike the opportunists and leaders of a day, his deeds were inspired by great ideas, and these ideas still live. He not only made a revolution; he wrote its history and explained the basic laws which govern all revolutions. In his *History of the Russian Revolution,* which he considered his masterpiece, he gave us a guide for the making of new revolutions, or rather, for extending throughout the world the revolution that began in October 1917.

Trotsky, the great man of ideas, was himself the disciple of a still greater one—Marx. Trotsky did not originate or claim to originate the most fundamental ideas which he expounded. He built on the foundations laid by the great masons of the nineteenth century—Marx and Engels. In addition, he went through the great school of Lenin and learned from him. Trotsky's genius consisted in his complete assimilation of the ideas bequeathed by Marx, Engels, and Lenin. He mastered their method. He developed their ideas in modern conditions, and applied them in masterful fashion in the contemporary struggle of the proletariat. If you would understand Trotsky, you must know that he was a disciple of Marx, an orthodox Marxist. He fought under the banner of Marxism for forty-two years! During the last year of his life he laid everything else aside to fight a great political and theoretical battle in defense of Marxism in the ranks of the Fourth International! His very last article, which was left on his desk in unpolished form, the last article with which he occupied himself, was a defense of Marxism against contemporary revisionists and skeptics. The power of Trotsky, first of all and above all, was the power of Marxism.

Do you want a concrete illustration of the power of Marxist ideas? Just consider this: when Marx died in 1883, Trotsky was but four years old. Lenin was only fourteen. Neither could have known Marx, or anything about him. Yet both became great historical figures because of Marx, because Marx had circulated ideas in the world before they were born. Those ideas were living their own life. They shaped the lives of Lenin and Trotsky. Marx's ideas were with them and guided their every step when they made the greatest revolution in history.

So will the ideas of Trotsky, which are a development of the ideas of Marx, influence us, his disciples, who survive him today. They will shape the lives of far greater disciples who are yet to come, who do not yet know Trotsky's name. Some who are destined to be the greatest Trotskyists are playing in the schoolyards today. They will be nourished on Trotsky's ideas, as he and Lenin were nourished on the ideas of Marx and Engels.

Indeed, our movement in the United States took shape and grew up on his ideas without his physical presence, without even any communication in the first period. Trotsky was exiled and isolated in Alma Ata when we began our struggle for Trotskyism in this country in 1928. We had no contact with him, and for a long time did not know whether he was dead or alive. We didn't even have a collection of his writings. All we had was one single current document—his "Criticism of the Draft Program of the Comintern."[13] That was enough. By the light of that single document we saw our way, began our struggle with supreme confidence, went through the split without faltering, built the framework of a national organization and established our weekly Trotskyist press. Our movement was built firmly from the very beginning and has remained firm because it was built on Trotsky's ideas. It was nearly a year before we were able to establish direct communication with the Old Man.

So with the sections of the Fourth International throughout the world. Only a very few individual comrades have ever met Trotsky face to face. Yet everywhere they knew him. In China, and across the broad oceans to Chile, Argentina, Brazil. In Australia, in practically every country of Europe. In the United States, Canada, Indochina, South Africa. They never saw him, but the ideas of Trotsky welded them all together in one uniform and firm world movement. So it will continue after his physical death. There is no room for doubt.

Trotsky's place in history is already established. He will stand forever on a historical eminence beside the other three great giants of the proletariat: Marx, Engels, and Lenin. It is possible, indeed it is quite probable, that in the historic memory of mankind, his name will evoke the warmest affection, the most heartfelt gratitude of all. Because he fought so long, against such a world of enemies, so honestly, so heroically, and with such selfless devotion!

Future generations of free humanity will look back with insatiable interest on this mad epoch of reaction and bloody violence and social change—this epoch of the death agony of one social system and the birth pangs of another. When they see through the historian's lens how the oppressed masses of the people everywhere were groping, blinded and confused, they will mention with unbounded love the name of the genius who gave us light, the great heart that gave us courage.

Of all the great men of our time, of all the public figures to whom the masses turned for guidance in these troubled terrible times, Trotsky alone explained things to us, he alone gave us light in the darkness. His brain alone unraveled the mysteries and complexities of our epoch. The great brain of Trotsky was what was feared by all his enemies. They couldn't cope with it. They couldn't answer it. In the incredibly horrible method by which they destroyed him there was hidden a deep symbol. *They struck at his brain!* But the richest products of that brain are still alive. They had already escaped and can never be recaptured and destroyed.

We do not minimize the blow that has been dealt to us, to our movement, and to the world. It is the worst calamity. We have lost something of immeasurable value that can never be regained. We have lost the inspiration of his physical presence, his wise counsel. All that is lost forever. The Russian people have suffered the most terrible blow of all. But by the very fact that the Stalinist camarilla had to kill Trotsky after eleven years, that they had to reach out from Moscow, exert all their energies and plans to destroy the life of Trotsky—that is the greatest testimony that Trotsky still lived in the hearts of the Russian people. They didn't believe the lies. They waited and hoped for his return. His words are still there. His memory is alive in their hearts.

Just a few days before the death of Comrade Trotsky the editors of the Russian *Bulletin* received a letter from Riga. It had been mailed before the incorporation of Latvia into the Soviet Union. It stated in simple words that Trotsky's "Open Letter to the Workers of the USSR"[14] had reached them, and had lifted up their hearts with courage and shown them the way. The letter stated that the message of Trotsky had been memorized, word by word, and would be passed along by word of mouth no matter what might happen. We verily believe that the words of Trotsky will live longer in the Soviet Union than the bloody regime of Stalin. In the coming great day of liberation the message of Trotsky will be the banner of the Russian people.

The whole world knows who killed Comrade Trotsky. The world knows that on his deathbed he accused Stalin and his GPU of the murder. The assassin's statement, prepared in advance of the crime, is the final proof, if more proof is needed, that the murder was a GPU job. It is a mere reiteration of the lies of the Moscow trials; a stupid police-minded attempt, at this late day, to rehabilitate the frame-ups which have been discredited in the eyes of the whole world. The motives for the assassination arose from the world reaction, the fear of revolution, and the traitors' sentiments of hatred and revenge. The English historian Macaulay remarked that apostates in all ages have manifested an exceptional malignity toward those whom they have betrayed. Stalin and his traitor gang were consumed by a mad hatred of the man who reminded them of their yesterday. Trotsky, the symbol of the great revolution, reminded them constantly of the cause they had deserted and betrayed, and they hated him for that. They hated him for all the great and good human qualities which he personified and to which they were completely alien. They were determined, at all cost, to do away with him.

Now I come to a part that is very painful, a thought which, I am sure, is in the minds of all of us. The moment we read of the success of the attack I am sure everyone among us asked: couldn't we have saved him a while longer? If we had tried harder, if we had done more for him—couldn't we have saved him? Dear comrades, let us not reproach ourselves. Comrade Trotsky was doomed and sentenced to death years ago. The betrayers of the revolution knew that the revolution lived in him, the tradition, the hope. All the resources of a powerful state, set in motion by the hatred and revenge of Stalin, were directed to the assassination of a single man without resources and with only a handful of close followers. All of his coworkers were killed; seven of his faithful secretaries; his four children. Yet, in spite of the fact that they marked him for death after his exile from Russia, we saved him for eleven years! Those were the most fruitful years of his whole life. Those were the years when he sat down in full maturity to devote himself to the task of summing up and casting in permanent literary form the results of his experiences and his thoughts.

Their dull police minds cannot know that Trotsky left the best of himself behind. Even in death he frustrated them. Because the thing they wanted most of all to kill—the memory and the hope of revolution—that Trotsky left behind him.

If you reproach yourself or us because this murder machine finally reached Trotsky and struck him down, you must remember that it is very hard to protect anyone from assassins. The assassin who stalks his victim night and day very often breaks through the greatest protections. Even Russian tsars and other rulers, surrounded by all the police powers of great states, could not always escape assassination by small bands of determined terrorists equipped with the most meager resources. This was the case more than once in Russia in the prerevolutionary days. And here, in the case of Trotsky, you had all that in reverse. All the resources were on the side of the assassins. A great state apparatus, converted into a murder machine, against one man and a few devoted disciples. So if they finally broke through, we have only to ask ourselves, did we do all we could to prevent it or postpone it? Yes, we did our best. In all conscience, we must say we did our best.

In the last weeks after the assault of May 24, we once again put on the agenda of our leading committee the question of the protection of Comrade Trotsky. Every comrade agreed that this is our most important task, most important for the masses of the whole world and for the future generations, that above all we do everything in our power to protect the life of our genius, our comrade, who helped and guided us so well. A delegation of party leaders made a visit to Mexico. It turned out to be our last visit. There, on that occasion, in consultation with him, we agreed upon a new campaign to strengthen the guard. We collected money in this country to fortify the house at the cost of thousands of dollars; all our members and sympathizers responded with great sacrifices and generosity.

And still the murder machine broke through. But those who helped even in the smallest degree, either financially or with their physical efforts, like our brave young comrades of the guard, will never be sorry for what they did to protect and help the Old Man.

At the hour Comrade Trotsky was finally struck down, I was returning by train from a special journey to Minneapolis. I had gone there for the purpose of arranging for new and especially qualified comrades to go down and strengthen the guard in Coyoacan. On the way home I sat in the railroad train with a feeling of satisfaction that the task of the trip had been accomplished, reinforcements of the guard had been provided for.

Then, as the train passed through Pennsylvania, about four o'clock in the morning, they brought the early papers with the news that the assassin had broken through the defenses and driven a pickax into the brain of Comrade Trotsky. That was the beginning of a terrible day, the saddest day of our lives, when we waited, hour by hour, while the Old Man fought his last fight and struggled vainly with death. But even then, in that hour of terrible grief, when we received the fatal message over the long-distance telephone: "The Old Man is dead"—even then, we didn't permit ourselves to stop for weeping. We plunged immediately into the work to defend his memory and carry out his testament. And we worked harder than ever before, because for the first time we realized with full consciousness that we have to do it all now. We can't lean on the Old Man anymore. What is done now, we must do. That is the spirit in which we have got to work from now on.

The capitalist masters of the world instinctively understood the meaning of the name of Trotsky. The friend of the oppressed, the maker of revolutions, was the incarnation of all that they hated and feared! Even in death they revile him. Their newspapers splash their filth over his name. He was the world's exile in the time of reaction. No door was open to him anywhere except that of the Republic of Mexico. The fact that Trotsky was barred from all capitalist countries is in itself the clearest refutation of all the slanders of the Stalinists, of all their foul accusations that he betrayed the revolution, that he had turned against the workers. They never convinced the capitalist world of that. Not for a moment.

The capitalists—all kinds—fear and hate even his dead body! The doors of our great democracy are open to many political refugees, of course. All sorts of reactionaries; democratic scoundrels who betrayed and deserted their people; monarchists, and even fascists—they have all been welcomed in New York harbor. But not even the dead body of the friend of the oppressed could find asylum here! We shall not forget that! We shall nourish that grievance close to our hearts and in good time we shall take our revenge.

The great and powerful democracy of Roosevelt and Hull wouldn't let us bring his body here for the funeral. But he is here just the same. All of us feel that he is here in this hall tonight— not only in his great ideas, but also, especially tonight, in our memory of him as a man. We have a right to be proud that the best man of our time belonged to us, the greatest brain and strongest and most loyal heart. The class society we live in exalts the rascals, cheats, self-seekers, liars, and oppressors of the people. You can hardly name an intellectual representative of the decaying class society, of high or low degree, who is not a miserable hypocrite and contemptible coward, concerned first of all with his own inconsequential personal affairs and saving his own worthless skin. What a wretched tribe they are. There is no honesty, no inspiration, nothing in the whole of them. They have not a single man that can strike a spark in the heart of youth. Our Old Man was made of better stuff. Our Old Man was made of entirely different stuff. He towered above these pygmies in his moral grandeur.

Comrade Trotsky not only struggled for a new social order based on human solidarity as a future goal; he lived every day of his life according to its higher and nobler standards. They wouldn't let him be a citizen of any country. But, in truth, he was much more than that. He was already, in his mind and in his conduct, a citizen of the communist future of humanity. That memory of him as a man, as a comrade, is more precious than gold and rubies. We can hardly understand a man of that type living among us. We are all caught in the steel net of the class society with its inequalities, its contradictions, its conventionalities, its false values, its lies. The class society poisons and corrupts everything. We are all dwarfed and twisted and blinded by it. We can hardly visualize what human relations will be, we can hardly comprehend what the personality of man will be, in a free society.

Comrade Trotsky gave us an anticipatory picture. In him, in his personality as a man, as a human being, we caught a glimpse of the communist man that is to be. This memory of him as a man, as a comrade, is our greatest assurance that the spirit of man, striving for human solidarity, is unconquerable. In our terrible epoch many things will pass away. Capitalism and all its heroes will pass away. Stalin and Hitler and Roosevelt and Churchill, and all the lies and injustices and hypocrisy they signify, will pass away in blood and fire. But the spirit of the communist man which Comrade Trotsky represented will not pass away.

Destiny has made us, men of common clay, the most immediate disciples of Comrade Trotsky. We now become his heirs, and we are charged with the mission to carry out his testament. He had confidence in us. He assured us with his last words that we are right and that we will prevail. We need only have confidence in ourselves and in the ideas, the tradition, and the memory which he left us as our heritage.

We owe everything to him. We owe to him our political existence, our understanding, our faith in the future. We are not alone. There are others like us in all parts of the world. Always remember that. We are not alone. Trotsky has educated cadres of disciples in more than thirty countries. They are convinced to the marrow of their bones of their right to victory. They will not falter. Neither shall we falter. "I am sure of the victory of the Fourth International!" So said Comrade Trotsky in the last moment of his life. So are we sure.

Trotsky never doubted and we shall never doubt that, armed with his weapons, with his ideas, we shall lead the oppressed masses of the world out of the bloody welter of the war into a new socialist society. That is our testimony here tonight at the grave of Comrade Trotsky.

And here at his grave we testify also that we shall never forget his parting injunction—that we shield and cherish his warrior-wife, the faithful companion of all his struggles and wanderings.

"Take care of her," he said, "she has been with me many years." Yes, we shall take care of her. Before everything else, we shall take care of Natalia.

We come now to the last word of farewell to our greatest comrade and teacher, who has now become our most glorious martyr. We do not deny the grief that constricts all our hearts. But ours is not the grief of prostration, the grief that saps the will. It is tempered by rage and hatred and determination. We shall transmute it into fighting energy to carry on the Old Man's fight. Let us say farewell to him in a manner worthy of his disciples, like good soldiers of Trotsky's army. Not crouching in weakness and despair, but standing upright with dry eyes and clenched fists. With the song of struggle and victory on our lips. With the song of confidence in Trotsky's Fourth International, the International Party that shall be the human race!

MILITARY POLICY OF
THE PROLETARIAT

September 28, 1940

This speech was given as the main political report to the SWP Plenum-Conference held in Chicago September 27-29, 1940. It concluded a two-month discussion on military policy conducted by the ranks of the SWP. The text is from a stenographic report, corrected by Cannon and published in the October 12, 1940, Socialist Appeal.

Our first word in formally beginning our deliberations today is devoted to the memory of our greatest teacher and comrade and our most glorious martyr. It is the proposal of the National Committee that we all stand for a moment in silent tribute to the memory of Comrade Trotsky.

We meet for the first time without him. I am sure that as we stood for a silent minute one common thought weighed upon us all. We all realize most poignantly that, whether we are quite grown up to it or not, we now face the appalling responsibility of leading and organizing the world movement of proletarian emancipation without the direct aid of the one who shaped and guided our movement, who instructed us, who raised us up and made men of us and prepared us for this great mission. It is up to us now to show that we have really learned what has been taught to us so patiently and so thoroughly. It is for us to take the tools that have been placed in our hands and use them no more as apprentices but as full-fledged journeymen.

We have confidence that we can do this because we have been left the greatest heritage that any political grouping in the history of the world was ever given. Never before did the workers' vanguard have such complete and thoroughgoing preparation, in a theoretical and programmatic way, as we have received. Especially in the past eleven years since Comrade Trotsky was exiled from the Soviet Union, eleven years so rich in historic events, we have had from day to day and from year to year the aid of his great Marxist brain. With his aid and guidance we have unraveled the mysteries of this epoch and found in every case the strategic and tactical road that leads the proletarian movement to higher ground.

We not only have now the task of leading the movement in this country. We also have on our shoulders a great international responsibility. In the nineteenth century, nearly seventy years ago, Marx and Engels transferred the center of the First International to the United States. Their action was then, so to speak, a symbolic intimation of the future international leading role of America. By a combination of circumstances the prophetic gesture of our great masters has finally been confirmed by concrete reality. The main political center and organizational base of the Fourth International, which is destined to complete the work begun by the First International of Marx and Engels, is in truth lodged here in the United States in the custody of those comrades who are gathered here and those whom they represent in all sections of the country.

A combination of circumstances, rather than any special merit of our own, has imposed upon us this international responsibility. First of all, we were fated to have the greatest amount of freedom for the open and legal development of our movement. While our valiant comrades in one country after another fell under the heavy blows of persecution, were stifled and repressed, we here in America have had now twelve years of uninterrupted preparatory work. We alone of practically all sections of the Fourth International were fortunate in beginning not entirely with new and inexperienced people. We carried over into the new movement of the Fourth International some substantial and experienced cadres who had been tested and who had learned in the Communist movement since 1918, and even before that. Our movement was thus prepared by its past and by these fortunate circumstances to establish an uninterrupted continuity between the movement of the present day and that which preceded it. All these things taken together have equipped and prepared us for the role which we must now play in aiding the further development of the Fourth International in all countries.

This movement is primarily the creation of Comrade Trotsky. He was responsible above all others for formulating its program and assembling its cadres on an international scale. But within the last few years our party has come to the front and played an increasingly important role. More and more Comrade Trotsky came to rely on us as the strongest pillar of the Fourth International. More and more the comrades in all parts of the world came to look at the combination of Comrade Trotsky and the American section as the main guarantee of stability in the leadership of the international party. And now, after the death of Comrade Trotsky, we can be sure that the comrades in all parts of the world—in China, carrying on their work in daily danger of their lives; the comrades imprisoned and in concentration camps in Germany; in illegality in France; in England; in Australia; in South America; in the Soviet Union; everywhere—they are now looking to the American section, to the Socialist Workers Party, to grow up to the level of its historic responsibility and assure the continuous functioning and development of our international movement. That puts a still greater responsibility upon all of us.

We cannot lag any more. Every one of us, I am sure, in the past years felt that if we erred, we had the assurance that we could be corrected by someone wiser than we. All of us, including myself, felt that if we shirked or slumped a little bit now and then, our laxity would be compensated for by the untiring energy of the Old Man. We permitted ourselves more than one luxury. That we cannot indulge ourselves in any more. The burden is on our shoulders. We must carry it. We must give the movement now more than ever in energy, in discipline, in faithfulness, and in efficient work.

We meet at a time of a great change in the world. Before our eyes, almost without our realizing it, there has been brought about a profoundly new world situation. A new period has opened up. The essence of the new situation is that capitalism in its unprecedented decay, in its death agony, has passed over completely from the relative stability and relative peace which characterized it as a growing and healthy social system into a state of permanent crisis, and the permanent crisis is now expressed in permanent war.

At the mass meeting last night I mentioned the new and significant development of the German-Italian-Japanese pact.[15] The announcement of this pact signifies above all other things that the war in Europe is due for an extension into Asia, Africa, and into the Western Hemisphere of the Americas. There is no prospect whatever for any more considerable periods of peace in the capitalist world. Just conjecture for a moment that some kind of peace could be effected in the European war. Nobody could believe that this would be a peace of any stability. It would only be a preparation for a new war of continents, of hemispheres, embracing the whole world. If a sudden, smashing victory of Hitler should enforce a peace with England, as was the case with France, no one would believe this would be the end of the war. If a formal peace should be declared and there should be a lull, during which there should be no war, it would only be an interlude.

We are preparing—our imperialist masters are preparing—night and day to challenge Hitler for world dominion. And Hitler, Mussolini, and the Japanese imperialists are preparing to meet that challenge. The outcome can only be a whole epoch of uninterrupted militarism and war. The proletariat, which is the sole power capable of lifting humanity out of this bloody morass, must face this fact. It cannot indulge in any more daydreams about the peaceful solution of the social problem. The workers' movement was dominated by this illusion for decades, for generations. It was thought and felt that through the day-by-day work of organizing trade unions, building reformist parties, casting votes, gaining some social legislation, that along these lines, working from year to year and from decade to decade they could gradually improve the conditions of the masses, and glide over peacefully, without violent collisions or shocks, into a new social order called socialism.

The workers can indulge in no such daydreams any longer because the world is on fire with war and militarism. The one big conclusion the proletarian vanguard must draw is this: All great questions will be decided by military means. This was the great conclusion insisted upon by Comrade Trotsky in his last few months of life. In his letters, in his articles, and in conversations he repeated this thesis over and over again. These are new times. The characteristic feature of our epoch is unceasing war and universal militarism. That imposes on us as the first task, the task which dominates and shapes all others, the adoption of a military policy, an attitude of the proletarian party towards the solution of social problems during a time of universal militarism and war.

The prospects of the United States remaining at peace are absolutely zero. You have before you the draft of our resolution on military policy. It has been printed in the internal bulletin and discussed in the branches for the past two months. We have elaborated in this resolution our conception of these new problems and tasks. In the very beginning we take up the question of America's participation in the war. It is completely absurd to imagine that there is some special policy—some legerdemain—that can make it possible for the strongest imperialist power in the world to escape participation in the struggle for the imperialist domination of the world. Nobody believes in this possibility except a few muddleheaded pacifists. And when I say muddleheaded pacifists I do not mean the bourgeois isolationists. I mean the fools, the people who belong completely to yesterday, like the Thomasite socialists, the Lovestoneites, the few religious fanatics.

That wing of the American bourgeoisie going by the name of isolationist are no less aggressive, no less military minded, than the wing which wants intervention right now in the present war.

The *Chicago Tribune* strongly criticizes the Roosevelt policy only because they have a different approach to the war. They think we should begin the struggle, the struggle of American imperialism for world dominion, by conquering first the Western Hemisphere and proceeding next to the East by way of a war against Japan, postponing the clash with Hitler till a later time. The more farsighted, the more conscious and, I am sure, the strongest section of the American bourgeoisie, who are called interventionists, believe that we must begin the struggle for world dominion by intervention in the European war. What divides the two camps at this time is only a matter of strategy. Now that they are confronted by an open military alliance of Germany and Japan their differences can easily be reconciled.

The only question will be how soon and at what point to begin open intervention. As a matter of fact, in all except the formalities of the situation, we are intervening in the European war now as much as we can. We are sending unlimited supplies of military materials to Europe. In my opinion the only reason we are not sending troops is that there isn't any place to land them. The Wall Street heroes and their political lackeys overslept the European situation. They underestimated the rottenness and weakness of the bourgeois democracies of Europe on the one hand, and the military strength of Hitler on the other. They waited too long, until the ports were occupied by the fascists. Nothing remains now but England. England has no room for troops, and there is a growing opinion among American capitalists and military experts that England itself is a lost cause.

When American participation in the war finally begins is only a secondary question. The very fact that we have appropriated approximately fifteen billion dollars in one year for military expenditures before any war was formally started; that we have instituted peacetime conscription for the first time in history— these facts can only indicate that the masters of this country are preparing for an explosion of military aggressiveness on a scale never seen in history before. Imperialist America is out to dominate the world. In its path stands Hitler Germany in the West. In its path stands imperialist Japan in the East. The conflict between these imperialist powers can in no case be resolved by diplomacy or good wishes or half measures, but only as all other things are decided in this epoch—by military force.

Now, confronted with these facts of universal militarism and permanent war, that the biggest industry of all now is going to be war, the army and preparation of things for the army— confronted with these facts, what shall the revolutionary party do? Shall we stand aside and simply say we don't agree with the war, it is not our affair? No, we can't do that. We do not approve of this whole system of exploitation whereby private individuals can take possession of the means of production and enslave the masses. We are against that, but as long as we are not strong enough to put an end to capitalist exploitation in the factories, we adapt ourselves to reality. We don't abstain and go on individual strikes and separate ourselves from the working class. We go into the factories and try by working with the class to influence its development. We go with the workers and share all their experiences and try to influence them in a revolutionary direction.

The same logic applies to war. The great majority of the young generation will be dragged into the war. The great majority of these young workers will think at first that they are doing a good thing. For a revolutionary party to stand by and say, "We can tolerate exploitation in the factories, but not military exploitation"—that is to be completely illogical. To isolate ourselves from the mass of the proletariat which will be in the war is to lose all possibility to influence them.

We have got to be good soldiers. Our people must take upon themselves the task of defending the interests of the proletariat in the army in the same way as we try to protect their interests in the factory. As long as we can't take the factories away from the bosses we fight to improve the conditions there. Similarly, in the army. Adapting ourselves to the fact that the proletariat of this country is going to be the proletariat in arms we say, "Very well, Mr. Capitalist, you have decided it so and we were not strong enough to prevent it. Your war is not our war, but as long as the mass of the proletariat goes with it, we will go too. We will raise our own independent program in the army, in the military forces, in the same way as we raise it in the factories."

We say it is a good thing for the workers now to be trained in the use of arms. We are, in fact, in favor of compulsory military training of the proletariat. We are in favor of every union going on record for this idea. We want the proletariat to be well trained and equipped to play the military game. The only thing we object to is the leadership of a class that we don't trust. We don't want stoolpigeons of the boss as officers in our unions. Just as we don't want them as officers of our unions so we don't want them in the military forces. We are willing to fight Hitler. No worker wants to see that gang of fascist barbarians overrun this country or any country. But we want to fight fascism under a leadership that we can trust. We want our own officers—those who have shown themselves most devoted to their class, who have shown themselves to be the bravest and most loyal men on the picket line, those who are interested in the welfare of their fellow workers. These are precisely the type of people we want as officers. In the period when the whole working class youth is mobilized for war, those are the ones we want at the head of our battalions.

So we simply make our independent demands upon the government. We will join the war as long as the workers do. We will say frankly to the workers in the unions and shops: "We would like to throw over this whole business of capitalist exploitation—military as well as industrial—right now. But as long as you are not ready for that logical solution we will join with you, fight by your side, try to protect the men from useless waste of lives. All that we will do, but we retain one privilege— the right to express our opinion day in and day out: That you must not trust the leadership of your enemy class. Don't forget that the government in Washington is a concentrated representative of the same bosses that you have to fight every day in order to live. It is nothing but the executive committee of all bosses who, together and individually, act as the exploiters and oppressors of the working class. Put no more trust in that bosses' government than you do in the individual bosses at home."

We will fight all the time for the idea that the workers should have officers of their own choosing. That this great sum of money that is being appropriated out of the public treasury should be allocated in part to the trade unions for the setting up of their own military training camps under officers of their own selection; that we go into battle with the consciousness that the officer leading us is a man of our own flesh and blood who is not going to waste our lives, who is going to be true and loyal and who will represent our interests. And in that way, in the course of the development of the war, we will build up in the army a great class-conscious movement of workers with arms in their hands who will be absolutely invincible. Neither the German Hitler nor any other Hitler will be able to conquer them.

We will never let anything happen as it did in France. These commanding officers from top to bottom turned out to be nothing but traitors and cowards crawling on their knees before Hitler, leaving the workers absolutely helpless. They were far more concerned to save a part of their property than to fight the fascist invader. The myth about the war of "democracy against fascism" was exploded most shamefully and disgracefully. We must shout at the top of our voices that this is precisely what that gang in Washington will do because they are made of the same stuff as the French, Belgian, and Norwegian bourgeoisie. The French example is the great warning that officers from the class of bourgeois democrats can lead the workers only to useless slaughter, defeat, and betrayal.

The workers themselves must take charge of this fight against Hitler and anybody else who tries to invade their rights. That is the whole principle of the new policy that has been elaborated for us by Comrade Trotsky. The great difference between this and the socialist military policy in the past is that it is an *extension* of the old policy, an adaptation of *old principles* to *new conditions*. In our conversations with Comrade Trotsky he said he considered the great danger to our movement is pacifism. The taint of pacifism in our movement is in part due to the left-socialist tradition of antimilitarism. In part it is also a hangover from the past of our own movement. We said and those before us said that capitalism had outlived its usefulness. World economy is ready for socialism. But when the world war started in 1914 none of the parties had the idea that on the agenda stood the struggle for power. The stand of the best of them was essentially a protest against the war.

It did not occur even to the best Marxists that the time had come when the power must be seized by the workers in order to save civilization from degeneration. Even Lenin did not visualize the victory of the proletarian revolution as the immediate outcome of the war. Just a short time before the outbreak of the February revolution in Russia, Lenin wrote in Switzerland that his generation would most probably not see the socialist revolution. Even Lenin had postponed the revolution to the future, to a later decade. And a few months later it exploded in all its power in Russia. Acute revolutionary situations developed in one European country after another.

Trotsky pointed out to us that even such valiant and honest antiwar fighters as Debs and others like him conducted a fight against the war as a protest, but never once did it occur to them that the war was directly posing the question of the struggle for power. This protest against the war had a semipacifist character. Our movement was affected by this, especially when it was afflicted with the petty-bourgeois element in the party. You can recall that when we were discussing and arguing with them, the prevailing tendency among them was expressed about as follows: "We want to know, how can we keep out of the war; if the war starts how can we keep out of military service." They were primarily concerned about the various ways of evading the draft. More than one expressed the idea of escape to Mexico.

A group of heroic minorityite students in Chicago bought a small boat and sailed for Tahiti or some such place to hide out there until the war would be over. While millions of young proletarian youth are on the battlefields getting all kinds of experiences, facing all kinds of dangers, becoming hardened and ready for anything, these heroes will be basking in tropical sunshine and waiting for their day of destiny. I suppose when the time comes to make the revolution these people will probably sail back from Tahiti and say: "Here we are, boys, ready to lead you." It is not difficult to imagine the answer they will get from the boys who have already selected their leaders in the test of blood and fire.

Only those who go through hell with the soldiers will ever get close to their hearts and be able to influence them. All those with experience in the labor movement know it takes more than fancy speeches to gain influence with the workers. You must be with the workers. And nine times out of ten, I think every trade unionist will testify, the best asset you can have is to be a good worker in the shop. If the workers say, "He is the best mechanic among us; he does his full share of the work, not because he loves his boss but because he doesn't want to load the work on his fellow workers, etc."—if the workers say that about a man his influence is transferred over into the union, and when he gets up to say a word on the union floor he is listened to.

Absolutely the same psychology will prevail in the army. A man scared, ready to run—he will never be able to lead the worker-soldiers by making a few speeches from his retreat. It is necessary to go with the workers through all their experiences, through all the dangers, through the war. Out of the war will come the revolution, not otherwise. The war manifesto of the Fourth International[16] declares: We didn't want the war—we are not in favor of the war—but we are not afraid of the war. In this very war we will hammer out the cadres of revolutionary soldiers who will lead the struggle.

We must remember all the time that the workers of this epoch are not only workers; they are soldiers. These armies are no longer selected individuals, they are whole masses of the young proletarian youth who have been shifted from exploitation in the factories to exploitation in the military machine. They will be imbued by the psychology of the proletariat from which they came. But they will have guns in their hands and they will learn how to shoot them. They will gain confidence in themselves. They will be fired with the conviction that the only man who counts in this time of history is the man who has a gun in his hand and knows how to use it.

The great advantage of the workers is their mass strength. "Ye are many, they are few," said the poet Shelley. All the oppressed masses need is the will to power. All that is necessary to transform this madhouse of capitalism into a world of socialism is for the mass of the workers and the poor farmers to get the one simple general idea in their heads that they have the power and it is time now to use it. The capitalist class puts arms in the hands of the working class. That will, in the end, prove their undoing.

Now war, as I remarked in my speech last night, destroys a lot of things that are useful and valuable. It is a terrible overhead cost humanity has to pay for the delay in instituting socialism after capitalism has outlived its usefulness. This delay of the revolution has visited a terrible plague upon mankind that is going to destroy not thousands but millions of human lives. It will destroy great accumulations of material culture that took decades of human labor to create. As one small illustration take the city of London today. Here is a great city with centuries of accumulated achievements of mankind being pounded to dust. Nineteen consecutive days of bombing, and it stands to reason that the city is already partially in ruins.

The war destroys a great many things which will take much labor to replace. But war destroys some bad things also. War puts an end to all ambiguity and poses every question point-blank. There might have been room in the past for doubt as to how the workers can best solve the social problem. There were whole generations of workers deluded with the idea that the best way was the gradual peaceful inch-by-inch trade union and parliamentary struggle. By that method they built up great trade unions and political parties with millions of members and tens of millions of votes. These organizations looked very imposing in times of peace. They were very important. But what happened to them, to these organizations, that hadn't learned how to do anything but pay dues one day and vote the next day? The moment they got one violent military blow they were simply finished. They were designed for peace, not for war.

How can anyone respect reformist parliamentarians and vulgar trade unionists after what happened in Belgium, Norway, and France? Millions of people organized, the whole proletariat virtually organized; paying their dues; contracts signed with the bosses; all equipped with full staffs of well-paid officials and business agents in the unions; many of the officers of long standing, substantial people in the community both physically and socially; everything going fine until the situation changed from peace, which is outlived and outmoded, to war which is the logic of the present day. All these organizations for peace were crushed like eggshells. Nothing of organization remains but the small body of revolutionary people who realized that war was on the agenda and prepared themselves to function accordingly. There is nothing left of the Jouhaux unions in France. Of all his contracts, his business agents, his treasury and his pseudoimportance—nothing is left. One decree of a decrepit

General Pétain, "We don't want these unions any more," and the game was up.

And that great Socialist Party of Leon Blum, the party that mobilized millions of votes and looked so big in times of peace. The war struck one paralyzing blow, and the French Socialist Party went down and out like a sledged ox in a slaughterhouse. Leon Blum winds up under arrest at Vichy practically like a vagrant picked up on the street and thrown into jail. They are finished people, these reformists, men of the past. Now times call out for new men and a new type of party, a party built for war.

They used to make fun of the Fourth International—this little group talking about war and revolution, which looked insignificant beside their numerically imposing organizations. They boasted of their own importance when their movements were already marked for ignominious death. The Fourth Internationalists, on the other hand, had an idea which contemplated the coming events and they prepared to survive them. I have the great pleasure to report to you that we have received word from our comrades in France—we were all greatly disturbed about the fate of our comrades—we received word that they survived the war up to now, that our comrades had slipped through the nets and were not only safe, but were functioning in little groups and in contact with each other. Even those in jail during the war made their way out at the time when everyone was running, including the jailors. They took advantage of the general exodus and mixed themselves with it and are still there. I am sure the same thing is true in other countries. Those who prepare in their own minds for the war are best qualified to survive and grow stronger. The philistines used to sneer: "The Trotskyites—there are only a few hundred of them." True, but they still exist, more confident than ever. Leon Blum could not today rally together a few hundred Social Democrats in the whole of the occupied and unoccupied territories of France. They were not organized for war. That is why they succumbed to the first blow. Only those parties adapted for war, ready to carry things through to the very end, to a military solution of the problem—only they will be able to survive and conquer.

Now I come to another phase of this problem—the transformation of this society from a peace to a permanent war basis as it affects the trade union movement. One thing is absolutely clear: The days of the old routine reformist trade unions are numbered.

They will not be able to survive the war as independent organizations. The trade union movement will be able to survive only insofar as it takes the road of resolute struggle against the capitalist system. The traditional nonfighting trade union in the United States will suffer the same fate as those in France, Belgium, and Norway, unless the revolutionary elements are able to vitalize them from within and inspire them with a spirit of revolutionary struggle.

And similarly the work of our own comrades in these unions has to undergo a change. We ourselves have been affected by the whole general perspective of long years of slow progress. Ninety percent of our trade union activity in the past had to do with little agreements and combinations with progressive and nonprogressive elements in order to gain a few inches in the economic struggle. We have to continue the struggle for immediate demands in the trade unions. It is necessary to continue all the patient day-to-day work, to guard every gain, watch every contract. In this work we collaborate with everybody—whether progressive or reactionary—in the daily interests of the workers.

But at the same time we have to realize, and make the workers realize increasingly, that there is not going to be the possibility in America for a long period of growth and stability of conservative trade unions. Such visions of the trade union bureaucrats represent a mirage. They are thinking in terms of the world of yesterday. America is going into the war with express train speed. The unions will be confronted with this alternative—they will either turn sharply, develop a revolutionary policy, begin a struggle for power hand in hand with the revolutionary wing of the army, or they will cease to exist. At best they will be relegated to mere appendages of the government, having no independent power. It is in this tone that we must speak louder in the unions and in the factories.

We have to look over our own party. All those comrades of the party who are in the conservative trade unions, who have in one way or another begun to succumb to that stifling atmosphere, who have begun to develop tendencies to avoid struggle and let well enough alone—all those party comrades who are sinking into that quagmire must be pulled up short. They must be reminded that the one most important thing in this epoch is to build a revolutionary party. Only a revolutionary party can inspire the unions to meet the test of the new times. We have to insist more than ever upon the party responsibility of every comrade.

Your strength in the unions is the strength of your party. Don't forget it. All these collaborators of the day; all these trade union militants who look so good in normal, peaceful times, who are good enough for a local strike but have no general concepts—how quickly these people can be transformed under the pressure of the social crisis. Only those will be able to stand up in the coming period who are fortified by great general ideas—not otherwise. You will have some bad disappointments if you believe for one moment that a man who has not yet broken his allegiance to capitalism in general will be able to stand up under the pressure of war. Not at all. Some of our comrades have already had some very painful experiences along this line. Those people can stand up under pressure who have anticipated pressure and can see beyond it to the goal of the new society.

Above all, we have to develop our party as a party of a new type. All the old party organizations were built for peace. They can't survive in this new epoch of universal militarism. The only party that can survive is the one that adapts itself to universal militarism and aims at the struggle for power. It can't be a sprawling, slow-moving, undisciplined organization. It must be highly centralized, with iron discipline in its ranks. It must be able to function, if necessary, under all kinds of persecution. It needs a strong leadership. We have to select out of the ranks tested and trusted people for leading positions and give them full authority. Only so will we be able to move fast and strike hard as a united, disciplined organization.

During the past year we made gains of historic significance. While Comrade Trotsky was still alive to help us we had the possibility of fighting out in our ranks a fundamental struggle which prepared us to build the party of a new type. We had people who set up a great howl about "bureaucratism." They wanted a party where one could do as he pleased; have the honor and badge of the Fourth International without any personal responsibility. And if the party at any time demanded anything of them, they raised a hue and cry about the injustices they were suffering. When these milksops cried about "bureaucratism" they really meant to protest against centralism and discipline. I thought many times, and I said many times to comrades, that the grievance the real proletarian revolutionists in the party held against us was that the accusations of the petty-bourgeois minority were not even half true.

The workers in the party want discipline. They want centralization. They want a party that doesn't permit anybody to make a fool of it. They want a party that demands of every leader that he put his whole life, his whole time, including his personal life, at the disposal of the party. Our movement is not playing for fun. It aims to take power in this country. For that we need a hard party, a firm party. It is a great advantage for us that we got rid of this petty-bourgeois opposition. We improved the composition of our party; we got rid of a lot of windbagism. We got rid of a lot of deadwood and are now in a position to take some real steps forward.

It is time now to bring the struggle with the petty-bourgeois faction to a definitive conclusion. You know the minority refused to accept the decisions of the convention. In order to be perfectly fair and give them time to think it over we allowed them a period of nearly six months of suspension, not expulsion, to accept the decisions of the convention majority and restore their party standing. They haven't availed themselves of this exceptional concession. In the meantime they have developed politically far away from us as a typical left-socialist, pacifist clique. Their ideological leader, Burnham, has renounced socialism. We haven't anything in common with them politically. They have more than used up the credit balance of probation we allowed them. We don't want any ambiguity and confusion in the public mind regarding them and us as two wings of the same movement. It is the unanimous recommendation of the National Committee that the suspension of the convention minority be changed to unconditional expulsion at this conference.

Our second recommendation is that we begin a closer checking up of party responsibility, discipline, and loyalty without permitting any panic in the ranks. We have two things to fear now, and we must steer a course between them. One is carelessness and irresponsibility, and the other is supercaution, a spy hunt, and general jitteriness in the organization. The second is by far the greater danger. We are proposing a measure that will tend to eliminate both of them. I have talked about a party that says it will stop at nothing short of the struggle for power and will fight to the end to overthrow capitalism. Such a party cannot exist with a leadership that is scared for itself or afflicted with nervousness of any kind.

We are under great pressure and will be under still greater pressure. We know that we are dealing with a murderous machine in Stalin's GPU. We know that Comrade Trotsky was not the first, and probably will not be the last, victim of this murder machine. Our party must also expect persecutions from the Wall Street government. Realizing all this, some comrades have wondered if we couldn't do something to preserve our leaders from danger—perhaps put them on ice, I suppose. From the very first hour since the assassination of Trotsky we have conducted a resolute struggle against this psychology. Scared people are not going to be able to lead anybody. One who takes part in the revolutionary movement by that fact has to encounter certain risks. Millions of young American workers are going to be thrown into the war. Many of them will lose their lives. These are dangerous times. But they are dangerous for everybody, not only for us. Revolutionists must face the hazards of our time, and not fear them. A good one-half or three-fourths of the objective of persecutions and assassinations is to terrorize others. Nobody can terrorize us. We will try to be careful, but not afraid.

I had an interesting talk with Comrade Dobbs about these two dangers of nervousness and carelessness. He agreed with me that jitteriness is worse than carelessness. "A careless man," he said, "is good as long as he lasts, but a jittery man is no good at any time." That is profoundly true. We must use the necessary caution and save ourselves as much as possible. But if you create an impression in front of the workers that you fear the hazards of the struggle you can never lead them. You can do without a lot of things in a revolutionary party but you can't get along without courage.

Now then, on the other hand, we have to check up on carelessness. We want to know who is who in the party. We don't want to have any universal spy hunts because that is worse than the disease it tries to cure. Comrade Trotsky said many times that mutual suspicion among comrades can greatly demoralize a movement. On the other hand, there is a certain carelessness in the movement as a hangover from the past. We haven't probed deeply enough into the past of people even in leading positions— where they came from, how they live, whom they are married to, etc. Whenever in the past such questions—elementary for a revolutionary organization—were raised, the petty-bourgeois opposition would cry, "My God, you are invading the private lives of comrades!" Yes, that is precisely what we were doing, or more correctly, threatening to do—nothing ever came of it in the past. If we had checked up on such matters a little more carefully we might have prevented some bad things in the days gone by.

We are proposing that we set up a control commission in the party. We are fully ready for that now. This will be a body of responsible and authoritative comrades who will take things in hand and carry every investigation to a conclusion one way or the other. This will do away with indiscriminate suspicions on the one side and undue laxity on the other. The net result can only be to reassure the party and strengthen its vigilance. We think the whole party now, with the petty-bourgeois riffraff out of our way, is ready for the appointment of such a body.

We have to strengthen our professional staff. We don't pretend to be a party of glorified rank and filers. The only reason we haven't got ten, twenty, thirty, or forty more people devoting their whole time, their whole energy, to the party is that we lack the resources for it. We need more money to engage more functionaries full time. This conference has to decide how big a forward step in this direction it feels able to take. We are not coming here with a proposal for specific quotas. We want each delegation to confer and decide what they can raise in, say, two months' time. Our general plan is that, as several branches have suggested, we raise a "Trotsky Memorial Fund" to build the party. We think it is a good plan. If it meets with the approval of the conference we can adopt a resolution to that effect.

We want to build the party henceforth in a more balanced way than in the past. In the past we gave an inordinate amount of our resources to the press. We had to do that. Propaganda had to go ahead of organization and prepare the way for it. In the next period we want to bend the stick a little for organization on the general principle of dollar for dollar—one for press and one for organization.

Since the last convention we have taken certain steps in this direction. You comrades in the auto field know we maintained qualified comrades in the field continuously. The same is true in other fields. The important step taken in St. Paul will have a national meaning for all of us. It shows the growing tendency of serious comrades to regard the party as the most important thing of all. I refer to the action of Comrade [Grace] Carlson in resigning her civil service job and accepting a post as party organizer. This is a good example. We should raise as much money as possible to put to work for the party on a full-time basis a great number of qualified party workers. It is appalling how many capable people we have who have to devote only a small portion of their time to the party because the necessary job of making a living takes so much of their time and energy. That is all right for the old party, but not for us.

THE STALINISTS AND THE
UNITED FRONT

September 28, 1940

*These were supplementary remarks during the discussion on the
political report to the SWP's September 1940 Plenum-Conference.
The text is from a stenographic report, corrected by Cannon and
published in the October 19, 1940,* Socialist Appeal.

It seems, comrades, that the discussion on the military policy is
pretty well exhausted. The small points of difference which have
been brought out can be answered in the summary speech. We
can now discuss the secondary question of the Stalinists and our
trade union tactics.

For some time we have been compelled to realize that the
Communist Party remains the greatest obstacle to the development of the revolutionary movement in the United States. The
Stalinists retain a powerful position in many trade unions and by
their new turn have still further confused things to our detriment.
The calculations that the Hitler-Stalin pact would result in the
annihilation of the Communist Party were not quite realized.[17]
This new line gave its bureaucratic leadership the opportunity to
put on the mask of pseudoradicalism once again. That appealed
more to the worker-militants in the ranks than the old policy. To
be sure, the cynical deal with Hitler repelled quite a large number
of Stalinist workers. But the great bulk of the losses, both
members and sympathizers, came from the petty-bourgeois
elements whom the Communist Party had catered to in recent
years. When the showdown came they were more devoted to the
bourgeois-democratic regime of Roosevelt than to the regime of

Stalin. The Stalinist workers, on the other hand, by and large, stayed with the party and stood up under a great deal of repression and persecution. These established facts must be taken as the point of departure in determining our tactical approach to this question.

We were aware for many months that we had not made sufficient inroads among the Stalinist workers. The Communist Party is an obstacle which the revolutionary workers must remove from their path. This cannot be done by frontal attacks alone. It is necessary to devise methods of flank attack to supplement our uncompromising and unceasing direct offensive against perfidious Stalinism. These thoughts were in our minds when we placed the question of the Communist Party on the agenda for a discussion with Comrade Trotsky on our last visit.[18] He was also of the opinion that our policy toward the Communist Party for a long time has been too negative, that we haven't devised sufficiently flexible tactics for flank movements in order to win over to our side a number of Stalinist workers.

Trotsky posed the question on the issue of the election campaign and put forward a shocking proposal. He said the CP leadership is talking very loudly in opposition to imperialist war, etc. We know they are liars and fakers simply carrying out current instructions in Stalin's diplomatic game. Tomorrow they will betray the fight against war. We know that, said Trotsky, but thousands of misguided workers are not yet convinced of it. "We must find a way to reach these workers as they are, with their present mentality. Let us take up the leaders at their word and state: If the Communist Party will maintain the position of real opposition to imperialist war we will propose to them a united front, and even give critical support to their candidates in the election."

Nobody in the delegation agreed with the Old Man on this drastic proposal. We had a long and at times heated discussion with him on it. We took the position that such a drastic change in the middle of the election campaign would require too much explanation, and would encounter the danger of great misunderstanding and confusion which we would not be able to dissipate. While we might conceivably win over a couple of hundred Stalinist workers in the course of a drawn-out tactic of this kind, we felt that we would run the danger of losing more than we gained.

We argued back and forth on this ground for several days.

Then Trotsky made a compromise proposal. He said that, after all, the main thing is the new military policy—the long-term strategical line—and not the short-term minor problem of our tactics in relation to the CP in the current election campaign.

He said, if we would take his proposal as one possible maneuver, and would devise some method of united-front approach which would really enable us to penetrate the Stalinist ranks, he would accept it as a compromise. We mulled over this a couple of days. I had a personal conversation with him before we left Coyoacan and restated my fears of misunderstanding and confusion from such a drastic policy as critical support to the CP in the coming election. He said he did not consider it of sufficient importance to make an issue; he did not want to provoke a party discussion which might divert attention from the paramount question of the new military policy. But we should think over the thing seriously and devise an effective united-front attack against the Stalinist bureaucracy.

The united-front tactics, as devised and perfected by Lenin, are in no sense the expression of a conciliatory attitude toward opponent organizations in the labor movement. The united front is designed to mobilize the masses—as they are—for common action against the class enemy on specific issues of the day. At the same time it is a method of struggle against alien currents and treacherous leaders. The tactic is not to be applied all the time, every day of the week, but only on suitable occasions. The main tactic of the Comintern under Lenin was the tactic of the united front. But Lenin knew when to employ it and when to put it aside. In the first years of the split of the Second International and the formation of the Comintern nothing was said about the united front. The Russians have a saying: "Every vegetable has its season." And the season of the war and the postwar period, following the Russian Revolution and the formation of the Comintern, was the season for head-on offensive against the international Social Democracy. The strategy was to complete the split in merciless warfare, and replace the reformist parties by revolutionary Communist parties.

That direct frontal attack was carried on from 1917, after the founding of the Comintern in 1919 and up until the fall of 1921. Then the leaders of the Comintern—Lenin and Trotsky—drew a balance. Lenin pointed out that we had succeeded in our strategy to this extent, that we had constructed independent Communist parties in all countries of considerable strength. But the Social Democrats still had big organizations of workers under their control; these workers were not as yet convinced of Communism. For the next period we must confront the reformist leaders with united-front proposals as an approach to the rank and file under their influence.

You can observe the same general pattern in the work of constructing the Fourth International in the fight against Stalinism. We have been conducting a long drawn-out frontal attack. In the course of that attack we have selected and drawn to our side hardened cadres of the Fourth International. But we must recognize that the CP still remains a powerful organization, many times more powerful than ourselves. It contains in its ranks a great many misguided but class-conscious workers. We are now obliged to resort to united-front tactics as a means of approach to them.

Nobody in our Political Committee wanted to sponsor the policy of critical support to the Stalinists in the election campaign. I think this is one time we disagreed with Trotsky correctly. Nevertheless we have all realized that we must devise a more flexible tactic towards the CP and look for suitable occasions, as long as they espouse this semiradical line, to penetrate their ranks, by means of united-front proposals. And here also we don't want to jump over to the other extreme, from leaving the CP alone to united-front proposals every day in the week. We should carefully discriminate, select occasions and incidents for approaches to the CP rank and file, through their organizations, for a limited, specific, united front. That we have agreed upon, and I think the conference should endorse it as a general policy.

It should be carried out, I repeat, in a most careful and discriminating manner. We already experimented, rather gingerly, with this tactic in New York at the time we were carrying out our struggle agianst the Bundists and Coughlinite organizations.[19] We addressed a letter to the district organization of the CP proposing to them a united front against the Coughlin-Bund bands. This was not followed up. We merely sent a letter and published it. But just the simple facts that we were out fighting the fascists in New York City, and that we appealed to the rank and file of the CP to join us, had good results. We were informed by our contacts in the CP that we created quite a ripple in their ranks. It caused the bureaucrats quite a little trouble. A good many rank-and-file Stalinists wanted to accept our united-front offer and join us in the fight against the fascists. Out of that single experience we won over quite a number of rank-and-file Stalinists to our party.

At the present time you have a situation out in California where, if I understand the facts, Governor Olson has proposed to the State Legislature the passage of a constitutional amendment to remove the CP from the ballot. Our Los Angeles local organization jumped on this right away. They proposed to send an appeal to the CP and other organizations for a united-front action to fight this attempt to outlaw the CP. The Political Committee unanimously approved the initiative of the Los Angeles comrades. As I understand it, they will push this action in the next few weeks.

It must be repeated all the time that the united front is a method of struggle. It does not mean friendship or conciliation. It simply means an approach to the rank and file of an opponent organization in the labor movement, through their official leadership, for a joint struggle for common immediate aims. Properly utilized, the united front creates the possibility to penetrate the ranks of organizations hitherto sealed against us. It is in this sense, and in this sense only, that we propose united fronts to the Stalinists, in the next period. We are, and we shall remain, the most consistent and most implacable enemies of Stalinism.

The Old Man was quite optimistic about the possibilities. He said, suppose you go into this and repeat these experiments time and time again on suitable occasions; in the end if you win over two hundred Stalinist workers to our party you have gained a lot. We raised the question of the enormous hatred of many honest workers in the labor movement against the Stalinists. There is a great grain of justice and sincerity in this hatred, although it is often confused with reactionary prejudices. We have to be very careful that we don't offend the sensibilities of these anti-Stalinist workers who are militant and partly class conscious in their attitude, but we must not let their feelings determine our political line. The moment we began to speak of a united-front approach to the Stalinists, we heard from all of our fractions in the trade unions a cry to go slow! Those in the trade unions know how bitterly the Stalinists are hated. We must be very careful. If we allow ourselves to become confused and mixed up with the

Stalinists, we will cut off our road of approach to the rank and file of the trade union movement, the anti-Stalinist rank and file, which, in my opinion, is a more important reservoir of the revolution than the Stalinist rank and file.

Here we had a little difference with Comrade Trotsky. He was inclined to dismiss the whole "progressive" movement as composed entirely of patriots and fakers. In fact he gave us quite an argument on [John L.] Lewis and [Earl] Browder. "What is the difference between Lewis and Browder? Is Browder a bigger scoundrel than Lewis? I don't think so. They are both scoundrels—of different types." One comrade there remarked, the Stalinists are very hostile to us. Trotsky said, "Yes, I know, sometimes they shoot at us." (This was shortly after the May 24 machine-gun attack.) He said, "Do you think Lewis or [William] Green wouldn't shoot at you? It is only a difference of circumstances, that is all."

We must classify the Stalinists and the reactionary and "progressive" patriotic labor fakers as simply two different varieties of enemies of the working class employing different methods because they have different bases under their feet. It brings us into a complicated problem in the trade union movement. It has been our general practice to combine in day-to-day trade union work with the progressives and even the conservative labor fakers against the Stalinists. We have been correct from this point of view, that while the conservative and traditional labor skates are no better than the Stalinists, are no less betrayers in the long run, they have different bases of existence. The Stalinist base is the bureaucracy in the Soviet Union. They are perfectly willing to disrupt a trade union in defense of the foreign policy of Stalin. The traditional labor fakers have no roots in Russia nor any support in its powerful bureaucracy. Their only base of existence is the trade union; if the union is not preserved they have no further existence as trade union leaders. That tends to make them, from self-interest, a little more loyal to the unions than the Stalinists. That is why we have been correct in most cases in combining with them as against the Stalinists in purely union affairs.

But our work in the trade unions up till now has been largely a day-to-day affair based upon the daily problems and has lacked a general political orientation and perspective. This has tended to blur the distinction between us and pure-and-simple trade unionists. In many cases, at times, they appeared to be one with us. It was fair weather and good fellows were together. The great issues raised by the war are rudely disrupting this idyl. Some of our comrades have already had revealing experiences of how a war situation puts an end to ambiguity and makes men show their real colors. Some people went hand in hand with us on almost every proposition we made to improve the union, get better contracts from the bosses, etc. Then all of a sudden, this whole peaceful routine of the trade union movement is disrupted by overpowering issues of war, patriotism, the national elections, etc. And these trade unionists, who looked so good in ordinary times, are all turning up as patriots and Rooseveltians. We now have a much narrower basis of cooperation with them. This new situation induces some of our comrades to say we should break off all relations with these patriotic unionists and progressive fakers. That is a very extreme position which we cannot endorse.

What we have got to do with our united-front policy, in the unions and in general, is to make it more precise. The united front does not signify political collaboration but joint action on specific issues despite political differences. The united front is based on day-to-day problems. It is nothing resembling permanent collaboration, but simply day-to-day agreements. Where we agree or half-agree with others we go along together; where we don't agree we go alone. Politically we have no ground for collaboration with the labor "progressives." We will have less and less as we go along, as the pressure of the war machine grows heavier.

A great number of our comrades in the unions have been working hand in hand with people who have been simply militant unionists and nothing else. In "normal" times they get along very well together. They will soon encounter the unpleasant experience of having many of these people, these fellows who have been coworkers, drinking companions, and pals turn up as direct enemies and informers against our movement. There is only one thing that binds men together in times of great stress. That is agreement on great principles. Good fellowship and chumminess is a very poor substitute. Those who don't know this will learn it in bitter experience.

All those comrades who think we have something, big or little, in the trade union movement should get out a magnifying glass in the next period and look at what we really have. You will find that what we have is our party fractions and the circle of sympathizers around them. That is what you can rely on. There may be cases where people who are united with us in principle will falter because of personal weakness. But those are the exceptions to the rule. There will be cases of men without broad political concepts, who, because of exceptional personal qualities will prove loyal to us in a pinch. They will also be the exceptions. The rule will be that the general run of pure-and-simple trade unionists, the nonpolitical activists, the latent patriots—they will betray us at the most decisive moment. What we will have in the unions in the hour of test will be what we build in the form of firm fractions of convinced Bolsheviks.

This military policy that we are outlining here will be the main line of our activity. We will have today a united front with Smith or Jones, together with Brown. We will agree with one or the other that such and such should be the demands upon the bosses, such and such proposals in the internal situation of the union. But we are bound to none of them and none of them are bound to us. We will fight against the Stalinist disrupters in the union every day in the week. At the same time we will approach the Stalinists on the broad political field for a united-front action, as, for example, in California, to fight the removal of minority parties from the ballot. Perhaps our progressive friends will say: "What are you doing? You are supposed to be working with us, and all of a sudden you come out against removing the CP from the ballot." We have a perfect right to reply: "You are supposed to be working with us 364 days of the year, but on one day you want to make an exception, to vote for Roosevelt, the agent of the bosses. And if you take that little privilege, you must give us one. We must have the same independence that you have." Maybe this will be a lesson in democracy to the democrats.

One point more on this and I will be finished. Many of our comrades in the unions who have become deeply integrated with this business of the progressive democrats, flinch away from the idea of offending them. Our party in this isn't as courageous as it should be. We are afraid of offending people, that is, their stupid, petty-bourgeois prejudices. That is only another way of saying that we are not yet real Marxists. The great Marxists—beginning with Marx and Engels—and ending with the last great exponent of Marxism, Comrade Trotsky—they all had a common characteristic: a complete indifference to public opinion. They did not care what the rest of the world thought about them. They figured out their line of policy in every case according to their scientific ideas. Then they courageously applied it and took the consequences. They made their own the motto of Dante: "Go your way and let the people talk." Perhaps this problem of the CP is a test for us. To the extent that we can deal with the problem correctly and carefully, but also courageously—disregarding philistine opinion—we will take a step forward, becoming genuine Marxists, genuine Trotskyists, who follow their own line and let the world make the best of it.

SUMMARY SPEECH ON
MILITARY POLICY

September 28, 1940

These excerpts from Cannon's summary of the discussion of his report on proletarian military policy at the SWP Plenum-Conference in September 1940 were published in the Socialist Appeal *of October 26, 1940. The stenographic transcript was corrected by Cannon and this is the only version now extant.*

In summary, I will take up the questions in reverse order of their importance. The Stalinist question is a question of tactics and is by far secondary to the main problem of our military policy. Nevertheless, it has considerable importance. The discussion has shown one thing clearly, that there is in our ranks today very little misunderstanding of the fundamental aspects of the question of Stalinism. That is far different from the situation a year ago.

It is important to remember in this connection that our fight with the petty-bourgeois ideologist Burnham began over the question of the characterization of the Stalinists. It will be recalled that almost two years ago, at the time of the auto crisis, the first real clash with Burnham and his satellites was precipitated by their attitude toward the split in the auto union. Despite the fact that the great mass of the auto workers were going with the CIO—and thereby at that time with the Stalinists—Burnham wanted to divert our support to Martin, even in the direction of the AFL, on the theory that the Stalinists were not really a part of the labor movement.[20]

The thing came to a head again over the invasion of Poland when Burnham wanted the party to take an outright stand against the Red Army on the theory that the Soviet Union is "imperialist." The issue grew sharper with the Finnish invasion.[21] Then, when Browder was indicted by the government on an obviously trumped-up passport charge, Burnham opposed any defense of Browder on the ground that he did not represent any legitimate labor tendency. He overlooked the fact that as an agent of the Soviet bureaucracy, Browder indirectly represented the biggest labor organization in the world, that of the Soviet state.

Burnham in this case was fundamentally motivated by the pressure of democratic imperialism in the United States. The Stalinists were for the moment at loggerheads with the Roosevelt administration, and the "intransigence" of the Burnham faction against the Stalinists simply represented a cheap and easy form of adaptation to the clamor of the bourgeois democrats. Their opinions were shaped against any kind of recognition of the CP as a tendency in the labor movement. We haven't heard such an expression here today from anybody.

Comrade Morton gave us a speech here today which was very informative about his experiences in the CIO union of Electrical and Radio Workers. He said something that we must heed—that the Stalinist rank and file in this union do not distinguish between us and the red-baiters, that they tend to regard us as a part of the general reaction. If that is true, we must take heed and correct such an impression.

First of all in the press. Our press must have a more precise line, a line that cannot be misunderstood. On each and every important occasion it must be made clear to the readers of our press that, while we are irreconcilably hostile to Stalinism—more now than ever before—we recognize that it does represent a current in the international labor movement, and as such we defend it against the attacks of the red-baiters. Our press is our most important medium of clarification. But the press campaign must be reinforced by united-front proposals to the Stalinists on suitable occasions which provide us the possibility of approaching the Stalinist workers and advancing the revolutionary cause.

Of course we must not forget that the present line of the Stalinists is only a year old. I will be very much surprised if it has another year to last. It was the opinion of Comrade Trotsky that Moscow is already turning in the direction of the Allies, and particularly in the direction of the U.S. The Soviet Union is caught in a vise between Japan on the one hand and Nazi Germany on the other. If the Axis powers suffer military reverses, if American imperialism moves more aggressively against them,

Stalin is very apt to shift over into the orbit of democratic imperialism led by the U.S. You can be sure, in this event, that the line of the Stalinists in this country will very soon change accordingly.

Such a prospect does not speak against approaching the Stalinists with united-front proposals on the basis of their present line. The more deeply we penetrate their ranks on a united-front basis in connection with their pseudoradical policy, the better possibility we will have to influence the workers against the swing back to bourgeois democracy and the Popular Front ballyhoo when the bureaucrats make the switch.[22] Such an overnight reversal of policy will inevitably provoke a crisis in the CP. We should strive to be in a good position to influence the revolting elements—and this time they will be the best, not the worst—in a revolutionary direction. Everything speaks in favor of a serious, carefully worked out, realistic, and practical united-front policy. It is obligatory that we devote a properly proportioned amount of our time and energy to the Stalinists.

But let us not go crazy over this issue. One could notice a slight tendency in the discussion to overemphasize this secondary tactical question at the expense of our main business, that of orienting the party for a military policy which has nothing in common with the policy of the CP. We must not begin to dance around this question like jitterbugs. We must not paint up the CP and make it appear to be something different than it is. We should correct our one-sided policy of the past, but not overcorrect it. There is a danger of our making a sort of panacea of united fronts with the CP.

I got a little bit scared today when I heard some of the speeches. I had a horrific vision of the party pacing back and forth and around in circles and so preoccupied with CP united fronts that we would not have anything else to do. Whiskey looks like tea but cannot be consumed so freely without bad effects. This business of united fronting with the CP is also a strong medicine. We must condition ourselves to the self-control of the man who can take it or leave it alone. Don't forget that Stalinism is an agency of imperialism no less than the bureaucracy of Green and Lewis. It is only another variety. Like the traitors of traditional reformism, the Stalinist bureaucracy also tries to defend its own interests against the imperialists. It is this contradiction in each case which opens the way for the united-front tactic. But never forget that the main blows of Stalinism are directed against the international working class.

Some comrades raised the question a little falsely, I think, today. They asked: "Who represents the main danger right now? What is the main danger? Is it represented by the out-and-out patriots of the Green and Hillman type? Or is it the CP?" And they came to the conclusion that it is the jingoes, not the CP. That only shows that the CP is an even greater danger than we realize; its duplicity creates a little confusion even in our ranks. Stalinism is the greatest danger to the international revolutionary movement precisely because the Stalinists discredit the great Russian Revolution and sow confusion and demoralization in the ranks of the proletarian vanguard which had rejected traditional reformism. A momentary diplomatic maneuver of Stalin—itself inspired by treachery—must not create the impression in our ranks that perhaps the CP is not as great a danger today as it was yesterday. Stalinism is treacherous to the core. It is the main obstacle in the path of the proletarian revolution. Our attitude towards Stalinism is that of irreconcilable war. We can conceive of the united front only in the sense of a flank attack against our most perfidious enemy.

The crux of the Stalinism question can be summarized under these five points:

First, where is the main reservoir of future recruiting for the revolutionary party in this country? Is it in the ranks of the CP? Or is it in the ranks of the half-awakened working class in this country that has not been defeated and that has not been corrupted? We consider it self-evident that the main reservoir for recruiting is in the ranks of these non-Stalinist workers. It is only incidental recruiting that can be expected out of the Stalinist party. This is also an important source, but it is not the most important. Every move we make in regard to Stalinism has to be weighed by the criterion whether it will help or harm our possibility of recruiting in the ranks of the young, uneducated but militant proletariat.

Second, we have to be more careful, more precise, and more militant in distinguishing our criticism of Stalinism from the attacks of the red-baiting jingoes. We must begin in earnest to emphasize this difference in our press. We have to clarify the whole problem for our membership, for our readers, for the Stalinist workers who sometimes read our press. We must make it clear on every occasion, sharply and categorically, that we have nothing in common with red-baiting attacks on the Stalinists by the capitalist newspapers, the old-style labor skates, and the Social Democrats.

The third point: Our chief problem in the political field is neither blocs with the Stalinists against the progressive jingoists nor blocs with the progressive jingoists against the Stalinists on incidental day-to-day problems in the unions. Our main problem is to bring forward and develop more clearly and precisely the independent line of the revolutionary party.

The fourth point: In the course of development, we will look for and take advantage of suitable and practical opportunities for united-front actions directed toward the CP workers. But this must not become the dominant side of our activity with regard to them. We will write ninety-nine attacks against the perfidies of the CP to one move that we will make in the direction of the united front with them. And even at the moment of approaching them for a united front, we will never relax for a moment, nor allow any worker to get an idea for a moment that this tactic signifies any kind of reconciliation, or any softening of our attitude towards the treacherous murder machine of Stalinism.

The fifth point: I am not as optimistic as some comrades about the number and quality of the recruits we will get from the CP. There are some members in our organization—quite a few—who came to us from the Stalinists in recent times and who have developed into good revolutionists. We've also had the experience of recruiting Stalinists more than once, more than ten times, who tried to become revolutionists, but who had become so demoralized, and to some extent so corrupted, by the CP that they were not assimilable. One of the greatest curses of Stalinism is the enormous demoralization, disorientation, and corruption of the minds of the advanced militant workers it has brought about.

Now I come to the decisive and basic question with which our party occupies itself, the question of military policy. During the discussion some comrades have asked: Was our old line wrong? Does the resolution represent a completely new departure and a reversal of the policy of the past? It is not quite correct to say that the old line was wrong. It was a program devised for the fight against war in time of peace. Our fight against war under conditions of peace was correct as far as it went. But it was not adequate. It must be extended. The old principles, which remain unchanged, must be applied concretely to the new conditions of permanent war and universal militarism. We didn't visualize, nobody visualized, a world situation in which whole countries would be conquered by fascist armies. The workers don't want to be conquered by foreign invaders, above all by fascists. They require a program of military struggle against foreign invaders which assures their class independence. That is the gist of the problem.

Many times in the past we were put at a certain disadvantage; the demagogy of the Social Democrats against us was effective to a certain extent. They said, "You have no answer to the question of how to fight against Hitler, how to prevent Hitler from conquering France, Belgium, etc." (Of course their program was very simple—the suspension of the class struggle and complete subordination of the workers to the bourgeoisie. We have seen the results of this treacherous policy.) Well, we answered in a general way, the workers will first overthrow the bourgeoisie at home and then they will take care of invaders. That was a good program, but the workers did not make the revolution in time. Now the two tasks must be telescoped and carried out simultaneously.

The main thing is that we must operate not under the old conditions of peace, but under the new conditions of universal militarism and war. We cannot avoid the new circumstances; we must adapt our tactics to them. In times of strike, we urge the workers to stay out of a plant. But when the majority decides to go back, we have to go back with them and accept with them, for the time being, the exploitation of the bosses. Sometimes the defeat of a strike goes so far as not only to smash a legitimate union but to drive the workers into the bosses' company union. We are against company unions; but if the workers are driven into them we go along and try to work there in the interests of the proletariat. Analogous tactics must be applied also in questions of war and militarism.

We had a great Marxist for a teacher, and a part of his genius was his never-failing application of Marxist tactics. He always took the existing situation, in its totality, as the point of departure. The Bolsheviks set out in 1917 to overthrow the whole capitalist world. They did overthrow the Russian bourgeoisie, but the other countries remained under the domination of the international capitalist class. So, at a certain point, the Bolsheviks drew the balance and said: "Here is the situation as it exists in reality. We cannot overthrow the other imperialist bandits at present. The workers are not yet ready. Therefore, let us open trade relations with the imperialist countries, gain a little breathing space, and overthrow them tomorrow." Comrade

Trotsky was prompted to elaborate and extend our tactics by the new situation in the world. A party which fails to adapt itself to this situation, to existing war, can play no role whatsoever.

One comrade here tried to justify a policy of antimilitarism. His remarks were, to my opinion, a reminiscence of departed days. Antimilitarism was all right when we were fighting against war in times of peace. But here you have a new situation of universal militarism. It is obvious that all over the world everything is going to be settled not by mass meetings, not by petitions, not by strikes, not even by mass demonstrations in the streets. Everything is going to be settled by military means, with arms in hand. So, can we now be antimilitarists? By no means! Just the contrary. We must say: "All right, the situation, not of our making, is that military force decides. There is only one thing left for the workers to do. That is to learn how to be good fighters with modern weapons." So we antimilitarists of yesterday become positive militarists today. The comrade who tries to represent our position today as still antimilitarist is, in my opinion, decidedly wrong.

I raised this question in our conversations with Comrade Trotsky. After he had elaborated his ideas, I put the question to him and asked him to make his answer as sharp and categoric as possible. I asked: "Can we call ourselves militarists?" And he said, "Yes. It might not be tactically advisable to begin with such a proclamation, but if the pacifists accuse you of it, if you are accused of being a militarist, you take the platform and say, 'Yes, I am a proletarian revolutionary militarist.'"[23] This doesn't contradict the somewhat different attitude we took in somewhat different times—when the possibility of preventing war by revolution could not be excluded.

Was the fight of the social-pacifist elements against conscription right in this last period? No, it was not right. It overlooked realities and sowed illusions. The workers were for conscription. The conscription bill was carried without any serious opposition whatsoever. The fight as we conducted it, for workers' control, was 100 percent correct. We are positively for conscription, but we do not want conscription of the workers by the bosses. We want conscription of the workers by a workers' organization. If some horrified muddlehead of a pacifist asks: "Do you really mean it? Do you want to compel every worker to take up arms and learn how to use arms?" We answer, "Yes, that is exactly what we mean." How do we justify such compulsion? By the necessities of the class struggle which justify everything. There is nothing new in such an attitude. A certain amount of compulsion has always been invoked by the labor movement against the backward, the slackers.

For example, trade unions always strive to make membership compulsory. The intelligent, loyal, and serious workers join the union voluntarily. Then they say to the backward, to the ignorant, and to the scab-hearted: Join if you will, peacefully, but join this union or else stay out of that factory. That's compulsion for you, my boy. We cannot allow your ignorance or mistaken conception of individual interest to interfere with the class interests as a whole. What is a picket line? Well, some that I have seen at least, had aspects of extraordinary persuasion. I have seen picket lines of such a nature that if anyone wanted to argue about it, he didn't even get a chance to argue. He either stayed out or got knocked out. Compulsion in the class war is a class necessity. We didn't invent it. It must be applied also to military training.

An interesting question, asked by some workers, was reported here: "How can you tell the workers to put themselves under the control of the unions for military training when the unions are controlled by people like Lewis and Green and Hillman?" Well, if we wait until the unions are led by the Fourth International, we lose all sense of the dynamics of their development. Green and Lewis and their similars—the whole upper bureaucracy of the labor movement at present—are agents of the capitalists in the labor movement, but they are not the same thing as the bosses. Their sole base of existence is the labor movement; and in spite of all the bureaucratism of the unions, they are subject to certain pressures, certain controls from below. When the worsening of conditions, supplemented by our agitation, raises a wave of radicalization in the masses, the workers will solve the problem of leadership in the workers' regiments as well as in the unions.

We always take the workers' organizations as they are. We join them as they are, support them as they are, try to remodel them from within. Of course, the very idea of a Lewis or a Green heading the military instruction of workers is farfetched. Correctly understood, our fight for military training under trade union control is a mortal struggle against the reformist, nonfighting bureaucracy. The adoption of our policy, or even a strong movement in favor of it, would spell the doom of the present leaders. Nobody would believe these scoundrels are fit for such a serious enterprise as the instruction of workers for military action.

In 1917, following February, the soviets of Petrograd and Moscow were controlled by the Social Democrats and the Social Revolutionaries, that is, men of the stripe of Lewis and Green, Hillman and Dubinsky; no better and no worse. In spite of that, because the soviets embraced the workers, Lenin raised the slogan: "All power to the soviets." In the course of that fight for all power to the soviets, the Bolsheviks won to their side the majority of the workers. And almost coincidentally with the uprising, the workers threw out the Mensheviks and Social Revolutionaries and placed the Bolsheviks at their head. That's the way things have to be conceived in this question also.

The question of the referendum on war in connection with compulsory military training was raised by one of the comrades. This question was propounded to the Old Man in a letter from Goldman, and answered by him. The Old Man said: "I don't see why we should drop the demand for a referendum on war. Before they actually enter the war, an agitation for a people's referendum is an excellent means of showing up their fake democracy."[24] It is a means of agitation against them. It is not so simple and automatic; one does not exclude the other.

Comrade Trotsky also answered the question whether our slogan of workers' defense guards is superseded by our military policy. He said he did not see why. He thought they were interrelated. Of course at the present time, the emphasis is entirely on the question of penetrating the military organizations. But, as the crisis develops, all kinds of reactionary attacks will be made on the unions. Gangs will be organized to break them up. The union members will be under the constant necessity to protect themselves. The workers must be on guard to protect their unions. The slogan of workers' defense guards can be raised at an appropriate time, not in contradiction to our military policy, but in correlation with it.

On the question of the role of women in the party after conscription. We must not get the idea that all our people will be in the army. Roughly speaking, the same percentage of our party will be in the army as the percentage of their class of the same generation. We have a young party. You will learn from Comrade Dobbs's comprehensive organization report that the average age of our party is twenty-nine years. This means that perhaps a majority of our men comrades are going to be in the army sooner or later. Some of our leading people will be taken out and in their places women comrades will come forward. We already have indications that we are not without resources in this field. And don't forget we have a few old codgers who are beyond the draft age. Maybe the party can make use of them. Lenin once said, and I always sympathized with him, that when a revolutionist reaches the age of fifty he should be shot. When men get older they usually get tired and conservative. But there are exceptions to all laws, and we come in under the exceptions. If we have the correct policy, and if we have the conception that every member of our party is potentially a leader, potentially a general in the army of the revolution, we will not lack leadership.

Comrade Birchman mentioned the question of the Negro workers in the militarization. Our attitude toward the Negroes in war, like our attitude toward all other questions, is the same as in times of peace. Our line is the class line. We stand for absolutely unconditional equality for every race and nationality. That's a cardinal principle of communism. We have to fight for and defend this principle under all conditions, including the conditions of militarism.

How do we work in a conscript army, someone asked. We work the same way as in a shop. Indeed, the main purpose of industry now is supplying the army. Where would you draw the line? There is hardly an industry that won't be mobilized either for the manufacture or transportation of materials for the army. The masses are in the army, or working to supply the army. The workers are subjected to military exploitation. We go in and defend the interests of the slaves of military exploitation, just as we go into the factory and fight against capitalist exploitation there. Our basic line everywhere is the class line.

The second point is to be careful, cautious. Make no putsches, make no premature moves that expose us and separate us from the masses. Go with the masses. Be with the masses, just as the Bolsheviks were in Kerensky's army.

Why can't we do that here? And how otherwise can we do it? How otherwise, in a world dominated by militarism, can we see our way to world salvation except through military means? And how can we get these military means except by penetrating the army as it exists?

We have one great assurance. I repeat what I said at the mass meeting. We have our opportunity before us in this country. Even if war is declared and a military dictatorship is instituted, even if all kinds of repressive measures are decreed—we must always remember that a dictatorship of the police and military forces, instituted by fiat, cannot be the same thing as a fascist dictatorship based on a mass movement mobilized over years of time after the workers have muffed their chance to take power. Before fascism can come in this country on a mass basis, according to the historical law elucidated by Comrade Trotsky, the great mass radicalization of the workers will take place. The workers here, as everywhere, will have the first chance to take power. That is all we need. We will have our chance, and we will not miss it.

SOCIALIST ELECTION POLICY IN 1940

September 28, 1940

This resolution, written by Cannon, was adopted by the SWP's September 1940 Plenum-Conference. It was first published in the Socialist Appeal *of October 5, 1940.*

Participation in the November elections is dictated to us by our Marxist conceptions of the tasks of a revolutionary party. Although the main energies of the party are devoted to the mobilization of the proletariat in mass action against the capitalist class and its state apparatus, that mobilization is served by participation in electoral activity. Revolutionary electoral activity takes the form of tribunes of the people summoning the masses to struggle, not merely at the polls on election day, but everywhere at all times. Electoral activity is a secondary but nevertheless important form of revolutionary activity.

One of the results of the capitalist preparations for the war has been the further development of almost insurmountable restrictions to prevent minority workers' parties from finding a place on the ballot, especially for candidates for the presidency. The National Committee was compelled to recognize that our party is too small to expend the funds and forces necessary to secure a place on the ballot for our presidential candidates because of these restrictions.

If our party did not itself formally participate in the elections, it might under certain conditions give critical support to the candidate of another party. Such a candidate would never be that of a bourgeois party. We no more support a Willkie or Roosevelt than support an employers' representative in a union election.

The only candidate we could conceivably support is that of a party representing a section of the working class whose augmented vote would be generally understood to signify progress for the labor movement. Unfortunately, however, no such party is participating in the present election campaign.

The Socialist Party is not such a party. It is a hopeless anachronism, a fading vestige of the past, a petty-bourgeois pacifist sect. It has scarcely any influence in any section of the labor movement. It would indeed be absurd for us to support in the elections a party which has far less influence in the labor movement than we have. Norman Thomas is rightly understood to be a personality with a personal following which represents neither socialism nor the labor movement. Any form of support for his candidacy cannot, therefore, aid the labor movement in any way. The same considerations hold for that grotesque sect, the Socialist Labor Party.

It is also impossible to give critical support in the elections to the Communist Party. Its union-smashing policies—which continue in its present pseudoleft period as in its openly pro-Roosevelt period—its role as Stalin's agent under the Hitler-Stalin pact, the subordination of the various Communist parties to the GPU as was glaringly revealed in the assassination of Comrade Leon Trotsky, make the Communist Party the object of hatred to many of the most progressive workers. The hatred of the honest progressive workers against the Communist Party must be distinguished from the patriotic hostility of the chauvinists against the Communist Party. The hatred felt against the Communist Party by many honest progressive workers testifies to their profound class instinct. These factors make impossible any electoral activity in support of Stalinist candidates.

At the same time, especially in the present election campaign, we have the elementary class duty to defend the rights of the Communist Party against the chauvinists who are attempting to rule it off the ballot, hound its election campaign workers, etc. Against the capitalist class and its agents, we unconditionally defend the Communist Party. A firm policy of defending the democratic rights of the Communist Party will also go far to separate the red-baiters from those progressive workers whose hatred of the Communist Party stems from their class consciousness.

So far as formal participation in this election is concerned the

SWP is participating in this election mainly through those state and local candidates whom some sections of the party have been able to place on the ballot. Our main activity on a national scale is to put forward our program on all the burning issues of this epoch of war and militarism.

We must recognize, however, that the 1940 election campaign means a lost opportunity for our party. The only way to prevent the loss of similar opportunities, not merely in the electoral field, but in others as well, is the speedy mobilization of our party to transform it from its present size and strength into a mass party of the working class.

LETTER TO THE TEXAS BRANCH[25]

October 15, 1940

This letter about a difference between an SWP branch and the party National Office is a representative example of the tone Cannon used in his relations with the branches and ranks of the SWP.

New York

Dear Comrades,

Your letter of September 23 was read and thoroughly discussed at the plenum of the National Committee in Chicago, despite the pressure of time in connection with the conference.

The plenum unanimously decided to uphold the position taken by the Political Committee in this matter. At the same time the national secretary was directed to write you a letter, explaining the reasons which motivate this decision.

1. The conditions under which the party works in a metropolitan center like New York are very different from those prevailing in other parts of the country, above all in the South which is practically virgin territory for the revolutionary party. Consequently, the methods employed in party work in New York, the internal life of the party, its tempo, etc., cannot be mechanically transplanted from New York into other localities where conditions are so different. Every attempt to do so brings bad consequences. We know these questions very well from abundant experience. That is why we try to see to it that when comrades go from New York to other localities they do not carry New York methods with them, but make a serious effort to adapt themselves to the conditions and the tempo of the new locality.

We explained all this at great length to Comrade Edwards

before he left New York. After receiving letters from him which indicated clearly that he was not carrying out our directions, we wrote him repeatedly and at length. We insisted that he modify his aggressiveness in the internal affairs of the branch, and go much slower in general, until he had lived in Texas long enough to learn more about its specific conditions and the outlook of the Texas workers.

He failed to heed our admonitions. Instead, he proceeded headlong on an opposite line. It was only after we became convinced from his own letters and reports that he was on the wrong track, and that he was not able or did not want to modify his methods in line with our advice, that we asked him to return to New York.

2. The question whether this decision should be complied with or not is not an issue between the Texas branch and the National Committee, but between Comrade Edwards and the National Committee. The plenum completely rejected the attempt to shift the thing around into a controversy with the branch. Comrade Edwards left New York for work in the field with the consent of the National Committee. That established his position as a field worker under the direct supervision of the National Committee. In our eyes whether field workers are paid or unpaid makes no difference in their status as far as their relations to the National Office are concerned.

We do not permit field workers to act as free lances. When their proposals or plans or methods conflict with those of the National Committee they have the full right to discuss the points with us but they have no right to carry out an independent line. They have to submit to discipline and conform to the instructions of the center. Of course the national leadership is not infallible. But it is far better to have the activities of the party regulated and controlled by a collective leadership that has been selected by a party convention than for every capricious individual to be permitted to decide and act for himself. Those who try to take such liberties will not be long in discovering that they have misunderstood our party and its methods of work.

3. It is extremely unfortunate that the Texas branch could not have a delegate at the conference. In addition to everything else, this most successful and inspiring gathering gave the party a sharp turn toward greater responsibility, centralization, and discipline. In bringing relations with the petty-bourgeois opposition to a definitive conclusion by expelling them unconditionally,

the whole conference felt an automatic impulse for more serious Bolshevik centralism and discipline. That is why the Edwards case struck the members of the National Committee like an anachronism, like a hangover of old days when the party was cluttered up with people dominated by the petty-bourgeois spirit of individualism and indiscipline.

We feel very sorry that such a young party organization as the Texas branch should be injured in its development by hangover manifestations of this spirit. We feel partly responsible for this because it was only by our consent that Comrade Edwards was transferred from New York to Texas. You can be sure, dear comrades, that we have been motivated in everything by the desire to help you, to help the Texas branch achieve a normal, steady development with a minimum of internal disturbances, and high-pressure methods. We will continue to do all we can to help you in every way possible.

As far as Comrade Edwards is concerned, we repeat that he remains under the jurisdiction of the National Committee and must account to the National Committee, not to the Texas branch, for the fulfillment of the instructions he has received.

With best comradely greetings,

Yours fraternally,
James P. Cannon
National Secretary

FIRST RESULTS OF OUR
MILITARY POLICY

Published November 23, 1940

This is the first of three articles on the SWP's military policy. It appeared in the Socialist Appeal.

The military transitional program, unanimously accepted by our recent Chicago conference after two months of discussion in the party branches, has provided our comrades with a most effective approach and means of agitation among the workers. Numerous reports and letters from active comrades in all parts of the country testify to the value of our program in this respect. It arouses interest and discussion precisely because it deals most concretely with the one big subject which dominates the minds of the workers, the subject of war and militarism.

All reports testify that the overwhelming majority of the workers expect direct participation of America in the war. This feeling of the workers is profoundly correct, and it is the duty of an honest revolutionary party to tell them so. Short of a revolution, for which the American workers are not yet ready, it is impossible to prevent or even halt the deliberate movement of American imperialism into the military struggle for world domination.

In the essence of the matter, America is already at war with the Axis powers at least three-fourths of the way. The policy of selling goods and war materials only to those countries who are able to carry them away in their own ships is simply a clever device to supply Britain and participate in the blockade of the others. The political and moral preparation of public opinion against the Axis powers is completed. The entire Western Hemisphere has already been marked off as the exclusive domain of Wall Street. To top things off, on the practical side, fifteen billion dollars have been appropriated for armaments while conscription has become a law and is being put into effect without any serious opposition whatever.

In the face of all these staggering facts it is a positive crime to lull the workers with a prospect of peace or to whine against universal military service which is already in operation. American imperialism has already entered with both feet on the path of war and militarism. This is the new reality, and abstract opposition cannot affect the course of events in any way whatever. It is the task of the proletarian vanguard to accept the new reality, to meet the imperialists on their own ground, the ground of militarism, and counterpose to their program the military program of the proletariat.

That is the task which our party, aided by the genius of Trotsky, has aimed to accomplish by the adoption of the Chicago resolution and the development of our agitation in accordance with it.

It is precisely because this resolution goes to the very heart of the problem of the day that it has aroused such widespread interest and discussion from the beginning. Our policy is realistic and profoundly revolutionary, but it strikes a new note and breaks sharply with the tradition of American radicalism which has been negative and essentially pacifist on the question of war. For that reason we devoted two months to internal discussion before publicly proclaiming our resolution. The unanimity and enthusiasm with which our party adopted the resolution is evidence that its years of Marxist education under the direct instruction of Comrade Trotsky were not wasted.

We are now only at the beginning of our attempt to popularize the policy in the general labor movement. There is a long road ahead, but the first results give reassuring proof that we are on the right road. We seek, first of all, an approach to the militant workers, whose patriotism—at least 99 percent of them are patriotic—is in large measure a confused expression of their hatred for fascism. These sentiments are now exploited by the imperialists. Our policy is designed to turn these sentiments in the direction of a struggle for their own class interests and liberation.

The first reactions of our resolution have been widely diversified. Our reports from the field show that some workers are sympathetic, some skeptical. Many workers want to know how the policy will work out in practice. They raise acute and penetrating questions of application which have not yet been adequately answered in our press. In this series of articles I shall comment on these questions and objections and undertake to answer at the same time the criticisms of the various radical political groups who, as was to be expected, neither understand nor agree with our policy. In some aspects of the question, the criticisms of our opponents provide an opportunity for the restatement and elucidation of our policy in a way to meet the objections of the workers and make our policy clearer to them. This aim, I hope, will justify taking space for an answer to factional polemics which would otherwise be stale and profitless and out of place in our agitational paper.

Our military resolution, it goes without saying, does not repeal the basic program of the party and the Fourth International, but is designed as a tactical supplement to it. It is not in itself a program of proletarian revolution, but a bridge toward it. It is designed to protect and develop the class independence of the workers who are dragooned into the imperialist military machine. It is, in effect, a proposal for a united front with the workers as they are today, patriotic and antifascist, not ready for the socialist revolution, but concerned to protect themselves and their class interests. We offer them a program of joint struggle for practical and reasonable demands which will protect the interests of the workers, preserve their class independence, and prepare the way, by the objective logic of their development, for the revolutionary showdown. That is why we call our military program a *transitional* program of *agitation* as distinct from our fundamental program of socialist revolution which we advance by *propaganda*. Once this distinction is understood—and no one who reads our resolution intelligently and conscientiously can misunderstand it—the criticisms of our political opponents, who accuse us of opportunism, fall of their own weight.

This is the case with the Oehlerites who have attacked our resolution in their official paper. These people are in favor of the proletarian revolution but they are really incapable of understanding transitional measures and demands which can take the workers as they are, not yet revolutionary, and advance them toward the revolutionary goal; a program which can form a bridge between the present consciousness of the workers and the ultimate logic of their struggle; in other words, a transitional program. That is why they cannot understand or agree with us today any more than they could understand or agree with the general transitional program of the Fourth International adopted at its world congress.[26] It is this sectarian mentality in general that dooms them to complete isolation from the current struggle of the workers and condemns them to utter futility despite all their intentions.

The SLP [Socialist Labor Party] will surely reject our military program if they have not already done so. (God forgive me, I don't read the *Weekly People* as attentively as I should and don't know whether they have yet expressed themselves.) The SLP will have nothing less than the "unconditional surrender of the capitalist class"—no immediate demand, no transitional program. But since the capitalist class, up to the present at any rate, has shown no disposition to surrender, the SLP remains aloof, unterrified and uncontaminated and, consequently, without the slightest influence on the course of development in the labor movement. Abstract propaganda for socialism is good and necessary. But such propaganda alone can never produce a revolutionary victory of the workers. It is necessary to supplement it by a practical program of agitation adapted to the needs of the day and the present stage of working-class development, in order to lift the movement higher and turn it in a revolutionary direction. That is why the revolutionary party needs a transitional program in general. That is why in the present world conditions it needs a military transition program in particular.

The Lovestoneites have not yet commented on our military resolution, as far as I know. But if they find it possible to take time off from their frenzied defense of Great Britain, they will surely attack our resolution "from the left," as they attacked the general transitional program of the Fourth International last year. We shall wait and see. Meantime we have a first-class substitute for a Herbergian[27] outburst of phony radicalism and pseudo-Marxism, embellished with irrelevant historical references and misapplied quotations, in a recent number of *Labor Action*, the official organ of the "Workers Party." This is the political group which the well-known Professor Burnham, with callous disregard of his parental obligations, abandoned, with a cruel remark that it "begins with foundations none too firm" and the parting salute: "I cannot wish success to the Workers Party." The author of this burlesque is Max Shachtman. And it marks his first utterance on controversial questions for a long time. After the double disaster of his polemic with Trotsky and the desertion of Burnham, Shachtman retired into silence and contemplation for many months. And that was the best thing for him to do. Total abstinence is the best prescription for a man sick from talking too much. But that couldn't last forever. Now he is at it again and, of course, as he himself says, his remarks are "sharply polemical."

When the announcement was made, with much fanfare, that Shachtman was returning to the political wars one might have thought that conscience and common sense would require him, first of all, to deal with the question of Burnham. Doesn't he owe his anxiously waiting public at least a few words of explanation on this score? How did it happen that Shachtman's mentor and "friend and colleague," with whom he fought shoulder to shoulder against Trotsky and the Trotskyists, suddenly—only two months later!—openly repudiated socialism and passed over into the camp of the class enemy? An explanation of this circumstance is what you might have expected from Shachtman—if you don't know Shachtman. But his "sharply polemical" article, full of sound and fury, is not directed at Burnham; it is intended to drown out the question of Burnham by shouting loud and long against others. It is not directed at the man who deserted socialism, but at those who in their stupid, ignorant way still remain faithful to it.

Only a few months ago, Burnham, with Shachtman at his heels, denounced Trotsky and the Trotskyites as capitulators to Stalin and as "the left cover for Hitler." So spoke Burnham, the spokesman of the minority, at our party convention a few months ago. Now, without so much as an explanation of our transformation, Shachtman describes us as capitulators to American imperialism, as almost-if-not-quite social patriots, as class collaborationists, as falsifiers of the "views and traditions of the Bolsheviks in the last war" which he, of course, defends.

An unsuspecting casual reader might easily imagine that the man is on a revolutionary rampage. But in reality he is only kibitzing. His entire article from beginning to end is a mixture of confusion and bad faith—a Shachtman "polemic." Not a single one of his "points" can stand inspection. In my next article I shall undertake to prove this, point by point. In doing so, I hope, as I said in the beginning, to contribute something to the clarification of the many and serious questions concerning our policy raised by workers in discussions with our comrades in the field. If I succeed in this the time spent on an otherwise distasteful task will not be wasted.

MILITARISM AND WORKERS' RIGHTS

Published November 30, 1940

This was the second of three articles in the Socialist Appeal.

Our resolution on military policy proclaims no new principle, but attempts to apply the old principles of Bolshevism to the new conditions. In line with all the programmatic documents of the Fourth International, the resolution says: "The imperialist war is not our war and the militarism of the capitalist state is not our militarism. . . .We are against the war as a whole just as we are against the rule of the class that conducts it, and never under any circumstances vote to give them any confidence in their conduct of the war or preparations for it—not a man, not a cent, not a gun with our support. Our war is the war of the working class against the capitalist order." (*Socialist Appeal,* October 5.)

So much for the principled position of Trotskyism, which alone among all the tendencies in the international labor movement remains consistently revolutionary in times of war as well as in times of peace. But, despite our opposition, we have the militarism and tomorrow we will have the war in full scope. That does not change our principle, but it imposes upon us a certain line of tactics since we do not want to remain aloof as mere oppositionists. We do not rest content with general opposition to capitalism and general advocacy of the socialist revolution and simply repeat our ultimate aims as a set of soul-saving formulas. We seek in each and every situation to devise the tactical slogans around which we may carry on continuous and effective agitation leading toward the goal. The problem of the hour is to find a realistic basis for our irreconcilable class agitation in the arena of war and militarism which now, and for a whole epoch, will dominate the world. This is the aim of our resolution on military policy.

Our military program is intended as a program of agitation. In order to be effective such a program must take into account not only the objective circumstance (the epoch of militarism), but also the present consciousness and mood of the workers. The American workers are against war, they are fearful of war, yet they are convinced in their bones that it is unavoidable and that the millions of young men who are being drafted and sent up for military training are destined to be cannon fodder. A comrade writes from Buffalo: "A large section of the working class, and perhaps all of it subconsciously, regards the draft for what it is— going to war. Even the National Guardsmen who left town last month were accompanied by weeping mothers and sweethearts."

The workers like to hear the promises of Roosevelt and Willkie that American boys will not be sent into foreign wars, but the great mass of them do not believe a word of it. Neither do they believe the isolationist and pacifist liars who say it is possible under capitalism to "keep America out of war."

The workers are profoundly impressed by the fate of the European countries which have been overrun by Hitler's army. They hate and fear fascism. So far they see it incarnated only in the foreign foe, and they are ready if necessary to go to war against it, especially if the war is presented to them, as it surely will be, in the guise of "defense" against a "foreign" attack. Facing the prospect of war it is obvious to the serious-minded workers that military training is needed. That is why they submitted universally to conscription; without enthusiasm, it is true, but also without any serious opposition. This attitude of the rank and file of the American working class is a thousand times more practical and realistic than that of the pacifist muddleheads who proclaim the necessity of socialism and yet oppose compulsory military training—in a world gone mad with militarism.

Our military resolution takes the foregoing circumstances, objective and subjective, as its point of departure and attempts to show the workers how to carry on their daily struggle against the bosses over into the new field of militarism.

The American workers have made great advances in the last six years. Millions of new recruits have been drawn into the trade union movement for the first time. They have had to fight every inch of the way to gain the smallest concessions, and then to fight all over again, and continuously, to keep them. In the course of these fights the workers have developed a fervent devotion to their unions. They have learned to hate and distrust the bosses who directly exploit them and the police and local authorities who help the bosses.

In strike after strike the militant American workers have demonstrated that they have no fear of direct clashes with these local authorities and police. But in their overwhelming majority, the workers still think of the national government as something different. They respect it and at the same time they fear it as a remote power, which cannot be combatted. The average militant trade unionist, who considers a battle with local cops as a part of the day's business in a strike, is inclined to flinch away from any conflict with "the man with the whiskers," the popular name for the federal government and its police agents.

"You can't strike against the government"—this is not only the dictum of Roosevelt, but also the feeling of the great majority of workers at the present time. Some of them think they have a right to do it, as was shown by the strikes against the WPA,[28] but the great majority approach any prospect of a conflict with the federal government with the feeling that "you can't get away with it." These illusions of the workers are the ace card up the sleeve of the American imperialists.

A letter from a Toledo comrade highlights this attitude: "I and other comrades have noticed in agitating at employment offices on our military program the following response. While workers agreed that military training is needed and express distrust of the methods of the present conscription bill, they are extremely skeptical of the *possibility* of getting the unions to control training or of winning union conditions in the army. 'You can't strike against the government.' 'If you agitate in the army you will be shot.' 'You need trained military men to have good training.' These are the three most common answers. . . . Even some of the politically developed sympathizers of the party say that our program has value only in an *agitational* sense but that it cannot be accomplished." (My emphasis.)

By such expressions—which are quite typical—the workers express the mistaken opinion that the class struggle ends when they leave the arena of the union and the factory and enter the new arena of war and militarism. They do not anticipate in advance the tremendous new experiences which are destined to make such a powerful impression on their minds, and that in a comparatively short time. Even the reported remarks of some of our sympathizers to the effect that our program "cannot be accomplished," reveal an unconscious tendency to accept as permanent a situation which is radically changing before our eyes and which will continue to change with increasing speed and sweep. Respect for the status quo is out of tune with the times. War and militarism will uproot the workers from the old environment in which their present convictions were formed, impose new and terrible experiences upon them, and compel them to think in new terms.

The workers have yet to learn that the government, which now appears as a sacrosanct institution standing above the classes, is in reality the executive committee of all the bosses. Experience under the conditions of militarism and war, aided by our agitation, will teach this necessary lesson in the coming period. In the course of these developments our program, if we present it with simplicity and clarity, will not only have success in an "agitational sense"; the awakening workers will pass over its extremely modest and elementary demands as advancing troops pass over a bridge to a new point of vantage.

The army of conscription will be different from the comparatively small standing army we have known, and the change will be all for the better. The "volunteer" army has been recruited for the most part from the ranks of the half-starved unemployed. They have been isolated from the people, helpless and unable to get a hearing. It was customary to think of these soldiers as having no human rights whatever, no means of redress. "If you agitate in the army you will be shot." Contemptible are those opponents of compulsory military service who, at the same time, directly or indirectly support this monstrous militarism of the "volunteer" variety.

In the army of conscription the situation will be radically changed. It will consist of millions of young workers—the proletariat in arms! They are accustomed to certain rights. Their mighty numbers will confer a sense of power upon them. It will not be possible to treat them like cattle for any length of time without creating a profound discontent in their ranks.

Our military transitional program is not for a day, but for tomorrow, for a long time. If only a part of the militant workers take interest in it and regard it as a good thing if it could be accomplished—that is already a gratifying initial success. It is up to us then to convince these workers that our demands are reasonable and practical in the present situation, and fully within their rights, as indeed they are.

Our aim, it must always be remembered, is not to convince quibbling factional opponents who wage a fictitious political struggle in the form of literary exercises, but workers who take the question, as they take all questions, seriously. That is why we hinge our agitation around illustrations from the life they know, that of the factory and the union. Their class attitude in the factory is the product of their experience, aided by the agitation of the more conscious elements. The right of the workers to organization, to have union officers of their own choosing, to be represented by shop committees of their own trusted people— these precious and necessary rights were not conferred upon our workers by benevolent bosses or an impartial government. In fact, they also were once "illegal," and more than one worker has been "shot" for advocating them. The workers' conviction that they need these things in the factory, in order to set limits to oppression and exploitation, is the result of their experience.

Their skepticism regarding the possibility of realizing analogous conditions in the field of militarism arises from the fact that for them it is as yet unexplored territory. But they will soon discover that the oppression, exploitation, and class discrimination, which are the substance of their daily lives as workers, reappear also in the Prussianized militarism of the capitalist state in a form that is more intensive, more brutal, and more contemptuous of human life. The military experience of the workers will come powerfully to the aid of our program, giving it a burning actuality, and make it the banner of their first struggles for a minimum of class independence and self protection. Our program anticipates this experience and attempts to prepare the minds of the workers for a speedier and more conscious reaction to it.

Our slogans carry the class line into the new conditions of militarism. In the factory a militant trade unionist wouldn't trust an employer or an agent of the employers as far as he can kick an anvil in his bare feet. But in the military machine, in the present setup, the officer corps from top to bottom is dominated by people of this boss type—class enemies who regard the workers in the ranks as cannon fodder, and have no regard for their welfare and safety. Why shouldn't the workers, in such a situation, put forth the demand for officers from the ranks of the workers and the unions?

Haven't the workers, who are risking their lives for "democracy," the right to a little democracy for themselves? Out of the billions of dollars of federal funds appropriated for military purposes, why shouldn't a certain sum be earmarked for the establishment of special camps to train workers to become officers? What's wrong about such a demand? And, for that matter, what is "illegal" about it? Indeed, if a serious militant worker who hates and distrusts the bosses and their agents for good reason will stop to think about it, he must be impressed by the extreme modesty of the demands of our transitional program. They represent not the last word, but rather the first. Most workers today have the illusion that the class lineup, which confronts him in the factory and on the picket line, is by some miracle eliminated in the domain of war and militarism. Our program of transitional demands, proceeding from the Marxist principle which never recognizes a suspension of the class struggle in the class society, is designed to break this illusion, this fetish. That is the purpose of our agitation around the program.

In my speech to our Chicago conference, I devoted a big section to our agitational approach to the workers who think it necessary to defend the country against fascism by military means, but imagine it has to be left in full charge of the bourgeois rulers. I argued against this prejudice in terms and by means of illustrations which I thought might be effectively employed by our party agitators. I summed up a whole section devoted to such arguments with the following statement: "The workers themselves must take charge of this fight against Hitler and anybody else who tries to invade their rights. That is the whole principle of the new policy that has been elaborated for us by Comrade Trotsky. The great difference between this and the socialist military policy in the past is that it is an *extension* of the old policy, an adaptation of *old principles* to *new conditions*."

From a reading of the text of my speech it is clear beyond possibility of misunderstanding that I was arguing against the prejudices of the workers and not against any principles hitherto maintained by our movement. On the contrary, I took pains to assert that our new concrete practical slogans are simply "an extension of the old policy, an adaptation of old principles to new conditions." My speech as a whole as well as the resolution adopted at the Chicago conference and the published letters and comments of Comrade Trotsky on the subject are all permeated with this idea. We stand, now as before, on the principles of Bolshevism and we aim to advance these principles by a transitional program in the military epoch.

Anyone who wants to conduct an honest dispute with us must begin by stating our actual position fairly and honestly and then criticize us from one of two standpoints: (1) the principles of Bolshevism are wrong and, likewise, the practical slogans designed to apply them; or, (2) the transitional program violates the principles of Bolshevism on war.

Shachtman, writing in *Labor Action* (November 4) employed a different method of attack, a method designed not to clarify, but to confuse. At the beginning of his article, as the first "point" which sets the tone and shapes the character of this article as a whole, he "lifts" my above-quoted statement out of its context and tries to make it appear that I am arguing not against the prejudices of the workers but against the *principles* of the modern Trotskyist movement! Then, with mock seriousness, he asks: "Of *which* old policy is our military program an extension?"—and solemnly pretends that I may have been speaking of the policy of the "Liberals, social-democrats and Stalinists." Then, after explaining to us that "Trotsky above all taught the movement that the workers themselves must take charge of this fight against Hitler," he ends the first "point" and premise of his article with the devastating question: "If that was the 'whole principle of the *new* policy' what was the principle of the 'old' policy?"

But I had explained in the sentences he quoted, and can only repeat here again, that we are not enunciating any different principle but simply attempting to apply "old principles to new conditions." But Shachtman obviously calculates that by the time he gets to the end of his juggled and misapplied quotation the casual and unsuspecting reader will be too muddled and confused to know the difference. To answer him it is only necessary to go back and show what we really said and what we really meant. The interested reader, who takes the trouble to read the quotations in their context—and that is an absolutely necessary precaution whenever Shachtman is "quoting"—can get the matter straight. He will also get an insight into the polemical methods of Shachtman which became so notorious in the factional struggle which he conducted jointly with Burnham against Trotsky and the majority of our party. He became known to the adult members of our movement as an unscrupulous "twister" of quotations and a perverter of historical incidents to serve factional contentions.

In his lengthy attack on the military policy adopted by our party, Shachtman runs true to form from beginning to end. The dubious methods which he employed in his premise are maintained throughout the article. Misrepresentation is followed by falsification and reinforced with a spice of outright literary forgery. In debating with Shachtman one needs not a pen but a pair of hip boots and a shovel in order to dig down and clear away the filth which he piles over the essence of every dispute. It is not a very agreeable task but in the line of duty, I shall return to it again, insofar as the exposure of these methods of the political underworld helps to facilitate the explanation and clarification of our military transitional program to workers who are seriously and honestly interested in the question—the most important and burning question affecting their lives.

LENIN, TROTSKY, AND THE
FIRST WORLD WAR

Published December 7, 1940

This was the last of three articles in the Socialist Appeal.

In advancing our military transitional program, we proceed from the point of view that permanent war and universal militarism have become the dominant characteristics of our epoch, and we visualize the social revolution as the immediate outcome of the imperialist war. We begin, as did Lenin, with a declaration of irreconcilable class opposition to the imperialists and their war. It is only by means of this principled standpoint of class opposition that the cadres of modern Bolshevism are formed and clearly delimited from all other parties, groups, and tendencies, which to one degree or another, tend toward conciliation or collaboration with their national ruling class in the war.

But the situation which confronts us today is not an exact duplication of that which confronted the revolutionary Marxists at the outbreak of the First World War in 1914. For one thing, the capitalist order has reached a far more advanced stage of decay and is more susceptible to revolutionary overthrow. In addition, we have the benefit of twenty-six years of the richest historical experiences which have been generalized by the great Marxist Trotsky. These circumstances enable us to go farther, with more concretely worked out slogans of agitation to advance the class struggle under conditions of war and militarism, than was possible for the revolutionary Marxist at the beginning of the First World War.

Trotsky, the author of our program, contributed extremely important thoughts to the workers' vanguard facing the Second World War: the immediacy of the revolutionary perspective in connection with the present war, and the necessity for transitional slogans which can serve to mobilize the masses for independent class action leading up to it. It is precisely this immediacy of the revolutionary perspective that makes the transitional program a burning necessity.

"Our policy," Trotsky wrote, "the policy of the revolutionary proletariat toward the second imperialist war, is a continuation of the policy elaborated during the last imperialist war, primarily under Lenin's leadership. But a continuation does not signify a repetition. In this case too, continuation signifies a development, a deepening and a sharpening." (*Fourth International,* October 1940.) He reminded us, and we repeated after him, that not even Lenin had visualized the victory of the proletarian revolution as the immediate outcome of the First World War.

At this point Lenin suddenly acquired an advocate in a camp which hitherto has not been distinguished by its fidelity to Leninism. Shachtman, comrade-in-arms of the avowed anti-Bolshevik Burnham, and the present leader of the "Workers Party" (the Burnham group minus Burnham), comes to the defense of Lenin against us. The "floating kidney," as Trotsky denominated Shachtman, bobs up in the most unexpected places!

However, we have committed no assault on Lenin, and he is in no way in need of the dubious "defense" of this attorney. It is necessary to take a little time out to prove this, because the authority of Lenin is one of the greatest treasures of the revolutionary movement. His name is written beside that of Trotsky on the banner of the Russian Revolution. We proclaim the extension of this revolution throughout the world in the name of Lenin-Trotsky. We must not permit the slightest confusion as to how we regard Lenin; and it is a matter of simple respect to his memory to protect him from the hypocritical support of an advocate who is known among Leninists only as a betrayer of Leninism.

It will take a little time and space, but this can't be helped. It is a simple task—mainly work with a shovel. His own confusion and instinct to sow confusion—two qualities always happily married in Shachtman's factional "polemics"—plus his unfailing twisting, falsifying, and misrepresenting the words of others and the events of the past are all piled together here also. It is simply necessary to dig this stuff away, and then to unwind the quotations and replace the historical incidents in their true position. Then nothing will be left of the dirty mess that

Shachtman has made of our alleged attack on Lenin and Shachtman's "brief" as attorney for the defense.

The defense of Lenin is the second "point" in Shachtman's indictment of our military policy. The occasion for it was the publication of my speech to our Chicago conference which adopted our resolution. Shachtman made a big "case" out of what I said about Lenin, or rather, what I didn't say. Here are the sentences which Shachtman quoted from my speech: "We said and those before us said that capitalism had outlived its usefulness. World economy is ready for socialism. But when the world war started in 1914 none of the parties had the idea that on the agenda stood the struggle for power. The stand of the best of them was essentially a protest against the war. It did not occur even to the best Marxists that the time had come when the power must be seized by the workers in order to save civilization from degeneration. Even Lenin did not visualize the victory of the proletarian revolution as the immediate outcome of the war."

Shachtman characterized this as a "monstrous falsehood," and as a "complete misrepresentation of the views and traditions of the Bolsheviks in the last war." He offers a number of "quotations" to prove that Lenin and the Bolsheviks advocated revolution during the war, he implies that Lenin expected revolution as the war's immediate outcome, and finally asks: "And above all, what in heaven's name was the meaning of Lenin's slogan, repeated a thousand times during the last war, 'Turn the imperialist war into a civil war'?"

Our quoter undoubtedly establishes the fact that Lenin was in favor of revolution, that he had a program of revolution. And he tries to make it appear that I denied it, or didn't know it. Shachtman's whole case rests upon this false construction. Lenin advocated the "program of revolution" not only during the world war but before it, before 1905, from the very beginning of his activity as a revolutionary Marxist. Shachtman's entire argument is directed against a contention which I did not make.

He makes his argument appear superficially plausible by the use of two well-known devices of literary charlatans. First, he mutilated the quotation from my speech, breaking it off short and eliminating immediately following sentences in the same paragraph which made my meaning more clear and precise. I wrote: "Even Lenin did not visualize the victory of the proletarian revolution as the immediate outcome of the war." Shachtman twisted it and distorted it into a denial that Lenin had "a program of revolution" during the war. But I think it is thoroughly clear to a disinterested reader that I was speaking of something else, namely, Lenin's expectations as to the immediate outcome of the war, and not at all of what he wanted and what he advocated.

My meaning was made more precise by the sentence which immediately followed: "Just a short time before the outbreak of the February revolution in Russia, Lenin wrote in Switzerland that his generation would most probably not see the socialist revolution. Even Lenin had postponed the revolution to the future, to a later decade." The context of my published speech, from which the sentences were extracted, makes it even clearer that the references to Lenin were concerned not at all with differences of program, but only with the immediate perspectives of the revolutionary Marxists in this war and in the First World War. I don't see how anyone can seriously dispute our contentions on this point because the words of Lenin himself constitute the basis for the reference. The October *Fourth International* cites two exact quotations on the point to which I referred without directly quoting.

"It is possible, however, that five, ten, and even more years will pass before the beginning of the socialist revolution." (From an article written in March 1916, Lenin's *Collected Works,* vol. XIX, p. 45, third Russian edition.)

"We, the older men, will perhaps not live long enough to see the decisive battles of the impending revolution." (Report on 1905 Revolution delivered to Swiss students, January 1917, idem, p. 357.)

That is not all. The main quotation from Lenin which Shachtman cites in his polemic against us—a quotation which he also mutilates to twist the meaning—shows that Lenin was not speaking of the revolution as an immediate perspective; that is, the quotation will show it when we restore the words which Shachtman cut off in the middle of a sentence. He quotes from the article of October 11, 1915, which appears on page 347 of the English edition of Lenin's works, volume XVIII: ". . . It is our bounden duty to explain to the masses the necessity of a revolution, to appeal for it, to create the fitting organizations, to speak fearlessly and in the most concrete manner of the various methods of forceful struggle and of its 'technique'. . ." There Shachtman ended the quotation, breaking Lenin's sentence off at a comma.

Here are the immediately following words which he left out: "This bounden duty of ours being independent of whether the revolution will be strong enough and whether it will come in connection with the first *or second imperialist war,* etc." Lenin obviously was not arguing about the immediacy of the revolution as we visualize it in connection with the present war, but about the necessity of advocating it and preparing for it.

If any further proof is needed one only has to read the rest of Lenin's article! In the very same article, on page 349 of the same volume, Lenin continued: "As to the untimeliness of preaching revolution, this objection rests on a confusion of terms customary with the Romance Socialists: They confuse the beginning of a revolution with its open and direct propaganda. In Russia, nobody places the beginning of the 1905 Revolution before January 22, 1905, whereas the revolutionary propaganda, in the narrow sense of the word, the propaganda and the preparation of mass action, demonstrations, strikes, barricades, had been conducted for years before that. The old *Iskra,* for instance, preached this from the end of 1900, as did Marx from 1847 when there could have been no thought as yet about the beginning of a revolution in Europe."

Shachtman took my remarks about the immediate perspectives of Lenin during the First World War, lifted them out of their context, mutilated the paragraph from which they were extracted, twisted them into an attack on the program and traditions of the Bolsheviks which was not intended or implied in any way by me, and then Shachtman attempted to bolster his thesis by quotations from Lenin which in reality prove the opposite—when they are honestly quoted without breaking off sentences in the middle, and without suppressing other sentences in the same article which make Lenin's real meaning even clearer.

To top off his exercise in literary skullduggery Shachtman refers to the "outlived" Lenin, using quotation marks to convey the impression that he is quoting me. That is an outright literary forgery. I never used such an expression and could not do so; it is not my opinion.

All this literary fakery and forgery in "defense" of Lenin has a fundamental aim which is not frankly avowed, but only thinly disguised. Against whom is Shachtman really defending Lenin? To be sure, he mentions only "Cannon," but it is perfectly obvious that Cannon in this case is only serving Shachtman as a pseudonym for the real target of his attack. My remarks about

Lenin's perspective during the First World War were no more and no less than a simple repetition of what Trotsky said on the subject. It was he who called our attention to the relevant quotations and explained their precise significance.

In the October number of our magazine *Fourth International* which Shachtman had at hand when he wrote his article in *Labor Action* of November 4—he refers to the Goldman-Trotsky correspondence contained therein—Trotsky wrote: Prior to the February revolution and even afterwards, the revolutionary elements felt themselves to be not contenders for power, but the extreme left opposition. Even Lenin relegated the socialist revolution to a more or less distant future. . . . If that is how Lenin viewed the situation, then there is hardly any need of talking about the others."[29]

Here is the real nub of the matter. Shachtman's attack on "Cannon" in behalf of Lenin is in reality aimed against Trotsky in a cowardly and indirect manner. He wants to set Lenin against Trotsky, to make a division in the minds of the radical workers between Lenin and Trotsky, to set himself up as a "Leninist" with the sly intimation that Leninism is not the same thing as Trotskyism. There is a monstrous criminality in this procedure. The names of Lenin and Trotsky are inseparably united in the Russian Revolution, its achievements, its doctrines and traditions, and in the great struggle for Bolshevism waged by Trotsky since the death of Lenin. "Lenin-Trotsky"—those two immortal names are one. Nobody yet has tried to separate them; that is, nobody but scoundrels and traitors.

Shachtman's article in *Labor Action* serves the same aim as the special "Trotsky Memorial Issue" of their magazine which was published only to defame the memory of Trotsky, to belittle him, to justify themselves against him, and at the same time— like any shopkeeper looking for a little extra profit—to claim his "heritage."

Trotsky, as if anticipating such attempts, gave this answer in advance. Here is what he wrote in the *Socialist Appeal:* "Only the other day Shachtman referred to himself in the press as a 'Trotskyist.' If this be Trotskyism then I at least am no Trotskyist. With the present ideas of Shachtman, not to mention Burnham, I have nothing in common. . . . Towards their new magazine my attitude can only be the same as toward all other petty-bourgeois counterfeits of Marxism. As for their 'organizational methods' and political 'morality,' these evoke in me nothing but contempt."

The literary manners and morals of petty-bourgeois dabblers in politics are no better than their theses. With such people, as Trotsky once remarked, it is not sufficient to check their theses; it is necessary to watch their fingers too! If we keep this salutary warning in mind the "theses" of Shachtman directed against our military transitional program can be disposed of without difficulty. As I said before, it is mainly work with a shovel.

THE VOORHIS ACT
AND THE FOURTH INTERNATIONAL[30]

December 13, 1940

This letter was mimeographed for distribution to members of the SWP National Committee nonresident in New York.

New York

Dear Comrades,

As you probably know, the Voorhis Act, which goes into effect the first of the year, requires all parties or groups affiliated with an international organization to register a list of all their members with the government under extremely heavy penalties for failure to do so. The same regulations apply to organizations "the purpose or aim of which, or one of the purposes or aims of which, is the establishment, control, conduct, seizure, or overthrow of a government or subdivision thereof by the use of force, violence, military measures, or threats of any one of the foregoing."

We here have unanimously agreed to make the following recommendations to the special convention which will meet in New York, December 21st:

1. To amend the party constitution accordingly and to eliminate references to the affiliation to the Fourth International.

2. To declare the present Declaration of Principles outdated and inadequate in several respects and appoint a standing committee to prepare a new Declaration of Principles for later consideration by party convention or referendum. (This task should have been undertaken by the last convention if we had not been so completely preoccupied with the other struggles.)

130

3. To adopt a suitable resolution or statement on the disaffiliation of the party from the Fourth International and our attitude towards the principles of internationalism.

We would like to hear from all nonresident members of the National Committee as to their agreement to these proposals which seem to us to be obviously indicated by the situation.

Fraternally yours,
J. P. Cannon
National Secretary

UNION WORK OR PARTY WORK

January 3, 1941

Excerpts from a letter to the Los Angeles Local of the SWP. Copies of the letter were sent to members of the National Committee.

New York

Dear Comrades,

. . .We here have been somewhat disquieted by the turn taken by your discussion of the aircraft orientation. We received several letters on one side of this question and had been awaiting a letter from Comrade Curtiss. . . . However, without having a rounded picture of the differences of opinion among you, we got the impression, from the letters we have received and from the decisions you have made, of a one-sided approach to the problem. We refer in particular to the decision that the party organizer must be mobilized for work in an airplane plant.

It is one thing to contrast the industrial and trade union orientation to a bad social composition in the party and an exclusively propagandistic activity. We could count a campaign along these lines as progressive even if, as is usually the case, a certain overemphasis is employed to bend the stick backward. It is something else again to push the shop and union orientation at the expense of the party apparatus. Such a line is false from the point of view of principle as well as practical results. Without the party, trade union work ends in opportunism and futility; and without a strong party apparatus there can be no party in the Bolshevik sense of the word. . . .

It is a profound mistake to imagine that a fraction in aircraft or any other industry will build the party in Los Angeles. On the contrary, a strong party nucleus, with a qualified professional staff, will build the necessary fractions in this industry, as well as others, ten times sooner. . . .

Yours fraternally,
J. P. Cannon
National Secretary

RELEASE PIERRE FRANK!

Published January 14, 1941

This letter appeared in the Socialist Appeal *a few days after it was sent.*

New York

Chargé d'Affairs
British Embassy
Washington, D.C.

Dear Sir:

We have received word from London that Pierre Frank, a well-known French revolutionist, has been sentenced by a London police tribunal to six months at hard labor. The charge was that Pierre Frank had failed to register, as a foreigner, with the authorities. Frank, however, explained to the tribunal that he had been condemned in absentia as a revolutionist by the French government and felt that, had he registered with the British authorities in the usual way, he would have been turned over to the French government, despite the fact that he was in England as a political refugee.

Frank's explanation appears to us as an eminently reasonable one for his failure to comply with a technical procedure required by British law. An explanation which should certainly have been accepted since he was being accused of nothing more than a mere technical violation. Instead, however, the explanation served only to harden the prejudiced tribunal against him. We are informed that the judge, upon hearing Frank's explanation, utilized it to denounce Frank as a "subversive person." Prejudice alone can explain the vindictive sentence of six months at hard labor for a mere technicality.

We protest this sentence and call upon the British authorities to release Pierre Frank and to accord him the democratic rights of a political refugee. Hounded out of France by the "democrats" who preferred Hitler to a resurgence of the French people, Frank now finds himself hounded by a government which claims to stand at the opposite pole to the Pétain government which still seeks to imprison Frank. Elementary justice demands that this fighter for French liberty be given his liberty by the British government.

Very truly yours,
James P. Cannon
National Secretary
Socialist Workers Party

TOBIN IS PLANNING A SERIOUS OFFENSIVE ACTION[31]

April 1, 1941

This letter to V.R. Dunne and Farrell Dobbs has not been previously published. The copy in Cannon's files was undated; the date is taken from a copy in the files of the SWP.

Jones [V.R. Dunne] and Barr [Farrell Dobbs]

Dear Friends:

I had been more than half expecting to be on my way East and to drop off either at Minneapolis or Chicago to see you before your April 8 meeting. That is the main reason why I have not written you before. Now, however, there are numerous reasons, outlined in another letter, which make it advisable for me to stay here a while longer, unless you think it is especially important for me to come along right away.

I assume also that you have taken my failure to write as a ,general agreement with everything that is being planned and done as related in your letters.

1. It has to be assumed that some kind of serious offensive action is planned against you by Tobias [Tobin], otherwise you can hardly explain his letter of March 21.

He does not refer to anything new that he has not known about all the time, and about which he had many complaints in the past. If he now thinks this conduct on your part has to be investigated—and actually proceeds to a formal investigation—it absolutely must be assumed at the start that some offensive action is contemplated. Moreover, we should not lose sight of the fact that this is in conformity with the general political situation

136

and the winds from Washington, to which Tobias as a civil service worker is most responsive.

2. The point you mention in the third paragraph on page 3 of your letter of March 22 can have some validity without in the least affecting the fundamental considerations referred to above, which must be our guiding line.

It is possible, and even probable, as Michael [Miles Dunne] suggests, that T may not be sure of what concrete action to take, but this does not in the least weaken the necessary assumption that he plans to do something and that the April 8 conference is a means of feeling out the situation and probing for an opening.

In my opinion, the one chance for him to conclude that the time is not propitious for offensive action lies in his being convinced that all of you, and especially your friends in the ranks, are set and ready for anything that may come, and that there is no chance for a pushover. From this point of view your special meeting with your most intimate friends on April 4 is of the most crucial importance. It's ten or a hundred times more important for them to determine their attitude in expectation of an offensive blow than that they begin to think of their course of action after the blow has been struck.

3. The most important question of all—and in my opinion the one that will determine the eventual outcome of your conflict—is your ability to put the conflict on its proper basis of trade union practices. The latest local attack against you is nothing but a supplement to the Fink suit and similar movements of the bosses who blame you because they have to pay 75¢ an hour to workers whom they used to get at 40¢ or less. That is the real issue, and at all costs the fight must be kept on that ground.

The attempt to rest the case on your alleged political association is obviously an attempt to divert attention from the real issue. In my opinion, it would be very foolish to allow the fight to be conducted to the end on this false basis. If any concessions have to be made, it is not so serious if they are made in this field.

As far as I know very few, if any, of your official circle have any actual political affiliation in the sense of actual membership, etc., being primarily sympathizers and supporters of the general ideas of the political group, in the same sense that those who voted for Roosevelt are considered Democrats, etc. Of course there may be a stoolpigeon or two who will attempt to prove the contrary and give evidence about "meetings," "assessments," etc., but the testimony of stoolpigeons never carries much weight, especially among good trade unionists.

Even Jones, who has been in the past an actual member and publicly known as such, is primarily a trade union man and should not allow the formality of his membership in a political association to be the issue upon which he would permit himself to be removed from a post in a mass movement where his presence is most necessary at the present time. His duty to the workers in the given situation is to remain at his post even if it involves the sacrifice of his constitutional right to belong to any legal political organization he chooses.

I am not suggesting of course that any such concession should be volunteered. However, in the course of the negotiations, if it appears that an offensive action is being determined upon, a way must be devised to draw out from the opponent the demands and conditions for an agreement to cease interference. At this point you and your intimate friends will be put squarely up against the most fateful decision. If you concede or even play with the idea of conceding any encroachments on your local autonomy, it will most likely prove fatal. One step of this kind will be followed by another and your troops, demoralized by the unjustified concession in the first instance, will most likely retreat step by step until there is nothing left of all the great achievements.

On the other hand, some political concessions such as I have mentioned above, the seriousness of which is not to be minimized, are nevertheless not fatal. Such things have been done before, and can be done again by people who know what they are about. Naturally, this presupposes that we are dealing with loyal men who do not change their principles at anybody's command, but like the early Christians, remain faithful in their hearts to the religion that was prohibited by the Roman law.

4. The suggestions I have made here apply of course most actually and most fundamentally to Jones himself. This is the problem I have been wrestling with ever since I got the news of your new trouble.

We are confronted here with a fundamental question which is bound to arise in other situations, and we must not make a mistake. The more I thought about it, the more I convinced myself to the very end that it is impossible for us in the coming period to allow a trade union fight to hinge on the right of formal membership in the club. I do not think such a fight can be successfully made even at the present time—and the difficulties and disabilities of such a position will increase from day to day with the general development of a reactionary atmosphere. We cannot play hide and seek with this question without injuring ourselves and our cause very badly.

The fact that the issue in the case of Jones is presented in the most acute and painful manner for all of us, including himself, does not enable us to evade the question. It must be faced and decided fundamentally. If worse comes to worst and there is no other way of maintaining his present post, the decision in his case must be made as indicated above.

This is my most considered judgment and I hope you all agree with it.

Best regards,
Martin [Cannon]

RELEASE SOVIET
POLITICAL PRISONERS!

July 1, 1941

This telegram for Stalin was sent to Constantine Umansky, the Soviet ambassador to Washington, shortly after the Nazi invasion of the Soviet Union. It was published in the July 5, 1941, Militant.

Trotskyists all over the world, now as always, are solidly for the defense of the Soviet Union. In this hour of grave danger to the achievements of the October Revolution, we demand that you release all Trotskyist and other pro-Soviet political prisoners who are now in jails and in concentration camps, to enable them to take their proper place in the front ranks of the defenders of the Soviet Union. Your crushing of workers' democracy has increased the terrible danger to the Soviet Union. We demand the revival of soviet democracy as the first step in strengthening the struggle against German Nazi imperialism and the capitalist world.

James P. Cannon
National Secretary
Socialist Workers Party

Left: Trotsky with Joseph Hansen and Natalia Sedova. Right: Cannon with Rose Karsner and Farrell Dobbs.

Left: Trotsky Memorial Meeting, August 1940. Above: Cannon and Farrell Dobbs in August 1941.

Top left: Carl Skoglund, Grace Carlson, and V.R. Dunne. Bottom left: Minneapolis headquarters of SWP. Above: Cannon addressing October 1942 SWP convention.

Farrell Dobbs addressing New York meeting protesting Minneapolis convictions. Others, from left: Rose Karsner, Cannon, James T. Farrell, and George Novack.

WHY WE HAVE BEEN INDICTED[32]

Published July 26, 1941

This statement in answer to the July 15, 1941, federal grand jury indictment of twenty-nine members of the SWP and of Minneapolis Teamsters Local 544 CIO appeared in The Militant.

Franklin Doublecross Roosevelt has systematically lied to the American people. He has broken promise after promise. At this moment the army training camps are seething with resentment against Roosevelt's latest broken promise: his solemn covenant with the draftees that conscription would be limited to a period of one year. And why is he seeking an indefinite extension of the term of conscription? In order to break his solemn promise of last November that no American soldiers would fight on foreign soil.

Couple with these broken promises Roosevelt's strikebreaking use of troops, his terroristic use of the FBI and other governmental agencies of repression against CIO unions and the Socialist Workers Party, and you have a clear picture of Roosevelt's foul scheme. By a combination of force and fraud he proposes to dragoon the American masses into a war which they do not want and for which they would never vote.

Roosevelt's typical combination of force and fraud is evident in the indictments drawn up by his Department of "Justice" against the leaders of the Socialist Workers Party. The basic motivation for those indictments was stated by Acting Attorney General Francis Biddle on June 28, when he sought to justify the FBI's Gestapo raids on the St. Paul and Minneapolis headquarters of the Socialist Workers Party. Biddle then cited and quoted from the antiwar sections of the Declaration of Principles adopted by the 1938 convention of the Socialist Workers Party.

But some strategist in Roosevelt's war party has since realized how unpopular would be a persecution of our antiwar party for our antiwar views. Hence, Biddle's assistants have now drawn up an indictment against us which makes no reference whatsoever to the antiwar sections of our 1938 Declaration of Principles—in fact, the word "war" appears nowhere in the indictment!

Carefully though they worked in preparing this indictment, Roosevelt's agents were not quite able to erase the telltale indications of the real motivation for this persecution. They give their game away in charge No. 4 of the indictment, which accuses us of urging, counseling, and persuading the workers and farmers "that the Government of the United States was imperialistic. . ."

Yes, we have explained and shall continue to explain to the workers and farmers that the Roosevelt government is imperialistic in its every move.

Imperialism is the motive force behind all Roosevelt's war plans. Like Hitler, he would be master of the entire world. Hitler seeks that mastery as political agent for Germany's bankers; Roosevelt seeks that mastery as political agent for America's Sixty Families, the DuPonts and Morgans and Rockefellers.

By his typical combination of force and fraud Roosevelt is intriguing to secure as cannon fodder and beasts of burden the masses of South and Central America. Next comes Dakar—that is, the Negro masses of Africa. By bribery and pressure upon Chiang Kai-shek, Roosevelt seeks to transform China's war of liberation into a war to serve American imperialism.

But before Roosevelt can hope to carry out this gigantic scheme of carnage and world conquest, he must first subjugate the American workers and farmers to his will. This is the aim of all his lies and deceit and broken promises. This is the aim of his acts of violence against the labor movement.

With a brazenness unprecedented in American history, Roosevelt has intervened on the side of Daniel J. Tobin to try to destroy the Motor Transport and Allied Workers Union, Local 544-CIO, sixteen of whose members have been indicted along with the Socialist Workers Party members. Thus Roosevelt pays his debt to one of his most servile agents.

But something more is involved. Tobin is a leader of the Fight for Freedom, Inc., which is yelling for immediate shooting war. The leaders of Local 544-CIO are resolute opponents of war. In indicting the Local 544-CIO leadership, Roosevelt's war party is striking a blow against the antiwar forces in the trade union movement.

As he plunges toward total war, Roosevelt would like first to destroy all leadership and potential leadership of the antiwar forces. Roosevelt and his war party understand very well that an honest workers' party like ours, with firm principles and cadres steeled and tempered in the class struggle, can tomorrow become the accepted spokesman for the great masses in the struggle to put an end to the war. The Roosevelt war party would destroy us before that tomorrow comes.

We have adhered to the Bolshevik tradition of struggle against war ever since 1917, as every politically literate person knows. But not since the notorious Palmer raids of 1920 has any government official pretended that we could be indicted for that. Only now under Roosevelt, only now that Roosevelt has become the ally of Stalin, and the Communist Party has become Roosevelt's most vociferous supporter in whooping it up for war— only now does our advocacy of Bolshevism against Stalinism become a cause for indictment.[33]

The "clever" strategists of Roosevelt's war party are thinking: "We are not going to make the same mistake that the tsar made. In November 1916 Lenin's party was small and apparently uninfluential. Yet a year later, thanks to its irreconcilable opposition to the imperialist war, it won a majority of the workers and peasants. Let us not repeat the tsar's mistake. Let us destroy Trotsky's party before it wins a majority of the workers and farmers of the United States."

This "clever" strategy of Roosevelt's war party is, in reality, the identical strategy that the tsar pursued. He hounded Lenin's party mercilessly, exiled, imprisoned, executed, and tortured its members. The tsar's cruelty became a byword in the civilized world. Yet all this did not prevent the great masses from abolishing the tsarist autocracy.

We do not fear Roosevelt's repressions, any more than Lenin and Trotsky feared the tsar's repressions. The war into which Roosevelt is plunging the country will be a fiery crucible in which millions upon millions of American workers and farmers will be steeled and tempered for the struggle against imperialism. For every fighter torn from our ranks by the class enemy, scores will come forward who, in this very struggle between us and Roosevelt's war party, will learn that every serious fighter against imperialist war belongs in the Socialist Workers Party.

We are no pacifists. We Trotskyists have shown, in China, in Loyalist Spain, in the Red Army, that we are ready to fight on behalf of a just cause. But Roosevelt's war is an imperialist war and we shall oppose it, and nothing shall stop us.

We are no pacifists. We shall not turn the other cheek to Roosevelt's attack on our party. On the contrary, we shall see to it that every worker and farmer in this country hears our true views and learns how Roosevelt has engineered this vile frame-up against us. This case will be tried by the government in a courtroom in Minneapolis and we shall defend ourselves there. Far more important, however, we shall defend ourselves before our true judges—the workers and farmers of this country. It is their verdict, above all, that concerns us.

And we are confident of their verdict, once we break through the fraud and deceit with which the Roosevelt war party seeks to conceal the true issue. The Socialist Workers Party is the antiwar party. The workers and farmers have no interest in this war. They want no part of it. The antiwar party and the tens of millions opposed to the war will join hands in the course of our battle to free the twenty-nine defendants from Roosevelt's Gestapo.

TROTSKYISM LIVES

August 22, 1941

This speech was given at a memorial meeting on the first anniversary of Trotsky's death, held at Manhattan Plaza in New York City. The text is from the August 30, 1941, Militant.

Comrade Chairman and Comrades:

In his theoretical elucidation of the post-Lenin reaction in Russia which swept the Stalinist bureaucracy into power, Comrade Trotsky referred to the history of revolutions and derived his thesis from that history. Revolutions throughout history, in the ebb and flow of history, have always been followed by counterrevolutions, but the counterrevolution has never succeeded in throwing society back to the original point of departure of the revolution. Every revolution has signified a permanent advance of mankind's social organization. Trotsky never departed from this thesis, but reiterated it at every new turn of events.

The reaction against the great French bourgeois revolution which, after Napoleon, went even so far as the restoration for a time of the monarchy, never succeeded in restoring feudal property relations, and consequently the revolution remained essentially victorious in spite of the long sweep of reaction against it. Capitalism was firmly established by the initial victory of the bourgeois revolution.

Here in America there was a tremendous reaction against our second revolution in the sixties, the revolution which overthrew chattel slavery. The reaction in the South went a long way in the years and decades following the military victory of the bourgeois North. The emancipated Negroes were virtually deprived of all political and social rights. But the reaction never went back so far as to restore private property in human beings which had been destroyed by the revolutionary victory of the Northern armies. Chattel slavery was not restored.

If we keep these historical facts and this thesis in mind, we can see more clearly beneath the superficial appearance of things and understand what is taking place in the Soviet Union, what is taking place in the world. Reaction set in against the Russian Revolution about 1923. The terrible event that we commemorate tonight, the assassination of the great leader of the Russian Revolution, was itself a product of that reaction, which is still sweeping the world today. But if we keep our theory in mind, if we understand the teachings of all the great Marxists that the march of history, in spite of everything, is forward and not backward, we can find our bearings even in these heavy days. And only we can do it.

In many respects one can find a certain analogy between events that are unfolding today, and those of twenty-four years ago this summer, when it seemed, indeed, that the blackest time had come. The world war had been raging in Europe for three years, devouring men by the million on the bloody battlefields of the war. The apparently invincible conquering army of the German Kaiser was then, like Hitler's army today, in occupation of the Ukraine. A stalemate had come in the war of the imperialist powers, and they poured out the blood of a million men in the madness of Verdun in an attempt to break it.[34] The United States had formally entered the war and the mad, patriotic mob spirit was running rampant in this country. Raids on radical labor organizations were taking place and the Department of Justice, under the same J. Edgar Hoover who is framing us today, was preparing the indictments against the IWW which were to be announced in the early part of September.

Then, out of the night of that black reaction, that time of desperation, a few months later came the brightest light the world had ever seen—the light of the October Revolution in Russia. Since that time we have lived by that light. And the whole world, friends and foes, whether they liked it or not, have also lived under the sign of the Russian Revolution of 1917. With that victory of the workers under the leadership of Lenin and Trotsky, the world revolutionary movement came to life again. The movement which had been beaten into the dust by the war and the capitulations and the betrayals of all the traditional leaders—then as now—the world revolutionary movement rose again, raised its head and began to recruit a whole new army of young people inspired by the Russian Revolution.

We felt it here in this country. We began again on one fundamental premise, established and demonstrated in Russia: that the way out of the madness of capitalist war is by the revolutionary victory of the workers; that the workers can and will accomplish that victory and free the world, not only from war, but from the horrible, decaying system of capitalism that breeds the war.

Twenty-four years have passed since that time. Those who have remained on the fundamental premise I have just mentioned—the premise of the adherents of the Bolshevik revolution—they can see the prospect of new advances throughout the darkness of the reaction. They understand that the reaction has set back but not yet overthrown the Russian Revolution. Those fainthearts, those traitors who said the Russian Revolution has been killed, that the Soviet Union is not worth defending, are being answered on the battlefields of Russia today by millions of men in arms. Millions of Soviet soldiers, pouring out their blood, say the revolution still lives and not even Hitler's army can kill it!

That is the meaning of this thing that is inexplicable to all the others, this tremendous Soviet morale. What did they all say? First, they said the two systems—fascism and sovietism—are so interlocked that Russia and Germany make natural partners against the "democratic" world. We heard such a monstrous thesis in our own party a little more than a year ago. We were informed by no less an authority than the great Professor Burnham that we Trotskyists were a "left cover" for Hitler because we wanted to defend the Soviet Union unconditionally. Burnham and his retinue never dreamed of the war that was to burst with full fury two months ago.

Then, when it happened, there was one universal expectation, one common prediction. Nobody believed in the fighting capacities of the Soviet army except the Soviet workers themselves—and the Fourth Internationalists. Stalin didn't believe in the fighting ability of the Red Army which he had beheaded.[35] The only reason he didn't capitulate to Hitler and give him all the concessions he wanted, is that he didn't get a chance. Hitler thought it would be so easy to smash the Red Army, he didn't bother to parley about it. All the statesmen and military experts expected and freely predicted a Russian collapse on the French pattern in a few weeks. What they all overlooked was the one most important and most fundamental element in war, the one that was elucidated by Comrade Trotsky in our last talk with him in Mexico, fourteen months ago, the element of *morale*.

In the course of our visit of a week or more—this was at the time when the great battle of France was raging, before Paris had yet fallen—we asked him more than once to give us his opinion of the military prospects of that fight. And again and again he repeated, "It depends on the morale of the French army. If the French army really has the morale to fight, Hitler cannot win, not even if he comes as far as Paris."

But the French soldiers did not have the morale to fight. That was explained in an article in our magazine, *Fourth International,* as well as by many other correspondents. Our own comrade who was there and had intimate contact with great numbers of French people in the course of his journalistic duties,[36] explained it about as follows: The French workers and the French soldiers, if you asked them if there wasn't some difference between the Hitler regime and the rotting bourgeois-democratic regime in France, would say, "Yes, there is a difference, but the difference is not worth dying for." That was one reason for the catastrophic defeat of the French bourgeois army.

Those who made an equation between fascist Germany and the Soviet Union could not understand the psychology of the Russian workers and peasants. You can write all the books, wiseacre theses, explaining there is no difference between the degenerated workers' state in Russia and the fascist regime in Germany. But the Russian workers and peasants think there is a difference, and they think the difference is worth dying for. They know better than all the renegades, better than all those who have turned their backs on the Soviet Union in the hour of danger, the hour when people are really tested as to the value of their ideas, opinions, theories, and promises.

Trotsky said more than once that the beginning of a war of imperialism against the Soviet Union would undoubtedly arouse a veritable outburst of genuine revolutionary patriotism and fighting spirit in the Russian masses. That is precisely what we have seen there. And as we wait breathlessly from day to day, and even from edition to edition of the newspapers, to see what is the further course, the further fate of the armies locked in combat, we know one thing for sure. We know that by their tremendous demonstration of fighting heroism, the Russian masses have said once again that the revolution in Russia is still alive, and still has the possibilities of reinspiring the world and starting a new upsweep of progress which revolutionary victory alone can bring.

The reaction against the Russian Revolution presented so many complexities, phenomena entirely new in history, that it was not easy to understand the real course of events and their meaning. The great service of Trotsky to humanity, to history, was that he *explained* to the revolutionary vanguard of the world the complex processes of the degeneration of the workers' state, of the rise of the privileged bureaucracy, of the reasons for it, and of what remained fundamental and secure in spite of the reaction of the bureaucracy. He explained it, he led the fight against the reaction, and even more than that, he organized on a world scale the nucleus of the revolutionary party of the future, which will complete the work which remained uncompleted in Russia. Trotsky's crowning achievement was the foundation of the Fourth International.

Here in the United States since 1928 we have fought under the banner of Trotsky. Thirteen years ago we raised that banner here. It seems but yesterday. The fight has been so intense, so uninterrupted, so full of interest and passion, we have never had time to reminisce about it. For thirteen years we have waged our struggle, and I think it is now clear to everybody, to friend and foe on both sides of the class barricades—it is now clear to everybody that the movement founded on the program of Comrade Trotsky in this country thirteen years ago, which is represented today by the Socialist Workers Party, is the authentic movement of Bolshevism, the movement that remains true to the Russian Revolution of October 1917, to the people who led it, and to the principles embodied in it.

The one authentic movement is our party. The hatred of all traitors, of all deserters and renegades against Trotsky and the Trotskyists confirms it. And it is now certified, so to speak, by the Department of Justice in Washington. Of all the parties and individuals in this country, the Roosevelt war party has singled out this group of disciples of Trotsky for special attention. Our organization is the first selected for persecution under the Smith Act and under another act passed in 1861 against the Southern Confederates.

We have suffered many blows since 1928. We have never lived or worked at any time without pressure upon us, without persecution against us, without hardships and material lacks.

But a year ago today the hardest blow of all fell upon our movement in this country and the Fourth International throughout the world, including its Russian detachments. The hardest blow of all that could possibly be dealt to us was the assassination of Trotsky a year ago yesterday by an agent of the traitor and murderer, Stalin.

You remember when we gathered in the memorial meeting a year ago, when we summoned all our courage and said, in spite of everything, we would survive that terrible blow because Trotsky had left us the program and the ideas and the example that will enable us to do it. Many people were skeptical. But we did survive. Just to have remained alive after such a calamitous loss, to have remained intact for a year, and not only in this country but on a world scale—that in itself would be a colossal achievement. But not only to have survived; to have made progress; to have gained in numbers and in activity—as we have done—that is the brightest promise for the future that this party which Comrade Trotsky founded cannot be destroyed!

In the past year we didn't do sensational things, but we moved forward on every front. Our trade union work was developed, better organized, more widely extended; the party became more firmly established with a larger percentage of its members in the trade unions than ever before. Our press did not go down; it went forward—increased its circulation, increased its size, its effectiveness, its popularity, and its influence throughout the entire militant labor movement. Our organization grew a bit. We took a number of young men and developed them into professional organizers. We have today a bigger staff on the organizational side of the party than we ever had in our thirteen years.

We didn't neglect our international obligations. Bearing in mind the more favorable position we occupy in the richest capitalist country in the world, we gave help to our Chinese comrades, to the refugees in Europe, to our comrades in Latin America—not by any means adequate, not by any means what we should have done, but more than we had been able to do before.

Mention has been made here tonight of our election campaign in New York. And indeed it is an epochal event that in the past year, on two occasions, we have raised the banner of Trotskyism in important elections. In Minnesota the Fourth Internationalists put a candidate in the field for United States Senate. They managed to get access to the radio, to carry on a fairly wide public activity, so as to arouse the interest of thousands of people and gain eight or nine thousand votes for Comrade Grace Carlson, senatorial candidate of our party in Minnesota.

And now, if we are able for the first time to have a candidate on the ballot for mayor of New York, if on the eve of formal entry into the war and in the face of the indictments in Minnesota, we are able to participate in the campaign with our own candidate on the ballot, we must say that for us it is a great step forward. It may not appear so important to others. If you judge things by comparative numbers, if you measure our party's numerical strength beside that of LaGuardia and Tammany Hall, it may seem a little ridiculous that only a few thousand people vote for the program of the Fourth International. But only the superficial people, only philistines, say that; only those people who see today prolonged indefinitely into tomorrow.

I venture to say that we will get more votes in New York, proportionately, for the candidate of the Fourth International than the Bolsheviks got in Russia in their first elections. We do not expect to get great numbers of votes in this election. We expect to put our program on record. We expect to take advantage of the time that is left us between the filing of the candidates and the trial in Minnesota to make part of our public defense against their trial. Our "defense" will be to accuse the prosecutors of responsibility for the destruction of millions of human lives in the war; to proclaim the downfall of their system and the coming victory of socialism. That is our aim in the campaign.

Everything will naturally be concentrated on the question that dominates the world. That is, the question of the war which every month or so draws new territories and new peoples into its bloody vortex. This war is the expression of the incurable bankruptcy of an outlived system; that was the fundamental theme of Comrade Trotsky's work in his last years—that capitalism is in its death agony. The great programmatic document of the Fourth International, adopted in the World Congress of 1938, written by him, bears that title, "The Death Agony of Capitalism and the Tasks of the Fourth International."

Comrade Trotsky never had the slightest confidence in the ability of world capitalism to escape from the war or to emerge from the war. He had no confidence in the ability of world capitalism to regain stability. He was not like those miserable Social Democrats, skeptics, and renegades from radicalism. They are the only people who see a rosy future for capitalism. Not the capitalists themselves! Not in any of their parties or groups have they the slightest confidence; they live in fear of what the future will bring.

Trotsky said and repeated time and time again that the war will put an end to all pretenses, to all ambiguity; it will destroy all parties and groups which try to play tricks with principles and to cheat history. They will be demolished, there will not be left one stone upon another. International Stalinism and Social Democracy will be victims of the war which their betrayals made possible. And the "London Bureau," that miserable centrist caricature which made its task in life to fight the "intransigence" of Trotskyism and its "sectarianism." Where are their mass parties? Where is the mass party of the centrist London Bureau in the United States? It was represented once by a clique of bankrupt sharpers who never had any masses but were always issuing promissory notes to produce them in the future—the Lovestone group. Where are they now? I don't think you could find them, because the group held a meeting and adopted a resolution to this effect: that the best thing we can do in the interest of socialism is to dissolve. And that was the first correct statement the Lovestoneites ever made.

I hear every week or so about some little pretentious sect that was more radical than Trotsky and bent on correcting the deviations of Trotsky, also, imitating the Lovestoneite example, "dissolving." And others don't even meet, they simply dissolve. And others make peace with capitalism, like the Social Democrats and the Stalinists. And others simply wither away, like the Socialist Party of Norman Thomas. We remain. We swim against the current. And that is not because of our personal superiority but because of the superiority of the program that we are organized to defend. Because we are the bona fide representatives of the one viable political current in the world—the current that was released by the great Russian Revolution of October 1917. The disciples of Trotsky are the people who really mean it when they say they defend the Russian Revolution and its conquests. Our struggle against Stalinism has always been a struggle in behalf of the Russian Revolution and all that it signifies.

Why, in the United States Senate, the other day, in that fountainhead of American political wisdom, you had the floor leader of the Roosevelt war party explaining to the muddle-headed isolationists the difference between Stalin and Trotsky. And after all these years, even [Senator Alben] Barkley knows the difference. I am quoting from the *Congressional Record* of August 5, 1941. Senator Barkley said:

"When they [the Russian people after the revolution of 1917] started out, they had a vague, fantastic notion that they would socialize or communize the world; and the fundamental difference between Stalin and Trotsky was over that question. Trotsky, as I understand the matter, was a world revolutionist, while Stalin took the position that the Russian Government owed its first duty to the Russian people . . . the fight between Trotsky and Stalin revolved around the question whether they should undertake to revolutionize the world or should concentrate on Russia. Stalin won, and Trotsky had to leave the country."

And they would not let Trotsky into this country because, while they never understood the difference quite so well before, they had a pretty good idea that Trotsky was the kind of a "counterrevolutionist" that would not do them any good.

We have been indicted. And the question is asked on all sides, why have they indicted the Trotskyists? Why didn't they indict somebody else, or why did they indict anybody? Have they completely lost their heads in Washington? This is the theme of the Social Democrats and liberals, supporters of the Roosevelt administration, who want to sell the advanced workers a war for democracy, and are somewhat embarrassed by this attempt to scuttle democracy even before the war begins.

Well, we are indicted for definite reasons, for essentially the same reasons that they have indicted the proletarian revolutionists in the past. Not because of our numbers, not because of our immediate power, but for what we represent, and because of the masters' fear of the future and the future things. They know in spite of all the noisy antiwar talk of the so-called isolationists, and pacifists, and Christian-Fronters, and America-Firsters— they know that the only real and serious opposition to their imperialist war, the opposition that won't stop when war begins, is represented by the Trotskyists.

They had an immediate occasion to attack us in Minneapolis as a result of a trade union conflict. One single union in the Teamsters International of 500,000, one union of 5,000 members, in a part of the country which is not decisive economically—it is on the edge of the prairie, it is away from the great industrial strategical centers—one single union came into conflict with President Roosevelt's principal labor agent, Daniel Tobin, and left the Tobin organization and joined the CIO. And everybody in the country seems to understand, practically every newspaper that has commented on the matter mentions the fact, that the indictment represents a political favor to Tobin in his fight with Local 544-CIO. There is something in what they say. This is undoubtedly the immediate cause of the indictment.

But that doesn't really explain the thing fundamentally at all. The question one must ask is, *why* did Tobin have a fight with the leaders of 544, and why did he try to drive them out of the union in Minneapolis? And then you come to the real nub of the matter. Tobin is a right-hand man of the Roosevelt administration, his chief "labor lieutenant," and a member of the "Fight for Freedom, Inc."—an organization which is campaigning for an immediate declaration of "shooting war." Tobin couldn't line up the Trotskyists in Minnesota for the war. The Trotskyists are that breed of people who don't line up. They are stiff-necked about principle. And when Tobin tried to put the pressure on them to be good fellows, to get in line, and to go along with the war, they said, "No, we do not believe in your war. We are going to fight against it." That was what prompted the struggle with Tobin which was followed by the indictments against us.

There is a parallel in our American history for the prostitution of the presidential powers to help trade union conservatives against radicals. In 1917 when the IWW was making some headway in different parts of the country as against the AFL, Gompers, who was the chief labor agent of Wilson in lining up the labor movement for the war, received, as his price for support, the prosecution of the IWW. That was a notoriously known fact at the time. It was common gossip among labor leaders that Gompers finally "got" Haywood through the Department of Justice.[37] I was reading Bill Haywood's autobiography again the other night, and he refers to the same thing. This is the historic precedent for Roosevelt's assistance to Tobin and the prosecution against us.

One of the counts in the indictment alleges that we advocate the formation of workers' defense guards, and that where we have the opportunity, having sufficient union support, we actually organize such defense guards, who make it their business to declare war on fascist bands and train and drill the workers to fight fascism. That is true, and our policy is 100 percent correct. There isn't any other antifascist tendency in the whole country that really intends to *fight* fascism. We do. The **Minneapolis unionists did actually organize a defense guard.**

Don't think for a moment, however, that President Roosevelt and his Biddles in Washington are foolish enough to imagine one group of defense guards or twenty-nine people were immediately threatening the government. No, that is a part of the frame-up. The ideas, and the knowledge that these ideas can really grow and become powerful when the conditions mature for them—that is what they are really shooting at. They want to put us in the penitentiary because we alone really proclaim the socialist society and summon the workers to fight for it. We alone counterpose to this bankrupt system of capitalism an alternative system of a classless socialist society. That idea they want to outlaw.

Of course what they are doing is against the Bill of Rights, against that part of the Constitution, those amendments to it, which were designed to secure the rights of the people to free speech and a free press. The indictment violates the Constitution, violates democracy. But do not have any illusions that because it breaks their own Constitution and because it breaks down their own pretensions to free speech and democracy, do not have any illusions that they are not going to go through with it. They are not interested in formality or consistency. They are interested in stamping out opposition to the war. They are interested in suppressing people who can't be brought into line.

The Social Democrats don't care very much about democracy except as a slogan to dupe the workers and farmers into a war in Europe. The Social Democrats who are supporters of Roosevelt, with a greater enthusiasm than Roosevelt himself in his sober moments could ever display, are somewhat at a loss to explain this indictment and they call it fantastic. "This little sect of twenty-nine people are going to overthrow the government? Ridiculous!"—and so on. They would like to make a joke out of it and lull us with the idea that because in their eyes it is utterly fantastic, nothing will come of it. Well, I will tell you something. If we were strong enough to be a "real and present menace" to the government, Roosevelt wouldn't be indicting us, he would have been disposed of a long time ago. If we were strong enough to threaten the Democrats or Republicans or the fascists, they would not be indicting twenty-nine people. Things would be at a far more serious pass, and the social crisis and the rise of fascism would have developed to a point where the transitory figure of Roosevelt would have been expunged from the political scene. The Social Democratic philistines pretend not to know that revolutionists who are persecuted and put in prison are always minority groups, as a rule small minorities. When we get big enough, we won't let them put us in prison.

The prosecution is no joke for us. The Haymarket martyrs represented a group no bigger than we. Sacco and Vanzetti represented a very small group.[38] The IWW in 1917 was by no means a powerful, million-strong movement. Neither were the pioneer Communists in 1919-20. All the cases in American history of persecution, of workers being arrested and thrown into jail and penitentiaries for long terms, have always been cases involving small groups, from the point of view of the relationship of forces, "fantastically" small.

The FBI is not joking in our case. They know very well that we were not "conspiring" to overthrow the government. That is the frame-up part of the indictment. And frame-up is an inseparable part of American bourgeois justice. Why, do you remember, it is just fifteen years ago tonight that Sacco and Vanzetti, two very good and honest friends of the working class, forfeited their lives to American justice? Fifteen years ago tonight they were put to death in Massachusetts on an absolutely false conviction for crimes they had no connection with.

The most outstanding cases of persecution of labor people and unpopular sects in America have always been frame-ups. The real crime in our case is quite clear. It is only the skeptics, the wiseacres on the fringes of the movement, the apologists for the Roosevelt administration—only such people profess ignorance as to what it is all about. The prosecutors know what our real crime is. They have absentmindedly put it in the indictment in one place, to remove any doubt. Paragraph 12 of the first count of the indictment gives the real crime of the SWP and the leaders of Local 544. If you haven't read it, I advise you to read the whole indictment in the August issue of the *Fourth International*. Paragraph 12 reads:

"12. The said defendants and their co-conspirators would, and they did, accept as the ideal formula for the carrying out of their said objectives the Russian Revolution of 1917, whereby the then existing Government of Russia was overthrown by force and violence, and the principles, teachings, writings, counsel and advice of the leaders of that revolution, chiefly of V.I. Lenin and Leon Trotsky, would be, and they were, looked to, relied on, followed and held out to others as catechisms and textbooks directing the manner and means by which the aforesaid aim of the defendants could, and would be, accomplished; and accordingly, certain of the defendants would, and they did, go from the City of Minneapolis, State and District of Minnesota, and from other cities in the United States to Mexico City, Mexico, there to advise with and to receive the advice, counsel, guidance, and directions of the said Leon Trotsky."

Count 12—that is right. That point is no frame-up. That is no false accusation. That is what they really accuse us of and that is what we are really guilty of! And we are proud of it, and we are going to continue to be guilty of that crime as long as we live, whether we are in jail or out of jail!

"The Russian Revolution of 1917 and the advice and direction of Lenin and Trotsky"—yes, that is what we stand for. *And that is the only way of salvation for America!* We know we are right, and we know that nobody can stop us. No Roosevelt and no Biddle and their whole hypocritical treacherous gang can stop the march of history that is represented by the Fourth International. This rotten bourgeois democracy, trying to crush our movement in this prosecution, will deal itself some blows from which it will never recover. It will be exposed in the eyes of tens of thousands of workers as a rotten, hypocritical fraud.

A year after Trotsky's death we remember his words and we remain faithful to his teachings, inspired by his memory. We will have our say at the trial to Messrs. Roosevelt and Biddle and their war party. We will go into the court and answer to their indictments not as defendants but as accusers, accusers of them and of the system that they represent. We will put them on trial and accuse them of conspiracy against mankind by trying to plunge the people into another war, a war which will devour people by millions and destroy a large part of the cultural heritage of civilized people accumulated through so many centuries.

We shall go into the court confident because we Trotskyists have no doubt of our historic mission. We have no doubt of the destiny of the class we represent to be victorious. And we know we are the only party that can represent this class.

Comrade Trotsky himself had a vast contempt for all other political organizations whether bourgeois or petty bourgeois or so-called workers' parties. In our last meeting with him a little more than a year ago we took occasion to discuss these questions with him—how in spite of all their adaptation and compromises, the reformists' and centrists' parties couldn't make any headway in this country. How the single party that showed continuous, even if modest, growth and stability, and retained its self-confidence, is our party—the party of Trotskyism. He said these other parties are completely hopeless because they all stand on ground that is crumbling away beneath their feet—the ground of bourgeois democracy. They do not stand on the rock of principle which alone could assure their future. They suffer by sympathetic action from all the diseases of bourgeois democracy and must perish with it. One blow of war can disperse their parties.

The real alternatives in America are Roosevelt's party—or we. That is what Comrade Trotsky said to our delegation a year ago. And then he corrected himself and said, that is not exactly precise. Because Roosevelt's party is a transitory thing which will be ground to bits as the social crisis develops. The real alternative in America, the real showdown, will be between the American fascists and the American Fourth Internationalists.

We believe that, and we are sure of our right to victory. Historical progress is not finished, but on the contrary is only beginning. Comrade Trotsky taught us to believe that. He taught us to believe in man, and his communist future. The memory of Trotsky, of all that he was and all that he left to us, the man, the teacher, the comrade; the memory of Trotsky which we and those who come after us will keep forever green, is our strongest support, our greatest heritage. Holding on to that heritage, we ourselves are strong and invincible. We can face any persecution, we can face any foe, with confidence that the future belongs to us. The future belongs to the Fourth International, which has the name of Trotsky written on its banners!

OUR PARTY'S ANSWER
TO THE PROSECUTION

October 11, 1941

*This was Cannon's main political report to the SWP's Plenum-
Conference held in Chicago October 11-12, 1941. The major part
of this speech was published in the November 15, 1941,* Militant.
*The section on work in the trade unions (pages 178-83) was omit-
ted from the published version. A corrected copy of this portion of
the speech was found in Cannon's files as well as an unedited
transcript of the entire speech indicating where this section
belongs and it has been restored in this version.*

Comrade Chairman and Comrades:

To judge by the turnout we have here for this Active Workers
Conference, if Mr. Roosevelt and Mr. Biddle thought that by
indicting a few members of the party they were going to scare the
rest, they made a miserable failure to start with. The Trotskyists
don't scare very easily. When we undertook to organize a
revolutionary movement to overthrow capitalism, we took it for
granted that along the road we would have to be prepared to take
a few blows. The real test of a workers' party is its ability to
stand up under the attempts of the class enemy to intimidate it
and to scare it out of existence. The Socialist Workers Party will
stand up.

This is by far the best gathering we have had in the entire
thirteen years since we founded the original nucleus of American
Trotskyism in 1928. Not only is it the best showing in numbers
but also in spirit and enthusiasm, in unity within our ranks, and
in the determination of all party members and leaders to respond
to the demands of the new situation with greater efforts and
sacrifices, firmer discipline, and devotion to the party.

One time, so the legend goes, there was a very spirited conference of the pioneer Communists in the early days of the Communist Party. One delegate got so enthusiastic that he stood up and said, "Comrade Chairman, I make a motion that this conference go down in history." Well, I am sure that this conference will go down in history without a motion to that effect. It marks a turning point, a new stage in the growth and development and integration of the invincible movement of the Fourth International in the United States. Nothing can break this party because it is founded on the solid rock of Marxism; it is inspired by the spirit of its great teacher and leader, Comrade Trotsky, and is marching forward in his spirit. This party is not afraid of anything or anybody. We can dish it out, as the saying goes, and we can take it, too. Biddle will find that out, and so will Roosevelt, and so will Tobin and all the little lackeys of these conspirators against the rights and interests of the workers.

I presume you have had an opportunity to study the resolution adopted and presented for your consideration by the National Committee. This is not a general economic and political survey but rather a special resolution to the occasion. The resolution undertakes to set forth, point by point, those specific concrete tasks imposed upon the party by the present situation arising out of the developments of the war and the federal prosecution of a number of our people.

Of course, this prosecution, as everybody knows, had its immediate initiation in the trade union fight in Minneapolis. But that trade union fight in Minneapolis was not just a trade union fight. It had its roots in the war situation. The conflict, as is pointed out in the resolution, and as is well known to all of us, between the Trotskyist leaders of 544 and Tobin, the warmongering international president of the Teamsters union, didn't grow up out of incidental trade union questions. The fight came to a head over the fundamental question of the conduct of trade union leaders in time of imperialist war. All over the country the labor lieutenants of the capitalist class have succeeded in pushing local trade union leaders into line for the war. They pushed over the Socialist Party trade unionists, without difficulty, like so many ninepins. The Stalinists are on the bandwagon, and so are the so-called "progressives" and "radicals." But they couldn't line up the Trotskyists. Why? Because they are people of a different breed; they are people of an entirely different type. The Trotskyists don't line up for war after they have said in time of peace that they are going to oppose the war. The Trotskyists are bearers of a glorious name. They feel obliged to make their deeds match their words.

The prosecution really, to put it on its right foundation, is a prosecution of our party because we remain loyal in time of war to the principles which we expounded in time of peace. This prosecution is a great new event. We are the first section of the working class to be singled out for prosecution. And not by some ignorant local prosecutor, not by some overenthusiastic provincial jingo, but by the federal government itself at the direct instigation of the president of the United States. This is the fact. And this fact puts our party right in the very center of the political situation in this country. It will remain there without question of a doubt because this prosecution will drag out for a long time, and it will echo for a longer time through the ranks of the American people.

The blow aimed against us—and it is a real blow; a deliberate and determined attempt to imprison twenty-eight people[39] for terms of years and to intimidate the others—such a blow can either make or break the party, depending on how we meet it. If we stand up and fight, regardless of the consequences; if we take the necessary risks, hold firm to our principles, use the trial for an aggressive defense of our principles—then our party is bound to grow in prestige, in influence, and in membership, in spite of anything that may happen to some individuals involved. But if the party tries to be clever, to run away, to disavow its principles under the fire of the enemy, then the party would be everlastingly doomed.

The political resolution which you have before you is designed to guide the party. It is your task here as members of the conference, in considering the resolution, to understand that we are giving the answer to all the party members and sympathizers, and to the working class generally, as to just what the Trotskyist party is going to do in the next period.

First of all we take up the question of the policy in court. We lay down in the resolution, clearly and categorically, that the policy, which is obligatory upon all party members involved, is not to renounce, not to water down the revolutionary doctrines of our party, but to defend them openly and militantly in court. That is the only program possible for us. When we are called to the witness stand to answer whether we did conspire to overthrow the government with armed force in the immediate future, we shall undertake to tell just what the party stands for and what it aims to do today and tomorrow. If we succeed in carrying out this program we will transform that courtroom, which is designed by our persecutors to be the scene of intimidation and terror for the party—we will transform it into a forum, into a sounding board from which we speak to the people of the United States about the program of our party.

That is the court policy laid down in the resolution, and I think it will be accepted unanimously by the conference, by the party, and by the party members among the defendants involved. And we should go further, too, even in this detail, in my opinion, and lay down lines of procedure for the comrades involved in the trial. That is, like Trotskyists in all situations wherever they may be, wherever two or more are gathered together, they act as one. All questions of procedure and policy, decisions that have to be made on the spot, are made in meetings after discussion, and in cases of differences of opinion, the vote is taken and the majority prevails. That is the way a serious party machine works everywhere and under all circumstances and must do there.

They have a wonderful plan up there in Minneapolis where they have a fine party headquarters with ample facilities. They are working out a plan for community feeding of the delegates— pardon me, the defendants. This system of community feeding, which we instituted last year at the Active Workers Conference and have again repeated this year, works out very well in keeping comrades together and promoting a good feeling among them. Twice a day in the commodious party headquarters the defendants will be gathered together for their meals, for lunch and dinner, which will be furnished by the defense committee. The party headquarters will also provide the necessary facilities and room for meetings of the defendants, social affairs, committee meetings and so on. Thus, from the beginning of the trial to the very end, the party defendants will be confronting their enemies as a solidly organized body, always together, always united, always striking in the same direction. That is the Trotskyist way.

Another aspect of the defense is the organization of the Civil Rights Defense Committee.[40] I am sure everybody in the party appreciates in the highest degree the work that has already been done by the people in charge of this committee. We are all grateful to the distinguished and celebrated men and women who have constituted themselves as officers and members of the committee. I note with appreciation that my old and esteemed friend Carlo Tresca is there, as always, in the front ranks of the fight for justice. Margaret DeSilver is there, worthily bearing the honored name of the wartime fighter for civil liberties, Albert DeSilver.

In agreement with us the Civil Rights Defense Committee has taken upon itself certain definite and limited functions. It will undertake to provide funds for the legal expenses of the trial. We must not overlook any possibilities to protect the legal rights and interests of the defendants. This costs a lot of money. We will have to help the Civil Rights Defense Committee to raise it. The other task of the committee is to secure publicity and create favorable public sentiment for the defendants in every possible way. The functions of the defense committee are limited to these two points.

The policy of the defense is determined by the party in cooperation with the defendants. We cannot transform the party into a defense organization. The party goes ahead with all its political and organizational work and tries to make such a distribution of the resources of our movement, between the necessary legal expenses and the necessary expenses of keeping the party functioning, that neither is neglected.

You hear a lot of chatter from some of the radical petty-bourgeois opponents of our movement about the necessity of a "broad united front" for defense. Don't take these windbags seriously. Nobody needs to agitate us about the importance of united-front formations when it is possible to get substantial organizations to take serious action. But we certainly don't intend, under the formula of united front, to permit the legal defense committee to be transformed into a forum for all kinds of factional disputes between all kinds of jangling groups. We want a defense committee that is a working body, that takes its defense tasks seriously and doesn't attempt to become a political organization or a debating society. Anybody willing to participate with us and help us in good faith along that line, in the committee which has been established, is certainly welcome to come along and help us. But if others, whose sincerity is suspect, think for a minute that we will permit them to make a factional football out of the defense of our case, they will be promptly called to order. We have a certain stake in the matter, namely, our heads. This gives us a right to some say about the procedure.

We would like to have a great conference of labor organizations supporting our defense, but it is utopian to think we merely have to proclaim it in order to get it. There is no possibility in the present state of affairs in the labor movement to enlist many important workers' organizations actively in our support. The Stalinists are not in favor of our defense. They are in favor of our prosecution. They give Roosevelt and Biddle critical support, friendly advice. They advise them to change the indictment, accuse us of being Nazi spies and make it a little bit stiffer for us. Is anybody here fool enough to think the Socialist Party wants to help us? The Socialist Party will piously announce its support of civil liberties in general and let it go at that. If you pass the hat around, they will, maybe, give us two bits. Even then you had better bite the coin to make sure it isn't counterfeit. The trade unions on the whole, up to now, are not bestirred to help the most extreme and persecuted revolutionary group in the country, the Trotskyists.

So we have to go along with this kind of committee of prominent individuals which has been set up. Later on, it is quite possible that with the further progress of the case and further developments in the labor movement, a real basis of support for the defendants can be established in the trade unions and supporting conferences organized in defense of our people. When such a possibility arises we will be the first to recognize it and the first to grasp it. But in the present situation we do not run after utopian programs and do not want to be bothered with such proposals.

I come now to the point which is stressed in the resolution and which I want to elaborate particularly here. What shall be the general attitude to the party in the event of a successful prosecution, that is, in the event of a conviction of the defendants involved in this case? Shall we accept this as a proclamation that our party is illegal, withdraw from the public scene, close down our offices, and establish underground corners and places of hiding, etc.?

That would be, in the opinion of the National Committee, the greatest mistake. We don't intend to surrender our possibilities of legal functioning at the very first blow. In spite of all they say, we are not "conspirators." We are a political movement and we want to work in the open. The advantages of public activity, agitation, propaganda, and organization are so superior and so much more economical than similar work carried out by illegal and underground means that a serious revolutionary party has to fight to the last ditch to maintain its legal rights.

I mentioned some weeks ago to the Political Committee the experiences of 1919, the postwar period. There was a tremendous wave of reaction stemming out of Washington under Attorney General A. Mitchell Palmer, the Biddle of his day. The Communist parties were no sooner organized—there were two of them; they began with a split, the Communist Party and the Communist Labor Party—they were no sooner organized than Palmer's persecution began. Palmer's agents arrested all the leaders they could find in one part of the country or another; there was hardly a leader of the movement who wasn't under indictment.

They staged raids on the meetings and arrested scores and hundreds of members within the space of two or three days. Under the impact of those blows, and under the influence of some leaders who were by no means cowards but who tended to draw their conclusions from the experiences in Russia where there never had been any democratic liberty, the parties automatically accepted an illegal status. They withdrew to the underground and stayed there two or three years, attempting to function with all the limitations and difficulties and multiplied expenses of illegal work.

A peculiar thing happened in connection with those events. Some judge—I forget the name—who had a case before him, proclaimed the Communist Party an illegal organization, and the party accepted his decision. But in another case, for some reason or other, some quirk in the judge's mind, he announced that the Communist Labor Party was a legal organization. This should at least have been the signal for the Communist Labor Party to say, "Thank you, Judge," and to open up its headquarters again. But instead of that, they considered the pronouncement an affront to their revolutionary integrity, a discrimination against them, and they issued a statement saying in effect: "By God, we are just as illegal as the Communist Party." And they remained "underground" on principle.

At the first underground unity convention in Bridgeman, Michigan—not the famous one in 1923,[41] but in 1920—when drawing up the constitution of the organization, the left-wingers insisted on having it stated in the constitution, "The Communist Party is an underground, illegal organization," so that there would be no doubt about it. In the light of later developments that attitude must be regarded as a mistake. The party was compelled later on to conduct an intensive struggle to regain its right to function legally, and in the course of several years, by experimenting with one form of organization and another, it succeeded in gradually extending its public activities. There was a change in the administration at Washington, and eventually the party restored its legal functioning although the laws remained the same as before.

In the United States, up to now, they have never worked out a formula to proscribe an organization as such. There is no reason why we should do it for them. We should not accept even a conviction in this case as a signal that the legal public activity of the party has to cease. It will not be so easy for our enemies, the Roosevelts and the Biddles, to wage a war for "democracy" and suppress free speech altogether. It is not our duty to simplify their task by voluntarily relinquishing our rights. We should continue as far as possible, step by step, resisting at every step, and striving, even at the cost of some casualties, to maintain a legal existence for our movement. I don't, of course, project the perspective of a party of our size being able to resist the whole concentrated weight of American capitalism against us, but we will do the best we can.

They are persecuting us and will continue to persecute us, but we must not immediately begin to develop an underground psychology. There are two sides to that underground psychology, and I have seen both of them in the course of my experience in the movement. One side of it is revolutionary, that is, it is inspired by the impulse to continue functioning in spite of overwhelming persecution. This was the dominating spirit of the Russian Bolsheviks under tsarism. It is the spirit of the comrades of the Fourth International who are working by underground methods in Europe today. On the other hand, some people seem to think there is romanticism, combined with safety, in an underground organization. When we finally found the possibility of restoring the legal functioning of our pioneer Communist movement in 1922 and 1923, we met with a great deal of resistance from various types of underground fanatics who wanted to stay underground out of habit and on principle.

We had a big battle over this question in Moscow. I was a delegate of the "liquidators" faction—that is, the faction which wanted to "liquidate" the underground party and form a legal organization—to the Third International in 1922. It was due to the intervention of Trotsky in the first place, then of Lenin and Zinoviev, that we finally got support for our program of legalizing the movement. In the course of the discussions Zinoviev told a story about some underground fanatics in the Russian movement who had become so accustomed to conspiring under the tsar that they wanted to keep it up after the tsar was gone. Even after the Bolsheviks took power, said Zinoviev, they had a woman in the party who used to go around with a false passport. She didn't feel comfortable without it. We will have to find our way between the possibilities and the necessities, and try in every case to make the best of it: that is, to do those things and take those steps which make it possible for us to survive as an organization and have the greatest possible freedom of action.

One of the ways pointed out in the resolution to facilitate our fight to maintain our legal existence is participation in election campaigns. You all know about the 1940 election campaign in Minnesota. That was one of the celebrated things of our conference last year. The campaign of Comrade Grace Carlson for senator and the sizable vote she received were certainly a great help and inspiration for the whole party. You have learned about the perennial election races of George Breitman in Newark, until they are beginning to call him a chronic office seeker. Breitman is running again this year. And this example finally caught hold in New York, and as you know, I stand before you today requesting your suffrage in my capacity as candidate for mayor of New York. And if elected. . . !

It is one of the greatest things that ever happened in the party, that the reaction of the New York party organization to our indictment was not to run for cover but to go out in the open, in the election campaign, with the banner of the indicted comrades. And they went out night and day, for weeks on end, and collected more than 15,000 individual signatures on the petitions. They must have interviewed not less than 100,000 people; and in almost every case there was the occasion to argue why they should sign, to tell them about the case in Minnesota and what our party stands for. I venture to say more propaganda, more agitation, for Trotskyism was carried out in concentrated form in those weeks of the petition campaign than ever before, by many times, in New York.

Now it appears that we have the petition filed with more than double the required amount of signatures. The first three days have elapsed without challenge and the indications are that we will be on the ballot in New York. This is an excellent means of propaganda and agitation and of struggle to maintain legality.

Our campaign in New York acquires exceptional significance now because of an account in today's paper that the Stalinists have withdrawn their candidate in order to help LaGuardia.[42] That's all right with us too. It means that the possibility can be created for our party, for the first time in New York, to rally around itself a real mass of militant antiwar workers.

This is a form of activity that must be emphasized more in the next period. Many comrades seem to take it for granted that we can't get on the ballot. We can't unless we work. We can do it in Newark; we can do it in Minnesota; now it has been demonstrated that we can do it in New York. It took us thirteen years to accomplish it. For thirteen years we thought we couldn't do it, but once this new group of young leaders in New York took hold of things, they organized the party to go out and get the signatures and put the party on the ballot. Let us think more seriously about election campaigns, particularly now in the light of our determined struggle to function legally as long as possible.

The party, in order to prepare itself for this blow and others yet to come, should get a word from the conference, which is contained in the resolution, about the internal preparation of the party. Some of the leading people of the party are put face to face with the prospect of prison terms; other activists in the party ranks may be confronted in the future with the same prospect. We have to ask ourselves, what does it take to enable men to stand up in the face of tests of this kind? Does it take courage? Courage has many kinds. Some kinds of courage, ordinary human courage, are by no means adequate for such tests as these.

During the last war a great number of IWW men were sent to the penitentiary, 150 to 200 of them. In the Chicago case alone there were a hundred.[43] These were the leading militants of the IWW and most of them served some years in prison—two, three, four years in prison. But only a small percentage of those IWW militants continued their activity for any length of time after their release from prison. A very small percentage. And that was by no means because they were poor material. On the contrary, they were first-class material, very good and courageous people. What the IWW men in prison lacked was a theoretical understanding and historical outlook that could sustain them under the pressure of the defeats of the day, looking forward to the horizon of the future. The complexities of the war overwhelmed most of those who had nothing in the way of equipment except the all-too-simple syndicalist philosophy.

In order for one to withstand persecution over a long period of time, he has got to have a theoretical understanding, a historical outlook, and a firm conviction that history is working on his side. He must believe he is serving a great cause whose victory is assured. This conviction will sustain us against all the blows of the class enemy in the years to come. And that is why we must devote special attention now to the new cadres of youth who are coming to us—that we educate them in the principles of Marxism; teach them the history and tradition of Bolshevism; and help them to acquire an historical point of view, which is the point of view of Bolshevism.

In general, the party in response to the new tests and the new tasks must of necessity be drawn tighter together, become more disciplined, demand more of its members, and particularly of its leaders. We cannot build a party and lead a revolution merely with clever leaders. In order to be a leader of the revolutionary labor movement, one must have Bolshevism in his blood. The leaders must have demanded of them that they set the example all the time before the party. The comrades must see the leaders always and everywhere out in front, not merely making speeches, but in tests and sacrifices. Only such leaders can have the authority and win the confidence of the rank and file of the party. The party must have leaders worthy of trust.

There is a section in the resolution about the internal preparation of the party. This section should be taken very seriously and reported at length to the branches on the return of the delegates. We must do more systematic educational work, not only for the rank and file and new recruits, but also for the second cadres of leaders who are coming up.

We have even talked in the [Political] Committee several times lately about the necessity of systematic study work on the part of our field organizers, as part of their duties. There should grow up an atmosphere in the party that the party expects a field organizer to be an educated Marxist; and that systematic study is part of his duties in the field. A certain number of hours of the day he should be assigned by the National Committee to retire to the library and study the theoretical works of Marxism and report on the progress of his studies. He should be paid for this activity by the National Committee as part of his functions as organizer in the field. We should eventually approximate the standard that all the leaders of the party, in the field as well as in the center, are informed Marxists. They will understand their philosophy, their doctrine, and their history, and they will communicate this respectful attitude toward theory and history to the rank and file of the party. Thereby the level of the organization will rise, and its ability to withstand the attacks of the class enemy will be greater.

They had a campaign of this kind once in the Comintern, along about 1924-25. The Communist International was swelled by the affiliation of parties in the various countries which had come over from the Social Democracy, and these parties were in different stages of political development. They had formally adopted the Bolshevik program but they were far from being Bolshevik parties. The Comintern worked out a program under a slogan called the "Bolshevization" of the party. The original aim, as announced, was to initiate a concentrated campaign of explanation and study of the history and principles of Bolshevism to aid in the assimilation of these new people into the Bolshevik current.

But, like every other good project of the Comintern as it fell more and more into the hands of Stalin, this excellent concept was perverted and caricaturized and transformed into a struggle against the best Bolsheviks in the Communist International. It became a campaign against Trotskyism. But the idea had an absolutely sound kernel. Trotsky mentioned it in his famous *Lessons of October.* He said, there is a great deal of talk about Bolshevization and it is very timely too, but what is Bolshevization? He said, *it is such an education of the party members and such a selection of its leading staff that the party doesn't leave the track when its opportunity comes.*[44] That, I think, is an excellent description of the campaign of internal strengthening which we want to carry out—to the end that the party membership should be so educated, and the leading people so selected, that the party will remain firm under every test which may confront it.

It is now my duty—and, God helping me, I always try to do my duty—to speak for a moment under the heading, "The Balance Sheet of the Split with the Petty-Bourgeois Opposition." This, of course, has nothing to do with the events or problems of today. It is like raking up last year's leaves. The split was carried out, as you remember, by them in spite of the extraordinary concessions, the unprecedented concessions, made by the majority in order to permit them to remain in the party. We made only one demand upon them: that they respect the decisions of the convention and obey the discipline of the party. Trotsky said they had a profound social impulse to separate themselves from the proletarian majority. From the point of view of every political experience, their split couldn't be justified anywhere but they felt compelled to break at any cost. When, a short time later, Burnham, the leader and inspirer of that whole contemptible faction, completely repudiated socialism and the workers' movement, we could see how really profound their social impulse to break from the proletarian majority really was.

It is a crime to break the unity of the revolutionary party. Not a few of the honest comrades who were duped into the split by Burnham and Shachtman are beginning to repent it and to reexamine the question of who was responsible for the split. They can find only one answer: the leaders of the petty-bourgeois faction were wholly and completely responsible. They say they were expelled against their will by the bureaucratic action of the Political Committee. That was along in the latter part of April, last year. Then a few months later, you remember, we had the Plenum and Active Workers Conference in Chicago. The time and place of the Plenum-Conference was announced in the press and known to the expelled leaders of the opposition. If they had been put out of the party only because of bureaucratic action of the Political Committee their next procedure was to appeal to the plenum, and to appear before the plenum and the conference in defense of their appeal, which they had a right to do under the party constitution. But they made no appeal.

Why? Because they didn't want to be reinstated into the party of Trotskyism on any terms.

After every bureaucratically engineered split I have seen in the past there unfailingly arose in the ranks of the party a criticism against the leadership for having expelled party members unjustly. And, thereafter, when the bureaucratic leaders got into difficulties, and when they would appeal for money to finance the party, the opposition would say, the party is in difficulties, the party is broke, because of the expulsions. There is an endless opposition around the heads of bureaucrats who force a split not politically motivated. That is a political law.

But we have not had in our ranks, from the time of the split a year and a half ago up till today, a single branch or individual who raised a reproach against the leadership for the expulsion of the petty-bourgeois opposition. One hundred or so comrades at last year's conference voted unanimously to confirm the expulsion and make an end of it. You have here approximately 150 delegates this year. I don't think a single one present wants to reopen the question.

It was a socially motivated split on both sides. It was a split of the petty-bourgeois elements from the proletarian. We didn't force the split, but we gained by it. Our party, from the very first day, went forward after that split. Our activities, our press, our organization, our finances,our morale, and our general digestion is a lot better ever since the petty-bourgeois opposition walked out on us. In the light of the experiences of the past year and one-half, one must say that of all of the splits in the history of our international movement—and there have been many of them, good, bad, and indifferent—the best split that ever came down the pike was the split between the proletarian majority and the petty-bourgeois opposition. There cannot be any semblance of concilia-tion toward them.

This does not mean we are not going to have some of the rank-and-file comrades back. Just as I stand here talking to you I received word from the West Coast that a group of eleven, the backbone of their second-largest branch, the Los Angeles branch, is waiting now for their convention, which is supposed to be in progress at the same time as our conference, to reject their resolution for the defense of the Soviet Union in order to come over in a body to join our Los Angeles branch on the basis of our program. Naturally, they will be welcomed back into our ranks. That is the kind of unity we can entertain with members of the so-called Workers Party. That is the only kind of unity we can have the slightest interest in.

Now I come to a very important point, the question of party work in the unions in the next period. You know that the unions are gradually undergoing a great transformation. Day by day the class-collaborationist leaders of the unions, cooperating with the government heads who have a deliberate design, are working to harness the unions to the war machine and to encroach upon their independence, to tie them up with no-strike contracts and agreements, to shift the center of their activity from strikes and class-struggle activities to negotiations by the government mediation boards, and so on. The program of harnessing the unions to the state is going ahead with full speed. Because of that our work in the unions becomes more important and, at the same time, more difficult than ever and requires more attention to the established Bolshevik principles of trade union work.

For years now we have been bending the stick in one direction: that is, we have been trying to take the party that was predominately petty bourgeois in its composition, in some parts of the country at least, and transform that party into a proletarian organization with its members rooted in industry and belonging to unions. We have waged a long and hard fight; the faction fight with the petty-bourgeois opposition was one of the episodes in that long struggle to proletarianize the party. We have succeeded so well that you can say offhand now that the average member of our party is a trade unionist. In many places the great majority of members of the party now are trade unionists. While we were carrying on that campaign to get into the unions, we naturally emphasized one side of the task. Comrades were cautioned not to go into the unions and begin making speeches about Lenin and Trotsky right away. They should be careful, integrate themselves, get some training in their trade, some standing as mechanics, workmen, etc. Instead of pushing them into exposure, we tended to restrain them at all times. We told them many times, there is only one way of carrying on trade union work effectively—that is inside the unions. And if you conduct yourself in such a way that you get bounced out before you really get in, you cannot carry on any fruitful trade union work.

This work of integration has been pretty well carried on. We have come to a new stage where the comrades should begin to develop systematic party political work. Trade unionism by itself does not amount to much in this epoch of wars and revolutions. Only insofar as trade union work is inspired and fructified by Bolshevik political activity does it afford some permanent benefits to the working class and lead them toward the path of revolution.

There is only one way to carry on political work in the unions, only one way to do any kind of serious work in the unions, and that is by means of fraction organization. It is by means of the fractions that the influence of the party is asserted, that policies are determined, that individual party members are controlled and subordinated to the party, and the full force of the party is brought to bear. You have in your conference folders, I think, a copy of a speech I made on the trade union question seventeen years ago, reprinted from the *Daily Worker* of that time. That was a speech to a party conference of coal miners in St. Louis in 1924.[45]

A project has been approved by the Political Committee to publish a book of my writings and speeches. This speech I refer to is part of the material dug up out of the old files. The one thing that struck me right in the eye, and other comrades when they read it, was that the speech, just changing a few names, would be 100 percent applicable to the present trade union problem of the party. Those were the days when we were just laying down the principles of communism and establishing the procedure by which the communists work in the trade unions. Without the fraction organization you cannot recruit for the party, and without recruiting for the party you never really influence the unions, you only have contact with them. An individual comrade who organizes a union, or gets a strategic position in a union, can lose that position for one of a dozen or more reasons. Then, if he has failed to recruit and build a party group in the rank and file, nothing remains to show for his work but a union for some business agent or bureaucrat to take over.

One cannot accomplish much in the present trade union movement without the help and direction of the party. The best comrades, the best Bolsheviks, become burdened by the weight and the detail of the trade union movement, which is a veritable breeding ground for opportunism. They have a tendency not to push party fraction work, but to postpone it, to pull away from it, to imagine that they can work out some shortcut to attain their ends which can only be attained by the means laid down by the party. This principle of party fraction organization is confirmed by all the experience of revolutionary Marxists in the trade union movement since Lenin first elucidated it. But time and time again you can find an individual comrade in the unions who becomes an official, who thinks Lenin's method is unnecessary in his case. Some of them take this attitude in the best of faith, thinking they know better than the party, they will do it differently.

You have other cases of comrades who get appointed or elected to some petty business agent's job and immediately begin to think they are bigger than the party and don't want to be controlled by the party. They don't want any fraction organization because they don't want the rank-and-file comrades to be able to call them to order. Of course, these are exceptional cases and the party always finds a way to deal with them.

It is no accident that the record of Trotskyism in the trade union movement is clear as crystal and clean as a hound's tooth. Our party never entertains for a moment the idea that a trade union official, or a trade union group, overshadows and dominates the party. The party leads the work of party members in the unions, as elsewhere, and that is the only way we want it. We don't want anything to do with fictitious influence in the unions. We want the real thing or nothing.

You had this morning a report of the magnificent fight that the comrades put up in Minneapolis. The whole country knows about it. The name of Trotskyism has been glorified by the magnificent stand of the leaders in Minnesota who would not knuckle down to the warmongers, who took the blows and fought back and defended their principles regardless of consequences. It is no accident that only the Trotskyists do that. Look at what happened to the others. Look at the Socialists. They had a big Socialist group in the auto union led by Reuther and Co. Dubinsky was once a member of the Socialist Party. Reuther, Dubinsky, Green, and VanGelder in the Shipbuilders union, all kinds of "socialists" in all kinds of unions—they have all gone over to the war machine. And the Socialist Party yet doesn't dare to criticize them because, you see, they are trade union leaders, and the Socialist Party has an inferiority complex in front of anyone who has influence in the trade union movement.

And look what happened to the Lovestoneites. They led Local 22 in New York, a very big union. They used to make fun of us as a splinter group with no "mass" basis, whereas they were—so they said—great trade union mechanics. The only trouble with them was that the business agents in Local 22 were willing to belong to the Lovestone faction as long as the faction shielded them from criticism and asked nothing from them. When the business agents decided to go 100 percent for the war, they dragged the Lovestone group with them. That is one of the reasons the Lovestone group had to dissolve in such disgrace. A political party which subordinates itself to trade union officials is doomed to die and deserves only to die.

We faced this question and fought it out in 1934 when the Communist League of America—that was the original Trotskyist group—was just beginning to come out of a six year period of isolation. We got our first chance in the trade union movement in New York in the hotel industry. We had a member at that time, named Field, who through a lucky combination of circumstances got himself elected secretary of a small independent union of hotel workers. This was the time of the first strike wave and the NRA. The union grew and mushroomed. In a short time there was a general strike of hotel workers in New York.

Field was known as a Trotskyist. The reputation of the party was involved. We sent in every possible force we could to help in the strike. We called Field to meetings with the National Committee to work out questions of policy and to bring to his assistance the experience that had been accumulated by the members of the National Committee in previous strikes. But Mr. Field, who had suddenly become a publicized trade union leader of thousands of people, thought it was beneath his dignity to confer with the leaders of what had already begun to appear to him as a small, insignificant political group. He rejected our suggestions, which would have enabled him to carry out the strike more successfully.

We tried day after day to persuade him to work with us, to let us help him. He rejected everything and thought we were completely at his mercy. What! A little group of Trotskyists down on 16th Street, telling me, the leader of a mass movement, how to run a strike? Well, do you know what we did with Mr. Field and Co.? We brought them up on charges of indiscipline in the middle of the strike and expelled them out of the party. We did that just to show them that they couldn't monkey with a Trotskyist party. The rank and file of the party warmly supported our action. That action was an extremely drastic one, but it was by that example among other things that we developed an attitude in party members of loyalty to the party when they get put in trade union positions.

If here and there you develop a trade union business agent who gets elected to office by strength of the party in the first place, and then begins to think he is bigger than the party, you have a way of reaching him. If you have organized a fraction in the union, you surround him with the fraction. Experience will convince you that in such conflicts the rank and file support the party every time. Without the rank-and-file fraction you have no means of controlling this fellow. He can compromise the party. But, you may ask, what shall we do if he will not submit to the decision of the rank-and-file fraction? The answer is simple, comrades: Kick him out of the party. Don't make big problems out of trifles. If our influence in a trade union rests on a disloyal man it is a fiction, and we don't believe in fictions.

In the next period this side of our trade union work has an extraordinary importance for another reason. Our task in the unions is not simply to play high politics. The main task of a party member in the union is to get acquainted with another worker beside him in the shop, and convert him to our ideas, and get him into the party. Unless we do that, unless we recruit continually into the party, we can never influence the trade unions, and without decisively influencing great masses of workers in the unions we can never lead the revolution.

Another point mentioned in the resolution is the defense of the Soviet Union, in reality the biggest problem of all for us today. The most important question, which overshadows by a hundred times the Minnesota trials, is the great military struggle taking place on the territory of Russia today. From all indications, Stalin and his gang are carrying their work to its predestined end. Stalin and Hitler together are dealing the Soviet Union what appears now to be its most catastrophic blow. The bitter truth can no longer be concealed by any blustering. The reality is too glaringly obvious now.

And you can be sure that more than one Stalinist bureaucrat in the United States, more than one careerist who has been serving the Stalin machine because it had power and prestige and money, is already beginning to draw the conclusions from the military defeat of the Soviet Union and looking for his own personal way out. You will see in the next period, if the tide of battle turns more decisively against the Soviet Union, great numbers of these treacherous careerists deserting what they consider the sinking ship and trying to find a place for themselves openly in the camp of American imperialism. They are very happy that they are on the Roosevelt bandwagon now, and there they want to stay.

But it is just such events as are happening now, just such a trend, that will break the hypnosis of the Stalinist rank and file. We musn't lose patience with the Stalinist worker. We must remember that the sentiment by means of which they held him, maneuvered him, and deceived him, was his determination to support the Soviet Union, to see in the Soviet Union some new hope in the world. Trotsky remarked in our very last talk with him that new events will break this hypnosis and make the rank-and-file workers see clearly what kind of leadership they have. These Stalinist workers—the honest and sincere but deluded workers—can't have any place to go except to us, or else into utter despair and disillusionment and inactivity. We should intensify our work among the Stalinists; try to reach them at all costs; fix the responsibility for the catastrophe of the Soviet Union where it really belongs—on the shoulders of Stalin and his gang; and try to win over every possible Stalinist worker to the movement of the Fourth International.

In such an hour as this, we see again how absolutely right were Trotsky and the majority of our party and the International in defending the Soviet Union to the very end; in establishing such a clear record that if we have now come to the catastrophe, nobody can justly say that one iota of responsibility clings to the Fourth International. We remain loyal to the Soviet Union in spite of everything, and that gives us the political and moral right to approach the disillusioned Stalinist workers.

It is not so with the petty-bourgeois elements who deserted our ranks on account of the Russian question. What position are they in to approach a sincere Stalinist worker who in his heart believed, and believed with justice, that the Soviet Union was a great fortress of the proletariat? Why, these wretched people addressed a leaflet to the Stalinists a couple of months ago in connection with the war turn and they didn't even mention their position on the Soviet Union. They felt so embarrassed and so helpless that they left out all mention of their attitude toward the Soviet-Nazi war.

We, on the other hand, can more and more aggressively, more and more confidently, approach the rank-and-file Stalinist workers who have believed in the Soviet Union and show them where the responsibility for the catastrophe belongs and lead them, or at least some of them, onto the path of the international revolution under our banner.

In the next period the shooting war may begin. Every day we get closer to it. Every day the effectiveness of agitation simply against war becomes diminished by the fact that more and more we are in the war. After the war starts formally, a mere opposition is not a practical basis of agitation. Then the proletarian military policy, adopted a year ago at our conference, comes to the front as the best practical means of agitation in a situation when the country is formally participating in a war. The demand for government-financed military training under trade union auspices, and for schools to train worker-officers, can be put forward with full confidence. As the experiences of the war develop and unfold, these slogans will get a wider echo and become ever more popular. The influence and the prestige of our party will grow with them.

I have given you, comrades, just an outline, a synopsis, of what the National Committee considers to be our most immediate problems and the concrete tasks which must be accomplished by the party members in the next period. I hope the suggestions we have made will meet with your approval. If any one has a contribution to make—an amendment, or a new proposal—I am sure that during the course of the discussion there will be ample opportunity to bring your ideas to the attention of the conference.

I want to close with the confident assertion that we shall go out of this historic conference firmly united on all important questions, sure of our future, and determined to answer the persecution of our enemies with better work, greater sacrifices, firmer discipline, deeper penetration into the trade unions. We have one common will: Everything for the party! All our work under the direction of the party! Every confidence that with this party and through this party we shall lead the American masses in due time to their liberating revolution!

IT IS TIME FOR A BOLDER
POLICY IN THE UNIONS

October 11, 1941

*This was Cannon's summary speech to the SWP's October 1941
Plenum-Conference. The text is from an unpublished and
uncorrected stenographic transcript.*

As I remarked in presenting the report today, our resolution is
not a general political and economic survey that touches upon
every question of importance. It is an attempt to answer what are
the most important questions that confront us in the present
situation. Now, the essence of political leadership is to answer the
question, what to do next. Only that kind of party and that kind
of leadership that can answer this question at the right time can
have political success. That is what we have attempted to do in
the resolution. In order to concentrate the attention of the party
on the burning and unpostponable tasks of the day, we left out of
consideration altogether a lot of other questions of considerable
interest and importance which we will deal with in due time
through the machinery of the National Committee.

We left out the question of the isolationists, priorities, the AFL
and CIO, the Hillman-Lewis controversy,[46] etc., only in order to
concentrate the attention of the party on those tasks which
confront it in connection with the federal prosecution and the
trade union situation. That is why we don't want to discuss here
today at detailed length the military policy to which we devoted
our entire conference last year. If we want to yield to that idea of
attempting to answer every question, we could have just an
omnibus resolution, with a section on the Negro question, one on
women, one on priorities unemployment,[47] one on Communist
work, another on the program for draftees, and all the other

186

questions which are important, but which are not burning for us at the moment and which would weigh down by quantity and tend to obscure and detract attention from the question of what does the party have to do in order to survive this blow and grow stronger under it. For that reason you will excuse me if I do not give detailed answers to some of those questions raised here. They will all be referred to the National Committee and dealt with in due time through the press. Questions of the labor party and demands on the government for appropriations, etc., I will leave out of consideration here for answer in the press.

Now the Stalinist question is for us again paramount. Stalinism is coming to the end of its rope. Stalin, hand in hand with Hitler, is finishing the work that he began many years ago with his renegacy from Bolshevism, his frame-ups, his purges, his assassinations, his whole system of lies and betrayals. We consider that the result, the catastrophic result of Stalin's policy, which is now piling up, must be the occasion for the complete departure of a large section of Stalinist careerists, functionaries, and trade union bureaucrats undisguisedly over to the camp of the bourgeoisie. And conversely, there must begin an awakening of a section of workers who have been under Stalinist influence because of their mistaken impression that thereby they were serving in some way the cause of socialism. The hypnosis that Comrade Trotsky spoke about can be broken now. We have to be alert to that problem.

All the time, since the beginning of our Trotskyist movement thirteen years ago, we have hammered more or less upon the Stalinist party because we recognized that it was the main concentration of revolutionary elements. Now it would be interesting to find out what percentage of the comrades attending here today at one time or another belonged to the Communist Party. Let's take a hand vote as to how many belonged to the Communist Party. At any rate, a substantial proportion of the comrades attending this conference and an overwhelming majority of the older pioneer members of our movement, had their origin in the Communist movement.

There are many new draftees, new people recruited by the Stalinists in recent years who can become for us a source of recruiting. And if you think, even if my calculations were not correct, if there is only 25 percent here who came out of the Stalinist movement, you are bound to remember that there are about 40 million workers in this country and if only 25 percent of our party came from the Stalinist party it gives you a rough idea, a comparative idea, of the recruiting possibilities from that section of the working class even for us yet today.

I don't think we can solve the problem of approaching the Stalinist workers and keeping after them by any mechanical device, or by any sensational proposal. I personally wouldn't be in favor of this idea of Comrade Stevens that we just bust out of this conference here, issuing a statement in defense of Bridges and Browder.[48] We have already done that in our press. We have made our position known. The matter was one of main consideration. We want a consistent policy of our party, oriented toward recruiting the disillusioned Stalinist workers. And don't forget that when you get a worker who has belonged to a political party, who has made sacrifices for it, who has habituated himself to revolutionary and disciplined work, you are getting a comrade who, if you can reeducate him in the spirit of Bolshevism, you have got a better piece of raw material than a worker without any previous demonstrated capacity to work in a disciplined formation.

The second point, now again, is the trade union question. Comrade Adler made an excellent point that the possibility of political agitation on the part of our trade union comrades is enormously enhanced by the new developments in the labor movement, in society in general. In the period of capitalist peace and stability, a comrade could work for years and years in a trade union and never be confronted in his daily work with anything more than the humdrum daily work of negotiating contracts, settling little grievances, routine, etc. Today politics has completely engulfed the trade union movement. In the old days the slogan of Gompers and Co.: "Keep politics out of the trade union movement," had a wide support. There was a tremendous impression among the workers that they had no reason to bring politics into the unions. But today with the development of the decay of capitalism, with its engulfment into the war and its permanent military program, Comrade Adler rightly pointed out that every question in the trade union movement leads today directly to Washington, to questions of the war, of priorities, of the mediation boards, and so on. And this opens up for us a political atmosphere which we can utilize if we know how to do so cleverly and successfully.

I think one of the funniest and at the same time most tragic [. . . examples] of how politics has caught up with some of the old-fashioned labor fakers is John L. Lewis. In the twenties Lewis was able to carry on a great crusade against the Communists and drive them out of the miners because they were bringing politics into the miners' union. Today he himself is facing annihilation because of the developments of the war between the Soviet Union and Nazi Germany and the war program of Roosevelt and one thing and another of that sort.

Generally, we can say that unions do not operate and can never operate again as they did in the old days of peaceful, stabilized, democratic capitalism. The traditional "business agent unionism" is dead forever. The new lineups in the labor movement, it must have struck you, which are repeated at every trade union convention, are the lineups on the questions of support of Roosevelt's war policy, for the defense of the Soviet Union, against any support of the Soviet Union, for isolationism—all questions which are in their very essence political, and the trade unions are compelled to make their lineups accordingly. And that makes an atmosphere for political interest of the workers who have been somnolent before, who never knew any political life before. They are compelled by the situation to think of political questions, and, to a certain extent, in political terms, and that is why I think we should try to develop our own political work in the unions with some hope of a better reception than we used to receive in the past. And, of course, by that we mustn't think that, as has been pointed out with a few words of caution, we will just run hog-wild; we will forget the relationship of forces; we will forget how weak we are . . . with the result that we will soon isolate ourselves and have ourselves thrown out. Now I don't mean that, whether some others meant it or not.

I do not believe in doing anything stupidly. I am convinced that any good proposition can become ridiculous if you apply it stupidly, and after my years of experience in this vale of tears, and my dealings with all kinds and types of humanity, I have evolved for myself a firm conviction on one point: there is absolutely no substitute for intelligence. If you go about developing our political work stupidly, naturally you will have bad results. I mean political work not in the sense of splurges, but in the sense of talking to the worker immediately next to you in the union or in the factory, taking advantage of problems arising over priorities unemployment, intervention of Mediation Boards, intervention of the Maritime Commission—as our comrades did on the Eastern Seaboard a few weeks ago, and utilized this occasion to do a little intelligent, careful, systematic political education, with the object of bringing people to the party, and, similarly, even open intervention in the union when the occasion is propitious. This can be done and should be done.

And I think that our comrades in the past year have carried out to the letter, and literally leaning over backwards, the injunctions we gave them to be careful and to get integrated in the shops and in the unions before they begin popping off too loud. But after they have been there for a year or two, after they have got their bearings and acquired a little prestige, to remain there year after year so careful, so cautious, so silent, and so invisible that nobody ever finds out that they have any political ideas, that, I must say, is carrying out the program of integration a little bit stupidly.

Now we must begin to bend the stick the other way and prod our comrades forward. And if somebody in some branch takes this as a signal that everybody who has not a strategic position in the union has got to run about with a bundle of *Militants* under his arm, you can just tell him what we said here, that you are supposed to do this, but do it cleverly and not stupidly. No mechanical politicalizing, no unnecessary and foolish exposure of comrades in the unions, who have to proceed cautiously in order to maintain their position; but to do the work, devise ways and means of strengthening the political work that we are doing in the unions. Meet in the fractions and discuss not only the high politics of the union but the simple question of how could we possibly recruit this man who is a good trade union militant and friendly to us, and bring him into the party. Assign a person to talk to him, two people to talk to him, work out a campaign for the approach and education of a single person in the union, to get him to join the party. That is political work which is ten times more important than any foolish splurging over a high question. What we want is new people in the party.

And the same rule of intelligence applies to the question of fraction organization too. I know that you can become so formal and so mechanical and get so wound up with the machinery of the fraction that all the energy of the comrades is involved with the fraction, and they never get around to putting the fraction to work. We don't want to do it that way. It is quite true, as Comrade Jones [V.R. Dunne] said, that fractions are no panacea; they are simply the Leninist mechanism of working in a mass movement. That is the whole thing. And the more formalized it is, the more the comrades get in the habit, whenever they have anything serious and important under consideration, of meeting together and talking it over and working out a policy and making decisions—in preference to the informal, lackadaisical method which is so easy to fall into in the trade union movement—the more success they will have.

Of course, neither a good policy, neither an acceleration of politicalization, nor fraction work, nor prayers will shield any organization from an occasional traitor. That can't be done. Every organization in all the historic experience in the labor movement, every great cause, has suffered from a certain percentage of renegades and traitors who under pressure turn over to the enemy. But we can keep it down to a minimum if our organization is tight and is disciplined and is prepared to defend itself. That is the whole score on the question of renegades, and by and large we haven't a great deal to fear from that. Every organization has had an occasional rat turn up. We have had a few turn up in Minneapolis—some careerists there, even though they are rank and filers, joined the party, stayed in a few months, then became disillusioned and go and peddle all they know, and a lot of things they don't know, to Tobin and the FBI. But serious defections anything like the parade of renegades who have risen up to confound the Stalinists everytime they get in trouble, I think we will be immune from because by and large we have accepted people of a different type and have not encouraged people to join the party with the object of self-advancement.

We have had some tests of the efficacy of fraction work just recently in the East Coast maritime situation. Problems of a complex political nature arose almost overnight over the question of bonuses for sailors going into the war zones, certainly a political [issue]. Then the Maritime Commission intervened and undertook to man some ships in the face of a strike. . . . Then the workers struck against the Maritime Commission and took a vote for a general strike and the question was taken out of the hands of the Maritime Commission and turned over to the hands of the Defense Mediation Board.

Our comrades could not possibly have found their way in that maze of developments if they had not met together. They came together in fraction meetings, they had the advice of the Political Committee, and I think everybody will agree that by virtue of that procedure—the fraction organization of the comrades in the union, and the political assistance of the Political Committee of the party—that our group came out of that tremendously difficult and complicated struggle with added prestige and strengthened position, while others didn't do so well, particularly those who didn't know how to work together. Why, it is really ridiculous when you stop to think, that the IWW tradition got wound up in this problem too, but we, working together, succeeded in breaking the IWW into different groups and fractions, because they don't believe in discipline, in giving up their individual liberties. We believe in discipline. We worked together and coordinated all our activities and practically scattered and demoralized them in favor of a more rational policy in the strike.

Fraction work is important for recruiting. I mentioned before, I have never heard that discussed much in the party, but it seems to me an excellent idea that if, for example, we decide here on a recruiting campaign, that the fractions in the various unions put on the agenda of the fraction meetings the question of recruiting, not in general but concretely, and really push the question of trying to draw into the party by the collective work of the fraction a few valuable individuals. That will be a great gain for us.

I had the very pleasant experience last Saturday night of spending an evening with one of our best trade union organizers, a young comrade who came out of Chicago, out of Indiana Harbor, and was appointed to an organizer's position with a big union. He first inquired of the Political Committee whether he should accept the post. It is one of those jobs which come up so frequently, of an appointment being made by a reactionary officialdom with a double purpose: one purpose being to try to win over to the machine a young militant who has been making a little trouble, put him on the payroll, soften him up a little bit, and integrate him into the machine; the other is, get him out of the field of activity, get him removed from his base in the rank and file, and if he doesn't go along a little later, throw him out. That is the way the wise labor fakers figure, and that is the way they ruined and demoralized many and many young militants who didn't have the advantage of a party education and party support. But in that case, as we almost always do with a comrade we trust, we said, go ahead and take the strategic position. Let them play their game with you, but you play your game with them. Use your position, however restricted the opportunities are, to acquire experience and to serve the party.

This comrade has now been promoted to a higher post and he again came to New York to consult us whether he should accept the higher position to which he was promoted. In the course of the conversation, he expressed great satisfaction. . . . One thing he was sure he had done which he counted more important than the organization of 10,000 workers was that he had gotten two of the organizers to join the party and he had a plan to collect some money out of his wages and the wages of the members he had recruited, to pay the expenses of a party organizer to go into that field and devote full time to the chasing down of contacts that he had secured for them. He, himself, naturally, because of his position, couldn't work in the open. But when one is really loyal to the party and when he understands that every time he does a job in the mass movement there has to accrue a benefit to the party in order for the work itself to be permanent; when you have that kind of attitude, you find a way to do the political work, to do the fraction work, and so on.

Trade union comrades operating in the trade unions in this day with the tremendous flux in the world, with the ups and downs, can suffer annihilation overnight as a result of some unexpected developments. One who is merely operating as a trade unionist today is operating with blinders on. That is not the case with the party. The party is not a local organization, not a trade union organization. It is an organization that is nationwide, that grows and thrives on the activity of comrades, even though that activity doesn't bring immediate success. Even a struggle that ends in defeat can only mean for party members an improved experience and a transfer to new fields of activity in the party and later back again to the trade unions.

I use the illustration, for example, in discussing this question of Bert [Cochran] who went into the trade union movement, acquired a position and certain influence, and then, in the future course of developments was ganged up on and defeated in his job as business agent for one of the Ohio Auto Workers' locals. Well, if he had been merely a trade unionist, disconnected from the party, his trade union leadership was at an end. Being there not as a trade unionist, but as an agent of the party, when that field became temporarily unproductive, it was no problem either for him or for the party. We simply transferred him to New York, to put in some time as party organizer. Then when the auto industry opened up again, we sent him back to Detroit.

In general, that is the way you develop real leaders, broadening their experience, moving them from place to place, letting them become more universal in their experience, and consequently in their understanding and their knowledge; and not to take it as a devastation or a catastrophe if we encounter here and there an inevitable setback in the trade union movement, not to think a whole world hangs on whether we win or lose this particular battle in this particular trade union.

I called your attention in my remarks this afternoon to the speech I gave in 1924 to the miners' conference in St. Louis. At that time the Communist Party had a tremendous influence in the Illinois miners' organization. At that time they were in virtual control of the needle trades unions in New York. In the further course of developments the party was completely wiped out of the mine fields due to their own stupidity and by the objective circumstances. . . . They eventually lost their base to a large extent in the needle trades, but the experience accumulated by the party in the trade union work in the needle trades, the prestige of these struggles that had brought some people into the party, opened up new trade union bases, and in the course of the next few years the CP, in spite of all its betrayals, mistakes, stupidities, and venalities committed by the bureaucrats, in spite of all of that, employing this technique of fraction organization, riding on the prestige of the pioneer Communist movement as a class-struggle organization, and exploiting the name of the Soviet Union, built up a tremendous power in the trade union movement of this country. So much so that just a few months ago the great John L. Lewis, who thinks it's possible yet to lead a labor movement without a political party, found that the Communist Party people whom he had been so cleverly using with fancy politics from the top, had been organizing fractions in the spots where he turned them loose and they came up with the power and not John L. Lewis. And if they can do it in the name of a false policy, in the name of all kinds of . . . betrayals and mistakes, what grandiose vistas open up for a genuine honest party of Trotskyism which has the wind in its sails in the union movement and organizes its forces and consolidates them at each and every step of advance.

I am in favor of the idea expressed here of colonizing, if we can find out where we can get the colonizers. The fact is that we have practically got the whole party now in industry. Why, only in the last few months we took twenty-five more comrades and shoved them into the maritime industry in New York. And we took them from the most unusual places and just hurled them in there and threw them into the bay, and they had to jump a ship in order to keep from drowning. And, by God, most of them turned out to be sailors and some of them did pretty good at it, and they became sources of support for us in that tremendously strategic industry and union. We are a small party and we can't go colonizing all over the lot. We must colonize in those places which offer the best opportunity at the time, and when this opportunity which we seize at one occasion proves later on to be not so fruitful, we have got to shift our people.

Right now we are colonizing more or less in one particular union in the maritime industry, because it is wide open for us. It is a new union with no entrenched bureaucracy and there are possibilities of our people exerting a tremendous influence there in due time. So we are trying to take some of our maritime comrades who were originally colonized in another union, and move them across 3,000 miles of country or around through the Panama Canal and transplant them to New York and ship them out through the other union. I am only sorry that we have encountered a little difficulty in doing this because some of the comrades have apparently settled down in San Francisco. I don't know of anything more disgraceful for a young revolutionist than to get settled down and get so encumbered in a place that he cannot move. . . . It would be a damn good thing for him if he had a fire. . . . to blow away some property encumbrance and make him footloose and revolutionary again. I hope that the comrades out there will get over this passing resistance and move around more to colonize this new position, and I cite that only as an example.

Our colonization must be strategic. We must take the occasion when it is opened up to us. We didn't, for example, acquire the great influence and prestige of Trotskyism in the Minneapolis trade union movement because we sat down and made a survey, and decided that was the most important center, and the most important union. The reason was that the door was open there and we had comrades in the situation who were able to get through the door and we took advantage of the situation. The same number of comrades of their caliber colonized strategically in auto or in steel would have made an even bigger splash in the American trade union movement. But they weren't in such a position; the road was not open; conditions were not propitious, so naturally they moved where they had the opportunity. And we must do that also.

Comrade Warde [George Novack] has made a proposal which

seems to have received a very sympathetic response from most of the comrades, that is, that the National Committee should constitute now an organized systematic recruiting drive, attempting to bring into the party nothing less than a few score or maybe a few hundred people who are already familiar with the party, somewhat friendly and sympathetic, who are known to our comrades; put on a systematic campaign, this to be the main point on the agenda of every branch and fraction meeting.

I think that would be a good idea, an excellent way of strengthening our ranks, provided it is not accompanied by such an excess of Bolshevization that every time we bring one person into the party we drive two others out by our impractical and unrealistic demands upon them. I listened very sympathetically to Comrade Carlson's remarks about this. We don't want to be chasing and driving people out of the party. Not at all. We've got to grow up to the level of political people who are able to make use of members who want to belong to the party. Lenin was a great master at utilizing material that wasn't 100 percent perfect and he even succeeded in making a revolution with this defective material. One of the best stories I have ever heard was the remark made by Serge Evrikoff, leader of the Left Opposition and secretary in the party under Lenin, when he was in this country.[49] He remarked to some American comrades, "You will never begin to understand the genius of Lenin or to appreciate him in his full stature. You know that he made a revolution, but you don't know the material he made it out of."

And every one of us should try to be a little like that and try to hold onto and utilize members of the party and kick them out only as a last resort. In general, I am not in favor of expulsion except in cases of disloyalty. That is the time to begin expelling people. But others, we should try to make the party attractive to them. You can get far more out of people by inspiring them than by nagging them and hounding them. That is the general manner in which our party operates, that is the way in which we get out of our party such sacrifices, activities, contributions—whatever it may be—such as no party in the history of America ever aspired to get . . . and let us try that with some of our laxer and backward members in the branches.

But even a sympathizer is worth holding onto. We are not so rich and powerful that we can afford to throw away material that could be useful. Comrade Kay made a very interesting report about the methods that the Stalinists use of attracting people and holding them and recruiting them, how they utilize all kinds of peripheral organizations to get hold of people, and she wondered if we couldn't use the CRDC [Civil Rights Defense Committee] for this purpose. . . . Except she made the qualifying remark that the Stalinist methods in general are so repugnant to us that maybe we shouldn't use it. But the Stalinists borrowed this method from us in the first place—the Leninist method of supplementary organization—and we have a full right to use it. And what are we going to go into any of these organizations for, except to utilize it in the first place for support of the party, for recruiting into the party, as well as for serving its own intrinsic purpose? Certainly we should do that. We are handicapped because we are small. The Stalinists have the advantage of a big movement and a big ramification of peripheral organizations; all kinds of publications that are either published by the party or by unions or by sympathetic—what they call, stooge—organizations, all of them contributing to the party and also making an atmosphere where they gather. They get hold of people, young men and women, bringing them into [activity] and confronting them with such an assortment of activities in the [orbit of the] party until their whole life becomes absorbed in and around the party. What's wrong about that? That is exactly what we must aim and aspire to do, try to make our party so attractive to those that join it, that once they are in, the pull is toward the party, not away from it . . . not a dull, narrow-minded, nagging party, but one of activities and ramifications that makes a new life for them. And what do we care if some centrist philistine says, "Oh, the Trotskyists have got another of their innocent clubs." We will get the members out of them for our party. [. . .]

Now I come to the last point, and that is about a realistic appraisal of what is before us. We mustn't let the enthusiasm of our conference and the confidence we all feel in the future of the party take us away from here with a mistaken perspective as to what is realistically possible for us in the next period. Certainly, with the war breaking upon us, reaction in full sweep across Europe, prosecution of our people in court, it would be unrealistic to think that we have a perspective of expansion all around us. No, we have hard times ahead. We are going up against the test of fire and our problem is to learn how to dig in, to educate our members, to harden them, tighten up the party, recruit individuals where we can, prepare for the turn of the tide that is surely coming, to have an organization that will remain intact and even grow a little under the worst conditions, so that when the new possibilities open up and the masses, in disillusionment with the war, turn toward a radical movement, our party can go forward and grow by leaps and bounds and become the leading party of the American workers. And whether we do that in the future or not is being decided by us now in this conference here. [. . .]

In the coming days, they will say of such a conference as this, that it was in that period when the Trotskyists faced their first test, when they braced themselves for it, and went forward in spite of it, that is when they made the decision that ultimately culminated in the victorious revolution led by the party.

THE PARTY'S COURSE
AFTER PEARL HARBOR[50]

December 10, 1941

These remarks were made to a special meeting of the SWP Political Committee two days after the U.S. formally entered World War II. The text is from an uncorrected and previously unpublished stenographic transcript.

We had quite extensive discussion in Minneapolis on this question since the hostilities broke out. We had a pretty strong representation of the National Committee there, as you know.

Now in the past, when we began back in 1938 to discuss more concretely just what our stand and our tactic, our technique, would be in the event of a war, we began to think in terms of a formula that would permit us to establish a clear record of what the party stood for and what its position was and, at the same time, not waste the cadres of the party in the first reaction to the war.

When war is declared, that is when the government is the strongest and the unity of the people behind it is most invulnerable, and when there is least of all reason to expect any immediate result from an antiwar agitation.

And the problem reduced itself, in our thinking, to the problem of establishing a clear record of what we stood for by some demonstration or declaration, and then we would begin to try to dig in and, keeping within the limitation of the restricted legal rights, try to keep a movement functioning and maintain some kind of contact with our cadres for more frank and outspoken discussions which wouldn't be at all conceivable in public.

We discussed this question with the Old Man in the spring of 1938.[51] Now, he wasn't in favor of the committee issuing a statement. We discussed it. He said we should be more economical; we should not make the whole committee, or the whole party, responsible for the whole blow. Very likely we should select one outstanding individual of the party and it would be enough if he would make a declaration for which the others would not be formally responsible. The object would be for the others to maintain their freedom and develop a civil-liberties case around the one or more comrades who were making the demonstration . . . not continue day by day to shout against the war and imagine that you can have any results and preserve the movement.

We have gone along in the three years since then more or less with that formula in mind. In fact, a year and a half ago, in talks with Farrell [Dobbs] and Vincent [Dunne], in Chicago and at the time the delegation was on our way to Mexico, we discussed even concretely who would make this declaration, and Vincent was very firmly of the opinion that I should do it. Well, in the meantime, we had something laid in our lap—that is, we had a sort of prewar prosecution which only wound up in its sentencing aspect the same day that war was declared. We had right at this moment of the greatest heat of the Japanese situation, we had from week to week four complete pages [in *The Militant*] of the most unvarnished declarations, in the form of testimony before the court, as to what we think of the war and their government, etc. And even this week, if we don't say anything else at all and just print the last four pages of the court record—an official record and hardly to be condemned—you have got a statement of our war position under cross-examination; that is, where the prosecutor attempted to probe deeper into our position and tear away any possible misunderstanding. And it is even more baldly stated in the cross-examination, and it has the effect of being printed this week, after the declaration of war.

Taking this into consideration—the fact that we had our case— we seriously discussed the question, first of all, is it necessary for us now to rush out the minute we are out of the court on bail and practically challenge them to give us another case? Is it necessary to do that? The opinion of everybody up there was that it is not necessary—at least not in the first issue of the paper. That to all intents and purposes we have done what we planned to do formally before—but in a court setting. We say it is not necessary in principle. That is the opinion of everybody there. Then the question is, would it be wise to do it? That is also another aspect of the question.

There is good reason to believe that if we jump out now, right in the face of the new situation, having just got through being sentenced in court for showing no loyalty to the government, having the judge say on the day war was declared that "as weeks and weeks went by I didn't hear a single one of the defendants say a single word of loyalty to this government and the flag,". . . and we having gone through that, and put up what I think everybody will recognize as a very good principled fight—transforming the court into a forum and really using it to broadcast our message—[. . . if we go out now and] invite another case, I am afraid that it can have a bad public impression. Instead of creating the impression of a heroic group defending principles at all costs, we would create the impression of trying to make martyrs of ourselves . . . and even lose sympathy from those who have supported us.

It is the unanimous opinion of the comrades in our discussion that it is neither necessary nor wise for the committee to issue in this week's paper any formal declaration of position on the war; that the testimony and the whole atmosphere that was engendered around the trial be allowed to stand as notice of our position for the time being. That is the first point.

The second point, then, is what kind of paper should we envisage for publication in the first period of the war? And what will be the big task we will set ourselves? Here, again, we had a unanimous opinion and that is we have a great deal to gain by trying to keep our organization functioning, at least in a seminormal manner. That is, we have a great deal to gain by not having the organization scattered and driven completely underground in the first period of the war when there is an absolutely unanimous public support of the war. That we devise ways and means of functioning—this is a comparatively simple thing to do. A choice of subjects can be found; the paper can give a lead; and pretty serious political activity can be carried on without running into the wartime legislation—as long as there is no hysteria against us.

And of course the decisive thing is the paper. It has always been the idea of the Bolsheviks that when driven into illegality [it is necessary] to devise ways and means of carrying out a limited activity within the law, depending on how severe is the persecution. . . . If [what was involved was] just simply a formal prosecution of the Communist Party . . . they didn't hesitate to form a Socialist Labor Party in Finland, and function through that. If any kind of party is impossible, you create some kind of literary society, or a union, or a fraternal order. I think they wouldn't even hesitate about working in churches as a means, not only of some kind of public expression, but of establishing contact with like-minded people, etc.

We discussed this also with the Old Man, as to whether we should try to preserve the existing press—at that time the *Socialist Appeal*—as a legal organ and publish surreptitiously another sheet or paper or something which would say what couldn't be fully said in the *Appeal;* or whether we should allow the *Appeal* to be suppressed for open defiance of the war policy, and then start a new legal paper—*Labor News,* or so on. His idea was that we should start a new paper. We took this up also for review in our discussions in Minneapolis and we came to the conclusion that in the peculiarities of this new situation we have something to gain by revising that. It is a tactical question. We have something to be gained by trying to preserve *The Militant,* at least for a time, with a careful editing policy . . . because it is well established, has second-class mailing rights [which amount to] about half of the possibility of publishing a paper legally without too big a deficit. To start a new paper means a great deal of expense, difficulty mailing, and the certainty that you would never get second-class privileges.

Then again, to come back to the peculiarities of the situation, we have made such a clear and indelible record—we could never hope to do that by a splurge. To have *The Militant* step out and practically invite suppression, it would not get nearly the play in the public mind [as the Minneapolis trial and it would] seem to be an anticlimax to it. . . . [People would say,] "The Trotskyists are popping out, challenging to be arrested again—maybe you had better lock them up and put an end to the nuisance."

We could reverse that conception, which is not at all a question of principles. And have in mind that it is going to be many months before there is any kind of public reaction against this war. The most fatal thing we could do is shoot our whole bolt in this period and then be silenced by having the whole backbone of the party locked up somewhere when we could be using it to be getting more deeply established, rooted in the unions, etc.

We can expect no public reaction against the war for a long time. This is an extremely popular war. Tactically, there is the advantage of having been attacked by the Japanese—a far-off proposition [. . .] a naval war for some time, etc. We have to anticipate a rather drawn-out period of this war before a serious public reaction against it. Our aim should be to have some kind of party functioning when public reaction will be more favorable.

We could supplement this paper by perhaps a monthly mimeographed bulletin or letter. I don't think you need a second paper, sort of an illegal paper, as in the CP days. For the time being, if we published a monthly letter, giving an unvarnished political review of the month in the light of the war itself, for careful distribution among party members and sympathizers— that would be sufficient to keep our people together and keep them assured that the center is not deviating when it follows a careful legal policy in the paper. There is more than one way to skin a cat. The greatest error is to fall into a tactical error and think you have to maintain that at all costs. Think of our experience in the SP. We were condemned by the Oehlerites in principle for having surrendered our press.[52] They maintained that it is impossible to have a movement without a press. Well, we got along very well with mimeographed and carbon copies from the center once a month. We kept the cadres together by letters from the center to groups throughout the country, giving tips on what to do and what the line was. And while the SP had a monopoly of the press, we had a big advantage.

In Germany in the early days of the war, the so-called Junius letters, which were not even signed by them, were passed around with tacit understanding that they came from Rosa, and were the medium by which they knew. . . .[53]

The rough idea we elaborated there was that it be signed by some pseudonym. That we will have time to work out.

Now, if that line is accepted by the Political Committee, like every other line it has got to be carried through to the end and we can't fumble with it. If we decide we don't have to rush out this week, in view of the record we have made in the trial, with a challenge to the government—outside of the court testimony which is a matter of court record—then we should begin editing the paper to maintain at least a pseudocompliance with the legal restrictions.

Automatic with declaration of war, the Espionage Act of 1917 goes into force. The amendment of it, which is the worst feature of it, does not go back into force. It penalized expressions, etc., more precisely. We should begin editing the paper to make at least a formal compliance with such federal legislation as there is. There is the Smith Act and the Espionage Act. And we thought that, of course, we can't publish the issue without reference to the war, but we would refer to it obliquely in a way to sort of tip off our people throughout the country. We could take this lead: that the declaration of war automatically reinstates the Espionage Act, and tell what this act is; how applied in the last war; what it prohibits, etc.—which is a way of informing our readers that the reason we are not saying everything we think is because this Espionage Act is in force.

Then, we should take another step and transfer the paper from the party to the Militant Publishing Association—that is, that the party ceases to take responsibility for *The Militant*. Instead of saying it is the official organ, we say it is a paper published in the interests of the workers and farmers, or something like that. Have a two-inch notice in this issue that, beginning this week. . . .

You see we have a pretty sophisticated radical movement. All these measures will undoubtedly be understood, and I think 99 percent approved. The only people who will complain will be the Oehlerites, who have a yes or no policy, and you don't know which it will be. Either they will come out this week and ask for a defeat of the American naval forces at the hands of the Japanese, or they will go underground and favor nothing at all.

The main thing to be concerned about is our own cadres. Will they understand these things and will they approve? We have had a priceless opportunity to prepare our members. We have a triple advantage in that we have cleaned out the petty bourgeoisie successfully; since the death of the Old Man we have had two wonderful conferences; we have had the indictment and the conference following it, at which we more or less conditioned the party with the idea of preserving its legality. I think the prestige of the national leadership is as strong as it might be in the light of the trial, so they will not get the idea that a capitulation has taken place. I think they will understand very well that this is merely a political preparation to make the very best of this situation without giving up any of our principles.

Here is the Espionage Act:

[(Reads) "(1) Whoever, when the United States is at war, shall willfully make or convey false reports or false statements with intent to interfere with the operation or success of the military or naval forces of the United States or to promote the success of its enemies,

["(2) and whoever, when the United States is at war, shall

willfully cause or attempt to cause insubordination, disloyalty, mutiny, or refusal of duty, in the military or naval forces of the United States,

["(3) or shall willfully obstruct the recruiting or enlistment service of the United States, to the injury of the service or of the United States, shall be punished by a fine of not more than $10,000 or imprisonment for not more than twenty years, or both."]

That is a very broad section, everything depending on how interpreted. Strictly and fairly interpreted, it would hardly touch us. But these were construed by the judges in the past war to cover every damn thing when they get ready to do it.

And then an amendment was adopted a year later to this act:

[(Reads from amendment, which added nine counts summarized as follows) (4) Saying or doing anything with intent to obstruct the sale of United States bonds; (5) Uttering, printing, writing, or publishing any disloyal, profane, scurrilous, or abusive language, or language intended to cause contempt, scorn, contumely, or disrepute as regards the form of government of the United States; (6) or as regards the Constitution; (7) or the flag; (8) or the uniform of the Army or Navy; (9) or any language intended to incite resistance to the United States or promote the cause of its enemies; (10) Urging any curtailment of production of any things necessary to the prosecution of the war; (11) Advocating, teaching, defending, or suggesting the doing of any of these acts; (12) Words or acts supporting or favoring the cause of any country at war with us. (This 1918 amendment was repealed on March 3, 1921.)]

This is on the question of the paper this week. That does not at all bind us not to issue a formal declaration, either in the name of the committee or in the name of an individual, next week or later as we see fit. The fundamental problem we have to solve now is whether it is politically and principledly necessary for us in the very first edition of the press to state a definite and categoric position on the war.

We had a lot of fun speculating on the Shachtmanites—they are in a different position, and they are afraid if they don't say anything it will be really taken as capitulation. And if they do, they will get in trouble. So they will probably have a great deal of trouble. But we don't have to worry about that, in my opinion.

It would be ridiculous in the face of this situation to think that we can begin expanding. Our problem is retrenching, and tightening up all along the line. We can't put on any splurges in the face of this situation. That dictates a return to the [*Militant* as a] four pager and corresponding economy and restraint all along the line. My personal opinion is that 99 percent of the comrades in the field will highly appreciate a policy in the center that makes it possible for them to continue their public activities and doesn't require a flare-up and then a setback, without considering it any kind of capitulation at all.

During the war, especially the first stages, there is nobody going to be talking against the war without being in the jug the next hour. You can't do it in the paper or in private conversation. . . .

Another important aspect of the trial is that we beat the first count. The jury acquitted us on the first count, which properly construed would mean that they had to show overt acts. And that is what the liberals were scared of. So when we beat this workers' defense guard business and all the implications of overt acts and conspiracy to do anything of a violent nature, and were convicted only on a free-speech issue, this gives them a better feeling to defend us. . . .

The rank and file appreciate it very highly if the leadership shows a little consideration for the problems they are up against.

A STATEMENT ON THE U.S. ENTRY[54] INTO WORLD WAR II

December 22, 1941

This statement was first published in the January 1942 Fourth International.

The considerations which determined our attitude toward the war up to the outbreak of hostilities between the United States and the Axis powers retain their validity in the new situation.

We considered the war upon the part of all the capitalist powers involved—Germany and France, Italy and Great Britain—as an *imperialist war.*

This characterization of the war was determined for us by the character of the state powers involved in it. They were all capitalist states in the epoch of imperialism; themselves imperialist—oppressing other nations or peoples—or satellites of imperialist powers. The extension of the war to the Pacific and the formal entry of the United States and Japan change nothing in this basic analysis.

Following Lenin, it made no difference to us which imperialist bandit fired the first shot; every imperialist power has for a quarter of a century been "attacking" every other imperialist power by economic and political means; the resort to arms is but the culmination of this process, which will continue as long as capitalism endures.

This characterization of the war does not apply to the war of the Soviet Union against German imperialism. We make a fundamental distinction between the Soviet Union and its "democratic" allies. We defend the Soviet Union. The Soviet Union is a workers' state, although degenerated under the totalitarian-political rule of the Kremlin bureaucracy. Only traitors can deny support to the Soviet workers' state in its war against fascist Germany. To defend the Soviet Union, in spite of Stalin and against Stalin, is to defend the nationalized property established by the October Revolution. That is a *progressive war*.

The war of China against Japan we likewise characterize as a progressive war. We support China. China is a colonial country, battling for national independence against an imperialist power. A victory for China would be a tremendous blow against all imperialism, inspiring all colonial peoples to throw off the imperialist yoke. The reactionary regime of Chiang Kai-shek, subservient to the "democracies," has hampered China's ability to conduct a bold war for independence; but that does not alter for us the essential fact that China is an oppressed nation fighting against an imperialist oppressor. We are proud of the fact that the Fourth Internationalists of China are fighting in the front ranks against Japanese imperialism.

None of the reasons which oblige us to support the Soviet Union and China against their enemies can be said to apply to France or Britain. These imperialist "democracies" entered the war to maintain their lordship over the hundreds of millions of subject peoples in the British and French empires; to defend these "democracies" means to defend their oppression of the masses of Africa and Asia. Above all it means to defend the decaying capitalist social order. We do not defend that, either in Italy and Germany, or in France and Britain—or in the United States.

The Marxist analysis which determined our attitude toward the war up to December 8, 1941, continues to determine our attitude now. We were internationalists before December 8; we still are. We believe that the most fundamental bond of loyalty of all the workers of the world is the bond of international solidarity of the workers against their exploiters. We cannot assume the slightest responsibility for this war. No imperialist regime can conduct a just war. We cannot support it for one moment.

We are the most irreconcilable enemies of the fascist dictatorships of Germany and Italy and the military dictatorship of Japan. Our cothinkers of the Fourth International in the Axis nations and the conquered countries are fighting and dying in the struggle to organize the coming revolutions against Hitler and Mussolini.

We are doing all in our power to speed those revolutions. But those ex-socialists, intellectuals, and labor leaders, who in the name of "democracy" support the war of United States imperialism against its imperialist foes and rivals, far from aiding the German and Italian antifascists, only hamper their work and betray their struggle. The Allied imperialists, as every German worker knows, aim to impose a second and worse Versailles; the fear of that is Hitler's greatest asset in keeping the masses of Germany in subjection. The fear of the foreign yoke holds back the development of the German revolution against Hitler.

Our program to aid the German masses to overthrow Hitler demands, first of all, that they be guaranteed against a second Versailles. When the people of Germany can feel assured that military defeat will not be followed by the destruction of Germany's economic power and the imposition of unbearable burdens by the victors, Hitler will be overthrown from within Germany. But such guarantees against a second Versailles cannot be given by Germany's imperialist foes; nor, if given, would they be accepted by the German people. Wilson's fourteen points are still remembered in Germany, and his promise that the United States was conducting war against the Kaiser and not against the German people. Yet the victors' peace, and the way in which the victors "organized" the world from 1918 to 1933, constituted war against the German people. The German people will not accept any new promises from those who made that peace and conducted that war.

In the midst of the war against Hitler, it is necessary to extend the hand of fraternity to the German people. This can be done honestly and convincingly only by a workers' and farmers' government. We advocate the workers' and farmers' government. Such a government, and only such a government, can conduct a war against Hitler, Mussolini, and the Mikado in cooperation with the oppressed peoples of Germany, Italy, and Japan.

Our program against Hitlerism and for a workers' and farmers' government is today the program of only a small minority. The great majority actively or passively supports the war program of the Roosevelt administration. As a minority we must submit to that majority in action. We do not sabotage the war or obstruct the military forces in any way. The Trotskyists go with their generation into the armed forces. We abide by the decisions of the majority. But we retain our opinions and insist on our right to express them.

Our aim is to convince the majority that our program is the only one which can put an end to war, fascism, and economic convulsions. In this process of education the terrible facts speak loudly for our contention. Twice in twenty-five years world wars have wrought destruction. The instigators and leaders of those wars do not offer, and cannot offer, a plausible promise that a third, fourth, and fifth world war will not follow if they and their social system remain dominant. Capitalism can offer no prospect but the slaughter of millions and the destruction of civilization. Only socialism can save humanity from this abyss. This is the truth. As the terrible war unfolds, this truth will be recognized by tens of millions who will not hear us now. The war-tortured masses will adopt our program and liberate the people of all countries from war and fascism. In this dark hour we clearly see the socialist future and prepare the way for it. Against the mad chorus of national hatreds we advance once more the old slogan of socialist internationalism: Workers of the World Unite!

LETTERS ON PRESS POLICY
AND ULTRALEFTISM[55]

January-February 1942

These are excerpts from eight unpublished letters about criticisms of the SWP's policy at the Minneapolis trial and of its propaganda on the war in the press.

To Barr [Farrell Dobbs]

[Los Angeles]
January 20, 1942

Dear Barr:

I received a letter from Franklin [Albert Goldman], enclosing the criticism of Munis on the trial. I also received a copy of a letter sent to Grace [Carlson] by N [Natalia Sedova]. Please ask F [Franklin] to accept this as a reply to his letter also as I want to take up a number of things with you, and my technical facilities are limited.

1. The questions raised by the criticism are too important to pass over. They should be answered in detail and the occasion utilized for the education of the party members and possibly even the sympathizers, on questions of political and propaganda technique in connection with prosecutions. This is especially important for the American movement, which is steeped in the half-Blanquist tradition[56] of the early CP. (This whole erroneous conception is expressed in classical form in the improvised title put on the 1922 American edition of Trotsky's book on terrorism and communism—*Dictatorship versus Democracy*.)

If possible, we should contrive to have our answer to all these criticisms published in the *FI*. If that is not possible, perhaps it should go into the international bulletin.

2. Together with Murry [Weiss], I am working on a comprehensive answer to all these criticisms. The criticisms are all wrong. We are right on every point. The design of our exposition will fall into two parts:

A. The aim of the testimony was to serve *propaganda* rather than *agitational* ends, in conformity with the present political primitiveness of the American workers and the elementary tasks of the party which flow therefrom. This accounts for the quiet, leisurely, and pedagogical pattern of the dialogue, instead of the agitational call to arms which might make sensational headlines for the bourgeois press, but not serve our propagandistic aims at this juncture. I think that we can prove that the present political situation fully justified and necessitated the schoolroom technique we adopted.

B. Our analysis of Munis's criticism so far discloses the following points which have to be explained: sabotage; defensive formulations; submission to majority; political nonsupport of war; military policy. We may extract a few more as our analysis is not yet complete. Each and every one of these criticisms will be answered point by point by the citations of Marxist authority. Thereby we will show that we have not employed any of our own innovations or improvisations but have simply translated Marxist formulas and techniques into practical action in the bourgeois court. What hits the sectarian formalist in the eye is the newness of the procedure. It was never done before in the American courtroom; certainly never so thoroughly and completely and self-confidently. We can show by chapter and verse that Marxist authority is on our side. The imposing list of quotations we are gathering will perhaps astound everybody who mistook in any degree Blanquist romanticism for Bolshevik realism.

3. I wish you would immediately gather up any comments or critical expressions on the conduct of our trial which may have appeared in the press of political opponents—in particular the press of the Oehlerites, Fieldites, or other sectarian groups. I hear the Oehlerites had a criticism of the trial. We must have this right away. It can give us the justification for a public answer to sectarian criticisms in the ostensible form of an answer to the Oehlerites, Fieldites, Marlenites, or others.

I also wish to receive *by return mail* full and complete copies of any letters you may have received from the south [Mexico]. It is obvious that N has not read the full dialogue and has been grossly misinformed and disoriented on the whole procedure. It is likewise obvious that Walter [Rourke] has demonstrated his political immaturity by permitting himself to be sucked into this Mexican whirlpool in a teapot. . . .

Martin [Cannon]

P.S. 1. The criticism of the trial and all correspondence relating to it should be strictly confined to the PC until the answer is prepared. Then we can consider further steps. . . .

To Franklin and Barr

[Los Angeles]
January 31, 1942
Confidential

Franklin and Barr:

I have been somewhat disturbed by your letter of January 24 referring to the discussion in the Club [Political Committee] about the policy of the newspaper.[57] I must say, however, that I sensed something like that coming up and have been thinking of ways and means to best deal with it.

If four such responsible people as those you mention take this position it must be assumed that a considerable sentiment of this kind exists in the membership, even if it is not expressed openly at the moment.

In my opinion it is somewhat artificial to center the discussion around the policy of the newspaper. For this reason I also think your explanatory answer is inadequate. The policy of the newspaper is only the focal point of the dissatisfaction. What is involved is the whole policy or rather tactic which we agreed upon.

In discussing this matter first in Minneapolis and later in New York, we said that we could permit ourselves to employ this somewhat unorthodox and highly complicated legalistic maneuver only because the leadership is firmly united and enjoys the full support of the ranks. I especially emphasized this motivating factor, and I think all the others were of the same opinion. To be sure, we thought of many practical advantages from our scheme—if it worked smoothly—but they all depended upon the primary consideration. Your report of the dispute in the Club should be taken as a warning signal. It shows that the major premise from which we proceeded no longer exists. It would be foolish for us to ignore this fact or to confine the discussion to the line of the paper which is only one element in the situation. Even if nothing else but the paper was involved I would say without hesitation: The legality and second-class mailing rights of the paper are very important and valuable but they are not worth a division in our ranks, especially a division in the leadership. If our decision in the first place was motivated by practical considerations of a positive nature we are all the less justified in overlooking practical considerations of a negative sort. A sharp dispute in the leadership—especially arising so soon—is by far too big a price to pay not only for the second-class mailing rights for the paper but for the other considerations also.

I think we must seriously consider the revision of our scheme and take a sharp turn to prevent the artificial development of an opposition "from the left." The flood of letters from the South which tend to nurture such a movement are also symptoms which should not be entirely disregarded. I am not in favor of pussy-footing with a genuine ultraleftist like M [Munis] but at the same time we should not close our eyes to the danger that an indifferent and stubborn attitude on our part with regard to the tactical scheme can push other comrades needlessly into such a position.

I would like to formulate my proposal as follows:

The complicated tactical scheme designed to serve practical legalistic advantages has already created serious dissatisfaction in a section of the leadership, which should be properly interpreted as a symptom of similar sentiments in the membership. If such a situation is allowed to drift it could easily develop into an artificial dispute in the party over principled questions when no principled issues are really involved.

All the practical advantages of the scheme put together are not worth such a price. Consequently it is necessary to make a radical change in our tactical procedure. A thoroughgoing statement should be issued by the NC on the war situation. The paper should publish it and thereafter sharpen its policy without, of course, throwing all caution to the winds and directly inviting suppression. The design, however, to preserve the paper on a more or less ultralegalistic basis should definitely be changed in favor of the original plan for another paper if and when the present organ is stopped.

I wish you would give close thought to these considerations and proposals and let me know your opinion.

I think we have finished the main work on the answer to M and the other critics of our trial policy. The list of authoritative citations we have gathered is somewhat imposing. Now remains only the problem of tying them together in article form. I think this can be done in the next few days. At present I am occupied with the preparation of my speech for tomorrow night.

Fraternally,
Martin

P.S. Perhaps a closed plenum should be called to issue the statement.

To Barr

[Los Angeles]
February 5, 1942

Dear Barr:

I am waiting anxiously for your reply to my letter proposing the calling of a plenum for the purpose of issuing a formal statement of the party on the war.

I am becoming more convinced every day that it is advisable to do this. The best time would be when Rodney is in New York. I could be there then too.

The question of a candidate in the St. Paul elections raises this question anew. I agree with R that we should do one thing or the other—either run on our full program or avoid the election.

We can gain tremendous advantages politically on a national scale by taking a clear-cut stand in this election. It would be an *action* in opposition to the war a thousand times more meaningful than a mere declaration—but we could not very well conduct such an action without the issuance of a formal statement by the NC. (We could even consider the advisability of issuing the statement in direct connection with the election, thereby associating the statement with an action and at one stroke cutting the ground from under the feet of the pip-squeaks who are boasting that they issued a "statement" before we did.) After all, a statement is nothing but a promise of action to come. It's the consistent line of action that impresses the workers and determines the real character of the party.

If we decide to run our Senator [Grace Carlson] as a candidate it does not necessarily follow, as R seems to think, that all Minnesota comrades would be obligated to speak in the election.

No, the campaign should be run from a national, far more than from a local, point of view. The public speeches should be made by a selected and limited number of speakers and all the speeches should be carefully written in collaboration with the PC. Perhaps one member of the PC should go there to speak at the final meeting of the campaign. The speeches should be written and made with an eye to their publication in the paper. The size of the St. Paul audiences at which they are delivered is entirely a secondary matter. Three or four meetings during the whole campaign, conducted under the auspices of the party, with prominent representatives of the party speaking—the Senator, R, and perhaps myself, would be enough—with the meetings strongly publicized in our press and the speeches printed in full, could yield us great political and moral gains. To be sure, there will be some risk attached to this procedure, but I am convinced that the political advantages far outweigh them.

The idea of an election campaign under the present circumstances on a limited program, remaining silent on the main question, would leave too big a hiatus between the last campaign of the Senator and this one. If the party in the meantime had been suppressed and the campaign was conducted by a new organization frankly attempting to function within a more limited framework, such a procedure would be understandable. But now I think it would harm us. Too many people would ask what became of the main issue of the Senator's last campaign.

Please send a copy of this and my previous letter to R; I do not know how to reach him on the road. I am very anxious to hear from you about these questions.

Fraternally,
Martin

To Barr

[Los Angeles]
February 12, 1942

Dear Barr:

. . . . I have been fairly busy here and I think my visit has been fruitful. Both meetings—the Lenin memorial and the CRDC affair—were very successful financially and otherwise. The movement here is in good shape, developing strongly along the lines of proletarianization and improving its contacts, especially in the CIO unions.

The former minority group[58] have brought with them somewhat of a leftist tendency, including an opposition to our military policy, from the pseudoradical standpoint of the WP and the Oehlerites. I have had several discussions with them which I think have been useful.

I have noticed a general tendency both of the ultraleftists (Oehlerites) and the pseudoleftists (Shachtmanites) to contrast Lenin to Trotsky and to refer to Lenin as the primary authority. This is nonsensical; Trotsky is Lenin, plus sixteen years of further experience and further development of Marxist thought. Our L.A. leftists were quite flabbergasted when I showed them that the kernel of our military policy dates back to Lenin. It is contained in his famous article on disarmament. You will find it in the third paragraph on page 498 of the volume of the Hoover Library entitled *The Bolsheviks and the World War* by Gankin and Fisher, published by the Stanford University Press. The same article was reprinted in the *New International* of August 1934, page 50. It is also contained in the volume entitled *The Proletarian Revolution* by Lenin and Trotsky, published in 1918 under the editorship of Louis C. Fraina (last paragraph on p. 142). Lenin, in this article, demanded among other things "the right for every 100 inhabitants of a country to select freely its military instructors, to be paid for by the state." Our demand for state-financed military training camps under the auspices of the trade unions simply develops and deepens this proposal and gives it a deeper class line.

I have reason to believe that we will liquidate the L.A. opposition to our military policy before my departure. This is very important because it will be necessary in the near future to begin expounding and popularizing this military policy more than ever, and to take the offensive against its pseudoradical opponents. . . .

I am working away on the exposition of our tactics in the trial and the answer to M. I feel very much worried about N's attitude and intend to write her a note. These things can make a devilish amount of trouble if they are ignored. The attitude of Walter is significant. He is obviously running a revolutionary fever accompanied by sweats, and Dr. Munis, instead of lowering the temperature in the room and applying cold towels to his head, is stoking the fire and forcing hot toddies down his throat. I hope that my article will cool some of these lads off or at least send them back to the books to see if they can find out what ails them.

In our dispute with the leftists, which cannot and should not be avoided, we must be careful to formulate our position precisely and not allow the leftists to make the claim, contrary to the essence of the matter, that they are defending orthodox positions against us. From this point of view, I think the expression in Felix's introduction to Goldman's pamphlet about "idol worshippers" is unfortunate.[59]

We are by no means iconoclasts or innovators in the realm of Marxism. We simply take it as its authors conceived and explained it, not as dogma or revelation, but as a method and guide to action.

I think Al's expression in his opening speech about our disagreement with some Marxian theory is disadvantageous for our coming discussion. Obviously it is not a question of important theories but of isolated expressions and formulas applicable in one concrete set of circumstances and not another.

Our critics do not know that the Marxian masters permitted themselves considerable latitude and flexibility in applying their secondary formulas under different conditions.

Munis, for example, makes quite a hullabaloo about my modification, in application to America of 1941, of Lenin's formula about the "extermination of civil and military chiefs" in his essay "The Revolution of 1905." I wonder what he will have to say about Lenin's own modification of this formula—in September 1917. Then, in a letter to the Central Committee *about the organization of the uprising,* he contents himself with a demand for the "arrest of the general staff and the government" (*Toward the Seizure of Power,* vol. 21, book 1, page 229 of Lenin's *Collected Works*). . . .

Fraternally,
Martin

To Nancy [Natalia Sedova]

[Los Angeles]
February 14, 1942

Dear Nancy:

When I was in Chicago on my way to California, Comrade Dunne and I discussed the question of a visit to Mexico by myself and R [Rose Karsner] who was waiting for me in Los Angeles. We did make such a definite plan, but unfortunately forgot to take into consideration the circumstance of my bail which makes it impossible for me to leave the country at the present time. I had hoped that we could go to Acapulco by boat and have another visit there where I recall such a pleasant and restful time last year. I still hope that sooner or later we will find a way.

I received from New York a copy of Munis's criticism of our procedure in the Minneapolis trial and was also informed that you expressed yourself in a critical sense on this affair.[60] I am bound to assume that this must be due to misunderstanding or inadequate information on your part.

I agree with you that differences of opinion on such a crucial question merit discussion and clarification even though the present political situation is not the most conducive to free discussion.

I am writing a detailed answer to the criticism of Munis for publication, along with his article, in the internal bulletin. I will send you a copy of my article, which would have been finished long before now if it were not for repeated interruptions arising from my work here, where we are making important gains in the trade union movement.

It seems to me, however, that on such a matter as the testimony, where everything depends on the precise meaning of every word, and even nuances of meaning, a condition for a correct understanding of our procedure and our point of view must require a complete and literally accurate translation of our documents in their entirety into French or Russian. If such a literal translation is not available to you there I will try to have it made in New York for your benefit.

I consider Munis's evaluation of the trial to be totally false. The assumption that there was a change in our policy between

Chicago and Minneapolis is without foundation. There has never been any change whatever.

During my testimony at the trial I considered that I had ample Marxist authority—in the first place the authority of Comrade Trotsky—for the formulations which I employed.

Contrary to Munis, who does not even think of such trifles, Trotsky valued our legal position and, in anticipation of attacks upon it, recommended to us a formula, defensive in form but correct in principle, for our answer in court. This letter, printed in the *Fourth International,* October 1940, page 126, was our guiding line in the trial.[61] I knew the formulations of our teachers on the questions in dispute and did not deviate from them. A further detailed examination of the classics of our movement, which I have made in the light of the criticism of Munis, only convinces me all the more of the correctness of our procedure.

I received your letter in the midst of the Chicago conference and asked Rose to acknowledge its receipt as I was absorbed in work of the conference and thereafter with the trial. Needless to say I read it attentively, and it never occurred to me then, or later, that my views of our task at the trial were different from yours.

I value your opinions in the highest degree and hope always to work in harmony with you. This can best be accomplished by a frank exchange of opinions on all questions which arise.

We think of you always with love and friendship.

[James P. Cannon]

To Franklin

[Los Angeles]
February 16, 1942

Dear Franklin:

This is in answer to your letter of February 4.

1. The important thing is to accommodate ourselves, by making the necessary concessions, to the legitimate dissatisfaction and criticism of responsible people in order to clear the road for an uncompromising fight against ultraleftism.

Along this line, we must issue a formal statement by the party and free our hands for a clear exposition of the question, and thereby for polemics with our enemies, in the paper.

We must not forget that the motivation for withholding an official statement was our feeling that we could take such a cautious and deliberate course without fear of repercussions in the ranks. In this we were disappointed and that can only mean that we must change around even at some risks.

The greatest danger of all is the danger of an artificial leftist formation being permitted to take shape in the party.

2. I note your remark that opposition is quite general among the refugees. This is also alarming from the international point of view. We must not sleep on this question but move decisively to separate comrades with secondary complaints from opponents in principle. I am sorry you did not specify who among the refugees are active in this opposition.

3. You will recall that our original plan did not contemplate any statement at all for the time being. The one printed in the magazine was decided upon afterward, in response to some dissatisfaction we sensed already then. Our tactical decision can be considered a mistake insofar as it produced dissatisfaction which we had not counted upon and is not justified by our political position on the main question, which remains what it was before, and is 100 percent correct.

There is absolutely no sense or necessity of any kind of an announcement of our change of tactics other than the change itself. We never said that our decision to refrain from issuing a statement in December excluded the issuance of a statement later. Our Senator's campaign can be taken as an occasion to make a declaration of our position in connection with a political action.

I think you are right in your statement that we did not think everything through in December, and perhaps we didn't all have the same primary motivation. You seem to emphasize the legal position of the paper in a primary sense. In my mind, that was secondary to the primary consideration of a formal statement at that time, considering it unnecessary in view of the record we had made at the trial.

Of course it is still possible to issue a formal statement and still maintain the difference between the two publications. But I personally am not in favor of making the difference in character between the two publications too sharp. This naturally represents a change in my opinion since December.

I have a feeling we are losing a lot of time and opportunity to make political capital, by keeping the paper under too tight a rein. There are risks, of course, but it's a question of relative values.

I am beginning to think of another side of this particular question which we could not evaluate very clearly in December, since we did not know what the policy at Washington would be in the first period of the new political situation. This is announced and practiced as extreme liberalism for the time being. In my opinion, while this lasts, nearly everything will be overlooked if it is expressed with a reasonable prudence. On the other hand, at the next stage, when they decide to change this policy, they will be apt to strike at us regardless of any restraint we have shown. Meantime, shouldn't we use the period of liberalism for the utmost political advantage? I get the definite impression that the paper is not *striking*.

Take the campaign of the Stalinists for example. Our position is purely defensive against their new frame-up campaign. We should on the contrary conduct a murderous offensive against them as betrayers. The paper seems to falter over this task. There seem to be psychological barriers in the way. As long as the paper itself has not taken a clear position on the main question, it is hardly in a position to attack the standpoint of other groups and individuals.

A new paper, coming out following the suppression of its predecessor, is much more justified in limiting its range. During the discussions in December I thought we could do just as well with the existing organ, but it does not seem to work out that way.

I fully agree with your disinclination to compromise with ultraleftism. I go further and advocate a fight even if in the essence it is mainly a preventative war.

Ultraleftism is fatal.

I vividly remember the early days of the CP and the devastation wrought by the sectarian mentality and the ultraradical phrasemongering. It was the chief disease also which prevented the growth and development of so many European sections. However, in order to fight them effectively, you must formulate our positions with the utmost precision from the standpoint of orthodoxy, in order to deprive the leftists of the slightest possibility of successfully appealing to the Marxist authorities.

As far as the famous question of defeatism is concerned, we can stand on paragraph 58, page 46 of "War and the Fourth International"; the formulation in the article "Learn to Think," printed in the *New International,* July 1938, page 207; our Declaration of Principles, and—if you can locate them—several other articles written by the Old Man in reply to Vereecken and similars.[62] These formulations are the crystallization of ten years' discussion in our ranks on an international scale. If the professional "Leninists" want to begin the discussion all over again as if nothing has happened, we can well afford to say "no, this is orthodoxy, the question is long settled in our ranks, and we are not interested in new formulations at this late date." I am going to speak about this question as well as the question of political opposition to war, sabotage, and military policy in the article I am writing—in every case from the point of view of orthodox positions.

This article, in reply to Munis, is turning into a pamphlet which I think we should publish in a special mimeographed bulletin as an opening gun in our war on ultraleftism. I have some suggestions as to the form and manner of this bulletin which I can discuss with you when I arrive in New York.

Martin

To Joseph Hansen

Los Angeles
February 19, 1942

Dear Joe:

I just received from Reba [Hansen] a copy of the letter you received from the South. I will be in New York soon and I hope we will have plenty of time to talk over this extraordinary epidemic of revolutionary virtue which has broken out below the Rio Grande. They are hotter than a breakfast of eggs rancheros, and that's getting pretty damn hot! I suggest you ask Farrell to show you some of the letters I have written him on this subject.

Obviously the question boils down to this: have we made or shown any disposition to make any changes in our central policy? If so, some alarm could be justified. But that is not the case. We stand on orthodox positions all up and down the line.

But since our aim is to influence a specific, known type of human, namely the American worker, we venture to take the privilege of approaching him in terms that he can understand and with arguments which can be of interest to him and lead him in the direction of action.

All sectarians have one thing in common: they always call for action but never think about the methods and tactics of preparing and organizing it, consequently their "action" never breaks out of the boundaries of a printed thesis.

Naturally, the tone of these letters is that of outraged virtue; and they toss off defamatory accusations as nonchalantly as a Kansas farm boy husking corn and throwing the ears over his shoulder with automatic motions while he is thinking of something else. Unjustified self-righteousness and groundless suspicion always seem to go with sectarianism in a trinity like the Father, Son, and Holy Ghost.

Walter has evidently read one article of Lenin's. He has not discovered yet that the sentences he complains about are literal translations from Lenin, expressions which he repeated more than once in order to disassociate the Bolsheviks from sabotage and other futile gestures which seek to substitute the action of individuals and small groups for the participation of the masses; ideas which are anarchist, not Marxist; expressions of impotent despair, not of revolutionary courage.

So, "the main enemy is at home"? That idea is extremely interesting even if not new. It isn't sufficient for us to say, as is said in the statement, that our position since the outbreak of the war is the same as before; that we cannot assume the "slightest responsibility" for the war; that "we cannot support it for one moment"; that "we advocate the workers' and farmers' government"; that "capitalism can offer no prospect but the slaughter of millions and the destruction of civilization"; that "only socialism can save humanity from this abyss"; that "we see the socialist future and prepare the way for it"; that "we advance once more the old slogan of socialist internationalism: Workers of the World, Unite!" These statements, it appears, overlook the location of the "main enemy."

But how do we approach the American worker who thinks Hitler and Hitlerism are the main enemy? A sectarian doesn't ask himself this question because he does not even think of approaching workers. He thinks only of writing theses to save his own soul.

What is wrong with saying to these workers—the very people who are going to make the revolution—that we are also against Hitlerism—and we are, by God!—that the way to deal with Hitler is to first get this gang of capitalists off our backs and replace their government by a workers' and farmers' government which will fight Hitler in cooperation with the German workers? The answer is, there is nothing wrong with that statement. It is 100 percent correct from the point of view of both principles and tactics.

And what answer shall we make to those "ex-socialists, intellectuals, and labor leaders" who are preaching with great success the idea that we must support the war against Hitler in order to save world democracy? What's wrong with explaining and proving that those who "support the war of United States imperialism against its imperialist foes and rivals, far from aiding the German and Italian antifascists, only hamper their work and betray their struggle"? That is 100 percent correct also, and the only way that we can counteract their insidious propaganda for "war for democracy" which is one of the principal factors in the mobilization of the American workers for the war.

The probability has not entered the heads of these hopped-up leftists that such paragraphs were put in the statement with the design to influence and aid the reeducation of the workers. They conclude instantly and automatically that it is intended as a "change of principles" in order to apply our military policy in a "nationalist sense" and consequently to capitulate to American imperialism.

Let them conclude!

Martin

To Barr

Los Angeles
February 19, 1942

Dear Barr:

I am enclosing herewith a draft proposal for the plenum as you requested I think it should be sent out right away. If other comrades want to send something too, it can be sent in separate documents. Obviously there is no time to formulate the thing more collectively.

I believe it would be a good idea to also send copies of the correspondence between me and you and Franklin to all plenum members, if it's agreeable to you both. I think the NC members would appreciate having all this collateral material to mull over before formulating their own opinions. If there are some parts of my letters which should be deleted, I have no objections. . . .

I . . . received Oehlerite material from Dave Stevens as well as the letters from the South, including some received by Grace, and one today received by Joe. All of them, pure Oehlerism! We did not fight Oehlerism for nothing. Besides that, I remember the tragic experiences of the first years of the American CP. I promise you one thing: nobody is going to sell me any ultraleftism—not even a nickel's worth!

Martin

PROPOSALS ON TACTICAL REORIENTATION

February 19, 1942

This document was mimeographed for the members of the SWP National Committee prior to its plenum in New York on February 28-March 1, 1942. It has not previously been published.

1. Our position on war was the basic cause of the prosecution against us. Our position on war was elaborated in great detail and with full clarity during the trial. The entrance of the United States into the war coincided with the finish of our trial. In fact, the declaration of war was being read to Congress on the same day and even the same hour that we were being sentenced.

2. Under these circumstances, in our first consideration of practical tactics following the declaration of war, we considered that our position had been made sufficiently clear in the court proceedings, some of the most important parts of which were being published after the declaration of war and all the essential parts of which were to be republished in pamphlet form. Under those conditions we thought it possible to dispense with another formal statement by the party for the time being, without running the risk of confusion or misunderstanding as to our position. We also considered that there were immense practical advantages and that we could gain time for serious propaganda work by keeping the expressions of the press within certain limits. It was our opinion that we could permit ourselves to employ this strategy because we were assured of complete unity in the leadership of the party and firm support of the ranks. We

believed that we could proceed along this line in the first stages of the war with the confidence of the membership and without any apprehensions on their part of a capitulationist change of fundamental policy.

3. This practical tactic was not laid down for all time but only as an experiment in the first stages of the new situation. We decided to put the emphasis on caution with the object of preserving the normal functioning of our cadres as long as possible. Needless to say, this strategy never contemplated in any degree whatever a change in the fundamental policy of our movement. We planned to feel our way along, to make a distinction in the contents of the two publications, and to supplement them by an informal bulletin which would speak with complete frankness for the orientation of the party cadres. The statement on the war, issued in the name of an individual as a substitute for a formal statement by the party, was discussed but not decided in our first consideration of the question. It was decided upon only later when we began to feel some dissatisfaction in the ranks.

4. Subsequent developments indicate quite clearly that our original plan has not worked out to the best advantage. The paper has been too much restricted, within the framework of our original decision, to strike the necessary blows against the Stalinist traitors, Norman Thomas, etc. On the contrary, up to now it had to take a rather weak defensive position on the new frame-up campaign of the Stalinists.

Within the ranks of the leadership, strong dissatisfaction has been manifested with the policy of the paper. This must be construed as a symptom of similar sentiments in the ranks. The fact that this criticism arose over the contents of the paper should not lead to the conclusion that the real source of the difficulty is located there. The paper is only filling the function assigned to it within the original tactical policy as a whole. The paper is thus only the immediate focal point of the dissatisfaction. The fundamental source is in the policy itself.

This criticism comes from responsible people in the party leadership. If similar criticisms are heard in the ranks we must take note of them. There are signs of an attempt to create a "leftist" opposition. We should not hesitate to confront and fight such an opposition if the lines are drawn clearly between Marxism and ultraleft phrasemongering. But we should not allow the issue to be confused and, by stupidly clinging to a practical policy that is not working out well, allow an ultraleft tendency to thrive on legitimate dissatisfaction.

5. For these reasons we should revise our tactical program, in such a thoroughgoing manner as to give complete satisfaction to all comrades who are making legitimate and responsible criticisms. This cannot be done by a nibbling alteration of the course of the paper from week to week. The change must be more fundamental, as follows:

A. If the personal statement previously issued is deemed inadequate, a formal statement should be issued in the name of the party, utilizing the occasion of the St. Paul election and thus associating the statement of the party with a political action.

B. This statement should be politically clear and at the same time carefully and even cautiously worded so as not to provoke or invite an immediate pogrom against us.

C. The press should immediately adapt itself to the line of this statement and, without running wild and throwing caution to the winds, begin to speak more sharply and decisively about the central political question, specially utilizing the attack on the traitors as an indirect way of indicating our contrary position.

D. This decision entails serious risks. There should not be the slightest illusion on this score. But such risks—suppression of the paper, another indictment, etc.—in the last analysis are small price to pay for the avoidance of an unnecessary and artificial division in the party, especially in the party leadership.

6. The party can compromise with ultraleft phrasemongering only at the peril of its existence as a revolutionary body. We stand, as before, on the orthodox position of Marxism on all central questions as they have been formulated in the course of experience and discussion since the foundation of our movement nearly fourteen years ago. We settled accounts with the petty-bourgeois opposition. We should be no more tolerant of ultraleft-ism, which is no less petty bourgeois in its essence. The criticism emanating from M. and others about our course at the trial, and now about the war policy, are chemically pure distillations of sectarian hysteria and unrealism. The reorientation of the party in its practical policy is not a "concession" to these tendencies. It is the way to clear the decks for a forthright and uncompromising battle against them.

Martin [Cannon]

WHAT THE PLENUM DECIDED

March 7, 1942

This letter to Murry Weiss, a member of the NC in Los Angeles who was unable to attend the February 28-March 1 plenum, reports the major plenum decisions for the information of the Los Angeles party members.

M. Merritt [Murry Weiss]
Los Angeles, Calif.

Dear Merritt,

The plenum went off very well along the lines that we discussed in Los Angeles before my departure. A little discussion clarified all the disagreements and misunderstandings, and unanimous agreement was achieved on all decisions as to the next steps. There was no support whatever for the criticisms of our course during the trial.

The most important political decisions were:

1. Endorsement of the St. Paul campaign and provision for Carlson's statement. (Printed in this week's *Militant*).

2. Editorial in *The Militant* supporting the campaign and the candidacy of Carlson.

3. Decision to open up a propaganda offensive against the Stalinists, labor fakers, and Thomasites who are betraying the interests of the proletariat in the war.

4. Provision for signed articles by myself and others which will appear on our personal responsibility. The paper hereafter will follow the policy of permitting expression of individual opinions in signed articles without necessarily taking responsibility for them. (See note in this week's editorial box.)

5. Decision to change the method of financing the party, by substituting monthly sustaining fund pledges for lump sum contributions in special campaigns. If the branches respond to this new program on the basis of the quotas we have assigned, we think it will be possible to restore the six-page paper, at least for a while. We plan to get out an experimental six-pager this week.

6. The PC is instructed to arrange a convention for about June if political circumstances at that time permit. This is the orientation, but the whole matter is left in the hands of the PC. Present indications are that we can have the convention.

Fraternally,
Martin [Cannon]

CRITICISM AND DISCUSSION
OF CURRENT PARTY POLICY

March-April 1942

These two letters were in reply to questions by branches of the SWP on the right to criticize party policy in branch discussions. Copies were sent to all party branches.

To All Locals and Branches

New York
March 5, 1942

Dear Comrades,

The National Committee received a communication from the Philadelphia branch, in regard to an issue which arose at their meeting, as to the form and method by which the branch could hear and discuss criticisms of current party policy which one of the branch members wished to present. Since this raised a question of general procedure which must be of general interest to all the party branches, we decided to incorporate the decision of the Political Committee on the matter in a circular letter to all party branches.

The following resolution was adopted by the Political Committee:

1. Questions of policy or principle which have been *previously discussed and decided by convention* may not be taken up for discussion again without a formal decision of the National Committee to this effect or the calling of a party convention which, under the constitution, provides for a preliminary discussion period and reexamination of any question even though it has been previously decided.

2. Any party member or branch has the right to *discuss and criticize current policy and procedure of the party leadership* at

any time, either in branch meeting or in the form of written communications to the National Committee. Branches, naturally, have the right to decide the form and procedure and the point on the agenda under which such discussion and criticism can be heard, but this formal right of the branch must not be employed in such a way as to unduly delay or postpone or make difficult the presentation of any criticism of current policy which any individual member of the branch wishes to make.

3. The National Committee welcomes communication from any comrade who has a disagreement on current party policy or wishes to present criticisms or suggestions for improvement. The same applies also to branches which may express their opinion in the form of resolutions.

4. If any criticism of party policy seems to be of a sufficiently serious nature or to express the opinion of a considerable body of party members, the National Committee, as a rule, if general political circumstances permit, will open a discussion of the given question in the internal bulletin in order to clarify the question.

> Yours fraternally,
> J. P. Cannon
> National Secretary

To the Akron Branch

> New York
> April 17, 1942

Secretary
Akron Branch

Dear Comrade,

This is in reply to your letter of March 31.

The National Office communication of March 5 was designed to explain party procedure with respect to discussions in the light of the party Declaration of Principles and constitution. This communication embodied a resolution adopted by the National Committee in response to some comrades who had asked for a clarification on this point.

Point 1 in the circular simply restated a provision of the party constitution as amended by the Third National Convention of the party in July 1939. Section 7, Article 8, of the amended constitution reads as follows: "Questions decided by the party convention may be subjects of new discussions only when such discussion is formally authorized by the National Committee, or in the established preconvention discussion period."

This is the party law. The reasons for it should be obvious. A party that goes through a protracted preconvention discussion—as is always provided for in our organization—and then makes a decision at the national convention, has the right and duty to declare the discussion closed for the time being and to obligate all party members to get to work on the basis of the majority decision. To allow further discussion after convention decisions would reduce the party to a permanent discussion club which would be attractive only to bohemian windbags. Revolutionary workers would have no respect for such a party. Bolsheviks do not discuss in order to discuss but in order to arrive at a decision and to act upon it.

Naturally, it is possible for a convention to err in its decisions and events may prove the necessity of reconsidering them. Or, decisions correct at the time they are adopted may require changes in the light of new developments. In either of these cases new discussions of the questions become necessary. But the right to initiate such new discussions is not left to every individual to decide for himself. The SWP is a proletarian party, not an anarchist madhouse. The authority to initiate new discussions is naturally delegated by the above-cited Section 7, Article 8, to the elected leadership of the party—the National Committee. This is not a usurped right, but a right conferred upon the National Committee by the party itself, acting through the national convention.

The constitution also provides a corrective in case the National Committee should refuse to initiate a new discussion when the necessity for it has become manifest to a substantial section of the party. Section 1, Article 10, states that "Special conventions may be called . . . on the demand of branches representing one-third of the membership." The call for a convention automatically reopens all questions for discussion.

From the above it should be clear that the party constitution has provided amply for free discussion of either new or old questions when the necessity for such discussions is manifest and, at the same time, protects the party against permanent discussion of settled questions by anarchistic individuals. These are ABC principles of Bolshevik organization.

You ask: "Are we right in interpreting point 1 as meaning that the convention decisions may not be discussed at all?" Only within the framework of the party constitution as elucidated above. Convention decisions are made to be carried out in practice, not to be everlastingly discussed as if no decision had ever been made.

You ask: "If new situations arise which might affect past decisions, might not the decisions be discussed within the various branches?" Any branch which is of the opinion that new situations require a reconsideration of convention decisions has a full right to propose to the National Committee that a discussion be formally reopened throughout the party. It does not have the right, and in a serious centralized party cannot have the right, to *initiate* the discussion on its own account without the consent of the party as a whole. That would be giving each individual branch the right to repeal convention decisions at will.

You ask: "If a new member comes into a branch, may he not ask for discussion on these decisions?" Presumably when a new member joins the party he has studied our program and convention decisions and expressed his agreement with them. If that is not the case, they should be discussed with him by all means; but during this discussion he should have the status of a contact whom we are trying to win over, not a new member who wants to subject convention decisions to criticism and review immediately upon his arrival. New members should have equal rights with old members, but no more.

You ask: "On point 4, what number of people would constitute a 'considerable body'?"—to prompt the National Committee to open a discussion. Naturally, it is not a mathematical question. The best answer is to be found in the procedure of the party. Discussion on the labor party question, for example, was initiated by the National Committee in 1938 on its own motion without any demands from the party branches. A new discussion on the Russian question was opened in 1939 on the proposal of NC members as well as a number of party branches. A discussion on the proletarian military policy was initiated by the National Committee on its own motion in the summer of 1940.

No important decision of a programmatic nature has ever been made in the history of the American Trotskyist movement without ample discussion of the membership. There has never been a time when the party refused to reopen discussion on old decisions when the necessity for new discussion was manifest to a reasonably numerous section of the party membership. This tradition and the party constitution can properly be considered as a double reassurance of party democracy. But individuals who want to discuss questions the year round until a convention meets and makes the decision, and then start discussing all over again as if nothing had happened, should join one of the numerous bohemian discussion clubs. A Bolshevik workers' party is not the place for them.

Fraternally yours,
J. P. Cannon
National Secretary

REPAYMENT OF A DEBT[63]

May 22, 1942

This personal letter gives a hint of the material poverty of the early years of the American Trotskyist movement and also Cannon's responsibility in ultimately repaying all obligations he had incurred.

New York

Mr. Morris L. Ernst
New York

Dear Friend:

I am enclosing herewith a money order for $100. This is in payment of the remaining half of the $200 which you so kindly loaned me years ago at a time of extreme personal difficulty. My unseemly delay in repaying this loan, as well as others which have also weighed heavily on my conscience, was due entirely to my unfavorable financial situation, which in turn has been caused by the unprofitable nature of the work to which I have felt obliged to devote myself.

I have always been deeply grateful for the help you gave me in a bad time, all the more so because your generous hand was extended to a stranger whose political views were, then as now, far removed from yours.

I hope you will accept this check as a settlement of the debt and strike off the interest for good luck.

With kind personal regards,
James P. Cannon

THE CONVICTION OF
KELLY POSTAL[64]

June 24, 1942

This letter was sent to all branches of the SWP.

New York

Dear Comrades,

By this time you all know that Tobin and the state officials of Minnesota have succeeded in convicting Kelly Postal on the trumped-up charge of embezzlement. The judge sentenced Postal to serve one-to-five years in prison.

This charge of embezzlement arose out of the decision of the vast majority of the workers of the Teamsters Local 544 in Minneapolis to secede from the AFL and join the CIO. As was their right, the membership voted to utilize the money in the 544 treasury for the necessary expenses of the new CIO union. This money was so used and this fact was seized upon by the state authorities to vote several indictments against Kelly Postal, Miles Dunne, and Moe Hork.

In the first trial involving one of the indictments against Kelly Postal, after the state introduced all of the evidence, the judge directed the jury to find a verdict of not guilty. Thereafter the prosecutors brought Postal to trial on the second indictment before a judge who, on the same evidence as was produced in the first trial, permitted the case to go to the jury and practically charged the jury to find Postal guilty. It is one of the greatest frame-ups in the history of labor.

The case must be appealed. Local 544, unable to stand the expense of the appeal, has requested the Civil Rights Defense Committee to help in the appeal and the executive board of the CRDC voted to do so. A letter will go out from the national office of the CRDC to all the local branches to raise funds immediately for defraying the expenses of the appeal. Altogether, approximately $1,500 is necessary. This money must be raised within two months, but at least half of it must be raised in the month of July and a good proportion of it is needed by the 15th of July.

All party branches are instructed to take up the question of having the CRDC branches raise the necessary quotas. The quota that the CRDC branch in your city has been assigned is $_____. The party branch is to assume the responsibility of seeing to it that the CRDC branch raises that sum within the next two months, and part of that sum by the 15th of July. Where there is no CRDC branch the party branch is to raise its quota and send it directly to the national office of the CRDC.

The CRDC has assured the defendants and Local 544-CIO that it will carry the case through to the Supreme Court and our comrades must see to it that the pledge of the CRDC will be fulfilled.

Fraternally yours,
J. P. Cannon
National Secretary

A RED-BAITING ATTACK
IN SAN DIEGO[65]

August 1942

These previously unpublished letters are from the archives of the SWP.

To Murry Weiss

New York
August 4, 1942

Dear Murry,

We received the copy of Fuzzy's statement. Also, the copy of her letter of July 28, 1942.

1. The statement is OK. We will not change it very much. At the trial she can speak along these lines. Our edited statement should reach her before the trial, but if not she can speak according to her outline and we will touch it up just a little bit for publication.

2. Naturally we will give no publicity whatsoever until the trial is over and we report the matter from a news standpoint, along with her statement. This means that we will wait for a news story from you about the trial before the membership before printing anything.

3. Fuzzy is right to emphasize the question of democracy. That is a very important point in matters of this kind.

4. While standing her ground firmly, Fuzzy should not provoke the situation. If the bringer of the charges or the board want to back down gracefully, there is no reason why we should force the matter to an issue artificially. Just let them move and we react accordingly.

5. Similarly if Henry butts in and tries to solve the problem with his well-known finesse. Fuzzy has no reason whatever to

confide anything to him. He has shown his treacherous character long before and it is little short of treachery for any member of our movement to confide in him or put confidence in him.

Fuzzy can take the position that she did not start any trouble; all this was provoked by the patriotic SOB who wants to curry favor with the bosses at the expense of the interests of the workers. For her part she doesn't sell her principles to anybody. She thinks unionism means democracy and she has a right to her opinion. Etc.

6. Between the office and my house I have temporarily mislaid Fuzzy's statement, otherwise I would be returning it with our editing herewith. I hope to locate it by tomorrow and send it along. If there is any delay, however, as remarked above don't worry about it. Fuzzy's original statement is plenty good enough for her speech to the membership. She makes a very important point about the necessity of making her speech understandable to the membership of this local union. It will do no harm if there is a little difference between the verbal address and the published report.

Fraternally,
[James P. Cannon]

P.S. Frank Lovell pulled in a few days ago. He was torpedoed. Another comrade also came in yesterday. Also torpedoed. These reports are becoming monotonous. We are waiting anxiously now for reports of a group of comrades who are on this dangerous Murmansk run.

To Murry Weiss

New York
August 5, 1942

Dear Murry,

In my haste I left out the most important point of my letter yesterday. That is, that it is not necessary or even advisable for Fuzzy to make her defense on the ground of her party affiliation, or to refer to it in any way. This narrows down the issue too much and would make her and us too vulnerable in similar fights.

She should represent herself as an individual with certain opinions and say nothing about her affiliations. Of course she should try to avoid denying affiliation if possible, and if baited on the question, should try to limit her explanation to the statement that what she belongs to or does not belong to is her own business and nobody else's, as she still thinks she has some democratic rights and doesn't have to ask the permission of any stoolpigeon as to what she should join or not join, as long as it doesn't interfere with her union duties. Etc.

This is a very important point. We decided already in the Minneapolis case, as you may remember, not to fight it out on the issue of party membership, but on the issue of the right of the individual members to have their own opinions, etc.

I just located Fuzzy's statement and noticed that she emphasizes the question of party affiliation. *All this material should be taken out.*

Fraternally,
[James P. Cannon]

To Murry Weiss

New York
August 13, 1942

Dear Murry,

We received your letter with the report on Fuzzy's fight.[66]

1. We are inclined to let the thing rest for the time being without any publicity since everything is in our favor as it stands. For us to publish the matter now might provoke the issue again from the International angle and we are not inclined to do this. Of course, if an attack comes from that quarter, we will meet it head-on. But meantime perhaps we had better let sleeping dogs lie. In any case, however, we plan to make an information report to the party a little later. Therefore, keep us informed of any new developments. Fuzzy should be a delegate to the party convention.

2. It appears to us that our position in the union situation is greatly strengthened by the outcome of the fight put up by Fuzzy. Our comrades should not be intimidated by this guff from Henry, but proceed to make up for lost time in recruiting some of these union militants into the party. Naturally this has to be done discreetly in this case, as in all union situations, but the important thing is that it be done and not neglected, and that we do not yield an inch to "trade union cretinism" especially now of all times.

3. We think you should proceed locally with the Control Commission matter. Let the Section Executive Committee appoint a strong commission to go to the bottom of this matter and clean it up. I think the procedure we used in the Michigan case of Dennis would be useful for you. First the Control Commission made a thorough investigation. Then, when it had decided on its recommendations, it called a meeting of all members throughout the auto district to meet in Detroit and hear the report and take a position on it. In this manner the membership was educated on the whole affair and participated in the decision. It is important not to let the thing drag out. The whole process—appointment of Control Commission, investigation, report to section membership meeting, and decision by the membership meeting—should not take more than a week.

4. If charges are to be made, be sure to follow the constitutional provision of putting them in writing. However, be sure to use a party name for the accused person and keep in mind all the time the possibility of anything written being handed over to our enemies, particularly the one with whom this person is accused of having relations.

5. By all means have a showdown with the one whose loyalty has been called into question. The one thing we can't tolerate is 99 percent loyalty. We want 100 percent. You have an excellent chance to educate the whole party on this incident. I don't know enough about the actual situation to pass any judgment, but it is barely possible that if the accused is confronted with the real determination of the party to put an end to all ambiguity of relationship, he may come to his senses and make a decision in favor of the party. Understand, I am not predicting this, but you should not exclude such a possibility unless you have definite information of real conscious treachery. Do not allow indignation against questionable conduct on his part during the affair to blind the comrades to the possibility of salvaging this individual. This again is stated on the assumption that the accused was not consciously and deliberately disloyal and that he was prompted only by syndicalistic muddleheadedness. In any case, the trial presents an excellent opportunity to clean out any remnants of this infection.[67]

Fraternally yours,
James P. Cannon
National Secretary

To Pauline Furth

New York
August 13, 1942

Dear Comrade Fuzzy,

We now have the final report of your fight. Everything was fine and you handled yourself like a real Bolshevik.

I would like to have a copy of the letter to Henry which he refers to in his letter to you.

Murry will show you my letter regarding the next steps in this affair.

Best regards,
[James P. Cannon]

THE WORKERS AND THE
SECOND WORLD WAR

October 2, 1942

*This was the political report to the SWP national convention held
in New York October 2-4, 1942. It was first published in* The
Militant *of October 31, 1942, and was reprinted along with the
political resolution adopted by the convention in the pamphlet*
The Workers and the Second World War *(Pioneer Publishers,
1942).*

Comrades:

Since we last came together in national conference a year ago
in Chicago we have had to record with sorrow the loss of
numerous soldiers of our cause who have fallen in the fight.

In far away China a brave and selfless revolutionist, the
pioneer of Chinese communism, Ch'en Tu-hsiu, succumbed at last
to the blows of persecution, imprisonment, slander, and poverty
which had rained down upon him through so many years of his
struggle. He died, as befits an honest revolutionist, in the ranks
of the Fourth International.[68]

In France a noble fighter for international communism, one of
the founders of the French section of the Fourth International,
Jean Meichler, perished before a Nazi firing squad. We do not
doubt that he died bravely.

Our own party has lost five of her best and most devoted sons
who served the party and the working class in the most dangerous posts as merchant seamen. Comrades Edward Parker, Carl
Palmer, David Udell, Ronald Tearse, Edwin Jaffe have lost their
lives at sea, our first victims of the imperialist war.

We honor the bright, untarnished names of our noble dead. The
Fourth International will carry on their work and keep their
memory green.

It is more than two years now since the assassin Stalin took the life of Comrade Trotsky and sought thereby to kill the movement that he had created and inspired. This present conference of our party, the largest and most imposing in our entire history, representing an active and growing party, self-confident, unified, and strong—this conference is living testimony, it is living proof, that the assassin failed in his main objective. The ideas of our greatest leader and teacher live and guide our work and struggle. The memory of our martyr is with us always, the inspiring force of our indestructible movement.

The Fifth Convention of the Socialist Workers Party, which is the tenth national convention of the American Trotskyists,[69] meets in the midst of the second imperialist war, a war in which the United States is now an open and active participant. The war, this terrible paroxysm of an outlived social system in its death agony, dominates everything in the world today. Upon the outcome of this war depends the future of humanity. But we must understand that this war is not an abnormal phenomenon. It is not an accidental catastrophe; not an interlude to be followed, in the course of events, by a long period of peace and normal functioning of capitalist society. On the contrary, this war is the most characteristic expression of bankrupt capitalism. The war is the very image of capitalism, as it is now, and as it will be until the workers and the oppressed peoples rise in revolution and make an end of it.

How unrealistic, how ridiculous, are those people who speak of settling problems "after the war"; who set up "Postwar Planning Committees," etc.; who proceed on the theory that the natural order of things is simply arrested now for a while, and then the war will end and then we will settle all questions and begin all over again. Utterly utopian are all such ideas. All the great problems will be settled in the war and through the war. That is the basic thesis of the Fourth International.

Capitalism today signifies permanent war and universal militarism. And from this conception we draw our tactics and our strategy. We foresaw the war. We prepared for the war, and we understood that the war would pose all the social problems for solution by military means. That is why our program is a war program, a military program, which excludes any form of pacifist abstentionism. That is why our ranks are animated by the conception that in the arena of militarism, which is today the main arena, we will learn how to participate and how to prevail.

We meet ten months after the formal entry of the United Sates government into the war. The Second World War is a continuation of the First World War, but not a simple repetition by any means. A continuation signifies, as Comrade Trotsky wrote, a sharpening and a deepening of all the features of the war. And just as this war is not a simple repetition of the first one, although a continuation, neither is the situation confronting the revolutionary vanguard, nor its tasks and its problems, a simple repetition of the situation and the tasks and the problems of the revolutionary vanguard at the outbreak of the First World War and during its course.

All the differences are in our favor, if we understand the situation to the bottom. The decay of capitalism, which was signalized by the First World War, has become the death agony of capitalism in the Second World War. The enemy, in spite of all superficial appearances, is weaker. On the other hand, the vanguard of the proletariat is better prepared and stronger today than it was in the analogous period of the First World War. If we are able to look beneath the superficial appearance of things we must see that this is the fundamental reality.

In 1914 the workers' vanguard met the war unprepared. The workers' parties and workers' organizations openly betrayed the proletariat in the war only at the last moment, not before. And the betrayal, the catastrophic collapse of the parties of the Second International and the trade unions, caused surprise even to the most perspicacious of the leaders of the revolutionary vanguard. When Lenin saw the edition of the Berlin *Vorwärts,* the official organ of German Social Democracy, with the statement supporting the war, he expressed the opinion that it was a forged edition, put out by the German general staff to deceive the people of other countries. He knew that the parties of the Second International were corroded with opportunism, but not even Lenin was prepared for their complete betrayal in such catastrophic form as took place on the fourth of August, 1914.

The First World War produced deep crises in all the workers' parties; the real discussion of the attitude to be taken toward the war began only after the war was under way. The war even produced discussions and splits in the ranks of the workers' vanguard. There were defections among the Bolsheviks. This is history that is perhaps unknown to many comrades because Bolshevism has been represented as something that was born perfect and carried through to victory without any internal difficulties or errors or defections. Not true at all. Bolshevism, like every other current in the workers' movement, grew and developed in the tests of action and took its final shape only in the fire of great events.

Just consider only these few facts among many which are recorded in the documented volume on *The Bolsheviks and the World War* published by the Hoover Library. The Bolshevik Committee of Organizations Abroad disintegrated. Of the five members, two enlisted in the French army; a third member withdrew. Lenin and Zinoviev remained as the representatives of the Central Committee of the Bolsheviks abroad to elaborate the war program of the party. At a Paris meeting of the Bolsheviks in August 1914, eleven out of ninety-four present favored a policy of defensism, more than 11 percent. The Geneva section of the Bolsheviks opposed with many objections the first theses submitted by Lenin and Zinoviev. Shliapnikov, a prominent Bolshevik worker from Russia, who spoke to the Swedish Social Democratic congress in November 1914, stated that the Bolsheviks in Russia had been taken by surprise; they had felt confident that the Socialist parties of Europe would be able to stop the war and were dismayed when the war broke out in full fury with the support of the official Socialist parties.

Needless to say, I mention these facts not at all to denigrate the Bolsheviks, but rather to show, on the contrary, what a heavy task confronted Lenin, even in his own party, in shaping the revolutionary policy toward war. Lenin's problem was the problem of clarifying the program of the vanguard after the war had started. It was the problem of rehabilitating Marxism on the international field and of taking the banner out of the treacherous hands of the petty-bourgeois opportunists and social patriots. Lenin had the problem of forming the first cadres, of getting hold of two, three, or five people, in order to begin all over again the work of building a bona fide revolutionary international party.

The situation confronting the revolutionary vanguard in this war is different in many important respects. That is why those wretched sectarians who consider it sufficient to simply repeat, word by word, what Lenin wrote in 1914 and 1915 are so far from the reality of the problem of the vanguard today. This time, for this war, the reformist organizations took nobody by surprise. In all countries there never was any question at all what position would be taken by the Social Democrats of the various varieties. They announced their betrayal beforehand. This is an important difference from the side of the Social Democrats.

Likewise, the Fourth International and its sections are not a simple reincarnation of the cadres created by Lenin in 1914 and 1915. The cadres of the Fourth International stand on the shoulders of the original cadres of Bolshevism which was reformed during the war. They are enriched by all the experience of that time and all of the intervening time. Therefore they were able to anticipate this war, and to prepare for it. The entire period, especially since 1929, when the Fourth International cadres were constituted on an international scale under the direction of Trotsky, after his deportation from Russia—this entire period since 1929 can be described as a period of clarifying the program, of drawing the lessons of the experiences, of sifting and selecting the cadres, in short, of preparing for the war and for the revolution which must issue from the war.

Consequently, the formal entry of the United States government into the war last December produced no crisis whatever in the ranks of our party. The war entry and ten months of participation in the war have found the leadership of our party united, the ranks firm. There has been no sign of social-patriotic trends or tendencies; no representatives of such tendencies have appeared or brought forward any proposals in our party.

It is from this reality that we proceed in discussing our war problems and tasks. We don't have to begin from the beginning by explaining what is social-patriotism and why it is wrong. We don't have to spend time gathering one, two, or three people wherever we can find them in order to begin anew. No, the situation is not the situation which confronted Lenin in 1914. The sectarians don't understand this. That is too bad. But then, if they understood how to proceed from the real and the concrete they wouldn't be sectarians.

War greatly intensifies and multiplies the pressure of bourgeois society on the workers' vanguard. All the force of material and moral pressure of bourgeois society is brought to bear in the most intensified manner at the time of the declaration of war and immediately following. With this is mind, and remembering the experience of 1914-18, Comrade Trotsky repeatedly warned us of a crisis in our ranks to follow the outbreak of the war. This in spite of our long preparation and our clarification of program. Trotsky warned that even in our ranks we must expect a crisis when the pressure of bourgeois society was brought to bear in full force with the entry into war. Now, this prediction of Comrade

Trotsky was not realized in the Socialist Workers Party. Sideline commentators and literary critics may point it out as one more flaw in Trotsky's infallibility. In reality, what is shown is that Trotsky built better than he knew. The ranks of the Fourth International throughout the world have stood up firmly against the war, against all the pressure and persecution of the class enemy. That gives us all the more assurance of our right to victory in and through the war.

Our unity is somewhat disturbing to certain people who don't seem to be able to take care of their own affairs but are very anxious to arrange ours for us. I am speaking of the medicine men of petty-bourgeois radicalism. Being politically unemployed otherwise, they have apparently settled down to the rather ungrateful and miserable occupation of unacknowledged physicians for our party. They are greatly worried about the fact that we have so much unity in our ranks, that we are free from crises and factional fights and feverish struggle over conflicting programs. These quack doctors don't understand that we are well, we are healthy, we are free from a war crisis, not by accident or the grace of God, but because we cured ourselves of the petty-bourgeois sickness in good time. We had the good fortune to have an *anticipatory* crisis before the United States entered the war, a crisis which we conquered with the help of Trotsky. We secured our internal peace by a timely *preventive* war.

As far as our leadership is concerned we have, so far, required no new discussion of fundamental program in relation to the war. Our problem has been much simpler, the problem of how to maintain our position and carry on our work to the best advantage and with the greatest possible utilization of legality under the conditions of war. These are not easy tasks, but they are minor and secondary. And their accomplishment is greatly facilitated by the fact that we are united on the basis of a principled program. Lenin's problem in 1914 was the problem of *clarifying* the program and of *selecting cadres* on the basis of it. Our problem is that of the *application* of the program, of devising effective propaganda approaches to the patriotic workers of today who will be the revolutionary fighters of tomorrow. Our internal cohesion, based on our programmatic unity, enables us to turn our attention outward rather than inward. Hence the emphasis in our press and in all our agitational work on our transitional demands, and on the slogan of our military policy addressed to the rank-and-file workers.

On the eve of the United States entry into the war we had a rehearsal in the Minneapolis trial. We were given the opportunity to test the firmness of the party leadership and the seriousness of its allegiance to principle under persecution and pressure on the very eve of the war. That was an advantage for the party, if you look at the trial from a broad political standpoint and disregard for the moment the possible consequences for some of the individuals. The trial was a stroke of political good fortune for our movement, but we were entitled to that, too, because we had lived right.

The trial was a forum for us, a forum from which to popularize our program and proclaim our attitude toward the approaching war. I think we made full use of the extraordinary opportunity. Never in this country, and never in history anywhere, did a political group make such full and complete political utilization of a prosecution in a bourgeois court as our party did. We were able to accomplish this, in spite of small numbers and resources, because we knew exactly what we wanted to do. We knew our program and had no trouble in explaining it. Out of the trial came two big pamphlets of a popular nature, especially devised to explain ourselves in the simplest terms to the ordinary worker, the rank-and-file American worker, and one pamphlet devoted to a discussion of the methods and propaganda techniques and principles involved in our defense.[70] These three pamphlets testify to a full and complete utilization of the trial for our purposes.

The war was declared on the very same day that we were sentenced—December 8, 1941. That certainly was a symbolic coincidence. Nothing could better symbolize our irreconcilable opposition to the imperialist war, and to the capitalist state preparing and waging the war; and nothing, also, could better symbolize our enemies' recognition of our attitude than this unexpungeable fact: that they declared war and sentenced the party leaders to prison on the same day and at the same hour—December 8, 1941.

There is not and there has never been the slightest possibility of misunderstanding our position on the war. We were given the opportunity on December 8—the day of our sentencing—to recant. On December 8, the very day that the radios were blaring with jingo speeches in Congress preceding the declaration of war, the defendants were given an opportunity to disavow what they had said in the trial. Nobody did it. Thus our first response to the war was an action in court, a thousand times more important from a political point of view than any ritualistic statement.

A statement, after all, doesn't constitute a fight against the war. There are some people who don't know that yet. A statement is a promise to oppose the war. But our stand in the Minneapolis courtroom was the thing itself. It was followed two weeks later by my formal declaration, as national secretary of the party, on December 22, simply restating what we had said before, recanting nothing, changing nothing. Again, a couple of months later, on the occasion of the St. Paul municipal election, Comrade Grace Carlson spoke out again in the spirit of the party program. Now the party convention, representing the whole organization, surveying the events which have transpired since the Emergency Conference of the Fourth International in May 1940, once again restates the program of Bolshevism in the political resolution which, I am sure, will meet with unanimous approval tonight.

So, I repeat, no misunderstanding has been possible. Neither friend nor foe could have any doubt of our position. Those who pretend otherwise are liars and provocateurs, not misunderstanding people and not honest opponents.

Our political resolution is not a new program. It is not even a complete restatement of the old program. It is intended only as a timely document, a timely supplement, summing up and interpreting in the light of our program, the most important events which have transpired since the "Manifesto of the Fourth International on the Imperialist War and the Proletarian Revolution," adopted in May 1940.

Trotskyism is the only tendency on the international field that has been able to survive the war. The Second International is completely in the camp of the imperialist democracies. The Stalinists put themselves at the service of one group of imperialists or another alternatively according to the deals or alliances they can make. They sell out the interests of the proletariat of any country, including Russia, in the interests of the diplomatic maneuvers and bargains of the traitorous bureaucracy in the Kremlin.

The "London Bureau"—I venture to say that even comrades present here have forgotten or, perhaps, never heard the name of this vanished ghost—the "London Bureau" was that pretentious international organization of centrists who fought Trotsky and the Fourth International tooth and nail on the ground of our "sectarianism" and their greater "realism" and their greater capacity, self-acknowledged, to build mass parties. And the strongest section of this centrist international, known as the London Bureau, was a rival of ours, an American petty-bourgeois group known, in its final phase before its disappearance into thin air, as the Independent Labor League, the Lovestoneites. The Lovestoneites agreed with us on one point, that is, they saw the war coming and they prepared in their own way for it just as we did. We prepared by sharpening and clarifying our program, cleaning up the remnants in our ranks of petty-bourgeois weakness. They prepared for it by dissolving their organization before the war started. Needless to say, the leaders of this group, who used to give us lectures on "Leninism"—with quotations— are beating the drums for the imperialist war. The "London Bureau" no longer exists on this mundane sphere.

Of the pretentious sectarian cliques and factions who used to shoot at the Fourth International from ambush and criticize us from the "left"—nearly all of them have disappeared from the scene, most of them in the most disgraceful manner.

But the Fourth International survives, struggles, and grows more confident because it alone has a consistent program. The Fourth International is the genuine historical movement, not made arbitrarily, but really expressing the historical course of development and this historic mission of the proletariat.

Our political resolution begins with a reference to an imposing series of programmatic documents of the movement of the Fourth International. We don't have to sit down now and rack our brains to write a program of Marxism for the present-day world. We didn't find ourselves thrown into a panic and crisis when the war started and having to begin then to discuss what we should do, as was the case with the vanguard in 1914. We have a program.

Just let me read this imposing list of documents, which are cited in the opening paragraph of our resolution: "War and the Fourth International," the fundamental theses, 1934, eight years ago; the resolutions of the foundation congress of the Fourth International in 1938; the SWP convention resolution on the Soviet Union, 1940, hammered out in the struggle against the petty-bourgeois renegades; the "Manifesto of the Emergency Conference of the Fourth International on the Imperialist War and the Proletarian Revolution," 1940; the SWP conference resolution on proletarian military policy, 1940; the manifesto of the Executive Committee of the Fourth International on the fall of France, 1940, and in defense of the Soviet Union, 1941; the

SWP manifesto on the Soviet-Nazi war, 1941; the manifesto of the Executive Committee of the Fourth International on American intervention and our defense of China, 1941; the statement by J.P. Cannon on the entry of the United States into the war, 1942; and the statement of Grace Carlson as a candidate of the party in the St. Paul elections of this year.[71]

I am not reading a list of journalistic articles. I am reading here a list of consecutively developed programmatic documents in which you can see from beginning to end one clear and consistent line of concept and principled policy. Our convention resolution is on very firm ground when it says that we have a correct program which equips us for the struggle and that we have only to apply this program to the events of the day. The resolution proceeds from there to analyze the events which have transpired since the adoption of those documents. One consistent program. We have no need of any innovations. The program answers the fundamental questions. All that was said before in these documents which I have mentioned is true and timely and pertinent to the problems of the day. We are not interested in any proposal to change, to modify, or to repudiate any part of our principled program which has stood the test of events and is more appropriate and burning in its application than ever before.

This applies to all the decisive questions that confront the vanguard in the world today. The nature of the war, the Soviet-Nazi struggle, questions of party organization, democracy and fascism, colonial struggle, China, India, Europe under the iron heel of the Nazis, the national question and the slogan of the Socialist United States of Europe—our program has an answer to every one of those questions in principle. We need only to read our program and understand it and we will find the way to answer the current problems correctly.

We proceed from the basic analysis of the war that is contained in the manifesto of the Emergency Conference of the Fourth International which is published under the title "The Imperialist War and the Proletarian Revolution," May 1940. We proceed from that analysis and apply it to four great new events which have transpired since that time. These outstanding events are: (1) the fall of France, June 1940; (2) Hitler's attack on the Soviet Union, June 1941; (3) United States entry into the war, December 1941; (4) the great upsurge of national self-confidence on the part of the peoples of the Orient, the mass of the majority of mankind who are beginning to stir and to make the whole world shake when they move.

In each of these four world-shaking events, the weaknesses of capitalism, its hopeless bankruptcy, its suicidal plunges into the unknown, are clearly demonstrated. Each of these four events reveal new and most promising revolutionary prospects for the proletarian vanguard.

France, which after the last war and the peace of Versailles was the master of Europe, is today a dismembered and oppressed nation. Hitler has conquered all of Europe and transformed it into a horrible concentration camp under Nazi domination. He has proclaimed a new order of permanent oppression and denigration of the peoples of Europe. Some see in these stupendous military victories of Hitler and his military conquest of the continent of Europe only cause for despair. They think that perhaps Hitler's victories are definitive, that Europe is thrown back for decades, or even for centuries, and they envisage Europe beginning again on all fours to crawl forward along the historic path through the medium of national wars. Others, despairing of the force of the people, of the proletariat of Europe, despairing of the one idea, the one program that will spell Hitler's doom, look to the Anglo-American imperialist bandits to liberate Europe from Hitler and transform it into a colony of Anglo-American imperialism.

Both of these perspectives, in our opinion, are utterly fantastic, utterly removed from the reality of things. And unfortunately the first tendency, the tendency to bow down before Hitler's conquest of Europe and regard it as definitive, merges all too easily with the second one of turning to the Anglo-American democratic bandits for relief from Hitler. That is the great danger of exaggerating Hitler's successes and Hitler's power and forgetting the power of the proletariat and the revolutionary program. You can be very sure that Hitler himself and his whole gang do not value their conquest of Europe half so highly as some despairing and disoriented people who are opposed to Nazism do. There is no doubt whatever that Hitler would gladly settle for half of his conquest if he could keep the other half undisturbed for the next period. What is the meaning of the speech he made the other day? It is an indirect way of saying: Let us have half of what we conquered and you can have the rest until we start the next round of the war.

But Anglo-American imperialism does not and cannot recognize Hitler's conquest of Europe. Hitler's domination of Europe means inevitably a further clash with America and England, as a minor partner, for the conquest of the world. Imperialistic interests forbid them to let Hitler have Europe in "peace" to exploit and incorporate in his so-called new order. That is why the war in Europe is still going on and will continue to go on until the workers end it by revolution. For this the workers need more than ever their own independent organization and their own independent program.

The resistance of the oppressed and doubly exploited peoples of Europe prevents any stabilization of Hitler's regime, leaving aside the interference of the imperialist rivals. The resistance of the oppressed peoples of Europe to Hitler can be the starting point for the revolutionary conflagration that will dispose of Hitler in passing and proceed to the permanent solution of the European problem by its socialist reorganization. The movement against national oppression can be, and may very likely be, the starting point of the inevitable European socialist revolution. But that is only on one condition: That the workers' vanguard sticks to its own program and does not adapt itself to the program of bourgeois nationalism.

Our resolution speaks very clearly and unambiguously on this point. We say the program of bourgeois nationalism is only another Versailles. They want only to turn Hitler's "new order" upside down, dismember Germany and return to the European madhouse of artificially divided states on a capitalist basis. That is the very cause of the war. The outlived national boundaries of old Europe have become insuperable barriers against the development of the productive forces. The system of private property combined with the system of national borders of the states, with their standing armies, and separate monetary systems and tariffs, strangled the economic development of Europe and plunged it for the second time in a quarter of a century into the maelstrom of destructive war.

It is sheer insanity to contemplate a return to this starting point. We say that under no circumstances can any section of the Fourth International adapt itself to these blind and mad people who want to go back to Versailles, who propose to solve the problem of Europe by restoring the very conditions which precipitated Europe into this war. Not backward, but forward!— that is the slogan Europe needs. Forward to the socialist reorganization of Europe. The leading and guiding slogan of that fight is, and can be only, "The Socialist United States of Europe."

Revolutionary Marxists are for self-determination as a principle of the program, and thereby they are for national freedom from all forms of oppression or national coercion. We are, and we should be, the foremost fighters and champions of resistance to Hitler. It is stated in our resolution that the workers of Europe must put themselves at the head of this movement of struggle against Hitler. The parties of the workers' vanguard—the sections of the Fourth International—should participate in this movement with their own program, and lead it to its socialist goal.

This is one of the most interesting and timely questions which we have formulated succinctly in our resolution; it is being dealt with at greater length in the international bulletin, as you have noted. It will be discussed further in our theoretical magazine. Our National Committee has participated in this international discussion by the adoption of its basic theses in those paragraphs of our resolution dealing with the question, and which will be elaborated and developed in future articles. We think our resolution indicates the correct line and have no doubt that it will prevail throughout the International when the discussion is completed.

We don't have to say much about the Soviet-Nazi war in our convention. We discussed that question at the last convention, if you remember. We had to debate with Professor Burnham there. Professor Burnham said that we were allies or indirect supporters of Hitler because we were defending the Soviet Union. Comrade Goldman did such a good job of that debate that we don't have to repeat it here. But I must say that, again on this point, we are the one and only political movement that does not have to retract anything or keep quiet about anything that was said before. We understood this question also and we prepared for it. And we alone were correct.

The fugitives from Bolshevism expounded a magnificent theory to the effect that the original Soviet-Nazi pact was based on an "affinity of ideologies." This theory, spun out of thin air, along with the theory of "Soviet imperialism," succumbed to the very real and substantial conflict of social systems and economic interests between German imperialism and the degenerated workers' state. We maintained all the time—it was stated already in 1934 in the theses "War and the Fourth International"—that regardless of how the Soviet Union may be allied in the beginning of the war, the war in the course of its development must inevitably lead to an attack upon the Soviet Union by one of the imperialist camps, whether allied with it in the beginning or not, or by all of them united. We held that the Soviet Union, standing even as the product of a strangled and betrayed revolution, is in the most principled opposition to the imperialist states, and that war between them couldn't be prevented. We were prepared for this eventuality, and we now only have to restate what we declared before, that we defend the Soviet Union for reasons that we have explained many times. The position taken in our last convention can be adopted in this convention with only a change of dates and a few supplementary remarks to bring it up to date. The principled line was absolutely clear and correct and remains so.

We don't support Stalinism, we support the workers' state. We support what remains of the greatest revolution in the history of mankind because we never abandon a conquest while it still has life in it. The worst and most despicable affliction—the characteristic malady of petty-bourgeois radicals—is this propensity to give up a battle before it is lost. Trotsky said, those who will not defend an old conquest will never be capable of fighting for new ones. The Soviet Union remains the greatest conquest of the proletariat in all its history. In spite of everything, it still stands. The Soviet workers know this. They still give the world a demonstration of heroism, of capacity for sacrifice, such as they could not even dream of in those countries where the workers do not feel that they have anything to fight for.

When we see what is done by those Soviet workers today, after all these years of strangulation by the bureaucracy, after all these years of bureaucratic degeneration, we get a glimpse of the boundless power of the proletarian revolution. We can see what miracles of energy will be released by the proletariat of Europe when it finally unites with the Russian proletariat on the revolutionary program. What could the state of the world be today if there had been just a little more energy and capacity in the vanguard of the proletariat to lead Germany to a successful proletarian revolution! All the objective conditions for the victory were present; only the leadership was lacking. Imagine the union of Soviet Russia and Soviet Germany as an economic and military power, with all the irresistible moral force that would be generated by such a union.

If the German revolution had not been defeated, if it had succeeded, we wouldn't be standing here today discussing the program of overthrowing American imperialism. We would more likely be discussing ways and means of finishing up the struggle against the remnants of the counterrevolution. The fact that the workers in Russia took power, the fact that they had a party able to lead the victorious struggle for power—this gives us the assurance for all time that the workers are capable of producing such a party and such a leadership in other countries and on an international scale. Even if the revolution failed once and twice, history is still pushing relentlessly in the direction of its eventual victory.

We are proud of our record on the Russian question. Whatever may befall, whatever future defeats may be in store before the Russian Revolution begins the ascending climb again, not one stain of dishonor will fall upon the banner of the Fourth International. It was the Fourth International, it was Trotsky and his disciples, who before any others began the struggle against treacherous and degenerating Stalinism. It was the Fourth International which explained, on the basis of Marxism, the causes of the degeneration. And in spite of all the slanders, the frame-ups, the persecutions, the blood of our comrades shed by the renegade bureaucracy, we never sought to take revenge on the Soviet Union; we never once faltered in its defense. If the Soviet Union should finally succumb to the strangulating grip of the bureaucracy on the one side, and the blows of imperialism on the other—even then no one can justly say by so much as one word that the Fourth International failed in its duty of defending the Russian Revolution to the very end. That is one of the proudest assets of our movement.

When the United States entered the war it certainly was no surprise to us. It was no surprise to any grown-up person. Our position on the war, as I have remarked before and as our resolution says, was stated in the Minneapolis trial on the basis of the programmatic documents that we had previously adopted. Our position today is the same. Not only are we opposed to American imperialism and consequently to its war; we are also opposed to the theory that American imperialism is invincible and will conquer the world and live a thousand years. We see the United States driven by contradictions. It is caught in the hopeless decay of capitalism as a world system and is going down with it. The formal entry of U.S. imperialism into the war is not an expression of its strength, but of its incurable malady.

They have daydreams in Washington of America replacing Britain as master of the world, of policing the whole of this vast globe with its teeming millions of people, of becoming the center of tribute and plunder to be extracted from the toil of all the peoples of the world. They dream, as this madman Hitler dreams, of a thousand years of world mastery. They will never realize their dream, and we will do our part to see that their disillusionment does not come too late.

The workers in the United States are the power; their power is far greater than that of all the masterminds, the exploiters, the generals, and the statesmen. The workers of the United States have been betrayed by their official organizations, they have been betrayed by their whole official leadership. But these leaders, after all, are only transitory, fill-in men. Their days are numbered. The real spirit and quality of the American proletariat are shown by the fact that they more than doubled the membership of the trade unions in the space of less than ten years. Five million workers organized themselves in a series of great class battles. The American workers give formal obeisance to the war mainly because they have been deluded into the idea that that is the only way to fight Hitlerism. They want to fight Hitlerism—and they are right in that impulse—and the revolutionary class way of waging the fight, the way outlined in our program, remains as yet unknown to the vast majority.

But in spite of that, in spite of their support of the war, the American workers, every chance they get, demonstrate their hostility to every encroachment of the bourgeoisie at home. They resist step by step every attempt to take from them those things they really value and treasure, which they have won in struggle—their unions, their working conditions, hours, wages, etc. With the further development of the war and the terrible disillusionment that must come to the masses of the people when the burdens of the war lie more and more upon them; when the fight for the very smallest economic question becomes of necessity a political struggle—then, we can be confident, the political awakening of the American proletariat will not lag far behind. That awakening can come long before the imperialists' rosy dreams of world conquests are realized. These dreams will be interrupted forever by the American working class.

The fourth great world event, or rather a connected series of events, which we mention in our resolution, is the upsurge of national self-confidence in Asia. In 1917 the imperialist chain broke at its weakest link, backward Russia. There are many indications that this time Asia, which in two countries alone—China and India—has a population amounting to two-fifths of humanity, will prove to be the weakest link in the chain of world imperialism. In the First World War the peoples of Asia were practically nonexistent politically, passive, scarcely heard from in the great reverberations of the world. In this war, from the beginning, the masses of Asia are in the very center of events and are exerting a decisive influence upon their further development. Here is the source of the most optimistic revolutionary hope.

We know Lenin's program, the program of the alliance of the proletariat in the advanced countries with the struggle of the colonial peoples for independence and free national development. In this trend of events in the Orient we see again a brilliant confirmation of this masterful idea. The proletarian revolution in Russia awakened the Asiatic people. Now the insurgent people of China and India, in turn, can stimulate a mass movement of the workers in the imperialist centers and, together with them, begin the upward march of humanity from the black abyss of imperialist reaction, decay, and war.

We alone expected these grave events and counted on them. The world congress of the Fourth International in 1938, considering the approaching war, said that some of the colonial or semicolonial countries would undoubtedly attempt to utilize the war in order to cast off the yoke of slavery. The world congress of 1938 not only anticipated that the colonial people would rise during the war, but in advance characterized their war as not imperialist but liberating. That is precisely what the peoples of China and India are doing. They are utilizing the war to the best of their ability to gain some freedom for themselves. We fully support them in every step forward they make, regardless of the initial auspices of the struggle. We are not champions of the colonial bourgeoisie. We are champions of the leadership of the colonial proletariat. But we support each and every forward step that the national bourgeoisie is compelled to take, insofar as it helps the movement forward.

The manifesto of the Emergency Conference of the Fourth International in May 1940 again stated: "By its very creation of enormous difficulties and dangers for the imperialist metropolitan states, the war opens up wide possibilities for the oppressed peoples. The rumbling of cannon in Europe heralds the approaching hour of their liberation."

What prophetic words were written two and one-half years ago by Comrade Trotsky when he drafted the manifesto of the Emergency Conference! He foresaw that precisely in backward Asia, the weakest link of the imperialist chain may snap and create the conditions for the breaking of imperialist domination everywhere.

Consider the Chinese fight. Five years of military resistance to the power of Japanese imperialism, five years of military resistance, not thanks to Chiang Kai-shek and his bourgeois regime, but despite it; despite the strangulation and restriction of the popular mass movement by the innately treacherous bourgeois rule. We see in that five-year fight, carried on under such difficulties, what latent powers reside in the Chinese people, what energies would have been released had the great Chinese revolution of 1926–27 been properly led and not betrayed into the hands of its enemies. One of the greatest crimes of Stalinism is the betrayal of the Chinese revolution.

We know Chiang Kai-shek as the hangman of the Chinese revolution, aided by Stalin. But despite Chiang Kai-shek and against him, the Fourth International and its heroic Chinese section has supported China in the war against Japan; and, in the opinion of our National Committee, there is no valid reason to change now. To be sure, the United States imperialists would like to take the place of Japan in China. There is no doubt of that. There is no doubt that their aims in the Orient are not benevolent but predatory. The replacement of Japan in China and the subjugation of China to the exploitation of the United States money gang is undoubtedly one of their great aims in the war. But it is far from realization yet. Meantime, China exerts more independence than ever, both in the attitude of its people and in the distorted expressions which this attitude finds in the policy of the bourgeois government of China.

We had wonderful gems of wisdom on this question from the ex-disciples of the late Professor Burnham. China was supported by the Fourth International and, from force of habit, they also continued to support China up until December 1941. And then what happened? The United States outpost in Hawaii was bombed by the Japanese; the next day America declared war on Japan; and then, *ipso facto*, as they say in legal circles, we learned that no more support of the Chinese war against Japan could be allowed. The fact that the very first military consequence of the war was the further isolation of China, the cutting of the Burma Road, and the necessarily greater reliance of China on her independent struggle—these *facts* counted for nothing. Our policy was supposed to be determined, automatically, it would seem, by the developments of diplomacy in Washington and Tokyo. Well, the very kindest thing I can say for that kind of theory is that it is absurd schematism. However, that is not a just appraisal, such as one might make of the position of a genuine sectarian leftist who is at least a revolutionist—as Trotsky said—in his own imagination. I think this is an artificial leftism, representing a belated attempt to compensate for errors made in the other direction, errors which amounted to crimes and betrayals. This pseudoleftism easily turns out to be political treachery on the part of people who are really beginning to be experts in this business.

We support China against Japan as we support India against Great Britain, as long as the war involves the Chinese masses and the element of independence predominates. We don't support the United States against Japan, and needless to say, we don't support Japan against the United States. We support China against all the imperialists, and in this particular case, against the immediate enemy, Japan. And in the further development of military events, if American imperialism replaces Japan, our attitude remains fundamentally the same. We won't quit supporting China; we will continue supporting it against the enemy of the moment, American imperialism instead of Japan. That is the Leninist policy which always seeks an opening for participation in the struggle, not a loophole to escape from it. Nothing has happened yet to change fundamentally the situation which prompted the Fourth International to declare its support of the Chinese war in 1937, five years ago.

India was awakened by the war and is properly taking advantage of the difficulties and weaknesses of the British Empire to advance her own rightful claim to independence. India's four hundred million people are rising. That is the great misfortune of world imperialism, and at the same time, it is the source of revolutionary hope and inspiration for the workers of the entire world. We foresaw this also. We prepared for it, we and our coworkers throughout the world.

The great struggle in India is beginning to develop under the leadership of the Congress, that is, the native bourgeoisie.[72] We support this movement, this action, because, as Comrade Trotsky wrote in his Open Letter to the Workers of India,[73] we support every single small forward step the bourgeoisie may feel obliged to take under the pressure of the masses. But what we see and what we count on is the sweeping movement of the masses. We support the first steps even though they are initiated or formally sponsored by others, in order to aid the mass movement to develop on a wider basis, break out of the narrow bounds of the program of the national bourgeois leadership, and eventually turn against them too, to the full unfolding of the movement of the masses on the program of the permanent revolution.

The workers' vanguard in India enters the struggle with a rounded-out program, with selected and capable cadres, with qualified leaders who have recently consolidated the groups in Ceylon, Burma, and India into one centralized organization, the Bolshevik-Leninist Party of India. This party has formally affiliated to the Fourth International.

The convention should formally send the Indian comrades our greetings and our promise to give them all possible help in their great historic struggle.

It certainly would be a good thing if this could be the keynote of our convention: an action of international solidarity in behalf of a section of the Fourth International which is on the line of fire. That would symbolize the gratitude we feel for all the good things that have been given to us by the international movement, and its great leader, Comrade Trotsky.

This is, properly speaking, our tenth convention. We are not a newly fledged party. It is fourteen years ago this very month that we raised the banner of Trotsky and the Russian Opposition in the Central Committee of the Communist Party of the United States. Then began the rebirth of the veritable movement of American communism under the banner of Trotsky. Behind us there are fourteen years of work and struggle; fourteen years of rich and varied experience, of the testing of programs and the testing of people. Out of that crucible has come a party that is strong and unified and confident of its future.

Next to the Russian section of the Fourth International—which lives we are sure and struggles in totalitarian darkness—next to the Russian section we are the oldest, and are universally regarded as the strongest and most experienced detachment of our international movement. That puts obligations upon us. From those to whom much has been given, much is demanded. We are obliged to give fraternal assistance, material and political, to our struggling comrades in other lands. We have done this since the beginning. We shall continue to do so. But the greatest gift we can give to them, the greatest service we can render to worldwide humanity, is to stick resolutely to our course, to our uncompromising and irreconcilable struggle against the most rapacious enemy of mankind, United States imperialism.

Ah, but the faint hearts say, American imperialism is so rich; it is so strong; who dares to challenge it? We do. We dare. We see not only its strength; we see also its internal weakness, its hopeless contradictions. We see the historic doom that has already been pronounced upon this imperialist monster. We know that this is their day, but we also know, with no less certainty, that tomorrow is our day. Our enemies are strong, but our program, our cadres, our discipline are stronger and will prevail.

We are inspired in our fight by the most completely self-justifying, the most powerful driving incentive that has ever been known—our faith in man and his grandiose communist future. Whatever may befall any of us individually, participation in the fight for the communist future of mankind is the only justifiable life in this epoch, the happiest and the most satisfying life. Whether we as individuals take part in the final victory—and many who are here in this hall will surely do so—or whether some of us as individuals perish in the fight—that is not of much consequence. That is only the soldier's hazard, it is not the most important thing. The most important thing is that we live in the fight and for the fight. Let all the other things take care of themselves.

ON SELECTING THE LEADERSHIP

October 4, 1942

These remarks to the October 1942 convention of the SWP were made under the point on the election of the National Committee. They are from a previously unpublished and uncorrected stenographic transcript.

Comrades:

We are now coming to the most acute problem involved in the general task of building the party. The political resolution has been adopted unanimously. Our organizational report, our trade union tactical line, have been discussed and approved. Politically and programmatically, the party has solved the tasks assigned to it by the convention call. And now we come to the most acute final task: the task of selecting the leadership to carry out the program. And I say it is the most acute problem because here the human element enters in very strongly, which is not so precise and uniform as a clearly defined political or programmatic document. We have adopted the program and we all know that it is the program that makes the party. But it doesn't make the party automatically. The party also is made by leaders selected on the basis of the program. And if we here fall down in this task, as so many other parties and groups, even in the Fourth International, have done so many times, the program is deflected, and instead of the party developing in a straight upward line, it goes through various zigzags and regressions. It is people who have to make the party, with the party program as their weapon.

And here, in the question of selecting the personnel of the leadership, differences of opinion arise among those who are completely united in their programmatic and political conceptions. Differences of opinion, they say, is what makes horse races and it is also what makes election contests, even in the most homogeneous and united party imaginable. Now the task of the leadership of the party is to lead the party in everything, including the question of selecting its successors. The leadership that has been at the head of the party was duty-bound to help the convention solve the problem of renewing the general staff of the party, to lead in this line also, not to pretend that it has nothing to do with it. But to lead the party doesn't mean to decide for the party. The party itself must decide. All that the leadership can do and should try to do is give a general direction and recommendation as to the method of selecting the leadership, rather than as to the complete personnel.

The ranks of a genuine Trotskyist party must be at all times completely free from any feeling of compulsion or coercion in selecting the general staff. The leadership is morally bound to give the party that freedom and not, by direct or indirect means, apply compulsion, pressure, and coercion with the result that the rank and file feel frustrated because they don't want to come into collision with the leadership on this question. The leaders must not control the party. The party must control the leadership. That is the task of the convention—freely to elect, to judge those who have been in positions of leadership, whether they deserve to remain, to judge those aspirants for leadership, whether they are qualified or not, and to make its decision freely.

Now, what was the best way to facilitate the free expression of the party opinion in the selection of the leadership without a general chaos and mishmash which could result from lack of any direction whatever? The best method, in our opinion, based on a wide and varied experience with this acute problem, the best method to have a free and unhampered selection of the new leading committee was through the medium of the nominating commission. This nominating commission was not a handpicked body. The recommendation of the plenum was, as you recall, that all the delegations should have representatives on it roughly proportionate to their strength—so that you had in this nominating commission really a microcosm of the convention. You had the convention in that nominating commission. For three days the delegates have been reporting back to their delegations, and the party membership, as represented by the delegations here, have had ample opportunity to bring their recommendations or their criticisms and to weigh them against the criticisms and nominations of other delegations.

Now, the nominating commission is not a sacrosanct institution. It is one method of selecting the leadership. There are others that have been used. For example, there is the method of having no slate whatever. That, if some of you recall, was the method of the Socialist Party. Their "wise" leaders of the party refrained from having any kind of slate. On the floor of the convention everything is apparently harmonious. And then they stay up to all hours of the night, running around to the delegations and making deals like horse traders, and one thing and another, and only the naive, the duped delegates, imagined there was a free selection. They were cooking up a slate behind the back of the convention without the knowledge of the naive section of the convention. Now, we are not such politicians as that. We don't make up that kind of a slate.

There is a second method, more widely used in the communist movement—that the outgoing National Committee presents its slate. That has not been done for this reason, that we were afraid that if we selected a slate in the National Committee, for the National Committee, and said, "Here is our proposal for the National Committee and alternates," that the authority of the committee is so strong, its weight is so great, that even though many delegates would like to make changes in it, they would feel a compulsion not to do it. There is a form of compulsion involved in a slate emanating from the National Committee. [. . .]

We didn't want to put pressure upon the convention by an official slate, so we said in our recommendation, get representatives from your different delegations, according to your strength, and make up your own slate and if we have something to say about it, we will say it either as individuals or representatives. We have no members of the National Committee on the nominating commission. If some members of the National Committee got on the nominating commission one way or another, it was on their own hook and not representing the National Committee or its decisions in any respect. We believe that the method we have devised and which was adopted by you is the best way for a free selection, and also for an approximation of the best possible slate for the leadership. But it is not a perfect method. The perfect method of selecting a slate of leaders has never yet been devised. The nominating commission is simply in our opinion the best method under conditions of more or less unity in the party, when there are not political conflicts in the party of great moment, no factions, and no point in selecting this or that person according to what he stands for, and everybody can stand on his merits because we are all of one mind on the political resolution.

And even here I say it is not a perfect method. We have to allow for a margin of human error, and I think, personally, some errors have been made this time. But I am afraid that if we try to correct any of these errors—and I speak only of my personal opinion—I fear that we may make worse ones. A free and honest democratic party can easily make errors in the selection of a leading staff. We made errors in the past. People who should have been put on the committee for some reason or another were defeated. Others were elected and later proved unqualified. . . .

I can cite you three examples of manifest errors made in the selection of candidates in past conventions which were corrected by the party without any difficulty because it is a free and honest party where merit decides in the end, and where no kind of machinations or combinations can do you any good in this party. In the long run you can't get to the leading posts of this party if you haven't got the stuff. That is what the history of our movement shows.

At our convention in Chicago in 1938 when we founded the Socialist Workers Party, the slate brought before the convention . . . rejected the candidacy of Comrade Breitman from New Jersey and put in his place another comrade, named Rosenberg, against the wishes of the New Jersey delegation. [We] made this error through lack of information and lack of knowledge of the two people and the haste of the last hour. Well, some of the comrades thought the world had come to an end because Breitman wasn't elected. But nothing happened. Breitman didn't make a big hullabaloo. He didn't go out to organize a Breitman for NC club. He just went back to work—that is all. And by the time the next convention rolled around, he replaced this unqualified [comrade] on the committee without any convulsion whatever.

The 1938 convention made an error later in removing Comrade [Sam] Gordon from the committee and many comrades resented that and thought some terrible casualty would ensue from this. [He] simply went back to work and by the time we came to the 1939 convention where . . . [comrades learned of] work done in the Painters Union in New York under the leadership of Gordon, it followed as a matter of course that the convention rectified the little mistake that had been made in this and returned him to the committee. Again without any trouble.

I don't know how many of you have stopped to consider that only two years ago at the convention in New York Comrade

Grace Carlson was defeated as a candidate for alternate; and just as in the case . . . [of Breitman and Gordon, the party] kept being reminded that she still existed and she was running for the Senate and we might need some political advice from her, so we didn't even wait for a convention. At the last Active Workers Conference in Chicago she was placed on the alternate's list, and today by unanimous recommendation of the nominating commission she is advanced from alternate to full member of the committee.

I cite these illustrations to show that there is no catastrophe in a free and honest party if an individual is defeated. That can easily be corrected.

Now, if I had my way about it—and I haven't got it—I would make some changes in the slate of the present commission. I could point out my personal opinion. For example, I think they were actuated from the beginning by a not entirely correct formula. Firstly, the formula, as I understood it, was that there should be no removal from the old committee or old slate of alternates, except for cause. [. . .] So unless they could find some very good reason . . . those on the committee before were practically cleaved to their posts, and the only chance for new candidates was a removal for cause. Two very worthy candidates were taken off the National Committee . . . [for] other reasons, the personal welfare of the comrades.

A third member of the past committee has been removed from the slate by the nominating commission because he lacked support in his own delegation, lacked the necessary support from those who have pushed him on the committee in the past. So that made only three vacancies, and didn't leave much elbowroom for the new aspirants. Now I think that is not entirely correct. We don't go into the business of tearing the committee to pieces in every convention. We believe in the continuity of leadership. But we also believe in its renewal and we want to have some new blood.

I would propose that at the next convention the nominating commission would sort of turn this formula upside down, to proceed in an opposite direction, at least for once, instead of no removals except for cause, we would say that no one should stay on the committee except for cause. . . . [Delegates should be asked to give] reasons why [each nominee] shouldn't be replaced by a more capable candidate. Quite often it is not at all a question of removing someone from the National Committee for cause. He may be a very good comrade and . . . [of] high quality. Meantime somebody developed with superior political or theoretical abilities who must be pushed forward into a more influential position. We must always have a formula that permits us to have more qualified comrades come to the front. That is what we hope we will do in the future.

Leaders must continually justify their position. There are some cases of comrades being elected to the National Committee—and I have seen it more than once—who are rightly elected because of their ability and qualification, who get on the committee and go to sleep and by the time the next election rolls around they are not qualified because they haven't lived up to the responsibility placed on them. We don't want any deadwood in our leadership. [. . .]

I would like to take the liberty, as an individual member of the party, not speaking in behalf of the committee, but on my own hook, I would like to give my personal criticisms of the present slate, or, rather, my appreciation and my estimation of the slate as it is made up. I think it is about as good as any slate that could be devised. I think, as a general rule, you couldn't get a nominating commission to come out of their sessions with a slate that would be materially any better. The central core of the leadership which is recorded there is unchanged. The only criticisms that can accrue to the slate are around the . . . minor questions of the relative merits of this or that individual comrade. The promotions that the committee has made have been all very good and I think will meet with general approval. They proceeded very cautiously, only advanced three people from alternates to NC—Carlson, Beidel, and Warde [George Novack].

I think the whole convention recognizes that these three comrades were first in line and it is the will of the party that if there are vacancies these three comrades should be the first to fill them. The three who would be added to the alternate list also, I think, were first-class selections. They were the best that were in action. Comrade Turner of Buffalo, New York, and Boston, well-known for his work, belongs on the alternate list. The same holds true for Comrade [Arthur] Burch, the organizer of the Newark branch, and the same holds true of Comrade Lang [Lovell] who is one of the oldest party members in the maritime fraction, who combines both trade union and political experience. As a representative, in a way, of the maritime section of the party, which is a very strong and valuable one, he is the one who is the favorite of the maritime comrades, and belongs on the list.

If I had my way I would have proposed the nomination of Comrade Henry [Ernest Mazey] as an alternate. I am very sorry that the Detroit delegation didn't nominate him, because he represented in the convention a political tendency, a nuance, that is in some ways different from that of the committee, and the committee ought to have that tendency represented in its ranks [. . .] and even more, the committee would have the opportunity to bring its ideas to bear upon him and it frequently happens that comrades who represent an antagonistic tendency end up by getting educated in the leading committee and change their opinions.[74] I regret that the Detroit delegation didn't adopt this point of view and were governed by local organizational considerations, rather than by the broad political considerations which would motivate putting a minority tendency forward.

It would have been a good thing, and insofar as I could influence anything I expressed my opinion quite freely to anyone who asked me, I was in favor of a representative of the group that came to us from the Workers Party.[75] The California delegation made such a recommendation, but it was rejected. But that is not fatal. I also was in favor of the recommendation made by California, [nominating] the present organizer of Los Angeles, who had a double right to consideration as a candidate . . . she is a woman.[76] We need in this period to pay special attention to talented women comrades who come forward.   But I cite this not as a big knock on the commission or as a proposal to overthrow its slate. Not at all. I am of the opinion that if the group which came from the Workers Party to us has qualified and able comrades in their ranks, as I think they have, they will so impress themselves upon the party in the next period that when we select the slate in the next period, I am sure they will find their way on it; they will impress themselves on the party without any difficulty. And here is where I come to my personal recommendation that despite the . . . [opinions] that individuals have about this or that comrade that we would like to see on there, the recommendation is that we take the slate as it is, by and large. And don't try to upset the slate in order to correct a small error, lest in the convention we make a greater error. Because, don't forget, if you nominate somebody to the list of alternates, [a] corresponding consequence is [that] somebody has to go off. Bumping is a railroad term which my old friend Adams [Henry Schultz] here can tell you about. Now if you try—and here is where you run into difficulties—to push forward a candidate for the alternate list, it carries the consequence that one of those thirteen is going to be bumped off. I personally don't know any one of those to remove . . . [in favor] of my special candidates.

If we have too much of that we will undo the work of the nominating commission and we will have a wild scramble here. You can't have everything, and you can't win every time. Harry DeBoer can tell you this. You just have to learn to be a good loser, that is all, and take it in your stride. The defeats that any of you as individuals may suffer are minor defeats and we have to look at the fundamentals here, at the big sides of the nominating commission. We have a slate that was freely selected by the representatives of the delegations. It was selected without any coercion, without any pressure behind the scenes. This slate as a whole, the work of this nominating commission, is a victory for a free party. We ought to look at it as a whole and support it as a whole. In my opinion, it is entitled to the unanimous support of the convention. We are not a great party by accident, we are not a great party only because we have a clear and firm programmatic line. It is also because we have learned how to solve the problem of the selection of the leadership of the party, . . . [a] method whereby . . . [we have] reduced personal friction to the minimum. Each one of us should look at the bigger, broader, more fundamental aspects of the whole method that has been devised for the selection of its leadership and give the nominating commission a . . . [vote of confidence] by accepting its slate as a whole.

A CENSORED SPEECH
IS BETTER THAN SILENCE[77]

November 16, 1942

These excerpts are from an unpublished rough stenographic transcript of remarks in a discussion in the Political Committee of the SWP.

Cannon: The whole idea of talking to the masses outside the circle of radicalism is finding an approach and subjects that interest them, methods of expression, and limits of your program to get a hearing from them. George says it is a problem of approaching new circles of workers. The stuff that we write in *The Militant* and the speeches that we make are as a rule speeches that we wouldn't make if we were talking to green workers. Those are the people with whom our membership today are in contact in the shops. The question is whether these speeches would be useful to them and how to approach the workers. . . .

I listen to Morrow. He wishes this speech wouldn't be delivered. What is the matter with that speech? The only thing is that it doesn't have the full program of the Fourth International in it. The speech is limited. It begins by saying that I want to discuss things that are of interest to the workers. The question of the poll tax is up and the workers should protest, and advocate the endorsement of [the bill to abolish it]. That is all perfectly correct. There isn't a line or a word in there that contradicts our program. It is just a small dose, that is all. In my opinion, you give thirteen small doses of a perfectly correct program if you can get an audience, and you will end up by getting some contacts for the movement. And I am convinced you can't get it otherwise.

I was thinking, before [John G.] Wright mentioned it here, of the Progressive Miners back in 1933, of that scandalous fight we had in the Communist League because I went out there in Gillespie, Illinois, and gave them a talk just on the trade union situation and didn't say anything about the CLA.[78] A tremendous hue. and cry was made in the party at that time, that I, the secretary of the party, hadn't advertised the CLA and unfurled the whole banner, etc. I don't think there is any merit whatever in those considerations. [. . .]

The question boils down to this: Are we going to speak through censorship or stay on our dignity and keep quiet? You can speak on the radio now only if you are for the war and if you don't call for revolution. Now, for my part, I will not stand on my dignity and refuse to speak through censorship. If I can only speak two words, I shall speak them and if two words are going to be spoken, the national secretary can speak them. What are we interested in? We are not interested in the wiseacres of Fourteenth Street, but if this will have any effect in bringing us nearer to any workers who up to now are not near to us, but suffering from a discontent.

Contrary to these dolorous predictions of a reaction from the rank and file, [the ranks know better] because day after day they talk to workers in the shop. From the point of view of serious propaganda work a speech such as this, and such as the one proposed on inflation, is precisely the way they have to talk to these workers if they want to lead them toward us. And don't forget you have a different membership than you had in 1933. Because you had a membership here in New York isolated from the workers. The members we have now are practically all in shops and confronted with the problem of getting the politically uneducated worker drawn closer to us. [. . .]

We voted enthusiastically and unanimously to get on the radio.[79] Did anyone imagine that we were going to get on the radio with the full program of the party? And we are just about to approach the problem of going down to see if we can get that through and all of a sudden we are going to begin to shy and move away. Bunk. I haven't the slightest consideration for these arguments. . . .

Al [Goldman] was incorrect in characterizing my speech as rot because, in general, I don't deal with rot and in this question, in particular, I am dealing very confidently with a subject that I know, both from experience and from study. The interpretation that it is solely a question of approaching new workers is not correct. That wasn't my contention. It is doubly a problem of approaching new people, plus the restrictions of censorship. I maintain that in any case, if you are going on the radio with the hope of approaching people whom you have never talked to before, you have to change your tone, your style, and your phraseology if you want not simply to express yourself and give expression satisfactory to your immediate associates and comrades. [. . .]

If the first lecture could influence only a few workers, only twenty who would become interested enough to hear the second and third one and send in for the speech and get not only a copy of the speech but of *The Militant* and be put on our contact list, then, I say, we would be making real headway. [. . .]

And I say it is foolish to engage in this venture unless we do it confidently and enthusiastically. It would be a fine business to jump into an expensive experiment of this kind with misgivings and fears as to whether we ought to do it or not. We are supposed to be leaders of the movement and know what we should do and should not do. I wasn't distorting when I said that this reminded me of previous discussions I heard back in 1920 or 1921. You couldn't get anybody to say he wasn't for legal work. But there was one element in the party that was pushing and driving for it and another element that every time you had a practical proposal you had a big fight on the question because the others were afraid that it wasn't in conformity with principle. They were concerned with the question of how their personal feelings would be affected by it, etc., while others were concerned with how can we reach new people and draw them toward us.

In its essence it is analogous. We haven't got here the poisonous factional motivations and one thing and another that was behind the Shachtmanites. But at the bottom a tendency toward timidity and holding back from experimenting. [. . .]

The speech here, I would say, is a good speech. I agree with Al that if there were no censorship I would make it better. But I think it is a good speech for the problem you have here, to talk to new workers, interest them in the struggle for democratic rights, and get it through the censorship of the radio. These statistics are information, something the workers really need to know about the poll tax. I venture to say that a lot of people, if they are interested in the poll tax, will say I never knew it before. And the conclusions that workers should be for democratic rights, that they should not support a system of that kind. The only thing I see wrong with it is that it is extremely limited. But this is the first talk approaching a new field of workers. The others will also be limited. If you take any one of them you can say this is kind of thin soup. But thirteen of them together, in my opinion, will convey a few ideas.[. . .]

Goldman: It is not a question of legality versus illegality. If it were, there would be no point to the discussion. Of course, if we can't say A we say B. That is to be taken for granted and I don't know why Charlie [Curtiss] raised that question about the Bolsheviks. That isn't the point. It is only a point insofar as now we want to try an experiment with the radio. We are not prohibited from saying things that we want to say right now. We are prohibited only on the radio. We could say things in written form, and if Jim's principles are correct, and now he has modified them—then our *Militant* which aims to be a mass paper would only be composed of statistics and American citizens' democratic rights, because that is the best way to approach workers. The point is that since we have an avenue—printed pamphlets, etc.— saying what we want to say, then should we spend money for the radio only because we have never done so before? We want to experiment with the radio. It is a new field. Maybe we can get new contacts through it. That is the point at issue. It is not a point of evading censorship.

Cannon: I don't agree that it is solely a problem of approaching new workers. I never maintained that. And I don't agree with Al that it is solely a problem of legality. It is both. And that is what determines the pattern I have fixed on for these speeches. I think you can say on the radio through the censorship a great deal more than is said in there, provided it is said in abstract form. I don't want to do that. [. . .] That is what the SLP does. . . . You have got a better chance of keeping the workers' attention if you are talking a little of something hot in the news, and insinuate a little something. . . . That is why I think the thing has to be considered from both points of view—the idea of trying to use a new medium and speak to workers, and speak through censorship.

And to come back to this question of, "This might be a good

idea but Cannon shouldn't do it." This seems to be a concession to the idea that this whole program is not very dignified. Let somebody, so to speak, take the rap for it. If I had that opinion of the program, I wouldn't want to saddle it on anybody else. [. . .]

But the whole question is if we are going to do this, we have to do it with conviction and not go spreading in the party a lot of defeatism before the program starts. At the end of the thirteen week course, assuming we get on, then we can say whether it was advantageous or not.

ON LEGAL AND SEMILEGAL WORK[80]

The Suppression of 'The Militant'

November 19, 1942

This speech to the New York Central Branch of the SWP is taken from an unpublished rough stenographic transcript, slightly abridged.

The immediate occasion for this talk by me was this contemplated radio program. You know that was announced at the last meeting and has been under discussion several times in the National Committee. And the immediate occasion which prompted us to put it on the agenda for discussion here is the problems and difficulties, also the opportunities, that are presented by this proposal to break out through a new medium. The new events, of course, complicate even that. I presume that you have all read this week's *Militant* and know what I refer to.

We were saying this afternoon that these new events add still further difficulties to the ones that we have already surveyed in the path of our breaking through with the propaganda of Bolshevism on the radio. For example, the project as we had originally devised it was that I should speak on the radio and my sponsor should be *The Militant*, a paper published in the interests of the working people, and I should speak as secretary of the Socialist Workers Party. But we were saying that after these things which have happened recently, my introduction would be a rather peculiar one. The announcer would say, "We now have Mr. Cannon, who has been convicted of conspiracy to overthrow the government, who has been accused of wrecking trains, and is now presented under the sponsorship of *The Militant*, a paper which has just been suppressed. Mr. Cannon's views are not necessarily," etc.

As I say, the question becomes a little more complicated, and more acute. Nevertheless, we do not abandon our determination to exploit this possibility and test it out, if it is possible. What we are really confronted with, both in the radio program and the press and public meetings, and all of our activities, unions, and affairs, is the fundamental question which could be formulated somewhat as follows: How does a revolutionary party conduct its work under conditions of illegality, or partial illegality, or through censorship? That is the problem that we have to solve, that I want to discuss this evening.

In one sense of the word, you can say we operate today under conditions of illegality. If you study the conviction in the Minneapolis trial and some of the laws on the statute books whose constitutionality has not yet been tested, you can say that our very existence is illegal. Since they have not been strictly enforced up to now, we have operated, and are now, with the new interference of the post office, at least under conditions of semilegality. We never know from one week to another now whether our paper will go through the mail at all. [They have] held up another issue. No paper can be mailed before going to Washington. Our general counsel was in Washington yesterday interviewing these gentlemen, and they have intimated very strongly that they do not care to approve any more issues of this paper.

Now, these are not easy problems to solve and many and many a group of revolutionary workers has broken its neck on the problem presented by illegality or semi-illegality. A group which is afraid of itself and really is revolutionary only in its own imagination, as is the case with the sectarian groups who fear above all that they will lose some of their revolutionary purity, confronted with all these difficulties retires into the shadows; they prefer to say nothing. That means to cease to exist.

Other groups have more than once solved the problem by simply adapting themselves to the requirements of bourgeois law and gradually ceasing to be revolutionary or to say anything that is forbidden or unpopular with the authorities. That is liquidation, in reality, of the revolutionary movement. In trying to find a path through these two dangers we have great advantages on our side insofar as we do not begin from the beginning. We are not approaching this problem empty-handed. There is behind us experience and also theory upon which we can draw to guide us and enable us to move with confidence in the situation, no matter how complicated it gets, knowing that we are doing what is correct and necessary to advance our cause in those devious ways which are possible under such handicaps. And doing it without in any way compromising our basic principles or adapting ourselves in any fundamental sense to the bourgeois order.

There is behind us the theory and practice of the Bolsheviks. That is the model party upon which our party draws all the time, and this Bolshevik party existed, as you know, from its beginning in 1903 up until the days of the revolution of 1917 in strict tsarist illegality. With the overthrow of the tsar in February 1917, the Bolshevik party for the first time came out into the open. It enjoyed a legal existence for [a] time. Then, in the July days,[81] the persecution became so severe that to all intents and purposes the party was driven underground, and then came up again and made a revolution. The Bolshevik party, which was strictly illegal under the tsar, nevertheless during a part of that time managed to publish daily newspapers in Petrograd and other parts of Russia, and carried on some kind of camouflaged legal activities. We in the United States had an experience from 1920 to 1922 during which the Communist Party of the United States was underground and considered illegal, during which we confronted the problems in our daily work of devising some ways and means of utilizing the partial legality that was open to us, without abandoning the communist program. And this experience in the United States, plus what we have learned of the history of Bolshevism, is what our National Committee is basing itself on all the time in making every decision—either to go this way or to wheel and go in another direction in confronting this problem of keeping up legal activities under the conditions of censorship, etc.

The problem can be boiled down to two points: one is to maintain our principled position, not to retreat from it or modify it, and to educate our new recruits and close contacts in the spirit of our program. But the other side of our program is no less important—that we not only maintain the members we have, but also strive to get new ones, assimilating new workers into the party.

The test of whether we are solving this problem correctly or not is whether in the development of our work we succeed in achieving both sides of this task.

We summed up ten months of work under war conditions at the

party convention. The convention showed that these ten months of wartime conditions of semi-illegality and persecution and censorship hadn't touched our program at all. The convention unanimously ratified the basic principled positions upon which the movement had been founded.

On the other hand, the convention reports showed that we had been gaining ground; the circulation of our paper expanded, new contacts—we took in eighty-seven new members since the trial, now expanded to ninety-eight, according to today's score. And from all parts of the country there is evidence and proof that the party is continuing its activities. So up to now we have been all right. But the indications are that the pressure upon us will become a little greater now.

We must not underestimate at all the significance of these recent events that are reported in this week's *Militant,* that two issues of *The Militant* have been held up. One issue has been ordered destroyed by the Post Office Department; the current issue is held subject to examination in Washington. We shouldn't be too optimistic about it being admitted to the mails, and our general counsel was informed down there that they are seriously considering making a formal application before the Post Office Department to deny *The Militant* to the mail altogether. That, to all intents and purposes, would kill *The Militant.* Second-class mailing privileges evidently would be denied us and then what would generally follow. . . .

[If] they make an arrangement with the express company that they should not deliver or transport any newspapers that are denied the use of the mails, you are pretty well suppressed. And, of course, that is not the last arrow in their quiver. They can proceed from there to indictments against the editor. . . . I confine myself to "overthrowing the government and wrecking trains." So they may put Breitman in jail. But somebody has got to make a sacrifice. So that we can contemplate the possibility that *The Militant* will be outlawed. Now, then, we will have to devise other means. It doesn't follow from this that we quit publishing. It doesn't follow from this that we discontinue our activity in our endeavor to spread our message. It only dictates to us the necessity of finding a new form and a new medium. On this point, the history of the Bolsheviks could be very instructive for us. In the worst days of the reaction in Russia, following the failure of the 1905 revolution, every form of working-class action was suppressed. In those days the party had very little propaganda medium except that of the underground press.

Then after 1907, especially toward 1912, when the workers' movement began to rise again, there was a tremendous relaxation of the severity of tsarist suppression. The tsarist administration conceived the idea of luring the revolutionists out in the open through permitting various forms of legal activities. At one time they didn't permit trade unions. They never legalized the party. But they permitted sick and death benefit societies, and the Bolsheviks became very aggressive "sick and death benefiters." They mixed themselves up with other workers who wanted sick and death benefits, and used these organizations as modified instruments for the class struggle.

At another time the government took the initiative to organize trade unions of a sort, sort of company unions which were designed in large measure to lure the revolutionary workers out into the open, where the tsarist police could get a chance to spot them. That didn't keep the Bolsheviks from going into them.

Then more legality was conquered, and the Bolsheviks put up candidates in the elections for the Duma [parliament] under the guise of labor candidates. At the outbreak of the war in 1914 there were six Bolshevik members of the Duma who fought against the war credits and were convicted and sentenced to Siberia. The Bolsheviks had daily newspapers published in Petrograd for several years. Sometimes these papers would be suppressed and they would change their name. . . .

These papers were not published as official organs of the Bolshevik party any more than *The Militant* is published as the official organ of the Socialist Workers Party. *The Militant,* as you recall, used to be the official organ of the SWP. After Pearl Harbor, when some new laws went into effect, *The Militant* was sold for "one dollar and other valuable considerations," and is no longer the official. . . . The party is in no way responsible for *The Militant,* and if *The Militant* gets into trouble they can't blame us for it—that is, they can't do it if they want to be honest and legal about it.

The daily paper of the Bolsheviks was published in what you call the Aesopian language. It wasn't a socialist paper that came out in print and said that the only party in the country is the Bolshevik party and the only thing to do was to overthrow the government by force and violence. . . . They called themselves "consistent democrats." And the paper did not espouse the cause of the Bolshevik party and did not propound its whole program.

It did this only by implication. It wrote in parables. It modified its language to get through the tsarist censorship. But they managed to do it skillfully enough so that around that paper the Bolshevik party was organized. So that when the time came, more favorable conditions, and the chance to break out in the open, the Bolsheviks had previously created a wide sentiment for their basic ideas among the advanced workers of Moscow.

All this time, however, they maintained the underground party. They did not confine themselves to this limited Aesopian legalistic propaganda; that was a supplement of the illegal program of the party. In the underground circles of the party they talked frankly about everything, clarified their program, and through it were able to maintain control over this vast network of legal activities.

These conditions created dangers. The Mensheviks, who adapted themselves to this tsarist illegality by practically abandoning the underground organization and the undiluted program, practically, in a sense, reconciled themselves to the existing regime, and thereby they destroyed their real authority with the revolutionary workers. The Bolsheviks, who were even considered hairsplitters at times on questions of principles, nevertheless were completely alien to all sectarian influence. They weren't afraid of themselves, and never hesitated to exploit even the smallest possibility to carry on camouflaged or modified legalistic work.

Here in the United States we didn't do so well in 1920 and 1921 because we lacked both this theoretical knowledge which was possessed by Lenin and his Bolsheviks, and we lacked the experience of the Bolsheviks, so that we were hampered at every turn under conditions of the government's persecution and the illegalization of the party, by the fears which beset a large section of the party that we would in some way compromise our program.

It was universally agreed in the party that you must exploit every possibility for legal expression. But every time we tried to do something concretely, we would run up against this sectarian fear that maybe we are going to commit a sin here. Larry [Trainor] gave us a perfect description of a sectarian, as one who is afraid of his subconscious impulses to be opportunistic, and that if he ever permits himself a little freedom, he will depart from the program.

It became clear to us that it is one thing to have a good

program, and to have an illegal organization, but if this illegal organization doesn't find some way of getting contact with the living mass of the workers, we die of stagnation. And it became clear to some of us that we had to break out of this charmed circle some way and, especially as the government persecutions were relaxing, we came to the conclusion that we had to find some way of getting a partial legalistic activity that would enable us to reach workers with at least a part of our message, with the hope that at least we would get contact with them. We had to go through several faction fights and splits before we could solve that problem. The more it became clear to some of us that we had to break through and find some means of legal expression, the more the sectarians opposed. . . .

First we used to try to develop forums. We organized in 1921 a committee to collect funds for the victims of the Russian famine and in the guise of this committee, we put on a wide propaganda campaign. But the organization was primarily a legalistic propagandistic medium for popularizing the Soviet Union and the principles of the Russian Revolution.

Then, we organized a series of clubs—Toilers Clubs—after the legal newspaper we were publishing, and these clubs would meet, hold open forums and discussions. . . . But the trend and the tenor of the speeches and the discussions were for the class struggle and criticism of the capitalist regime, etc., from which the implications led one toward communism. Then we decided to federate these clubs. We called a little convention and organized a National Association of Toilers' Clubs and announced that we were going to run candidates for office.

Then when we got away with that without any prosecution, the next step was to work out a devious [plan]: to have two parties in the United States—that is, the conditions were such that we could not have a completely legal communist party. So we decided we would have two parties: an underground communist party with an absolutely undiluted program, and a legal party which does not say anything wrong, but just doesn't include the whole truth in its program, it stops just short of those statements which are complete and necessary to round out the communist program. By this means we would have a legal platform whereby communists and communist sympathizers would speak in public, and only give a part of the program—that part not yet outlawed—and remain silent on those questions subject to legal prosecution.

[This would enable us to] create a periphery of half-communists through which the Communist Party with its illegal press can penetrate.

We had a tremendous faction fight in the party before we could realize that program, and eventually had a split—lost three or four thousand members in the split in our ruthless determined drive to push through this program. It was necessary for the salvation of the party.

For a time we had two parties in this country, and had two official organs—a weekly paper called the *Weekly Worker,* that was admitted to the post office and was carefully edited so as not to conflict with the law too much; and then, an official organ of the party called *The Communist,* which devoted itself to discussion of theoretical questions of the program without any thought to the censorship. This was intended to complete the educational work started by the legal press and the legal party. By that means the Communist Party began to grow and gain contacts in the trade union movement, and later, when legal conditions became better and prosecutions ended, . . . the party as a whole became legalized and remained so all the years since then.

Similarly with us. We operated, beginning with 1928 as the Left Opposition, with complete legality. There were no prosecutions by the government up until 1941, thirteen years. It would have been very foolish for us to come to the conclusion that the communist program is illegal—which almost any lawyer will tell you—according to the laws of the statute book, but which were not enforced. And why should we go underground when it was possible to operate legally?

In 1941 they convicted us. [. . . That decision is still being appealed.] In the meantime, we maintain we are a perfectly legal party and we don't go underground. We prefer to keep out in the open and carry out our work as best we can, at the risk of further prosecutions, rather than at the first attack to retire from the public field, organize ourselves underground, and hope that some way or other the workers will discover our whereabouts.

At the plenum in Chicago in October 1941, when we were on our way to the trial, the plenum laid down this line in a resolution: that we do not give up our legal rights. We do not admit that we are an illegal organization. And even if we are convicted in the trial we will still attempt to function legally in the next period. We don't promise that we would be able to maintain this position under a thousand blows from the government. . . .

Well, we not only got the conviction that we kept talking about, but we also got the declaration of war on the same day. Simultaneously our party came under a shadow, so to speak; the general status of the Trotskyist movement came under a cloud. We had been convicted of a crime and the war had been declared, which automatically reinstituted the Espionage law, and our legal status began to be a little bit shaky. Nevertheless we met after this and the national convention laid down the line that we are going to [continue to act as a legal party]. We were compelled to turn *The Militant* over to a publishing association and *The Militant* then became an independent publication for which the party was not responsible. And if they find that the leaders of the party are [guilty of holding illegal views] that does not make *The Militant* an illegal paper, because it has nothing to do with the party except that some of the party leaders write for it. That is the way the thing has developed up until the present time, but the thing is turning a little now. You must have noticed that *The Militant* changed its tone a little bit after it ceased to be the official organ of the party. It began to carry out the function of a legal paper—that is, it advocated and propounded parts of the communist program but not the whole program.

But *The Militant*, of course, was the most important means of our propaganda because it keeps the whole periphery of our movement together. All the workers who lean toward us or are sympathetic toward us saw in *The Militant* the ideological center which represented in general the most important elements of our program. *The Militant* was pretty radical in spite of that. Perhaps it crowded the legalistic interpretation of the law and the policy of the administration right up to the limit, and that was the design. We didn't intend to publish a paper just to publish a paper. The object was to say just as much as could be said under the given law, and perhaps a little more; to feel one's way— because the law is not an absolute quantity at all. It is on the books, but the interpretation and enforcement of the law—that fluctuates a great deal according to the attitude in the country, of judges, etc. So that one cannot say exactly what is legally permissible, etc., until you test it out.

If you want to keep in existence a legal paper. . . . Let us assume that *The Militant* is suppressed. Then you have no public journal. What do we do then? Two things. We can stand on our dignity and say, "By God, if we can't say what we want to say, we will say nothing. We will spite you." Or we will say, "We can't say as much openly and legally now as *The Militant* said up to December 7, but we can say three-fourths of that, and since *The Militant* is a suppressed paper, we will try to get three or four people to start a new paper." That is what probably would happen. Or assume, then, that a second paper—maybe a paper called *Truth*, would be suppressed because it didn't tell the whole truth, but told too much of it. Then the problem would confront the realistic Bolsheviks as before: It is no longer possible to say what the old *Militant* said, which was everything, or what *The Militant* since December 8 said, which was nine-tenths of everything. But at any rate, the workers are entitled to some kind of paper that gives some attention to the workers' problems and we will try to interest some people in starting a paper called *Workers News,* which doesn't even run editorials any more.

As a matter of fact, when we talked with Comrade Trotsky in Mexico in 1938—that was a year before the war started—we were all expecting its outbreak and discussing what we would do in the event of war and what our techniques would be. This very question of the press was discussed. We anticipated that the prosecution would be swifter and more severe than it has been, that the leaders of the party would be arrested, *The Militant* suppressed, and we had already decided what we would do in that event.

Even if conditions became very severe we would still find it necessary to interest some people at least in the project of forming a paper that would give workers some news in the darkness, and thereby keep a semblance of the movement together. We looked forward to various vicissitudes, changes of the situation, with a certain definite line guiding us all the time. We are going to keep our movement out in the open as long as possible. We are going to develop as much public activity as we can, and we are going to try to exploit even the smallest possibility of keeping open contact with the workers, and the workers' movement, even at the cost of further prosecution, because if we fail to do that, we lose our contacts.

All this is background for the proposal to develop a new propaganda medium through the radio. It may sound a little incongruous on our part for us at this time . . . that we should begin to develop the idea of getting on the radio. [We became convinced this was a realistic possibility] after the broadcasts in the New Jersey election.[82] And we have perhaps been a little slow in realizing this and trying to utilize it. When the question was being discussed, one of the comrades in the National Committee said, "By God, that is right. Radio is the coming thing." He was answered, "No, it is here." The radio program aroused big enthusiasm because everybody could see at a glance that this offers the possibility of reaching new circles, of getting a hearing from people who never heard our message before, and naturally this is what we are looking for all the time because we must be continuously striving to grow, expand, and get new people into the movement. But it is not such a simple question to just stand up on the radio and say, I represent the Socialist Workers Party, which advocates the overthrow of the capitalist government, because the radio has a very strict censorship. . . .

In view of the fact that Breitman was a candidate for the Senate, he was given a little more latitude and when we went back to that same station after the election was over and our comrade said we want to talk to you about putting on a whole series of programs for Cannon to speak, they immediately chilled and said, what does he want to talk about? "Oh," he said, "just problems of the day—taxation, for example." "Taxation? You know the tax bill has been passed by Congress. You can't criticize that any more. This is an American station. We don't want to get into trouble with the government."

The point is that the censorship of the radio is perhaps ten times more severe than the censorship of the post office has been up to now. And on top of all that, the jitteriness of the radio stations and their own private censorship, self-imposed on top of the government censorship. [. . .] The best we can do is to go in there as sort of, if not convicts, at least people who have been convicted and gotten into trouble with the Post Office Department, and under suspicion. We don't go there under the best of auspices.

Now, the question is, in spite of all of that, should we try it? It is obvious there is only a very thin crack of radio censorship through which we can hope to penetrate. We can't hope for more than one-tenth of the latitude that even the restricted *Militant* has had in the period since the declaration of war. But, in spite of that, should we try to break through the censorship with a series of speeches which would appear to the educated communist very modest and . . . by this means get some contacts that we haven't got now? That is what we would have to do and that would be the maximum.

We would have to go into the project with the understanding that the speeches we make are of an extremely limited and outwardly appearing moderate character. However, not speeches which tell any lies or reconcile themselves in any way with capitalism, but simply limit the contents of the speech and the criticism and proposals to the requirements of the censorship, with the object that you do not tell the whole program in one speech, but give only a small dose. [. . .]

The question is, would the members of the party understand and approve it? Would they feel disappointed that we can't say everything we want to say, [that we] must restrict our program in content to such a narrow ledge, and even then present it in a tone that is different from the forthright tone of our unrestricted propaganda? Would it be disappointing? That is what we would like to hear an expression from you about. Because it would be foolish for the National Committee to embark upon this kind of a program if the members didn't understand what [it was aimed to accomplish].

There are risks involved. For example, that I, as the speaker on the radio, speaking in such "refined" language, which is by no means expected of me, and limiting criticisms more than we are accustomed to doing in our public speeches—that this might be creating the impression that the Trotskyists are getting very tame and not as revolutionary as they used to be. But there are also possible gains. Some of the wiseacres, and so forth, might find these speeches somewhat lacking in their standard of revolutionary doctrines. On the other hand, there is the possibility of a few hundred workers who never heard anything about the class struggle or socialism or its implications might become interested. [. . .]

You know that following the July days in Russia the hue and cry was started against the Bolsheviks and Lenin was denounced as a German spy and a big hue and cry arose for Lenin to go into the court and demand that they prove the charges against him. And instead of that, Lenin put on a disguise and went over to Finland, and stayed in hiding, because he wasn't ready yet to be arrested. And he suffered the attacks of some of the philistines, that he had run away from the accusations. But the court was not an honest court, so instead of that, Lenin, disregarding all the philistines' pretensions toward prestige, judged what was necessary in the interests of the movement to do: keep himself out of their hands and do the work necessary to prepare for the revolution.

We shall be governed, we ought to be governed, by the simple criterion: can we gain or lose more by going through with the radio program within the very limited possibilities offered to us, or shall we abandon the project? And we really would like to have an expression of the sentiments of the comrades on it.

If it is decided finally that it is not advisable to exploit this medium on such a limited and narrow basis, we will return the money to comrades who have pledged it. On the other hand, if you really feel the enthusiasm to try it, then we will in the next few days go down to the radio people and see what kind of arrangements can be made. We probably will have to change the sponsorship.

OPEN LETTER TO
ATTORNEY GENERAL BIDDLE

Published November 21, 1942

This letter about FBI harassment was first printed in The Militant.

Mr. Francis Biddle
Attorney General of the United States
Washington, D.C.

Dear Sir:

A few days ago two agents of the Federal Bureau of Investigation appeared at my office at the headquarters of the Socialist Workers Party, 116 University Place, New York City, and inquired of me whether I had had anything to do with a train wreck that occurred about a year and a half ago. They also expressed their intention to question other leaders and members of the party on the same subject.

What is the meaning of this fantastic inquisition? How could the FBI ever arrive at a theory that we, members of a workers' political party with openly declared political aims, could be interested in wrecking trains? All our writings show clearly that we are opposed to individual violence and sabotage.

It appears that in the train directly following or preceding the one that was wrecked there was a car carrying engineers and officials of the Soviet Union.

It is possible that an agent of the FBI, completely unacquainted with what our movement stands for, assumed that the Trotskyists, being enemies of the Stalinists, might have recourse to violence and sabotage. But it is also possible that, when Stalin became friendly with Washington and London, the GPU became friendly with the FBI, and that the GPU has suggested to the FBI the concoction of a typical Stalinist frame-up against the Trotskyists.

In either case, I want to protest at being subjected to questions which imply that Trotskyists resort to sabotage and violence against individuals. The American workers, and all decent citizens, must recoil with horror from the implication that the federal government is going into the business of imputing fantastic crimes of violence and sabotage to political opponents and critics, and of framing up such charges against them, when the real purpose is political persecution.

Our political ideas can be read in all our papers and pamphlets openly published and distributed. Any attempt to attribute ideas and practices to us outside of those that are openly advocated by us must be publicly called by its right name: a prelude to a frame-up.

> Very truly yours,
> James P. Cannon
> National Secretary
> Socialist Workers Party

THE ATTACK ON "THE MILITANT"

Published November 28, 1942

This article was printed in The Militant.

During the same week that the American authorities clasped hands with the French quisling, Darlan, in Africa and sought collaboration with the fascist Franco in Spain, here in the United States they took the first steps to suppress a bona fide antifascist workers' paper—*The Militant*.[83]

As reported last week, the issues of November 7 and November 14 were held up by the post office authorities. Since then the November 7 issue has been destroyed at the post office on orders from Washington, and the issue of November 21, which carried a report and protest against these arbitrary actions, has likewise been held up. We have learned from attorneys of the Post Office Department that *The Militant* has been subjected to these persecutions because of its editorial policies and criticisms of the administration.

The Militant thus has the honor of being the first workers' paper to suffer a reactionary attack on the freedom of the press, just as the Trotskyist movement was singled out for the first prosecution under the notorious antilabor Smith Act. But the Trotskyists are hit first only because they are the spearhead of militant resistance to the developing reaction. These attacks against the Trotskyists are, in essence, aimed at all workers' rights and against the labor movement as a whole. The entrenched reactionaries are feeling their way toward a general assault on the constitutional rights of free speech and free press. They want to silence all criticism.

The arbitrary, bureaucratic violation of *The Militant's* mailing rights is only the latest in a series of actions against the

Trotskyist movement in the United States during the past year. They all fit into the same pattern.

1. In June 1941 FBI agents raided the headquarters of the Socialist Workers Party in Minneapolis and St. Paul, seizing literature which was on public sale there. Three weeks later the Department of Justice secured indictments against twenty-nine members of the Socialist Workers Party and leaders of Local 544-CIO. After a five-week trial before a jury which did not contain a single trade unionist, in Minneapolis in October-November, eighteen defendants were found guilty of violating the Smith Act of 1940. These were sentenced to prison terms of one year to sixteen months. Appeal of these convictions has just been heard in the circuit court at St. Louis, and will be carried, if necessary, to the Supreme Court.

2. Several weeks ago the Department of Justice apparently sought to lay the basis of a new frame-up against us, when two FBI agents questioned me about a train wreck that occurred over a year and a half ago. The obvious implication of the inquisition was that Trotskyists engage in such acts of violence and sabotage, although the whole record of our movement, and its literature, prove the contrary.

3. The inquisition about the train wreck fits in with the announcement that a motion picture of ex-Ambassador Davies' *Mission to Moscow*[84]—a brazen whitewash of the monstrous Moscow trials of 1936-37—is soon to be released with the obvious design to prejudice public opinion in favor of the hangman, Stalin, and against the victims of his frame-ups. The quasi-governmental auspices of this motion picture of the ex-ambassador's doctored book present a most sinister aspect of this affair.

4. In the November elections this year the Socialist Workers Party ran as its candidate for U.S. senator from Minnesota, Grace Carlson, who had received almost 9,000 votes in the previous election. Although other candidates received their returns, *the vote given the SWP candidate was uncounted and unrecorded by the election authorities.*

5. Now the post office authorities have struck at the mailing rights of *The Militant* without even specifying which articles or editorials are objected to.

To cap these crimes, news of these suppressions has itself been suppressed. The managers of the paper were not notified of the suppressions and were informed of them only after they had inquired concerning the nondelivery of the paper. None of the big capitalist papers has published reports of this blow against the freedom of the press.

Thus Trotskyists have been the first to be indicted and tried under the infamous and unconstitutional "gag" act of Poll-Tax Representative Howard Smith. The Department of Justice is apparently trying to devise a "train wreck" frame-up against us. A "propaganda" frame-up is soon to be unreeled on the motion picture screen. The SWP candidate in Minnesota is the first to be deprived of electoral rights. *The Militant* is the first labor paper to suffer suppression since this war began. Finally, the authorities have tried to suppress news of this suppression.

Such are the facts in the sustained campaign of prosecution directed by the Roosevelt administration against our movement.

In a featured article in the *New York Times,* Sunday, September 21, 1941, Roosevelt's Attorney General Biddle was quoted as saying: "Insofar as I can, by the use of the authority and influence of my office, I intend to see that civil liberties in this country are protected; that we do not again fall into the disgraceful hysteria of witch-hunts, strikebreakings, and minority persecutions which were such a dark chapter in our record of the last world war."

We could quote similar declarations of intent from President Roosevelt and other high officials of his administration.

These declarations flagrantly contradict the policy of persecution initiated by Roosevelt's administration against our movement. Despite their promises Roosevelt and his aides have set their feet upon the path of persecution blazed by the Wilson administration in the last war. President Roosevelt takes up where Wilson left off; Attorney General Biddle, with his raids and prosecutions, imitates Attorney General Palmer; Postmaster General Walker suppresses socialist and labor papers like his Democratic predecessor Burleson; OWI [Office of War Information] head Davis suppresses the news of our suppression like propaganda minister Creel during the last war. They "use the authority and influence" of their offices, not to protect civil liberties, but to abridge them. Persecutions speak louder than promises.

The administration claims that it is waging this war to defend democracy against the fascists and to preserve the four freedoms, among them the freedom of speech and freedom of the press. But what are they actually doing? They attack free speech. They attack the free press. While dealing with quislings and fascists abroad, they strike at genuine antifascists at home.

The uncompromising antifascist policy of the Trotskyists is known to every informed person. The Trotskyists of Spain fought in the Spanish Civil War against Franco's fascist dictatorship[85]; they are fighting against him today while Washington seeks an alliance with him. Under terrible persecution the Trotskyists of France fought against Darlan and all the other men of Vichy. Jean Meichler, a Trotskyist leader, was executed by a Nazi firing squad in France. Leon Lesoil, leader of the Belgian Trotskyists, has just died in a German prison for fighting against the Nazis. The Trotskyists in Germany fight under the most adverse illegal conditions for the overthrow of Hitlerite imperialism.

Roosevelt's Department of Justice knows precisely what we stand for. The leaders of our party explained our program and policies in full detail to the judge, prosecutors, and jury at the Minneapolis trial. This testimony has been published and distributed in thousands of copies to workers all over the country, all over the world in fact.

Our program and our record demonstrate that we Trotskyists are antifascist to the core. We are unremitting fighters in the interests of labor. We fight for the preservation of all democratic rights and civil liberties, against every form of inequality and injustice. As revolutionary socialists, we are principled opponents of the Roosevelt administration and criticize it from the standpoint of the socialist and labor movement.

These are our crimes in the eyes of the administration, and they add to their crimes in attacking us for them. The Roosevelt regime claims to oppose fascism but it collaborates, when expedient, with the fascists. It claims to be defending the four freedoms while trying to deny these freedoms to its political opponents. We Trotskyists, however, are defending democratic rights here at home against Roosevelt's assault upon them. We are fighting for the freedom he hypocritically pretends to be safeguarding.

But we are not defending these rights for ourselves alone. We are fighting on behalf of the entire labor movement in the United States. We are only the first to be attacked. If the government can put through these initial moves without a wide protest, prosecution of others will surely follow.

If *The Militant* can be suppressed, any CIO or AFL paper can be likewise suppressed. If our party's candidates are not given their electoral rights, other parties can be similarly disfranchised. If the leaders of Local 544-CIO can be convicted under the Smith "Gag" Act, this law will be used against other militant trade union leaders. If the FBI can succeed in their frame-ups against us, they will extend the frame-up system to others.

The persecution against the Trotskyist movement is simply the first step toward an all-out campaign against the militants in the trade unions and the civil liberties of all working-class critics of the administration. The workers have already been denied the right of collective bargaining and the right to strike. Are they now to be deprived (by the powers that be) of the elementary right to express their convictions, to criticize the acts of the government and the reactionary plots of the profiteers, to defend their interests *even in words?* Wages have been frozen. Are civil liberties also to be frozen? The cost of living is mounting daily. Is the wave of reaction to be permitted to rise along with it?

These are the issues involved in our fight against the persecution of our party and the suppression of *The Militant.*

These are the reasons why our fight should be supported by the whole labor movement and every sincere believer in democratic rights and civil liberties.

Over 100 years ago, when William Lloyd Garrison started his famous Abolitionist newspaper, *The Liberator,* he wrote in its first issue: "I am in earnest—I will not equivocate—I will not excuse—I will not retreat a single inch—and I WILL BE HEARD."

With this same spirit, we intend to wage our struggle against the censorship of today's reactionaries. It is with this call that we summon to action every individual and organization determined to fight for the preservation of genuine democracy here in the United States.

From left: Felix Morrow, Albert Goldman, and Cannon.

Above: SWP picket at showing of *Mission to Moscow*. Below (left to right): Miles Dunne, V.R. Dunne, and Oscar Coover at New York farewell banquet. Right: Minneapolis defendants (from left) Farrell Dobbs and Harry DeBoer (standing), Cannon, Emil Hansen, Oscar Coover, Carl Skoglund, Carlos Hudson, Jake Cooper, Clarence Hamel (standing), V.R. Dunne, and Max Geldman.

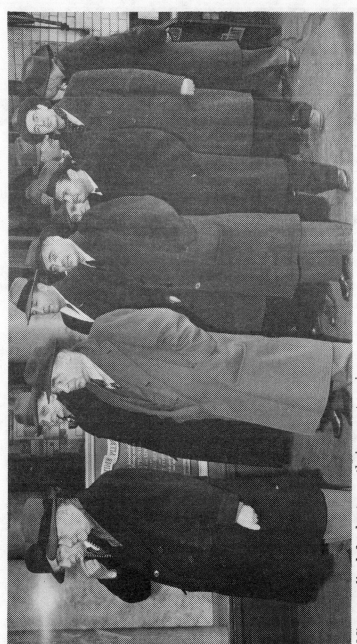

Minneapolis defendants on their way to prison.

CAMPAIGN FOR A LABOR PARTY

November 1942

Cannon's proposal for a labor party campaign was presented to the Political Committee of the SWP on November 25, 1942. His remarks on the campaign were made at a meeting of the PC on November 30. The two pieces were first published in an SWP internal bulletin and then in the August 1943 Fourth International.

1. Outline of Proposal for a Labor Party Campaign

We must make an important political turn without delay. It is time to start an aggressive campaign for the formation of an independent labor party, to transform the *propaganda* slogan into a slogan of *agitation*. This is the most important conclusion we must draw from the recent elections in the light of the present situation in the labor movement and the attitude of workers and the changes which are sure to come in the not-distant future. The labor party is the central issue around which the drive of the workers for class independence can be best expressed in the next period. By becoming the active champion of the labor party the Socialist Workers Party will link itself to an instinctive class movement which is almost certain to have a tumultuous growth, and thus multiply its influence and recruiting power. A brief review of our experiences with the labor party slogan since its adoption in 1938 up to the recent elections will show that now is the time to strike.

I

The adoption of the labor party slogan in 1938 by the Socialist Workers Party was predicated on the stormy development of the elemental mass movement of the workers through the CIO and the assumption that this movement, in the next stage of its development, must seek a political expression. The enormous disproportion between the rate of growth of this mass movement of millions, and that of the vanguard party, showed that we could no longer hope for our party to be the medium for the first expression of political independent action by the mass of the workers.

We concluded that this first expression would take the form of an independent labor party based on the trade unions. Hence, in order for us to link ourselves with the next stages of the political development of the American workers, we had to adapt ourselves to the trend toward a labor party; to work within it in order to influence its development in a revolutionary direction, and, at the same time, build the Trotskyist party. Our estimation of the most probable next stages of development, and our reasoning as to the role our party would be obliged to play by the circumstances, were correct. The development was slower than we anticipated at that time. But if we examine the causes which slowed down the labor party development, it will be clear that the movement was only arrested, dammed up, so to speak, in order to break out with still greater strength after some delay. The causes for the delay were transitory and are already passing away.

II

Just about the time that we adopted our labor party position, the economic conjuncture began to improve. This checked the discontent of the workers which had been rising up till that time. Roosevelt still appeared to the workers as their champion and his social reform program was taken as a substitute for an independent political movement of the workers. At the same time, the entire leadership of the CIO, including the Stalinists, who had been the most aggressive proponents of the labor party idea, supported Roosevelt in a body. They squelched all organized expressions of the sentiment for an independent labor party. The labor party question was thus taken off the agenda of trade union meetings and conventions, and to superficial reasoners the movement seemed to be killed. The campaign of agitation for a labor party which we had planned did not find a favorable field in these circumstances. Foreseeing future developments, we did not abandon the slogan, but in our practical work we had to change it from a slogan of agitation to a slogan of propaganda.

III

War conditions—the huge preparatory development of the armaments industry and later the actual entry into the war—

introduced two factors which served to militate against any immediate response to the labor party slogan. The preliminary war prosperity tended to dampen the interest of the workers in the labor party for the time being. They still regarded Roosevelt as their political champion and supplemented their support of him by economic action against individual employers and corporations.

Then began the process of blocking off this economic outlet of the workers' struggle. By a combination of cajolery, threats, and treachery—granting of some wage increases, institution of the War Labor Board, labor leaders' pledges of no strikes—the workers have been stymied on the economic field. Once this was accomplished, wages were virtually frozen, while the cost of living rises at a scale which amounts, in essence, to a monthly wage cut. Meanwhile, the employers, taking advantage of the situation, resist the settlement of virtually all grievances. These grievances pile up in the pigeonholes of the War Labor Board and the workers get no satisfaction.

The workers' discontent is already evident and is bound to grow enormously as the cost of living mounts, as taxes and other burdens are piled upon them and they are denied corresponding wage increases, and they feel balked by the denial of the right to resort to the strike weapon. The entire history of the American labor movement shows that the workers tend to resort to independent political action when they find themselves defeated or frustrated on the economic field. There is every reason to believe that this tradition will assert itself more powerfully than ever in the coming period.

IV

To a certain extent—positively, and especially negatively—the workers asserted a tendency to resort to independent political action already in the recent congressional and state elections. For the first time the Gallup poll was badly upset and the calculations of all the political experts were refuted by a factor which had not been anticipated—the unprecedented abstention from voting by the workers. The smallness of the workers' vote can be attributed, in part, to the military mobilization, the shifting of vast numbers of workers to new locations, their failure to register, etc. But a very important factor, if not the main factor, in the mass failure of the industrial workers to vote, was their attitude of indifference and cynicism toward the two capitalist parties.

On the other hand in New York, where the leaders of the American Labor Party found themselves, much against their own desires, conducting an independent campaign, the workers turned out in great numbers to support the American Labor Party. In New York City the ALP polled 18 percent of the vote, despite the fact that it had an unknown nonentity from Tammany Hall as a candidate, and despite the appeals of Roosevelt—and of Hillman, his chief labor lieutenant—for the Democratic ticket. The vote of more than four hundred thousand for the ALP in New York is a rather convincing demonstration of the deep sentiment of a considerable mass of workers in New York for independent political action.

In the Minnesota election somewhat the same phenomenon is to be observed. Despite the terrible disintegration of the upper circles of the Farmer-Labor Party there, the treachery of the Stalinists, the support of [Minnesota Governor Harold] Stassen by the official heads of the CIO and considerable sections of the AFL bureaucracy—despite all this, the Farmer-Labor Party polled a bigger percentage of the vote this year than was the case in 1940 or 1938.

From these two examples, we must conclude that a strong sentiment for independent political action by the workers reveals itself wherever they have a chance to express it through the medium of an independent party.

In the light of the election results in New York, the correctness of the position taken by our party in support of the ALP ticket, and the absurdity of the boycott policy of the Workers Party juveniles, are equally demonstrated. The Workers Party decided to boycott the ALP ticket just at the moment when it was demonstrating its greatest appeal to the workers under the most unfavorable conditions. We, on the other hand, by our policy, linked ourselves to the movement of the future. The lesson of this experience will not fail to impress itself on the minds of the class-conscious workers who are observing developments.

V

We should draw the following conclusions:

1. The elections in New York and Minnesota positively, and in the other states negatively, show the beginning of a trend of workers' sentiment for independent political action.

2. The mass sentiment of the workers in this direction must grow tumultuously, as the gap widens between frozen wages on

the one side and rising prices, tax burdens, and enforced contributions on the other.

3. The sentiment for independent political action may, and to a considerable extent will, take a very radical turn. To many workers, burning with indignation over grievances which cannot find an outlet for expression on the economic field, the demand for a labor party will signify in a general way the demand for a workers' government—for a change in the regime!

4. The time is opportune right now for the SWP to start an aggressive campaign of agitation for an independent labor party. It would be a great political error to lose any time in establishing our position in the forefront of this movement.

VI

Our campaign should be developed according to a carefully worked-out practical program, designed to swing the entire party into activity and to mobilize its energies for the advancement of the campaign, step by step, in coordination with the tempo of the mass movement itself. The main points of such a practical program are approximately as follows:

1. Make the labor party the central campaign issue of the party in the next period.

2. Stage a formal launching of the campaign by means of a plenum, an eastern conference, or a New York membership meeting at which a thoroughly worked-out motivating speech will be delivered and published as the opening gun in the campaign. The emanation of this published speech from some kind of a formal party gathering will give it more weight than a mere article or statement.

3. Our literary forces will have to be organized to prepare an abundance of propaganda material on the labor party question— factual, historical, argumentative, and perspective. The propaganda material should include a comprehensive pamphlet and leaflets, as well as abundant material in the press. Our comrades in the trade unions must be adequately supplied with information and arguments to meet all opposition on the labor party question.

4. The campaign should be directed from the center in an organizational, as well as in a political way, following the developments of the work of each branch and giving systematic directions for next steps, and so forth.

5. At a given stage in the development of the campaign, we should go over to the formation of *labor party clubs* in the unions

where circumstances make this feasible, and use these clubs as the center of organization for the labor party fight. These labor party clubs will tend to become, in effect, left-wing caucuses or progressive groups. At the right time, regulating the tempo of our campaign always in accordance with the internal situation in each particular union, we should begin to introduce labor party resolutions. If we can succeed at first in having a labor party resolution passed by a prominent and influential trade union local or body, we can then use this resolution as the model for other unions. From a practical standpoint there is a big advantage in being able to say to a local union that the proposed resolution is the one previously adopted by such and such a trade union organization on the labor party question. Our trade union department, in cooperation with the fractions, can work out this end of the matter without difficulty.

6. We must proceed according to the conviction that all developments in the trade union movement from now on must work in favor of the development of the labor party sentiment; that the slogan will become increasingly popular; and that we must become the leaders of the fight. Our labor party campaign can be the medium through which we bring the elementary ideas of class independence into the trade union movement. This is the indicated approach for the gradual introduction of our entire transitional program.

VII

Our labor party campaign must be understood as having great implications for the building of our party. *We must conceive of it as our third big political maneuver,* the first being the fusion with the American Workers Party, and the second the entry into the Socialist Party. This maneuver will be different from the others, but the differences will be all in our favor, and the prospects of gain for our party are vastly greater.

1. This time we will undertake the maneuver with a much better internal situation in our own party. Each of the other maneuvers had to be undertaken at the cost of a fierce factional fight and split in our own ranks. This time, we can enter the campaign with completely unified cadres and without the slightest fear of any internal disturbances as a result of the step. On the contrary, the announcement of the campaign can be expected to call forth enthusiasm throughout the party and a unanimous response to the directions of the center.

2. The quality of the recruits, on the whole, which we will gain from the labor party maneuver will be different from the recruits gained by the fusion with the AWP and the entry into the SP. To be sure, in each of the other two cases we were dealing with the prospect of recruiting politically more advanced people than we will gain directly from the trade unions in the labor party campaign. But in return, the recruits from the other two ventures were in the majority centrists who brought with them the baggage of bad training and tradition and preconceived prejudices. That was why the attempt to assimilate them into the Trotskyist movement produced in each case a second factional fight and split. The heterogeneous composition of the Trotskyist cadre of those times also hampered this work of assimilation. The Abern clique based itself on the backward section of the Musteites, and both Abern and Shachtman (not to mention Burnham!) based themselves on the unassimilated elements from the SP and the Yipsels.[86]

From the labor party campaign we will get fresh workers whose political education will begin with us. They will come in as individuals without factional attachments from the past, and their assimilation and education will be facilitated by the united cadre of our present party which, in the meantime, has accumulated considerably more political experience.

The third important difference between the labor party campaign and the two previous political turns we have made is in the magnitude of the prospects. This time we must think in terms of thousands—and eventually of tens of thousands—of recruits who will come into our party from the labor party movement. And, given the facts that they will come to us not as a previously constituted faction or party, but as individual recruits; that they will enter a party which is homogeneous in its composition, whose unified cadres have serious political experiences behind them, we can confidently expect to assimilate the new members without an internal crisis.

There is no doubt that the key to the further development in the next period of our party and the expansion of its membership lies in the self-confidence, speed, and energy with which we plunge into an organized labor party campaign. Big successes are possible for us along this line; even probable, I would say. Naturally, we cannot promise ourselves any miracles overnight. There will be favorable returns from our campaign from the very start, but we must plan a long-time fight.

We can expect big results within a reasonable time. But even the first big results will only be a down payment on the unbounded prospects which lie ahead of us along this road. The modest recruiting campaign we are now conducting should be conceived, in the light of a labor party campaign, as a mere curtain raiser. We may hope to recruit thousands in the course of the labor party campaign, and our work from the start should be inspired by this confidence.

2. Remarks on the Labor Party Campaign

You all have the outline. I don't have much to add except that some of the points can be elaborated.

The first point, about changing the slogan from a propaganda slogan to a slogan of agitation, I think is an important one to understand. In our work, generally, we ought to distinguish between three types of slogans: slogans of propaganda, slogans of agitation, and slogans of action. A perfectly correct slogan can be either effective or ineffective according to how it is applied in a given situation.

For example, the slogan of workers' defense guards during the height of the fight with the Coughlinites, Silver Shirts, Nazi Bundists, etc., was a slogan of *agitation,* in some cases leading directly to *action.* But with the temporary slowing down of this fascistic movement, we have moderated the tempo with which we press the slogan of workers' defense guards. The practical necessity for them is not clear to the workers. It is now a *propaganda* slogan. We don't conduct an active campaign because there is not enough response in the present situation. A little later, when reaction gets more aggressive, and the labor movement runs up against fascistic hooliganism again, we will have to renew our agitation for the guards.

Similarly, with the labor party. We have been talking about the labor party, but only in an educational, that is propagandistic, way because the movement didn't seem to have any wind in its sails during the last year or two. In the next period things will be different. We draw this conclusion from two points of view.

The fundamental point of view: the situation in which the workers find themselves—with increasing pressure and difficulties upon them, and the fact that they are stymied on the economic field—must push them into the direction of political expression through a labor party. We should anticipate this and begin to prepare our campaign so as to get full prominence in the movement.

The second, subsidiary, point of view: the results of the elections, especially the negative demonstration, showing the indifference of the workers to the Republican and Democratic parties, should be construed as the preliminary symptoms of a movement in the direction of an independent political expression.

Now is the time, in my opinion, for us to begin beating the drums for a labor party, with the confidence that we are going to get a response, if not right away, a little later. The more active we are right now, when no other tendency in the labor movement is agitating the question, the more we will gain.

Point 3 under section 5 of the outline is a very important point. When the workers begin to make a break from the capitalist parties toward a labor party, it is quite possible that they will not give it the reformistic connotation which has been associated in the past with the labor party, but that it will symbolize to them, even if vaguely, a break with the whole regime and a move for a new one, a regime of workers' power. This idea was first mentioned by Warde when he came back from Detroit. The more I have thought about it, the more it has impressed me as a very plausible deduction. Under present conditions the labor party idea can have far more revolutionary implications than in past periods when it was advanced as a reformistic measure.

There is no need at all for us to speak about a reformistic labor party. What we are advocating is an *independent* labor party, and we are proposing our own program, which is not reformist. In the past, the assumption has always been that a labor party would surely be a reformist manifestation. It may, in some instances. But in others it may have a more profound meaning in the minds of many workers who adopt the slogan. In England, for example, the slogan of "Labor to Power" has no doubt the same double meaning for many workers. For some it can mean a purely moderate demand that the reformist labor leaders take over the government as agents of the bourgeois regime. For others it can indicate a call to the workers to take power and change the whole system. These things should be taken into account when we weigh the feasibility and effectiveness of the labor party slogan in the present situation.

It is very important that a resolution or other political document considered by the National Committee be clearly motivated; that it be completely objective and properly proportioned. That is, it shouldn't be an "agitational" document in any sense of the word. I have this conception about all documents concerning policy and line and if my outline proposal appears to contain agitational optimism, I don't mean it in that sense at all. The outline is intended as an objective appraisal, from my point of view, of the situation and perspectives.

Comrade Henderson [Joseph Hansen] has reminded us of Trotsky's conception that the economic basis for a successful reformist labor party is undermined. That, of course, is the materialistic foundation for the idea which Warde expressed—that the workers will take the move for a labor party, in a vague way at least, as having revolutionary implications.

I don't speak in the outline about existing labor parties, because our tactics in these cases can be easily decided. Naturally, we are not going to propose to start a new labor party in New York or Minnesota. We work within the existing parties. But I should point out, however, that we haven't been working within the ALP. The clubs are scattered all over the five boroughs. The Stalinists are quite active in these clubs and so are the Social Democrats; but we have not gotten around to them yet. Where there are existing parties, we certainly must participate in them if our campaign is to have any serious meaning.

When I speak of labor party clubs in the outline, I don't mean them in the sense of these ALP clubs. These latter are assembly district organizations required by law, the legal basis for the election machinery. The labor party clubs suggested in the document are groups formed in the unions to fight for the labor party. For example, in a progressive local union a club would be formed for the object of propagating the idea of the labor party in the local. Such clubs will, in the nature of things, become the natural centers of left-wing organization. They will represent a direct challenge to the whole regime—to the state administration, as well as the trade union bureaucracy—without exceeding, in a formal sense, the legalistic bounds. I have the idea that these labor party clubs can become in the next period a tremendous mechanism for the building of the left wing in the unions.

The question has been raised in the discussion whether there is a trend or only the beginning of a trend toward the labor party, whether the election results are exaggerated in the outline. I tried to state it very carefully, that the elections should be taken as representing the *beginning* of a trend. I emphasized the negative manifestations—that is, the abstention of the **workers** from voting throughout the rest of the country—more strongly even than the positive vote for the labor party in New York and Minnesota. Obviously, it is not yet a very conscious movement for a labor party. But it is a half-break with the old parties, and that necessarily has its logic. This, together with the fact that we are all confident that the next period must promote a politicalization of the workers, justifies us in asserting that there is the beginning of a trend toward a powerful labor party movement.

The ALP vote keeps coming up to plague those who have any reservations in this regard. The fact is that the ALP got 400,000 votes in New York, under the most unfavorable conditions. The leaders were scared of themselves; the candidate, a Tammany hack, had never been heard of before; the pressure of Roosevelt and of Hillman, who was, you may say, the cofounder of the party, swung the whole bureaucracy of the Amalgamated [Clothing Workers] away from the ALP. In spite of all that, the ALP got 18 percent of the votes in New York City and over 10 percent of the votes in the state. That must signify something. I think it has to be taken as signifying in part that these workers—those who voted the ALP ticket were mainly workers—have something in mind different from the old idea of voting for the Democratic Party.

I don't think it would be correct to say these are votes against Roosevelt. I would venture to say that 90 percent of them are still pro-Roosevelt. But this vote shows that the workers, still largely for Roosevelt, *are not for the Democratic Party*. That is the important thing. They don't give a hoot for the Democratic Party. All during the time they were led in behind Roosevelt, they weren't led in behind the Democratic Party. On the contrary, their hostility is perhaps greater today than before. I think if you look back at this period of the Roosevelt regime you will see that Labor's Non-Partisan League, the ALP in New York, and other manifestations showed that even then, in order to dragoon the workers to support Roosevelt, they had to provide some kind of labor or pseudolabor machinery for it. They couldn't just unfurl the banner and say, Vote for Roosevelt.

This election was the greatest test of all. The workers in New York—400,000 of them—stood up independently for the first time. I can't read anything else into this ALP vote except a strengthening of the impulse of the workers to have a party of their own.

I come to a point here which has been discussed and which I

am quite insistent upon: that I want to describe this proposed labor party campaign as a *maneuver,* comparing it to the two other big maneuvers we carried through: the fusion of the Trotskyist organization with the AWP and the entry into the SP. Of course, I don't mean to equate the labor party campaign with the fusion and the entry. It is not the same thing at all. But it is the same *kind* of thing.

What do we mean by a maneuver? It is a tactical turning aside from a predetermined path which has been blocked off, in order to accomplish the original objective, to reach the same goal by another road. The thing in common between the proposed labor party campaign and the other two maneuvers in our history is that which is basic: the attempt to build a revolutionary party through another party.

Normally and logically, when you organize a party and adopt a program and invite people to join it, that is the way you build up a party—by recruiting people directly. We came up against the fact in 1934, however, that there was another group developing on the left-wing road. They didn't come over to us, so we had to go over to meet them. This fusion with the AWP was a departure from the line of direct recruitment. Similarly was the entry into the SP. It was a maneuver, a turning away from the path of building the party by direct recruitment, because a certain set of circumstances confronted us where the most eligible and logical candidates for Bolshevism refused to come into this party. We had to turn about and join them. In the same sense, the united front can be called a maneuver. In the early days of its existence the Comintern reached a certain stalemate in its struggle against the Social Democracy. The majority remained in the Social Democratic ranks and didn't come over and join the Communist Party. Then the Comintern devised the medium of the united front as a means of approach to the Social Democratic workers. This was not a fusion or an entry, but a coming together for concrete actions for specific immediate aims, etc.

What are we trying to do here? It was not a historic law that we must have a labor party in this country, and that we have to become advocates of it and work within it. As a matter of fact, in the early days of our movement Trotsky refused to sanction the advocacy of the labor party. He said, *It is not yet determined* whether the workers will seek their first political expression through a revolutionary party or through a reformist party based on the unions, and we should advocate the revolutionary party based on individual membership. The socialist movement over most of Europe and the world was built up that way. It was only during the stormy development of the CIO, which began to show political manifestations, when it became pretty obvious that the rate of development of this new mass movement of the CIO was so much faster in tempo and greater in scope than the development of the Socialist Workers Party—it was only then that the Old Man revised his conclusion.

The new movement of the masses was developing outside the SWP, on a vastly wider scale. This trend is even clearer now than it was in 1938 when Trotsky first recommended the labor party tactic. In order for us not to be left on the sidelines, we have to go into the labor party movement without giving up our own independent organization. That is what is contemplated in this proposal here. We are going to try, once again, to build our party through another party. We will be inside of it for a long time, although not in the same technical and precise way as in the other two maneuvers. This time there will be no fusion, and no entry. We will maintain the independence of our party all the time. But in some places we can conceive of the SWP being affiliated to the labor party, in other places, where we may be denied entrance as a party, we will participate in the labor party through the unions, etc. But, in every variant, we will be trying to build a revolutionary party through a political movement of the masses which is not yet clearly defined as revolutionary, or reformist, or in between.

From an internal point of view, it is very important, in my opinion, to explain to the membership that we conceive this campaign as a maneuver. On the one hand, we must show them the great scope of its possibilities; on the other hand, that we are maintaining our independence all the time. And we are working, not to build the labor party as a substitute for our party, but to build our party as the party that must lead the revolution. The labor party may never come to full-fledged shape at all. The conflict of the two wings—the revolutionary and the reformist— can reach such a state of tension that the movement will split before the party is fully formed on a national scale. I can even conceive of the existence of two kinds of labor parties for a certain time—a labor party with a revolutionary program and a labor party with a reformist program—which would engage in election contests against each other.

In the past, under the pressure of circumstances, parties based on the unions have taken a far more radical turn than the ordinary reformist conceptions. The Norwegian Labor Party was almost a replica, in its structure, of the British Labour Party. But, following the war, it formally adopted the communist program and joined the Comintern. The Comintern tried to transform it from a loose party based on delegates from unions into an individual membership party. In the process, eventually, a split took place and the Norwegian Communist Party was carved out of the body of the Norwegian Labor Party. When the revolutionary tide receded and the mass of the workers returned to reformism, things fell back into their old place again. The developments of the labor party movement in the United States, with the stormy developments of the class struggle which are clearly indicated, will least of all follow a predetermined pattern.

I think it is correct to characterize what is proposed here as a political turn. A campaign of agitation, as is proposed, requires a radical change in our activity and, to a certain extent, in our attitude. We have to stir the party from top to bottom with discussion on the labor party question and show the party members that they have now a chance to participate in a fight, in a movement. We should aim to inspire them with the perspectives of the big possibilities which are by no means stated in an exaggerated fashion. At the appropriate time our comrades will begin moving in the unions step by step; perhaps to form a labor party club, perhaps to introduce a resolution, perhaps to circularize this resolution to other places, according to circumstances in each case. All this represents a turn from what we have been doing up to now in our purely routine propaganda in the press without pressing or pushing the issues in the unions.

If we had been imbued with this conception a few months ago we would have taken a different attitude in the New York election. We would have been campaigning for the labor party in New York from the very beginning if we had been as sure then of what was going on as we are now. I personally couldn't support such an idea then because I didn't know; I needed the results of the election to convince me that the ALP was not going to fall apart. It is clear now that we underestimated its vitality.

Comrade Charles [Curtiss] has pointed out that the trend of the war, the Allied victories, promoting reaction on the one side, will also provoke more resentment and discontent, and perhaps revolt, in one form or another, by the workers. The assumption is that, in general, there will be a sharpening of the class struggle.

How can this manifest itself in the next period? Possibly there will be a wave of outlaw strikes. But I think its strongest manifestation will be in the political field. The two may go together. But, in any case, we should absolutely count on a sharpening of the class struggle and help to give it a political expression.

We must appraise correctly the workers' attitude toward Roosevelt. I believe, also, that the abstention of the workers from the elections in the big industrial centers did not signify a break with Roosevelt. It showed that they want to make a distinction between Roosevelt's social reforms and the Democratic Party's war program. Their tendency is to support the war under the leadership of Roosevelt, in payment for the social reforms they think they got from him. The thing they consider most is the social reform program. From their standpoint, at the present time, the ideal political situation would be a labor party with Roosevelt at the head of it. Their sentiment is for a labor political expression, but they haven't broken with Roosevelt. We have to be very careful that we don't overestimate that question or conclude that the elections showed a break with Roosevelt.

The "New Deal" of Roosevelt was a substitute for the social reform program of Social Democracy in the past. That was the basis of its hold on the workers. The bankruptcy of the New Deal can't possibly, in my opinion, push the workers back into an acceptance of traditional capitalist party politics. Their next turn will be toward a labor party.

Once more about kinds of slogans: We must carefully explain to the party the difference between a propaganda slogan and an agitational slogan, and an agitational slogan and a slogan of action. I am especially sensitive on this because, in the early days of the Communist Party, in those furious debates we used to have on the labor party, we fell into all kinds of mistakes on the question. In a situation such as there has been in the past few years, the labor party could only be a propaganda slogan. If we had been beating the drums all over the labor movement and tried to form labor party clubs, we would have simply broken our heads. The time was not ripe, there was not enough response, to justify intense agitation for the labor party. It was necessary to confine it to a propaganda slogan. But now there are possibilities, and even probabilities, of a rising sentiment of the workers and a favorable response to a concentrated agitation for the labor party. In the new situation we would make the greatest error if we were to lag behind events and continue with the routine propaganda of the past period.

There is a difference also between slogans of agitation and slogans of action. This is illustrated by one of the classic errors of the early communist movement in the United States. Propaganda for the idea of workers' soviets is, now as always, a principle of the program. But in 1919 the editors of the New York *Communist,* growing impatient, issued the slogan of action in a banner headline: "Organize Workers' Councils." Sad to say, the soviets did not materialize. The slogan of action was premature and discredited its authors.

It wouldn't be out of order, in connection with the educational preparation of the party for this campaign, if we impart to the whole membership a better understanding of the different ways of applying slogans—as slogans of propaganda, of agitation, or of action—according to the situation, as it is in reality.

A LETTER TO CARLO TRESCA[87]

December 8, 1942

Cannon remained friends with many figures of the pre-World War I radical movement who did not share his Trotskyist views. This personal letter recalls one such friendship.

New York

Dear Carlo,

I just heard the sad news about the death of your brother who has been so close to you and meant so much to you through these many years of turmoil and struggle. I deeply sympathize with you, dear friend, in this heavy affliction.

I know through my own experience that tobacco is sometimes the best consoler. Therefore I am sending you a few cigars.

Rose asked me to invite you and Margaret [DeSilver] to have dinner with us sometime very soon. If this is convenient and agreeable to you, give me a ring.

I clasp your hand warmly,
[Jim Cannon]

A DANGER OF CLIQUISM

December 13, 1942

These remarks were made near the end of a convention of the New York Local of the SWP. They are taken from an unpublished and uncorrected stenographic transcript.

Comrades:

This is the first time that I have spoken in a local New York discussion since the spring of 1939. After the petty-bourgeois opposition left the party and the proletarianization process got under way, I was of the opinion that the natural course of events would work in favor of the development of the New York organization, and that the national leaders should stand aside and let the party work its way out. By and large, I think that was the correct policy and if I speak now in the internal discussion, it is because I have been taking some note of recent developments in the New York organization and I consider that a reversal of the forward process has been going on, to the point where it is time for every national party leader to show where he stands and help the New York organization by frank, outspoken talk, to prevent it from sinking back into the morass from which it climbed two and a half years ago.

Now the essence of the matter, as I size it up, is that the proletarianization of the party in New York—that is, the real proletarianization—has not been completed. Technically it has made very satisfactory progress, but the proletarianization in the sense of the eradication of the petty-bourgeois mentality and ideology and political habits has by no means been completed. And this discussion and convention is to me adequate proof of it. The atmosphere of the convention, especially in the latter half of it, which has taken so many comrades by surprise, is to me reminiscent of the atmosphere of the early days of factional explosions which we saw in the past, having the same kind of roots. To paraphrase Marx, I was reminded of the fact that great historical events are always enacted twice—first as tragedy, and then as farce. And I believe if we understand this correctly and if each individual of the national leadership shows where he stands, that this repetition of past unfortunate events can be reduced to a farce.

What do I mean by a reminiscent atmosphere? You have here the appearance of an opposition without a clear basis. What are the indications of the appearance of an opposition without a clear basis? Well, first, you have a unanimous report of the leadership of a year's work, compiled and voted for by the entire City Committee, adequately presented here. And then on the basis of this unanimous report, you have a little exception: (1) on Stalinism; (2) on organization; (3) on the election campaign; (4) on party educational work; (5) on the necessity for political-ization; (6) on financial management; (7) and this always comes—demand for freedom of criticism and protest against suppression, and the tendency to encourage all who are aggrieved or appear to be aggrieved.

So the total result of the unanimous report, summed up together, amounts to an apparently concerted drive to discredit the leadership. The remarkable thing about this, which reminds us so much of experiences we have had in the past, is that all these criticisms are different. They are not organically tied together at all. Some of them are valid—or at least partly valid—all of them I would consider minor to the main question of the record of the leadership. All of these questions are not necessarily related and yet you see in the atmosphere of the meeting here a sort of touching solidarity of all the critics. The criticisms are not máde within the framework of a general agreement. No, they are within the framework of a general opposition atmosphere—I don't say conscious, at least not on the part of all the comrades, but I speak of the total effect of the atmosphere on one who comes in from the outside. You have in the New York organization here the appearance of an opposition—I don't say an organized and conscious opposition—and you don't see any serious platform for the opposition—not yet. Even if you take all these criticisms together they don't constitute a serious platform for an opposi-tion. I could support every single one and really be on the side of the leadership—I mean really, not hypocritically.

I have seen a lot of comrades in my time duped into opposition without knowing what they were getting into, and that is why I think it is time to point out to them what the tendency of this atmosphere appears to be to a more experienced observer. We know something about factions. We know that when serious political differences reach a point where they can't find adjustment in normal channels, a dispute within committees, discussions in the branches, conventions, etc.—that they sometimes lead to a necessity to conduct a factional struggle in the name of these principles. Now, such an organization deserves the name of a faction—that is, a body that is based on principles which do not get adequate consideration without a faction fight.

On the other hand, we know something about cliques. We know that the organization of a group that acts in concert in the party without a principled basis is the most abhorrent phenomenon the revolutionary movement can know. That is, an unprincipled clique formation. And, as I repeat again, often comrades not knowing the objective logic of a situation in which they are placed, by a combination of grievances, first informal solidarity, and so forth, can be maneuvered and duped into a clique formation and their usefulness for the movement destroyed for a long time to come.

Let us take up this question of Stalinism. I don't want to discuss the merits of that question because I think, from that point of view, it is a little bit out of date now. I was ready to discuss Stalinism or any other political question two months ago at the national convention of the party which decides these things. Nobody appeared at that convention with anything new. We had nothing new to say. So you must say that, at least by default, the convention reaffirmed the policy which had been followed up to then.

Has the New York Local been out of step with this national policy? Not at all. So you have to say that the convention should have resolved this question, and discussion is out of date until something new has transpired which would justify reopening of the question. Nevertheless, we had a discussion in the local organization on it. Now you have a local convention which also discusses it. And I hear from Comrade [Lou] Cooper that after this convention we have to have still more discussion. What kind of attitude is this about national conventions and conferences? At what point will this be resolved? If discussion is fully in order after this convention is adjourned, then you can draw one of two conclusions: either we are people who discuss for the sake of discussion or we must continue this discussion until it is decided in a way satisfactory to Comrade Cooper. I call this a completely irresponsible attitude and an attitude which the party convention must reject out of hand—to disregard the decisions of the national and local conventions and think that any discussion on the question of Stalinism can begin again, either on the open floor or in secret, in informal conversations, without showing disrespect for the party.

What Comrade Cooper demands of the party on the line of Stalinism isn't really very much, not worth a discussion, in my opinion. What does he want? It boils down to the question of two people being assigned to Local 65, one being left in Local 302 . . . I don't care how they decide that. It is by no means serious enough to warrant turning the party upside down. Furthermore, the guardian of party policy between conventions is the National Committee. If anybody in the New York organization seriously feels that the city leadership is out of line with national party policy, he ought to put in a complaint. We never refuse a hearing to any complaint of any kind and see if we can resolve it in the National Committee. But up to now the National Committee has fully supported the work of the New York organization in this field.

What is the duty of the national leadership in this incipient situation? I think the leaders have got to take a position on a certain number of questions. I, for one, am going to do it, and propose that the national leadership do it, and what I do will be done out in the open and everybody will know it.

On the question of discussion, we discuss only to decide, not to discuss everlastingly. If anyone leaving this convention considers any question so important that it must be discussed again, I suggest he put . . . [his request in writing, so] the National Committee [can] decide whether it merits opening a discussion or not, and on that basis. . . .

I think the National Committee has to take an attitude on the local leadership here, whether to support it or not. Up to now we have supported it because I think it has shown good progress in all fields. That is not to say without errors or derelictions, because you can't have any leadership. . . . But we don't believe in building mountains out of molehills. As far as the record stands now—and we know and we have observed things—we support the local leadership and we are not going to leave it in the lurch against an opposition.

On the question of Stalinism we have already in the National Committee taken a clear position. If anybody again wants to raise the question, I think the National Committee will again consider it and take a definite position [on whether to open] discussion on the point.

We should take an attitude toward serious criticisms that are made by comrades in the rank and file or in a section of the leadership here. I don't think we should discourage criticism at all. [It is] not out of order, not wrong, or in any way disloyal for comrades to stand up in branch meetings and make their criticisms. But after this convention, the leadership elected by this convention is entitled to loyal support and deserves [it], not in the framework of undermining.

I think the national leadership should take an attitude toward cliques, that cliquism is poison in the revolutionary party and the organizers of cliques are criminals and will make no bones about it. I don't know how far this business has developed in the New York organization: further than we realize, or whether we exaggerate it. I don't know whether the warnings given at this meeting today will cause some comrades to pause and consider where they are going. But I will tell you one thing: you will never get experienced people into clique formations. Once you take the cure of that terrible experience you are immune forever. We had the experience over years and years in this movement because of its petty-bourgeois composition and atmosphere, which is the natural soil for clique politics, of a permanent chronic clique called the Abern Clique. Everyone ought to read over again the history of this clique.[88] We used to notice that as years went by this clique would flourish on tidbits, minor complaints, etc., until you would bring this out in the open and call for a political showdown. . . . Green and inexperienced comrades seem to have to go through this experience before they know what they are getting into.

If there remain any comrades who haven't done it, we will do our best to help them in the next period. I am speaking now for myself, and I think the National Committee generally will agree with me. I don't think the situation is fatal or even dangerous if we face the reality and don't let anyone deceive us. Don't tell us we are only imagining things.

You may underestimate or you may exaggerate a little bit, but where there is a great deal of smoke—and there has been a little smoke in the New York organization—there must be a little fire. We want to put that fire out before it burns down the house. I think the way to do it is to insist on more real proletarianization. Here is where I have to disagree with the educational comrades. We want to proletarianize the minds of the comrades in the party as well as their hands. We want to ask to have all cards put on the table, no hidden cliques, no shooting from ambush, no ambiguous oppositions. Come out in the open if you have got something to come out in the open for, and if you haven't, discontinue opposition a d rally loyally about the leadership that is elected, no matter who it may be. Comrade [Morris] Stein, at the party convention, uttered what I am sure will be a famous aphorism. He said, "Unfurl your banner or pull in your horns." That is what I say to incipient tendencies in the New York local.

THE SITUATION IN THE
NEW YORK LOCAL[89]

December 23, 1942

*This speech was given to a New York SWP membership meeting.
It is from an uncorrected, unpublished, and incomplete stenographic transcript.*

Comrades:

We had a discussion in the National Committee about the New
York City convention. We had my report and the report of
numerous other members of the NC who had attended the
convention. And we discussed the question and we came to some
conclusions which we want to present to the comrades of the New
York Local as recommendations. In doing this—presenting it
orally rather than in written form, we want to avoid formalizing
the intervention of the National Committee as much as possible,
and we want to keep the whole episode within its proper
proportions—so what we are doing is done in this informal
manner because of that. Our aim in presenting these recommendations is, first, to try to help clarify two questions: First, the
objective logic of artificial factionalism and, second, the question
of freedom of criticism in the organization and the duties of the
leadership in answering critics and in providing the atmosphere
and securing freedom of criticism in actuality as well as in
formality.

Our second aim is to promote peace and the restoration of
harmonious relations between the comrades who have been
engaged in the recent war between the states, as they say in the
South. I say peace in a very inoffensive manner, but you must not

take that as a pacifist attitude on our part. We are like the Irishman back in Kansas City who said he was going to have peace, by God, if he had to fight for it. More or less, that is our attitude.

Now, on the question of why factionalism and factional atmosphere are out of place in the present situation in the New York organization, I want to give you some arguments which we have discussed. The record of the New York organization during the past year, since the past convention, has shown progress in the most important fields. New York has many, or I think even more than its quota of new members compared to the organization nationally. The work of proletarianization, integrating the comrades in the factories and unions, which we considered the foremost problem and task of the party here, was carried out not badly. The work of the whole year was in general accord with the party line. We have never had any occasion during the past year to bring any serious criticism against the political activities of the New York organization. Now this we consider to be the outstanding fact in the whole situation—that ought to outweigh all other considerations. When a local organization is going forward and is not committing any serious political errors, there isn't much ground for any serious opposition from the party. That isn't to say that there have not been differences and that the differences didn't have their own legitimacy—not at all. But as we have examined these differences as presented in the convention, and discussed there, we have to tell you that they are not greater than the usual differences that occur in any normally functioning party organization, including the National Committee; rather, less.

The New York delegation unanimously supported the political resolution of the national convention; the report of the City Committee was a unanimous report, and also was voted for unanimously by the convention. All these are convincing proofs that there is political unity in the New York organization on the most important questions. Consequently, in the differences that have been discussed—which are not greater, as we say, but rather less than you can normally expect to accumulate in the year's functioning of an ordinary party organization anywhere—there is no ground for any really serious opposition, and certainly no ground for any concerted opposition, in view of the fact that not all the comrades had the same criticisms: some were on one point, some on another. What is dangerous in the situation was a tendency toward a concert of the various critics, the generation of a factional atmosphere which, if allowed to run its course without some guidance and instruction in such matters, could lead by its objective logic only to one place, and that is to the blind alley of artificial and unprincipled factional formations, which are known in our movement as cliques.

When it is said, as I said it at the [city] convention, that the objective logic of such tendencies is the development of unprincipled factional formations or cliques, that is not meant at all to accuse specific comrades, either individuals or in numbers, of a conscious or deliberate plan of such organization or activity. That is not to be taken that way. It is to be taken only as a warning of the objective logic of these tendencies. And we think that if that warning is taken properly, the question can be eliminated.

Now, the second point upon which we want to clarify our position is on the question of freedom of criticism within the ranks of the organization. This is a very serious and important point. We are not only a centralized and disciplined party, but we are also a democratic party and what we need at all times is the proper harmony and equilibrium of these two elements of democratic centralism: freedom of criticism, and at the same time, discipline and centralization. And we have to define the rights and limits of party discussion correctly so there can be no question about it. When we say that criticism and discussion in our party are free, we do not mean to say that we are a bohemian discussion club. We don't want any anarchistic claims to discuss at all hours of the day or night, year in and out, after conventions and before. We have had such experiences in our movement and a lot of fights about it, but that has nothing to do with democratic centralism. That is anarchy. I think it goes without saying for all comrades educated in our movement that discussion which is carried to the convention and differences which were considered by the convention have to discontinue when the convention adjourns. If we could go on the day following the convention as though nothing had happened, then there is no sense in having conventions. The criticisms that were made at the convention and considered there must properly be discontinued in the next period out of respect for the party as a whole and the party convention.

But that does not mean to say that the party has to be transformed, then, into one of these religious orders or prisons where the silence rule is observed. Not at all. Everything has to be done intelligently and that doesn't apply at all to new differences that may arise, new differences of opinion. And we have always in our party tradition, a tradition we have always cherished, the tradition of keeping not only the formal right of criticism, but the proper atmosphere for it. It is perfectly possible for slick leaders to write ten constitutions guaranteeing freedom of criticism in a party and then create an atmosphere of moral terrorization whereby a young or inexperienced comrade doesn't want to open his mouth for fear he will be made a fool of, or sat on, or accused of some political deviation he doesn't have in his mind at all. Every criticism must receive comradely consideration from the leaders. An atmosphere must prevail where even the newest and greenest member feels free to get up and state his criticism. That is a point which the National Committee discussed and thought should be made clear alongside of the other fundamental point I have discussed concerning factionalism.

It is quite possible that excesses have been committed on both sides of these questions, some sharpness of expression that doesn't take place in normal times, perhaps some excesses. We are not in a position to judge because we don't attend all the party meetings. But the mere feeling of some comrades that such things have taken place justifies us, I think, in saying that, in our opinion, we had better lean backward on this question. If there is the slightest feeling in the ranks of the organization that criticisms will not be attentively heard and received, or that every effort would not be made in the future to give satisfaction to any comrade or group of comrades who bring complaints to the party, then we have to turn the rudder the other way and eliminate every fear or suspicion of that kind. We want to have a disciplined and centralized party, but we want to have one with a free, comradely atmosphere and I am sure that this will be carried out.

Now I come to the question of why peace should be made now in regard to the recent unpleasantness; why it should be crossed off and relegated to the past. There is a basic political motivation, and not mere sentimentalism at all, even though we are talking in that season of the year. That is not it. It is more serious than that, because that is only temporary with them until the holidays are over. But we would like to have it a little more permanent.

The basic political motivation for our recommendation of peace and the restoration of comradely and friendly relations among all the comrades are the following:

1. All the questions which were in dispute are unripe for any further controversy. The most that can be said from a political point of view on either side is that one could discern certain tendencies in one direction or another which might in the future develop along a certain line and crystallize into a deviation—a serious deviation. For example, the generalization in some of the documents and in some of the unofficial and informal criticism that [there has been] a nonpolitical approach to questions on the part of the leadership; and on the other side, a generalization either formal or informal that the critical comrades represented a petty-bourgeois approach to questions. Both these questions, I say, are by no means sufficiently clear and fully developed to warrant or even make possible a serious fight along these lines.

It is one thing to say, for example, that the tendencies manifested in the convention toward concerted opposition without a serious political motivation and similar tendencies which were manifested even before the convention—it is one thing to say that the objective logic of this practice may lead in the long run to an unprincipled faction formation. To say that it is now a fully crystallized unprincipled faction is another. You can't fight it out on that basis because the comrades deny any such formation or intention and further fight about the question can only degenerate into recriminations, accusations, and denials. Similarly, on the question of the nonpolitical approach, generalizations contained in the documents of Comrade [Abe] Stein and the other two comrades. They made some concrete criticisms and then proceeded to generalize that this shows a lack of appreciation of the problems from a political point of view. I think that is a hasty generalization too. At any rate, there is not sufficient [evidence] to demonstrate it. And if you continue the fight you will only set the party backward and not forward. You must wait, even if one feels in his bones that this tendency will develop full-flowered in the direction you suspect, you must wait until it is a little clearer to the rest of the party and you cannot conduct a fight in the party on this basis. That applies on both elements of the question.

Therefore we say that the dispute now has to be discontinued, the controversy discontinued, and in the course of common work and practical cooperation, we have to have further experience in order to demonstrate whether the incipient tendencies are absorbed and done away with, or whether they develop such lines as to necessitate a further political struggle. So because we say both these questions, these generalizations, are premature and the tendencies upon which they are based are by no means fully developed, the controversy should be discontinued.

The second reason for discontinuing the fight now is to give all the comrades involved who may have made some errors a chance to correct themselves without any humiliation, without dragging the thing out endlessly, and affecting their standing and injuring their feelings. Anybody who had made a mistake and wants to correct it has done all that a political person can ask of him. If he wants to do it quietly, that is all right. We don't want to have disputes in the party develop in such way that in every little dispute there are victors and vanquished. We must not forget that even in conducting disputes over the most serious political questions, we are not two rival classes fighting, we are a communist family discussing differences among ourselves and we must keep that in mind all the time and regulate our attitude accordingly. And how much more does this have to be taken into consideration in discussing these comparatively minor and trivial disputes which have divided the comrades in New York!

Members of the party, especially new members, can't learn anything from prolonged faction fighting over issues that are not clear. The only thing that can result from such struggles over issues not absolutely clear to the new members is poisoning the atmosphere, lining people up on one side or another, not according to what they have learned in the political sense, but on a personal basis with the result that the atmosphere of the organization is poisoned and the issues not clarified. I am telling you this as a result of a good deal of observation and experience in the past, and some instructions also from a great teacher.

We had a lot of fights in the communist movement since 1919 and even in the early days of the Left Opposition, and some of them were very intense. At one time in the early days, the so-called Cannon-Shachtman fight, which was conducted with all the intensity of the final struggle with the petty-bourgeois opposition and even with more acrimony—in that struggle Comrade Trotsky made the comment that the two factions each anticipated too much.[90] They fought each other not on the ground of the political merits and qualities which were fully demonstrated as of that day, but from a point of view of a generalization as to what the ultimate development of the political tendencies on each side would come to. And he said when you anticipate too much and fight over issues that are not clear to the members, you result only in a poisonous and almost insoluble factional situation and don't educate the new members. In such a situation, Comrade Trotsky said, the most progressive tendency is the conciliatory tendency—those who propose to make peace and test out in further common action what is the basis and merit of the accusations on each side. That advice of Comrade Trotsky was accepted in the old fight. Some people accepted it diplomatically and some honestly, but, in general, the prescription was to plunge the party into mass work, stop the faction struggle, disband the faction organizations, and test out in political action what were the tendencies of the two groups.

And eventually we came to a solution of it in the year 1940—but the fight had begun ten years before, and if we had tried to solve it in 1933 by means of a split—which is the only way you can solve irreconcilable faction fights—there is no way the movement might have profited by it, because we would have had to explain to the workers outside the movement what the fight was about. And if we couldn't make this clear to comrades inside the party how could we make it clear to the nonparty people we wanted to join? The result would have been the stagnation of the movement as was the case in England.

We have a way of conducting disputes in the Trotskyist party. We ought to know how to do it, and do it properly. The way, especially [in the case of] a dispute in its incipiency, in its beginning, is first to set precise aims for the dispute, determine how much of a difference has been established, how clear it is, and what one demands in the situation. If you have a dispute as to whether you should rent another floor in the headquarters or economize, we don't conduct that dispute with the intensity that you fight over the principles of trade unionism, for example. But sometimes inexperienced people do. It doesn't merit that. Such a dispute normally should be settled by taking a vote in the committee or branch, and then letting the majority decide, and let experience teach further. I cite this as an extreme illustration.

Precise aims should be set for the dispute and the dispute limited to these aims. If the aim is to correct what one considers to be a disorganization of the branches by shifting people around a good deal, more will be gained by fighting on this question than by formulating a thesis that shows that from this little incident. . . . If you do that, if you set precise aims for the dispute and limit it to the acceptance of those aims, and then take into consideration the necessity of helping membership to learn from these disputes and not to be confused by them, and avoid premature generalizations, I believe that in the next year— if God saves us from more differences of opinion on current questions— they can be disposed of as routine matters, or at least with less distubance than this year.

It would be a funny committee, if you stopped to think about it, who all come to the same opinion at the same hour on every question. But our National Committee had enough experience with these matters to keep in mind fundamental questions and our fundamental unity. We were able to go to the national convention with a unanimous political resolution and to give the party throughout the entire country a demonstration of unity and harmony in the leadership. And don't underestimate the importance of that to the party. The party values that in the national leadership and values it in the local leadership too. There are tremendous wastes in factionalism; [it is] the main problem of every organization outside of ours. That may sound like a tremendously drastic statement, but it is an axiom among all organizers and leaders that the biggest problem is keeping their own forces in order, keeping them from flying about.

I was a member of the communist movement of the United States from 1919 and this movement was different from other voluntary organizations only in that it was better because it had the most idealistic people in it and more self-sacrificing and selfless people in it than the churches and lodges, etc. Yet the United States communist movement in all the years I belonged to it consumed not less than 75 percent of its energies on unnecessary factional struggles, personal friction, animosities, clique fights, etc. When disputes developed in the beginning, as they invariably did, people didn't know any other way than to start a fuss about it, gather people around them to help them fight for this or that issue, and these formations always—and this is the terrible logic of unprincipled or unmotivated factionalism—these formations always create counterorganizations, and the party from top to bottom becomes wracked by these factional formations, sometimes formed only over episodic matters.

And the internal life of the party year after year was devoured by this corrosion of unprincipled and unnecessary factionalism.

That led the CP the only place it could lead—into a complete blind alley in the end, when people who didn't want to be fighting all the time, especially when they didn't have anything very important to fight about, fell out of the party in great numbers. A lot of people dropped out—I don't say they were the best—perhaps the best were those who endured and stuck it out in spite of everything in discouragement and despair over the. . . .

THE END OF THE COMINTERN
AND THE PROSPECTS OF
LABOR INTERNATIONALISM[91]

May 30, 1943

*This speech to a meeting at Irving Plaza, New York, was given
shortly after the Communist International was dissolved. It was
published in the June 12, 1943, Militant.*

Comrade Chairman; Comrades:

The formal dissolution of the Communist International is
undoubtedly an event of great historical significance, even
though everybody understands that it is simply the formal
certification of a fact that was long since accomplished. Some of
the bourgeois commentators and politicians may exaggerate a bit
when they speak of the dissolution of the Communist International as the greatest political event since the beginning of the
war. But, in any case, there is no question of its transcendent
importance. This is recognized on every side, and the event has
called forth discussion from every quarter.

There are two ways to view the question. One is from the
standpoint of the United States and Allied capitalist powers in
their war against the Axis powers and their struggle to maintain
the capitalist system of oppression of the workers in the home
countries and enslavement of the great masses of the colonial
world. The other standpoint from which the dissolution of the
Comintern can be discussed is from the standpoint of the
liberation struggle of the workers, which has had a conscious
expression now for ninety-five years, since the publication of the
Communist Manifesto in 1848.

The discussion has all been one-sided so far. All the discussion

335

outside our ranks begins from the premise of its effect upon the fortunes of American imperialism, with particular reference to the war. It is remarkable how so many people, in so many supposedly different camps, take this as their starting point in analyzing the burial of the Comintern. It was to be expected that the bourgeois press would take this point of view because all their interests lie in that direction. But we notice also that such labor leaders as have pronounced themselves show the same bias. They inquire, with straight faces, whether Stalin's action is sincerely meant as a gesture of help and cooperation with our war leaders in Washington and London, or whether it is a mere maneuver. No other aspects of the question seem to concern them.

The same thing is true of the Social Democratic press. You might think that people who used to have an International of their own would have something to say about the unburied corpse of the Second International, but they pass over that as a matter of no interest. Perhaps they are right in this respect. They sagely discuss the recent events in Moscow and put seriously to themselves—these "socialists"—the question: Will this help America in the war or not?

Even the Stalinists, who up to a few days ago were the adherents and representatives—even if not formally, owing to the Voorhis law—of the Communist International, solemnly discuss the action like imitation congressmen. They defend the burial of the Comintern without reference to its effect on the struggle of the workers for better conditions and eventual liberation—the original aim of the Comintern—but solely from the point of view of the interests of the American ruling class. Browder writes a letter to the *New York Times* and attempts to reassure this extremely perspicacious organ of America's Sixty Families that the action taken in Moscow is in good faith and in their interests, and that it is not quite sporting of them to raise a questioning eyebrow about the fact.

So far nobody has discussed the question from the point of view which brought the Communist International into existence, that is, from the point of view of organizing and furthering the worldwide struggle of the proletariat for emancipation from capitalism. But it is this point of view that I want to bring to the discussion here this evening.

Of course, the announcement of the formal dissolution of the Comintern is simply the news account of a burial that is ten years overdue. It serves a certain purpose in that it puts an end to a fiction and clears the air of illusions and misunderstandings, to say nothing of very bad odors.

This belated burial of the corpse of the Comintern is a climax, we might say, to a long sequence of events which has extended over two decades. These events, in their highlights, can be noted: the death of Lenin; the promulgation for the first time, in 1924, of the theory of socialism in one country; the bureaucratization of the Comintern and all of its parties; the expulsion of the Bolshevik-Leninist Opposition, first in the Russian party and then in the other parties of the Comintern; the capitulation of the Communist Party of Germany, with its 600,000 members and its six million voters, without a struggle and without a fight, to Hitler fascism in 1933; the organized, systematic betrayal of the proletariat of the world in the interest of the diplomatic policy of the Kremlin; the murder of the Old Bolsheviks; the assassination of Trotsky; the betrayal of the proletariat in the Second World War, first to Hitler and then to Roosevelt and Churchill.

Since the beginning of the war the Comintern, the unburied Comintern, was silent as the grave. Now it is formally buried, and that, at least, is a good thing. It is somewhat late, but the old proverb says, "better late than never." By the formal burial of the Comintern, Stalin, for once on the international arena, has unconsciously performed a progressive act.

The bourgeois press and public generally, the political leaders and spokesmen, are very well pleased with the recent pronouncement, even if they understand that it is only a formality. They have good reason to be pleased. The dissolution of the Comintern, and the cynical repudiation of internationalism and the international proletarian organization, is an ideological victory of vast importance for capitalism and reactionary nationalism. They have been quite true to their interests in hailing this action and pushing aside the quibblers who wonder if, after all, it isn't another maneuver.

They have good reason to applaud the action of Stalin, taken through his puppets in the so-called Executive Committee of the nonexistent Comintern, because the renunciation of internationalism is a renunciation of the basic premises of scientific socialism. It is a renunciation of the cardinal doctrine which has guided and inspired the struggle of the workers for generations, since Marx's day. The modern movement of international socialism began with the *Communist Manifesto* in 1848, ninety-five years ago, with its battle cry: Workers of the World Unite!

The *Communist Manifesto* proclaimed the doctrine that the emancipation of the workers could be achieved only by their common actions on an international scale. Against the cardinal principle and battle cry of Marx and Engels, and of all revolutionary socialists since that time—Workers of the World Unite!—Stalin has announced a motto of his own: Disband your international organization; give up all thought of international collaboration; support your own imperialists; and confine your activities to the national framework of the country in which you are enslaved.

Internationalism was not a dogma invented by Marx and Engels, but a recognition of the reality of the modern world. It proceeds from the fact that the economy of modern society is a world unit requiring international cooperation and division of labor for the further development of the productive forces. The class struggle arising from the class division between workers and exploiters within the countries requires class unity of the workers on an international scale. From the beginning, the program of scientific socialism has called for the international collaboration of the workers and oppressed peoples in the different countries, with all their different levels of development, in order that each might contribute their strength as well as their weakness to a unified world program and world cooperative action. The *Communist Manifesto* called for common efforts of the workers in all countries for the common goal of workers' emancipation.

After the downfall of feudalism, the national states played a progressive role as the arena for the development and expansion of the forces of production in the heyday of capitalism. But these very national states, whose sanctity is proclaimed by Stalin in 1943, became obsolete long ago. They have become barriers to the full operation of the productive forces and the source of inevitable wars. The whole pressure of historic necessity is for the breaking down of the artificial national barriers, not for their preservation.

Just as the petty states and principalities and arbitrarily divided sections of the old countries under feudalism had to give way to the consolidated, centralized national states in order to create a broader arena for the development of the productive forces, so, in the same way, the artificially divided national states have to give way to the federation of states. In the future course of development this must lead eventually to a world federation operating world economy as a whole without class and nationalistic divisions. From this it follows irrevocably that such an order can be created only by the international collaboration and the joint struggle of the workers in the various countries against their own bourgeoisie at home and against capitalism as a world system. So preached and so practiced the great founders of socialism, Marx and Engels; so preached and practiced their great continuators, Lenin and Trotsky.

Among the immortal achievements of Marx as a revolutionist, side by side with his monumental work on capital, will always stand his creative labor in the building of the first international organization of the workers, the International Workingmen's Association. From the time that the ideas of internationalism were propounded in the *Communist Manifesto* to their first realization in 1864 in the First International, up until the present time, the conflict within the labor movement between revolutionists and reformists has revolved around this fundamental question. At the heart of every dispute, socialist internationalism on the one side has been contrasted to nationalistic concepts on the other.

We can see in the whole period down to the present day the deadly parallel between revolutionary internationalism, pointing the way to the socialist future, and opportunistic adaptation to the decaying order of capitalism. Marx and Engels were the champions of this idea of internationalism and of corresponding action. The nationally limited, narrow-minded trade union reformists of Britain and other places renounced the idea of internationalism. With the idea of gaining small favors for the day at the expense of the interests of the class as a whole and of the future, conservative trade unionism, even in Marx's day, took a nationalistic form and had a nationalistic outlook. In the First World War of 1914–18, the great resounding struggle which took place between the revolutionary wing, headed by Lenin and Trotsky, on the one side, and Kautsky & Co. on the other, had as its great criterion, its touchstone, the question of international organization.

Lenin, the Russian, living as an emigre in Switzerland, with no more than a dozen or two followers that he could name and place, rose up against the whole so-called Second International and the Social Democratic parties in the war. He rose up against the bourgeois world and announced the necessity for the Third International in 1914. Similarly, in the period of the decline and eventual decay and death, up to the formal burial of the

Communist International, the great dividing line between the real inheritors of Marx and Lenin on the one side, and Stalin and his cohorts on the other, has been this principle we are discussing here tonight—the principle of internationalism.

Since it was first proclaimed nearly a century ago, in the historic ebb and flow the idea of internationalism and the organization of the international workers has suffered three great defeats. The organizations have been destroyed, but always the idea rose again after each defeat, corresponding to historical necessity, and found the necessary organizational form on higher ground.

The First International, that is, the International of Marx and Engels, was founded formally in 1864. Seven years later came the tragic defeat of the Paris Commune.[92] Along with that great defeat and the great impetus it gave to reaction on the continent of Europe, there was the unprecedented rise and expansion of capitalist industry. The productive forces began to expand and develop on a capitalist basis at an unprecedented rate. This temporarily weakened the revolutionary movement. It was the expansion of capitalism still reaching toward its apex of development which decreed the end of the First International by its formal dissolution in 1876. But the First International didn't die like the Second or like the Comintern. It was dissolved with its honor unsullied. It remained an inspiration and an ideal which still continued to work in the vanguard circles of the workers and in time bore good fruit.

The Second International followed. It was formally launched in Paris in 1889, thirteen years after the formal end of the First International, and died as a revolutionary organization on the fourth of August, 1914. The fourth of August was the day when the Social Democratic deputies in the Reichstag voted for the war credits of German imperialism. But between the manner and form of the end of the Second International and that of the First, there is a great contrast that we should not forget. The First International succumbed to external conditions, to the defeats, the spread of reaction, and the expanding development of the capitalist productive system. It went down gloriously. The Second International, on the contrary, ended as a result of the betrayal of the leadership in a period when capitalism had already long passed its peak and had entered into its decline and bankruptcy. The Second International capitulated at a time when the necessity and urgency of international revolutionary organization were a thousand times more apparent than in the case of the First International.

The Third International was born of war and revolution and struggle against nationalism in March 1919, twenty-four years ago. This International, too, died ignominiously from a false theory, from capitulation and betrayal, and is buried in 1943, without honors, without regrets.

As far as the revolutionary vanguard of the proletariat is concerned, the formal event was anticipated and nobody was taken by surprise. We have been struggling against the national degeneration of the Comintern for a long time. This struggle, as a matter of fact, began in 1923. That is twenty years ago. It is startling in these days, in contemplation of this final ceremony of burying the nonexistent Comintern, to read the polemics of Trotsky written twenty years ago in Russia. At the very first signs of national degeneration, Trotsky, like a physician, put his finger on the pulse of the organization and detected the fever of nationalism and pointed out what it was and what it would lead to. He began a struggle twenty years ago in the name of internationalism against the theory of socialism in one country, against the conception that the workers could find any other way to salvation except through international organization and joint struggle against capitalism on a world scale.

This fight began in the factional and ideological disputes of 1923. The fight took international form in 1930 in the organization of the International Communist League,[93] shortly after Trotsky was exiled from Russia and began, from his refuge in Turkey, to communicate with cothinkers on a world scale. The unceasing struggle of Trotsky and his disciples was climaxed by the world congress of the Fourth International in 1938.

Trotsky, the unfailing champion of internationalism in the uncompromising struggle against every form and trace of nationalist degeneration, was finally assassinated by an agent of Stalin. But his imperishable ideas are incorporated in the new international organization of the communist workers, the Fourth International.

Stalin's action, formally dissolving the Comintern, was taken in the midst of the Second World War, an appropriate time. The international organization which was presumably formed to enable the workers to take advantage of the difficulties of national capitalist states to promote the international revolution, is dissolved with a cynical explanation that it doesn't fit the conditions of the war. Kautsky, in 1915, explaining the collapse of the Second International when the war started, said that the International is an instrument of peace, not of war. Kautsky was the originator of this monstrous theory. Stalin simply repeats it, nearly thirty years later when it is thirty times more false.

Lenin said in 1914: *"Because of the war,* we must build the Third International in order to coordinate the activities of the workers in struggling against the war and in all that will follow from it."* Stalin says to the workers of the world in 1943: *"Because of the war,* dissolve international organization and confine yourselves to the framework of your own bourgeois fatherland."* In this contrast between the words of Lenin, who thought the war was a means of underscoring and emphasizing the necessity for an international organization of workers, and the words of Stalin, who says the war is a sufficient reason to disband international organization—in this contrast you have the measure of the two men and of what they represent in history.

Already in 1914 the First World War had demonstrated beyond all question that the bourgeois national states, as an arena for the development of the productive forces of mankind, were already outlived and had to give way to a broader basis. National capitalism had already entered into its bankruptcy in that time, more than twenty years ago. The most tragic expression of the bankruptcy of capitalism was the fact that it could find no other way out of the conflicts between outlived national states than in the explosion of the terrible war that cost ten million lives and crippled and maimed twenty million more.

And it was precisely the demonstration by the terrible fact of the war, it was precisely the war that caused Lenin and Trotsky, and such as they, to realize that even the Second International as it had existed before the war—as a rather loose federation of national parties—could not be rebuilt. As Trotsky expressed it, the war had sounded the death knell of national programs for workers' parties. They drew the lesson from the experience of the last world war, 1914-18, not only that the workers must reconstitute their organization on an international scale, but also that they must base this reorganization on an international program and not on the sum of national programs.

Thus, the war of 1914, which signalized the bankruptcy of the national capitalist states, was, in the eyes of Lenin and Trotsky, the greatest motivation for an extension of the idea of internationalism in program as well as in form of organization. Now, a quarter of a century later, when the bankruptcy of capitalism has developed into its death agony, when an explosion takes place in the form of a Second World War, an even more tragic loss in human life and material culture—now, after this, Stalin and his traitor gang have the cynical effrontery to tell the workers that there is no need of international cooperation and international organization.

There isn't a shadow of logic or reason, if you proceed from the point of view of socialism and the cause of the proletariat, in any of the explanations given by the Stalinists for the renunciation of internationalism. The explanation given by the bourgeois press and bourgeois political leaders is more correct and honest because it frankly proceeds from the point of view that is of interest to them, that is, to the capitalist world order, and they can see in it a very good thing. But that it is no good for the workers is quite obvious.

Even the bourgeoisie recognize internationalism in their own way. The bankruptcy of the national limitedness has become so clear to the bourgeoisie that all their most perspicacious leaders have been compelled to renounce the idea of national isolation altogether. Isolationism as a political tendency stands discredited in bourgeois politics. And in this situation, in this terrible war that is caused by the artificial prolongation of the life of national states as separate economic units, Stalin and his puppets tell the workers: "Confine your efforts to the national limits in which you find yourselves. Support one set of bandits against another set of bandits." That, workers of the world, heirs of Marx and Engels, heirs of Lenin and Trotsky and the Russian Revolution, that is your destiny in 1943, pronounced by Stalin and his gang.

This treacherous advice not only defies Marxist doctrine and tradition but it violates the most fundamental features of the prevailing world situation. It betrays the workers in the metropolitan centers and even omits any mention of the many-millioned masses in the colonies and the semicolonies who were awakened by the Russian Revolution and the Communist International to the struggle for life and freedom.

I think that the frankest and most heartfelt expressions of opinion by the chosen leaders of the democratic world bourgeoisie—Mr. Churchill and Mr. Roosevelt—really were off the record. They didn't have the heart to put down in public print what they really think of Stalin and his order dissolving the Comintern. They could only make fun of the explanation that the time has come in 1943 to go back to the national boroughs and forget the world arena at the very moment when they, the leaders of the bourgeoisie, are looking over the whole world and talking only in global terms. Stalin's explanation, intended to deceive trusting workers, can cause only the most cynical amusement to Churchill and Roosevelt, tinged with contempt plus a little appreciation for a very valuable favor. They at least have no illusions about national limitations either of economy or of politics, and certainly not of war.

If you take down from the bookshelf that imposing library of polemics, manifestos, appeals, and analyses written by Lenin from the fourth of August, 1914, on, you see running through the whole collection, like a red thread, the idea of internationalism. His manifesto, the manifesto of the Bolshevik Central Committee against the war, raised the demand already in 1914 for the creation of the new Third International. His atttitude led him and the Bolsheviks to the Zimmerwald Conference in 1915, to Kienthal in 1916, and then to the revolution in 1917 in Russia.[94]

Now, in all the plans of the Social Democrats, to say nothing of the imperialists, in 1914—in all their plans to do away with international organization, to harness the workers to the war machines of their respective capitalist masters in the different countries, the one thing that was not counted upon occurred in Russia, a little surprise—merely a revolution. The revolution that first overthrew the tsar in February and then overthrew the bourgeoisie in October was one of those unheralded events of the past world war which upset all calculations.

We do not see any mention of that in the order of dissolution, as we may call it. There is no talk about revolution. There is no talk about socialism. There is no talk about anything except winning the war against Hitler. Lenin's steps, from 1914 on, led through these events I have mentioned to the Russian Revolution, the conquest of power by the proletariat of Russia, supported by the peasantry and led by the Bolshevik party of Lenin. That didn't end Lenin's fight against the theory of Kautsky, that internationalism is an instrument of peace, not of war. In view of the collapse and bankruptcy of capitalism, as well as in anticipation of another war, Lenin and his party sponsored in 1919 the formation of the Comintern.

So, you see, throughout the whole course of Lenin's work, his manifesto after the betrayal of the German Social Democracy, his participation in the conferences at Zimmerwald and Kienthal, in the revolution of 1917, and the formation of the Comintern in 1919—every act of Lenin from first to last took place under the banner of internationalism. The premises of the Third International were that the dissolution and collapse of the capitalist world order made necessary the organization of the proletariat for the seizure of power in the capitalist states, the federation of the socialist states into a world federation, and the inauguration of the world socialist order.

Lenin saw the Russian Revolution as only the beginning of this worldwide process. Lenin and Trotsky and the Bolshevik party as a whole understood that Russia could not stand isolated in a capitalist world; it could not remain as a national utopia. They saw it as a fortress of the world proletariat. Their policy was to unite the Soviet Union, representing the fortress of the world proletariat, with its allies in the world. And who were the allies of the Soviets as Lenin and Trotsky saw them? Not Churchill. And not even Roosevelt. Their allies were the world proletariat in the developed capitalist countries, and the colonial peoples. Under this leadership the workers of the war-torn countries lifted their heads again. They were reinspired with socialist ideas. They reorganized their ranks. They formed new revolutionary parties. They made heroic attempts at revolution in Europe. The colonial masses were awakened for the first time to political life, to revolt against age-old slavery, and were inspired to throw off the imperialist yoke altogether.

Such was the course of development under Lenin's leadership of the Comintern. Under Stalin's leadership, which was tainted from the start with narrow-minded nationalism, the world movement was betrayed; the Soviet Union was isolated; the services of the Comintern and its parties were sold like potatoes on the market to the various camps of imperialists for dubious pacts, for dribbles of material aid, at a very cheap price. Lenin and Stalin—the creator of the Third International and its gravedigger—these two represented ideas and actions which are in polar opposition to each other. They can in no way be reconciled. I notice that while they had the effrontery to refer to Marx in the order dissolving the Comintern, they left unmentioned its founder. That, at least, was a wise omission, because Lenin's name would have been out of place there, as Marx's was also.

In the course of twenty years, from 1924, when the fatal theory of socialism in one country was first promulgated, to the sorry, dishonorable end of the Comintern in 1943, in that whole tragic degeneration, we can see above everything else the decisive role of theory in political action. Stalin didn't begin with the dissolution of the Comintern. He began with the theory of socialism in one country. From this false theory everything else has followed—the betrayal of the world proletariat, the isolation of the USSR behind her national barriers, the purges, the Moscow trials, the mass murders, the assassinations, and finally the dissolution of the Comintern.

There is a profound lesson in this terrible sequence of events for all the generation of the young proletariat awakening to political interest and political life. Trotsky explained it in 1928 in his book, which was here referred to by the chairman. In the "Criticism of the Draft Program of the Comintern" [in *Third International After Lenin*] he explained to the communist workers of Russia and the world that precisely this theory of socialism in one country, with its inevitable nationalistic implications, would inevitably lead to the degeneration and downfall of the Comintern. When this was written fifteen years ago, the great majority of Communists considered this a great exaggeration and even an insult to Stalin and his co-workers in the Russian party. But Trotsky, who did not impute design but only ignorance to these people at that time, explained that good intentions cannot help you in politics, if you proceed from a false theory. It is like a mariner setting a false course that can only lead the ship to an unintended destination.

The struggle against the theory of socialism in one country was conducted in the name of internationalism. And in the name of internationalism Trotsky and his disciples struggled against its disastrous consequences, as they began to reveal themselves in life. As the tragic course of events unfolded, Trotsky, step by step, analyzed; he explained; he threw the Marxist light on all the great events as they happened, before they happened; and afterwards he drew the necessary conclusions. He was not deterred by persecution; he was not dismayed by the fewness of those who surrounded him, nor by the renegacy of others, nor by the sneers of philistines.

Trotsky did not consider in the first place numbers, popularity, success of the moment, any more than did Marx and Engels, and Lenin. He considered historical necessity. He considered the task of formulating for the proletariat the program showing the shortest road to the realization of its historical goal. His work and struggle bore fruit in the creation of an international nucleus of revolutionary fighters, and eventually in the formal organization of the Fourth International, in the world congress in 1938.

At the time it was formed, the great politicians of the mass parties of the Social Democracy used to sneer at Trotsky's little handful and his insignificant Fourth International. The heroes of the London Bureau, the centrists who, if they could not organize mass parties could at least talk about them, used to argue against Trotsky that he didn't have many followers. And the Stalinists, backed by the limitless material resources of the Soviet Union, with money, a tremendous apparatus, a subsidized bureaucracy, and the GPU murder machine at their disposal—with all this tremendous weight at their side, they derided, hounded, and persecuted Trotsky and the Fourth International.

But in the brief period since the Founding Congress of the Fourth International, in a brief five years, every other international organization of the workers has been hurled down to ruin as Trotsky predicted they would be, without one stone left standing on another. This was the fate of the Second International of the Social Democracy, of the London Bureau of the centrists, and now it is the fate of the Stalinists, admitted and acknowledged by themselves. They have all been destroyed by the war, as Trotsky said they would be. But the Fourth International remains. And with it lives the principle of internationalism, which alone can show the tortured masses of the world the way out of war and slavery to the socialist future of humanity.

In this past period since 1864, each international organization of the workers, in passing from the historical scene, left something accomplished, left something behind upon which its successor could build for the future.

The First International left an imperishable ideal, an unsullied record, as an inspiration for the workers from that day to this, a glorious memory.

The Second International died ignominiously through betrayal in 1914. Nevertheless, in the period from 1889 to that fatal day in August twenty-five years later, it built great mass organizations of the workers, and handed on experience in organization of incalculable value, upon which the Third International was able to build. Also, the initial cadres of the Third International didn't fall from the sky. They came right out of the heart of the Second International. Thus, in spite of everything, the Second International left a great heritage.

The Third International, which has ended now in shame and disgrace, has nevertheless left behind the richest treasures for the future. Its founders, Lenin and Trotsky, belong to us; nobody can dissolve the tie that binds the new generation of revolutionary workers to Lenin and Trotsky, to their teachings, their example, their beautiful memory. The record of the long internal struggle from 1923 to this date, the struggle of Trotsky and his cothinkers and disciples, belongs to the proletariat of the world. The record of that struggle is the basic literature upon which the whole new generation which is destined to lead the world will be educated and trained. The first four congresses of the Comintern, held under Lenin's leadership in 1919, 1920, 1921, 1922—four congresses in four years—produced documents which are the basic program of the movement that we uphold today.

And, in addition to that, out of the Third International, before it died and long before it was buried, came the initiating cadres of the Fourth International. Thus, looking at the thing always from the standpoint of the international proletariat and disregarding no elements in the whole survey, whether they are positive or negative, we have a right to say that the balance sheet of the Communist International, in spite of everything, shows a great historical credit balance.

Stalin can bury the dead organization but he cannot bury the great progressive work the Comintern accomplished in its first years. He cannot bury the Fourth International, which has risen, phoenix-like, from the ashes of the Third. We know very well and we don't try to conceal the fact that the numbers of the Fourth International are small. But its ideas are correct, its program represents historical necessity, and, therefore, its victory is assured. Its program consciously formulates the instinctive demands of the workers and the colonial peoples for emancipation from capitalism, fascism, and war.

Even today, striking workers who never even heard of the Fourth International, are denounced as "Trotskyists" whenever they stand up for their rights, just as the workers and soldiers in Russia in 1917 under Kerensky were denounced on every side as "Bolsheviks" and heard then, for the first time in the denunciations, the word "Bolshevik." Trotsky relates in his *History of the Russian Revolution* how they began to say to themselves, "If what they are accusing us of is Bolshevism, then we had better be Bolsheviks."

So it will be again wherever workers stand up for their rights, express their instinctive will to struggle for a better future, and are denounced as Trotskyists. In good time they will learn the name of the Fourth International, its meaning, its program, and ally themselves with it.

No one can dissolve the Fourth International. It is the real Comintern and it will keep the banner unfurled in the faces of all traitors and renegades. And we assert confidently that it will be strengthened and grow and triumph until its organized ranks merge with the whole mass of humanity. The song that no Stalin can render obsolete ends its chorus with the words: "The International shall be the human race." And this chorus has a profound political meaning. It is not merely a poetical expression.

The peoples of the world in the various countries, through coordinated international effort, will pass, in their great historic march from capitalism to socialism, through the transitional period of the dictatorship of the proletariat. As they progress toward the completely classless socialist society, all the various workers' organizations which have been instruments and mechanisms of the class struggle, that is, the parties, the unions, the cooperatives, the soviets, will gradually lose their original functions. As the classes are abolished and class struggles consequently ended, all these instruments of class struggle will tend to coalesce into one united body. And that one united body will be the organized world society of the free and equal. The International shall really be the human race.

We disciples of Marx, Lenin, and Trotsky, we partisans of the Fourth International, retain undimmed that vision of the future. To see that vision even now, to see it clearly through the fire and the smoke of the war, is simply to be in accord with historical development, to foresee the inevitable march of events and to prepare for them. To fight for this vision of the socialist future, to hasten its realization, is the highest privilege and the greatest happiness for a civilized man or woman in the world today.

THE PROBLEM OF PARTY
LEADERSHIP[95]

November 1, 1943

*This was a speech to the Fifteenth Anniversary Plenum of the
National Committee of the SWP, held in New York City, October
29-November 1, 1943. From an unpublished, uncorrected stenographic transcript, slightly abridged.*

As I understand the problem that has been under discussion,
comrades, it is the whole problem of the selection of the
leadership of the party. It is not a question of criticisms of the
faults or shortcomings of the different individuals, in the main. If
that were so, we could have reduced the discussion in scope and
even have perhaps referred it to a subcommittee. But it was quite
clearly established, I think, that the criticisms of individual
comrades that have been made in the presentation of the question
by Comrade Morrison [Goldman] and in subsequent discussion of
others, that this criticism was related to a conflict of ideas over
methods of selecting the leadership of the party. I believe that is a
fair presentation of the problem and we have to discuss it on that
plane and discuss the merits or lack of merits of the individual
criticisms back and forth within that framework.

It is an important question because the selection of the
leadership of the party is decisive for the party itself. I have
always held this view and, much as I deplore any personal
element that enters into this discussion, I welcome a discussion
on the question itself because I have always maintained—that is,
always since I became a self-confident Trotskyist—I have
maintained and I have repeated many times to comrades in my
efforts to inculcate this idea in others, that if, as our theses amply
established, the decisive problem of the proletariat in this
revolutionary epoch is the party, then with almost the same

weight one can say the problem of the party is the leadership. And the leadership does not form itself automatically. It must be formed consciously, just as the party itself must be built consciously by the Trotskyists.

We have to begin with a concept of organization and a concept of leadership. That is true of all workers' movements regardless of whether this concept is, you may say, conscious or unconscious. The movement in which I received my first training, such as it was, the prewar socialist and syndicalist movements, were organizations without a conscious concept of the selection and functions and development of leadership. It was an automatic, sprawling process. From that unconsciousness of the prewar socialist and syndicalist movements in which my first activities took place, up to the present moment in our party, you see a development which long ago became qualitative in the sense of consciousness. [We have invested] the highest degree of consciousness in the question of selecting the leading staff of the party, and I believe if one should estimate what part I have played in the development of our movement, if it would be of interest to anybody, it could easily be established that my most important contribution was that I introduced the element of consciousness into the question of selecting the leading staff, of training it in a certain manner, educating it in certain methods, and developing it into a staff of professional revolutionists. And my great advantage over others, in the fifteen-year history of our movement, has always been this, that I was animated by consciousness on this question; I knew what I wanted.

That is my trend in the discussion today. I know precisely what I want and it is in accord with a concept which has been fixed in the course of study and experience and I believe it is a correct one. And it is from that point of view that I think this discussion can be made very fruitful, in contrasting what I may say is my concept, to Comrade Morrison's which I don't think is as fully conscious or as worked out as mine. . . .

[We are] not a self-educating circle, not a discussion club, not a sprawling electoral machine like the Social Democrats, not a headless movement like the IWW, but a combat organization, and it is from this that we derive the concept of democratic centralism, to which we all subscribe in our basic doctrines. Democratic centralism is a profound conception. We cannot devote too much time in the instruction of our party, and especially its new recruits, in the great significance of this profound conception of Lenin, that a party must have this double quality of democracy which makes it possible for the rank and file to exert its will and control, and of iron centralism which makes it possible for a leadership to act and for a party to act unitedly.

We have to go back and check against this marvelous contribution of Leninism to see whether we are really, in our approach to the problems of the party and its leadership, understanding fully this dialectical combination of democracy and centralism and making them both fit together and making them yield to each other in accordance with the stage of developments and specific activity of the party at a given moment to understand when democracy must have the dominant role.

It isn't a question of 50 percent democracy and 50 percent centralism. Democracy must have the dominant role in normal times. In times of action, intense activity, crisis and approach toward crises, and swings of the party such as we took toward proletarianization after the split, and so forth, centralism must have the upper hand, as it had in the last few years.

Now the Leninist method and form of organization flows from the program, the tasks and the aim that is set for the party, in complete harmony, a completely harmonious conception.

Now, Comrade Morrison, in my opinion, and everything that I say I want understood as the deductions and implications that I draw from his speech and from the conceptions he defended, and if I exaggerate them or appear to, I assure you it is not intentional. I have this conception of the basic source of Comrade Morrison's differences with us, the basic source—secondary and personality factors later. The source of the conflict is this. Comrade Morrison is for the program of Bolshevism not less than we are. That was emphasized even in the discussion on the political resolution when some of the amendments that he made strengthened the resolution in the sense of the program, the amendment which he made—which Comrade Bell also mentioned—about the possibility, or even probability, of the revolution taking such sweep that it would proceed to the organization of soviets and so forth.[96]

Now, that is Comrade Morrison's programmatic position. But the source of his difference with us—and here again I say it is my deduction rather than any specific statement that he made—is that, while Comrade Morrison adheres to the program of

Bolshevism, that the proletariat is going to make a revolution successfully in this epoch by one means or another, there is in his mind a certain doubt about the rightness of the organizational methods of Lenin. Now, that is the way the thing appears to me. It is not justified to suggest or draw any deductions, any inference of a departure from the program of Bolshevism. But there is a justification to deduce that he is becoming doubtful or skeptical about the organizational methods and principles of Lenin. How illuminating on that score was his remark, in the course of his speech, about how some novelist must appear who will explain this psychological phenomenon of honest revolutionists becoming transformed in the course of their party work and submission to discipline and one thing or another—revolutionists who have been able to withstand the pressure—succumbing to the pressure of their own party and turning into the opposite of revolutionists, as in the case of the Stalinists. The problem of the danger of the Leninist party becoming, in the process of development, a Stalinist party. Now, that is my inference, from his speech, and a whole series of incidents and disputes we have had.

Comrade Keller's [Art Preis] speech, I think, was beside the point entirely because it completely oversimplified the question and trespassed beyond the legitimate bounds of the differences which Comrade Morrison has presented, which I have defined as in the sphere of organizational method, and presented the question in such a way as to create the implication, at least, that Morrison was departing from the program of Bolshevism. That was by no means justified. The dispute is strictly limited to this narrower proposition I have made here as to whether or not the Leninist methods of organization are correct or whether they present a great danger which we must begin now to guard against by some special safeguard about democracy, some weakening of centralism, and some modification of this die-hard ruthless drive to select a cadre that is really going to be held together and stay together and will not permit itself to be dispersed.

Now we must criticize ourselves, that is, each other, and not only each other, but each should criticize himself in this discussion within the framework which I have presented here. This is the way I am prepared to. . . .

Are our concepts being properly applied in the sphere of organization, and particularly, in the sphere of selection of the leadership and its methods of work, etc.? If some of the criticism can be established as justifiable, then the most I can concede is we must change ourselves and improve ourselves in our methods of carrying out the Leninist concepts to which we are in allegiance.

Now, the task in regard to the selection of leadership as we see it can be presented in such a way, I believe, as to narrow down the dispute still further so as to see, one, that our task is to select as leaders of the party those who are most capable and independent-minded. I will accept that premise. Point two, that it is our task to educate the party in the habit and practice of critical and objective thought. Critical and objective. Of course critical thought cannot take place without objectivity, although some comrades seem to think so, so I link those two together to leave no doubt.

Objective, critical attitude toward everything and everybody, including the leaders and including all events that transpire. But that is not all, now. I grant that as a premise—that is what our task is. But I want to tack on an amendment, and here I want to bring in the element of Bolshevik realism. Let us undertake to carry out this task with the material that we have at hand and not with some imaginary material that we hope exists somewhere else. That, I think, is a necessary amendment to the premise, which I think will be agreeable to you. To select the most capable and the most independent minded, to educate the party in objective, critical thinking, but to do it with the material at hand.

Now, how have we been proceeding? How have we selected out the cadre that sits in this room, in the course of fifteen years of struggle? I doubt whether anybody will contest that it was selected freely at a democratic convention a year ago. Nobody would contest that, I am sure. I don't believe anybody would contest the further declaration—I think it was of Comrade Frank [Cochran] and others I heard mention it—that if we were in a position to call a convention tomorrow that the committee selected out of that convention, without any pressure or manipulation, as there was none last time, would be substantially the same, with an individual or two different here or there, but certainly the central core—not only the central core, but the overwhelming majority, 90 percent of the comrades sitting here would be reelected.

But that is only the formal side of the question of the really true representative character of this leading cadre. They weren't elected at the last convention by accident or for the first time. They were prepared as candidates for the election by fifteen years of contest and struggle against the stream and quite a few of the committee have been continuously in the leadership from the very beginning, or from very close to it. So that, you may say, this cadre is organically rooted in the party and has full right to speak for the party. Now, that is the National Committee as it is here, and I doubt whether any comrade who will think critically and objectively about the question will deny the correctness of my assertion that this committee is the representative of the party.

But this full committee does not conduct the daily work. How is the Political Committee selected? Our present system is that the Political Committee is not elected in this body, as we did in previous periods, at different times. Our present system is that all comrades who are resident in or near New York or are temporarily in New York are automatically members of the Political Committee. So there is no manipulation or shenanigan work of any kind in getting a Political Committee that is unrepresentative of the National Committee. And I believe it is reasonable to say that by and large, the Political Committee that we have in New York represents the mind and the will of the plenum, subject to certain criticism and cautions that have been received at the plenum about the basic line. But the ways of thinking and conceptions are so closely united that you may say the Political Committee is the true representative of the plenum. That is the way we select our leadership—complete freedom and democracy that makes it possible for those to come to the top circles of the party unobstructed.

Now I go back further and say that not only is it the free election of a convention and that these comrades were prepared by fifteen years of work and struggle—not only that, but that there is employed in this method of ours a system which facilitates, doesn't hamper but facilitates, the passage of the most qualified and learning, capable comrades to come from the ranks into the ranks of alternates, and eventually into the ranks of the National Committee. Complete freedom, with a deliberate program of facilitating the way for any individual who shows promise of developing leading capabilities. Now that is a representative body. It didn't take place by accident but is the crystallization of a method and a system. Is any able member of the party excluded from the National Committee? Is there one comrade in the party who is known to the party members as qualified for national leadership who isn't here? I have not heard that accusation.

It is possible you may say John and so-and-so in Detroit would make good material, but you wouldn't say it in such a way as to say that he is being kept out artificially because the minute you establish the fact that there is a comrade developing in Chicago or Detroit who looks promising, you know very [well that] at the next convention the doors will be wide open and he will very probably be included, first as an alternate. I have heard no accusation whatsoever of an exclusive attitude towards people of ability or developing or showing promise of leadership ability.

Now, where did you ever see a party like that before? Where and under what auspices was a leadership—and I am speaking now of the democratic side of the problem, I will come to the other later—where was a leadership elected or selected by such a thoroughgoing and undiluted democratic method as ours? Where? You never saw it because it never existed, and those who can give the best testimony on this point are those who have had any experience in any other workers' organization whatsoever. We have developed that art and that method of selecting the best and most qualified, and only the best and most qualified, to the highest degree of consciousness, and apply it undeviatingly in the selections of the leading staff. That is one of the elements that insures the authority of this leading committee and assures that if in the ranks of the party we have latent talent and other qualities of leadership, and talent is only one of them, that they will come to the committee in the natural course of events and make their contributions to the further strengthening and improvement of the committee.

I take up Comrade Lydia's [Lydia Beidel] speech for a moment, and I am sorry she is not here, and I don't want to speak of her New York experiences because they are an individual matter of adjustment which are entirely beside the point and, in my opinion, have nothing to do with the problem at issue. She is very much concerned to awaken the ranks of the party, to stimulate its intellectual life by means of discussion, arguments, and so forth, and she protests against any sentiment of contrasting discussion to activity, which, of course, is entirely correct. Now, I believe there can be a certain kernel of justification for Comrade Lydia's concern—a kernel. I myself have been thinking about this very problem for some time because the party is not what it used to be, and the precise method—I am not speaking now of the system of methods as a whole, but the precise methods of shaping and forming the party that we employed yesterday—may require application in a slightly different manner today, for the following reasons, that the party is not today what it used to be.

It is quite a different party. It is not what it was four years ago. In 1939 it was a madhouse of conflict between the proletarian and the petty-bourgeois tendencies. It was an asylum of discussion and argument gone mad, and had been for a long time. It was a party in which the system of speaking one's mind and expressing one's thoughts and controverting one's opponents had been developed to such excesses that it was devouring the party and holding it back from the task of proletarianizing itself and was attracting to it a type of petty-bourgeois adapted to such an atmosphere and repelling the proletarian who will not belong to an organization that is talking all the time. So we conducted an historic battle in defense of our program. Naturally, in such an atmosphere and with such a composition we eventually came to a crucial fight in the party orientation, democratic centralism, and so on—a thoroughgoing fight, the like of which has never been seen in our movement in its theories, in the amplitude of the issues, in the clarity with which they were defined and discussed, and in the documentation which we have compiled from that fight for the education of the membership.

Now, you know the outcome of that fight was a gigantic purge of the party. As a result of the victory of our proletarian section, the split amounted to a tremendous purge of not less than 40 or 45 percent of the membership. I have seen lots of splits, but in almost any other circumstances a split of from 40 to 45 percent of the party would paralyze it for a long time from sheer loss of blood and throw the members into discouragement. You know the result with us was different. We emerged from that purge with renewed energy and conviction. We didn't lose, you may say, even one day's time in speeding up the tempo of the party's work. The membership was so sated with discussion and so sick of discussion fanatics and experts that they turned unanimously to the proletarianization task and concentrated themselves upon practical work and activity. I don't know the party ranks now as well as I should because I haven't traveled the country lately, but I can see the possibility, or even the probability, that this bending the stick backwards as we did in the split, with such a mighty wrench and proletarianization following, that the practical side of our work has been somewhat exaggerated.

And on top of that we have recruited 230, I think, new members since the Minneapolis trial and these 230 people haven't come out of the SP discussion clubs or out of some other discussion organization. They have come right out of the class struggle, raw material, the great majority of them who are receiving their first ABC lesson in politics now, in our party. So the type of the party has been different, its activities are different, and I am willing to grant an objective survey of the party internally as to whether we should do something to stimulate educational discussions and a reemphasis of that side of our work.

I have been thinking about that. I thought about it so much that I seized the occasion when the Akron branch wrote in [asking the] same question [which] arose there as to what was permissible to discuss, to propose in the Political Committee—no, it was in Philadelphia, where a question arose as to whether it was permissible to discuss the tactics in the Minneapolis trial.[97]. . . [Some comrades in the branch were of the opinon that the comrade who had raised the criticism was out of order and that he should be prohibited from discussing the subject on the branch floor.] Our committee naturally rejected that proposition and told him he could discuss and criticize it to his heart's content. I took advantage of the situation to propose that we send that circular to all the branches throughout the country explaining that they could discuss if they wanted to all current questions and that we welcome and encourage them to do that, but under the constitution they must not undertake discussion of principled questions settled by the last convention.

I don't know what the result of the circular was in stimulating discussion in all the branches. In Akron . . . they saw a prohibition of the discussion of program that had been decided at the last convention, and that they considered bureaucratic. I gave a perfect illustration of how utterly impossible it is for some people to understand what a Bolshevik party is and where democracy ends and centralism begins. That is a premise that I am willing to take out of Comrade Beidel's speech and make an inquiry on the question and consider it. Not to make a snap judgment decision that we can stimulate a lot of discussion— maybe it is not necessary. But if it is necessary, if there is a stagnation, too much one-sidedness on practical work and not enough on political education, then we must step in and bend the stick back. Because we do not want only activities; we want communist workers, and that requires other things.

Now I come to my next point—the accusations against the majority of the Political Committee. The accusations as I sifted them out would come under these heads: one, lack of independent thinking on the part of the great majority of the comrades; two, personal domination by an individual and a leader cult, or at least an incipient leader cult; three, bad methods and morals on the part of some of the comrades that—if I put a modification on the accusation—give an indication of showing a tendency in the general direction of Stalinism. In other words, bad methods and bad morals, lack of integrity.

I will undertake to discuss these questions both in general and concretely and see to what extent we can agree and to what extent we must disagree. Independent thinking. Now it would be pretty hard to get me to vote against independent thinking. I won't do it. I would vote for it and I believe everybody will vote for it and, as I say, I am willing, in the preface of my remarks, to define independent thinking more precisely, saying that what we mean is that we want an objective and critical attitude toward everything and everybody, and nobody and nothing excluded. That is the way we want to educate the party.

But now to what extent and how much and within what framework is independent thought possible or probable in the party? That we have got to define, and here you run up against another element of realism or reality—which is very dear to the Leninists within the party, especially on the question of the party—with the material that you have, not ideal material on the moon, but the people we have now on hand and can appreciably expect to get in the near future. Comrade Hansen wrote a brilliant contribution to this question in the last party conflict, in the fight with the petty-bourgeois opposition.[98] He wrote it when he was in Mexico and I don't doubt that Comrade Trotsky, if he didn't help him with it—I know in any case, Comrade Trotsky praised it highly.

Comrade Hansen pointed out that the grain of originality in most human beings is very slight. We imitate, we get from others, and the art of independent creation is strictly limited; even the creators of our theory were independent only within a certain framework, not utterly and completely as has been demanded of us many times in the past. They were conditioned by the times, the environment, the culture, upon which they had to base themselves. Similarly, in our international movement we have developed only two independent creators in the field of theory, to my knowledge, in the period since the *Communist Manifesto*. I don't know of any others. I know Lenin and Trotsky. I know of many great, distinguished revolutionists and politicians who brilliantly applied the ideas of Marx and Engels, but I don't know anybody who made new and original contributions to Marxism except Lenin and Trotsky.

I know many other people who made original contributions, but they weren't any good, so I rule them out. So, observing them—and I have preoccupied myself with that question consciously for many years—I have come to the conclusion that creative originality in the field of theory is a very rare thing and that gift was not bestowed upon me by my creator. I haven't got that gift. And I have that defect in common with the whole movement of the entire world, that I know of anyway, so that it doesn't depress me so much, and that is one reason why I brought down my heavy hand against anybody ever calling me a theoretician.

I called myself an agitator and I didn't do it with false modesty either. Because I am not troubled with that sickness. I considered myself able within the limits of my capacities to apply what I had been taught by my masters. [. . .] You may say, the maximum you can demand from a leader [is], assimilating all that has been taught by the masters, he would make [independent contributions of his own]. But people who are sufficiently at home in the doctrines and methods of Marxism to be able to orientate themselves in a political situation and give an answer without too much delay, that is a necessary and valuable thing, and not only in the leadership but in the rank and file. But you get that not too widely.

The tendency of the rank and file is more cautious than that of the professional discussers. Why? Because they associate their thinking on political questions with what the party is going to do, and they don't want merely to express themselves, that is not their idea of what the party is. Their idea of the party is that it is going to take an action against the class enemy and they don't want to make a mistake that will cost them dearly. So the tendency of the rank and file of the party is to be cautious to this extent: that they will wait for the initiative of the leaders.

The caution of the rank and file expresses itself in that they will wait to see what *The Militant* says before definitely making up their mind. They will discuss what *The Militant* says and get their orientation from that. That is the tendency of the great majority of human beings in our party and will be, no matter what you decide in this plenum as to what kinds of minds you want to have in the heads of our party.

Now I am in favor of independent thinking and I value every comrade, whether in the leadership or the rank and file, who is independent to this extent, that he tries to think out a problem and that he will argue and discuss with others, and even be convinced by them; that he will try to make up his mind on the basis of objectivity and not just merely pretending to agree, or submitting against his will to somebody else. I want to distinguish between that and deferring to somebody else. And the workers will defer.

You will find the average worker who will think about events in the class struggle, maybe have an opinion, and he will see that the party Central Committee says, no, this is the line, and he will change his position even though he may not be completely convinced, because he thinks the party must not make an error, and they have more facilities, more information, more experience—and he wouldn't want to risk . . . for fear he might do the party an injury. That kind of deference is necessary in any party or you will never have a combat party. And that kind of deference is unavoidable, even in the leading staff, to a certain extent and in certain respects. [. . . Party leadership rests on many kinds of people with different skills and areas of work. A capable leader] will defer to more experienced people. As Trotsky would and as Lenin would. You think that I am making an extraordinary statement that Trotsky would defer? Trotsky deferred to Lenin in the Brest-Litovsk peace. . . . [He had his own independent position] but in order to give Lenin a majority to carry out his line, he abstained on the vote.

Now I am for, I say, the maximum of independent critical thinking and for the amateur independent thinker. What I am against now, as I have been in the past, is the professional independent thinker. I never, as they say out where I come from, I never saw any good come from that. The professional independent thinker—and we have had lots of them in the past, and I see incipient tendencies in this direction now, and I don't mean Morrison—[holds] that independent thinking means disagreeing with Comrade Cannon. Just the reverse side of independent oppositionists. I don't encourage that tendency. They never contributed anything in the past in our movement and they never will.

I said that Trotsky was capable of deferring to others. I know, because he deferred to me more than once. That may seem an astounding revelation to you comrades who have been told so often about my automatically raising my hand every time Trotsky opened his mouth. I don't say that he deferred to me as many times as I deferred to him, but it wasn't altogether a one-sided question.

Comrades Dunne, Gordon, [Morris] Stein, and Collins [George Clarke] remember the big dispute we had in the case of Field. When Field originally became a member of our party—a petty bourgeois, but a very talented fellow, a statistician—in a few months he organized a class for the study of Marxism at his house and he got a group of young comrades around him to educate them. The local branch had nothing to do with it. The National Committee had nothing to do with it. The local branch of New York didn't like this independent method of operation. They said, you can conduct a class but it must be made an official class and open to any comrade who wants to join it. I won't discuss the merits of their demand, but that is the nature of a political organization, that it does not like people operating on a pinwheel. I am sorry Morrow didn't hear that remark. Well, Field said he refused to obey the decision. So the Local New York organization threw him out. They expelled him just like that. You see, there were some good points about our organization even away back then. They knew how to throw someone out if he monkeyed with discipline. Field packed his grips and went to visit Trotsky. . . . [The next thing we knew we began to receive] articles written by Field with an introduction by Trotsky on the world situation. He sat down there and began to write. Well, this stooge of Trotsky here in New York [Cannon] went into the committee and made a motion that we write to Comrade Trotsky and tell him that we would not tolerate such an action, that an expelled member of our party cannot be [given access to the internal life of our movement in another part of the world].

At that time I didn't know Trotsky as well as I knew him later. I must admit at that time I was somewhat impressed with the great wave of propaganda about Trotsky's domineering the movement and his ruthless pushing aside of people who didn't carry out his will. And the Old Man *was* a little imperious. He had a way of commanding and in his impatience to get things done, making a shortcut through organization even more than I do. And I was so determined that we would not permit the rights of our section to be violated that I told Comrade Trotsky, Dunne, and others. . . . And I remember—talk about soul-searing periods—in that period I was brooding in my mind that I was not going to under any circumstances tolerate such a thing and if Comrade Trotsky was going to insist upon such arbitrary methods, he would have to find somebody else to carry them out. And I lived in the most terrible apprehension of what he would write back, that he would write a sarcastic . . . and that would be the end of it as far as I was concerned.

Instead of that he wrote back a most conciliatory and apologetic letter and agreed with us and begged our pardon and indulgence—that it really was a mistake on his part. The fellow [Field] really wanted to come back, informally, and he [Trotsky] begged us if he could use him in his secretariat in preparing mail, on the following conditions: that when he came back to America in the following months, he would not be taken back in the organization. No, he had to be further disciplined. He should be accepted as a sympathizer for six months and if at the end of six months he showed signs of having learned something, then we could consider the question of taking him back. That was a time when, you may say, Trotsky deferred.

Trotsky deferred to Cannon on the question of the name of this party. I never told anybody this before. Trotsky didn't like the name of the party. He didn't like "the compromising name socialist." He wrote me quite strongly about it. But I wanted that name. I wanted to continue the name "socialist" and thought that it would be a little better cover for our comrades in the trade union movement. I thought it was necessary for us in the trade unions, so I didn't motivate my answer, but I just simply told him no. The Old Man dropped the question. He subsided and let it go. He didn't rush out into the *New International* with an article on the question. A couple of years later he raised it again.

A third time that Trotsky didn't agree with me but deferred to me, not only to me but to others who were with me—Sam [Gordon], myself, Farrell, Joe [Hansen], and Comrade [Antoinette] Konikow—in the summer of 1940 a couple of months before he died. You all know that Comrade Trotsky proposed to us in that session that we should give critical support to the candidacy of Browder on the Communist Party ticket and presented it very forcefully. And we didn't agree with it, and I especially emphatically opposed it. He was not impressed by our arguments. But the Old Man wasn't worried about independent thinking because he had it. He didn't have to worry about it and he knew that if you haven't got it nobody can give it [to you].

Trotsky thought far more highly of me and valued me far more highly than I value myself—because he said so, and more than once. He valued me far more highly than I have been valued here in this plenum or I have been valued in the PC. I think, as I say, more highly than I value myself because just as I, in trying to play a leading part in assembling a leading cadre of leading people, I try to know what these people are. I try to know these men, what they are and what they are not. And I try to know myself. I don't know how much I succeed, but I think I know my limitations and shortcomings as accurately as anybody, and that is why I am not willing to attempt to assume rights or to assume titles, and I don't want anybody to demand of me something that I can't do. You have got to take me as I am, just as I take you. I spoke before about this. [. . .]

The Bolshevik worker has the primary concern, when he sees a political event unfolding, to find the right answer for the party—that is his concern. And if in arriving at that answer he finds that the National Committee or some of the national leaders have presented a different answer than his, even though the reasons are not all clear to him, he will usually defer, not because he is a stooge or a dope but because he is so highly responsible to the party that he doesn't want to take the responsibility of the party's making an error from his immature judgment. That is the primary concern, not only of a Bolshevik worker, but also a Bolshevik leader. If, when an important issue is presented, and he has a first impression and he is not too sure of it and others are more sure or positive of it, he will defer. I do it practically every day in one question or another in practical work. I am deferring right now on the auto policy of the party. I don't know whether that line being developed by Frank is entirely correct or not, but I am not familiar at the present time with the developments in the auto situation, I have confidence in his judgment and, in a manner of speaking, I defer to him. And you have to have in the leading committee such an interchange of deference . . . not who evolved the policy or how it was derived, but whether it is right or not, because if it is wrong the party will suffer; if it is right, the party will gain. I have seen this independent attitude, professional independence, ruin more people than subservience. In fact, I haven't seen many people spoiled by subservience in the derogatory sense of the term, not in the regime that I have had anything to do with, because I don't [encourage it]. I like rebels around me. I like men of spirit. I don't like sycophants, even if they attach themselves to me for a time, because I am concerned with the problem of creating a cadre that can lead the party in case a streetcar would run over Cannon some day. And I challenge you, by God, and think it over, as to the qualities of the people in this leading committee, which, I say again, have been elected freely by the membership, and in another sense of the word, they have been selected. . . . Conditions have been created which made it possible for people of this type to be elected and for the rejection of other types.

I have seen people who got nettled by the accusation that you are dependent on Cannon. And this is a petty-bourgeois, not a proletarian trait, to be so self-concerned that you are worried about what somebody says about you, so much so that in order to prove the accusation is false you do something that is not wise. Shachtman used to be associated with me for years and years, and if Shachtman ever had an independent thought, I never caught him at it. Neither during the time he was said to be Cannon's right-hand man nor the time when he was to write the analytical. . . . [It was] not his fault—you couldn't blame him. Shachtman is an interpreter and popularizer and adapter of other people's ideas, and was a tremendously valuable man when he occupied himself with that task of applying the great ideas of Trotsky on the one hand, and Cannon on the other . . . [until he began to worry that his own originality was suffering from neglect.]

I have seen that become the downfall of others too. And I advise everybody to be themselves. Be yourself and don't pretend to be something otherwise, and think the best way you can and bear in mind all the time that what is decisive is not whether you are always expressing yourself to complete satisfaction, but whether what you are doing and how you are doing it is helping the party to do the right thing. I remember and I think many of you do—it is really out of place to labor this point because Stein made it so clear in his speech—that a problem you present about an individual comrade, after a certain period of experience and so on, acquiring more experience than others [and beginning to exercise a great deal of influence over the opinions of other comrades]. . . .

It is a phenomenon of Chicago, of Detroit, of any place where any one of you comrades of the committee in your local work have a preponderant influence. If that weren't so, you probably wouldn't have been elected on the National Committee as the representatives of your district. But I recall the arguments in the international movement of the Socialist Workers Party of Germany [SAP] who used to write all the time this nauseating dribble that the Fourth International is all right but it has one fatal defect—the preponderant dominating influence of Trotsky. The Lovestoneites in this country used to sing this song all the time. They couldn't be in the International because Trotsky decides too much. His authority is too great. I commented on that in one of my letters to Trotsky that is printed in my book.[99] It never impressed me, that argument never impressed me at all although it was true.

But there was nothing to do. I expressed my opinion on it this way in a letter. I am ready to agree with you that ten leaders with outstanding influence are better than one, and two are better than one, but if I can't get ten and can't get two, I will be damned if I will throw the one away until I get two. That's your problem right here in this committee—the problem is to develop here. You have got them on the PC but you can't see them because you are blinded by subjectivity, and you are not sufficiently objective and critical in your appreciation of the qualities of the comrades we have on the Political Committee. Wasn't that the old song about Lenin and the Bolsheviks? And I want to say, all proportions guarded, because this idea goes all the way from the [time] of Lenin and Trotsky to the Detroit or Minnesota organization: It is a phenomenon of all workers' organizations, more or less. Trotsky used to argue [against] that, but he learned better and he saw that Lenin's methods built a party and he was man enough to come over to Lenin, and that is one of the greatest historical benefits the workers ever got.[100]

Now I say that you can build this leadership only out of the material you have got, and that you must quit talking or even thinking about an image of an ideal committee because you are playing with an idea you can't realize. Where in the name of heaven are you going to get it? There isn't time now to try to recruit a new cadre. Stop and think how long it took to get this material you have here. It took fifteen years of pounding to get this cadre, and I use that word with full consciousness of what I say. This cadre was not picked up on the street and made what it is overnight. It was pounded into shape through fifteen years of battle, and those who had the mettle in them constitute, you may say, the residue of all the people we have had in the committee all this whole period of time. And if you try to play or dabble with the idea of a new leadership, then I say that you are presenting a problem that has no solution, none whatever. I don't see how you could do anything but demoralize the party with such a suggestion.

For heaven's sake, study Lenin and try to learn from Lenin, not only on all the great questions, but on this question because, don't forget that if Lenin hadn't known this question—how to build a party and how to select a leading staff—all his other contributions could never have been realized in life. The revolution couldn't have succeeded. . . . [On the] question raised by the German comrade [Walter] Held, about the case of [Paul] Levi and the Communist Party of Germany in connection with the March action.[101] Held criticized Lenin for having expelled Levi and supported the majority of the Central Committee, who had the party with them. Comrade Van [Jean van Heijenoort] controverted Held on the ground of discipline, that Lenin was enforcing and demonstrating discipline. . . . Although they [Lenin and the Bolshevik leaders] thought Levi was right in his political position, in the main, they supported the Central Committee and confirmed the expulsion of Levi.

My contribution to that would be that the discipline was the secondary side of the question. It was not impossible for Lenin to have found a way around discipline if he could have found a way around the other questions. That was those who had committed the terrible blunder of the March action which had such catastrophic results for the party. Those who had led that action, they were the leaders that he had at hand, and Levi had none. And he had to take that material that had committed that terrible error, the March action, and support them and try to make something out of them because Lenin made his cadre out of the material he had at hand, not out of cadres that existed in his imagination. And this is the important lesson to draw from this discussion. And that is the way I approach the question all the time.

I am convinced we have the best people we can get at the present time in the committee. We are troubled, we are dealt heavy blows by two factors arising out of the war. Comrade Charles [Curtiss], who had developed as a very important contributor, and by no means a regimented yes man but a very promising and talented comrade, and Comrade Breitman who, after all, is only a mere boy, who is developing with leaps and bounds and gives promise of being a first-class Bolshevik leader, have to go into the army. Bert [Cochran] is on the skids for the next month. Joe [Hansen] and Sam [Gordon] and George [Clarke] have to be in this maritime [situation] so we haven't got anybody but those who are here. I believe that if these comrades I name could be present, if Stein could be in New York, it would strengthen the committee in all respects, including the element of independent and critical thought on the question. [. . .]

If these people are taken away by the war or by prison, and we have to take a second line, it won't be a first-class one but by God it will give first-class answers and keep the party together. You have to have that in mind all the time. I will make a Political Committee out of them, and from the whole committee, the whole leadership of the party—I will even take people out of the secretarial staff of the office and the New York branch—I will make a Political Committee. It may not be a first-class committee, but it will keep the party together.

Now I want to come to the next point of criticism, on the leadership cult, and I have to admit that I had a certain distaste for this whole discussion. It is distasteful for me not only to hear what is said against me, but particularly to have to listen to comrades speak in defense of me. It is a rather irritating question. I think one's personal influence and authority in the movement in the long run doesn't depend on who boosts him or who knocks him. I have always had the attitude—I don't know whether you believe it or not—from the very beginning I was clear on this point: Let things take their due course. I neither push myself nor do I suffer from false modesty. Let things take their course. I have watched very carefully every one of the men who come in the PC. I watch them—I watch especially their development from the point of view of their indifference to themselves, or their willingness to let things take their course and to fall into whatever place is assigned to them without pressure and manipulation, and I think that is the right thing and the right attitude for everybody to take.

I don't like people who push themselves. And if they only knew it, it doesn't do them much good, because while I don't determine everything in this party, I play a hell of a big role in stopping any careerist from getting to first base, or I would, if any appeared. I don't think careerism is a serious matter in our party. On the other hand, I don't believe you can have a leaderless movement, a combat movement without leaders. Leaders must be armed with weapons. One of the weapons is the constitution which gives them the power to decide questions by the convention. But that is not enough. They have to have the weapon of prestige. And they not only must have prestige in the party, but as the party tasks develop, they must have it outside.

Let things take their course and those leaders who develop a certain influence and authority and show a certain loyalty, they should be given their due, they should be afforded that prestige and that public recognition that is necessary for them to carry out their tasks. I speak of this in connection with the evidence that was adduced about an artificial inflation of me by the promotion of my book [*Struggle for a Proletarian Party*]. This is protested against here by Morrison. I could hardly believe my ears. And then, by young Oscar [Schoenfeld]. I was prepared to hear Cassidy [Morrow] say the same thing, but I guess he left it out of his notes. Now I say you have approached that as you have approached everything else in this direction, to a large extent subjectively.

The question about the book is, what do you think about the book? Was it worth something? I thought so. I believe the overwhelming majority of the committee thought so. I think the rank and file of the party thought so. I think the majority of the party thought so. So why shouldn't it be published? Just because Morrison does not think it of any value? That would be a bad criterion. Morrison doesn't think anything that his colleagues write is worth publishing. He lacks respect for his colleagues. But if the book was worth publishing, it should be published. It just happens, and here I am a sort of victim of my own Frankenstein, I began hounding the editors of our *Militant* months and months ago because they don't campaign for our publications. I would bring in a paper of political opponents and I would see two or three pages about their own published material, descriptions about it, promoting and selling their own stuff—Why don't we put on a campaign for some of Trotsky's stuff? I demanded reviews, not only of books but pamphlets. Every time Pioneer Publishers got out something, I firmly [demanded of] the editorial staff that they should make a campaign to sell and advertise it to get money back to publish others. Wright went to the New York City Executive Committee to raise holy hell because they weren't conducting an energetic enough campaign for Comrade Trotsky's book [*In Defense of Marxism*]. I created this atmosphere and in the midst of my influence came my book and it rode on the crest of the campaign spirit and got not one review but several. I can assure you that if I thought there was anything in the form of phony inflation of my significance or the importance of the book, I would surely protest. I don't think that. I think the book is OK and deserved the publicity it received.

It is the first book our party ever published by one of its members.[102] If the book had been written by some other comrade you wouldn't find me on the sidelines, opposed to giving it a real play. That is all there is to it. Nothing else, and I am certainly sorry to see that issue magnified out of all proportion. I am not surprised to see Shachtman's attitude toward the book because this book didn't do Shachtman any good. Shachtman had to notice the book some way and he couldn't review it because if he did he would have to say what does he think about the chapter on "War and Bureaucratic Conservatism,"[103] the chapter on leader cult, and so forth. He burned his fingers once on this document. And nevertheless Shachtman knows that that book is a mighty weapon, not only today but for the future, that the awakening generation of workers coming toward communism who are going to be burning with a desire for knowledge of the past of the movement is going to stumble across that book among others and that is never going to do the Shachtman tendency any good. It will do us good and that is why we should be in favor of promoting it and if you can find some way of doing it without mentioning my name I will agree to that.

Have you given any thought to this question of leadership outside of the question of whether I am being promoted too much, of whether Cannon is getting too much publicity or not? This question is not to be discussed abstractly in a vacuum. You are discussing certain situations and concrete situations. Don't you know that something has happened to the leadership of our party in recent years? Here is what has happened, perhaps unbeknown to you: the prestige of all the leaders of our party, especially the more prominent ones, increased enormously in the recent years, mine among them, perhaps a little more, but all of the comrades have greatly increased their prestige in recent years. Now Shachtman protests against the special expression of this fact, with good reason, but I don't see why any member of our party should. The factor which raised the prestige of our leadership so high in our ranks was the fact that when the party was subjected to an attack that threatened its existence, these leaders rallied around the party and defended it and protected it.

And they were appreciated by the party more than they ever were before, because the members saw in times of crisis when the life of the party was at stake in the face of the war, we came forward and acted like Bolsheviks. A qualitative change in the leadership took place, and a change in the attitude of the rank and file toward the leadership took place in that process. And then came the trial and the comrades conducted themselves in the trial in a way that was approved by the rank and file of the party. They are more deliberate and conscious in their regard for the leadership than they ever were before. I am not in favor of inflating that—but I am not in favor of suppressing it. In this period we have grown in the eyes of the membership into the, stature of leaders of whom they are proud, who defended their party in time of crisis, and who defended it before the bourgeois courts. And our rank and file go out proudly with Cannon's book because they know that Cannon is OK. [. . .]

If you have got any fears that I am going to be a party to any artificial manipulation and advertisement of party sentiment for the promotion of myself or anybody else, then you have got a very poor appreciation of me, you don't know me. I want the thing to develop normally. When there is a justification to put a comrade's picture in the paper, put it in there, popularize him. My method is the normal honest method. [. . .]

Heavens alive, some comrades were apprehensive that this trouble we have had here would shake the party. Why, you couldn't possibly do it. Not even a comrade with the prestige and authority of Morrison could make a dent in it. They would see the whole committee, or most of them, rising up and saying Morrison must be called to order. I don't say that Morrison wouldn't have a chance in the end to convince a majority if he has a good case. The first reaction of the party will be for the committee, that is, the leadership. It mustn't be broken up. That is a great element of stability. That is why friction in the spinners [maritime] fraction or friction in the Detroit branch can be quickly isolated or cut out and stopped from spreading because the leadership is so powerful that it can do that. That helps to keep stability in the party.

Now I was raised the hard way in politics. I was raised in the Communist Party from 1919-28—you know that is nine years of uninterrupted factional struggle. That is, unless you call an interruption a peace to catch your breath and reorganize your forces. Nine years that devoured the energy of the party. That was one of the principal factors in that lack of authoritative leadership. In the beginning there was no individual leader with sufficient [authority], there was no group of leaders with sufficient authority and ability to command the confidence of the party, and one was challenged by others and the fights became struggles for influence and power in the party. Philistines write about this as a wholly negative thing—look at all the fighting. The only difference was that that took place in every party where the leadership has not become consolidated. And up until 1928, when we were expelled, we had not consolidated an authoritative leadership, not in any way approached the homogeneity of this. What we were [was a federation of factions:] Foster, Lovestone, and Cannon, and these leaders had authority in their own faction and only there. Each faction was so strong, the other two couldn't crush the third, and so we had a coalition group each time— sometimes one group was in the majority and sometimes another.

Now in the course of fifteen years of fighting and struggle, we have consolidated quite a homogeneous leading group that enjoys great authority and that is why faction fights would be hard to create. . . . I don't mean by going down and cutting people's heads off.

But in the old days we didn't know that. You see we had to learn how to be leaders while we were already leaders formally, and God knows the movement suffered from that. And we have to value, in my opinion, the leading cadre that we have constructed and try to do whatever we want or hope to do with this cadre. By God, if anybody knows the barrenness of personal rivalry and the barrenness of fights in a party on a personal basis, I ought to know because I have seen it and I have suffered through it. That was the nature of the fight that took place in the Communist League of America almost from the beginning until 1933 to '34. Why, comrades who took part in that then feel, I believe, as I do, that the greatest thing we ever gave to the movement was the blood we gave in going through the barren fights. Shachtman-Abern on one side, Cannon on the other. What is the issue? Cannon is domineering in the committee, and we have got to defend thinkers. Political issues? None. Nothing serious. Young comrades, inexperienced in the movement, lined up. Independent thinking sounds OK, let's go for it, collective leadership is better than one man.

Before they knew it they were in a faction lineup and then— fight it out before the membership. Lewitt and Weber in one faction; I and Clarke, Dunne, Gordon in another—standing up and arguing about who is the better leader.

I look back with horror upon that nightmare. By God, the hardest time I have had in the movement has never been the persecution of the authorities, or the fight with the petty-bourgeois opposition. It was that goddamned barren fight over questions of personalities. We finally extricated ourselves from it with the help of Trotsky. And one reason I know a good many things that other comrades haven't learned is that I had to learn it on my back.

There is no profit in such fights because the membership cannot learn anything from it. They can only learn which group of leaders they think is better than the other and they group themselves according to sympathies and antipathies, and the struggle, devoid of a serious base, no program or principle, inevitably develops the most. . . .

One side begins boasting, denigrating the others. All the leaders lose prestige and the authority of the leadership as a whole. I don't want to see any suggestion of such a thing in our party and I hope there will not be that. And I hope that we will get out of this difficulty by concession and compromise on the personal question. I wouldn't be able to compromise much on the question of method and principles—in fact, not at all—because that is in my bones; I believe that if you develop a loose attitude on the question of assembling the cadres, you lose the party—it will fall apart.

I can join you in the hope that we will have—and, as a matter of fact, before your eyes it is developing—that you have other comrades developing in the committee who have independent influence. I have listened to a half a dozen people speak in this plenum who, as everybody knows, have independent influence, who are not waiting to see what Cannon has to say. As a matter of fact, my speaking on this whole question here is just redundancy. The question was fully covered and fully illuminated in the discussion from the floor by other comrades, but as the comrades get increasing experience they not only get increasing influence, but increasing influence on each other too. You talk of Collins. He has developed. Sure he has. Fifteen years is a long time. He learned and grew and developed a little and he still has some way to go. He is no more the same as he was then than I am the Cannon I was then. I have learned a whole lot, the hard way. . . .

The most you can be talking about is what I used to be. When I came out of the nine years of the CP I was a first-class factional hoodlum. If not, how would I ever have survived? All I knew when somebody started a fight, let him have it. That existence was all I knew. I think Trotsky is right when he says that in that long drawn-out fight between Cannon and Abern that historical right is on the side of Cannon. But that doesn't mean I was right about everything. No, I was wrong about many things, including my methods and my impatience and rudeness with comrades and repulsing them. My past record—but that is years ago. I don't do that anymore. I don't insult comrades. I don't persecute them or even give them grounds for thinking I am doing it. I know more about how to lead a party than that. I have had responsibilities on my shoulders and I have had the Old Man's instruction and some day I am going to publish the Old Man's correspondence on this question and it will be very illuminating as one of the great sources of my information and change. I improved myself, cleaned myself up, and you have got to judge me as I am today.

What we have got to do is continue the method we have now. I think this method is unassailably correct, and I only hope if someone abler comes along he will build on what we have, and won't start from scratch.

I said that in this room, the National Committee, are the ablest and strongest people in the party, and everybody is of that opinion. Isn't it? Where did you ever hear of a leadership being constructed on that principle of getting the ablest and strongest around you? That has never been done. It is only Leninism that makes that possible. What is the leadership of the United Mine Workers? A leadership subservient to John L. Lewis, who surrounds himself with the machine of personal adherents. And that is the machine of every trade unionist in this country and the machine of every socialist organization in this country.

As soon as a stronger pressure than Lewis, the pressure of Roosevelt, interfered, he lost his right-hand men. And then he lost Van Bittner right out of his own organization which appeared to be so indestructible, a monolithic machine.[104] This machine is far superior to the Lewis machine because it won't crack under pressure. If it were handpicked, if there were any truth whatsoever that I look for hand-raisers and handpicked people, I could have done it to a certain respect. The leader of a party has a certain advantage. I could have manipulated things. . . .

That kind of committee will go to pieces. The only way you can hope to build a party that will stand up under any circumstances is the method that Trotsky had: build them around ideas and concepts and let them become of the flesh and blood of people and they will carry on even though the originator is not there. And that is why we are able to carry on to a certain extent after Trotsky, and everybody here is confident that they will be able to carry on when we go to prison. Did you stop to think about that?

We have on the agenda here the question of the substitute leadership. Where are we going to find it? In whoever is left of these twenty-five. Not on the streets. And we have confidence that these comrades, although they may be stumped a bit, but with the concepts and what they have learned in the fight, they will go forward.

Now Comrade Cassidy developed a thesis here today, I heard that from him before. He didn't take me by surprise. He talked to me about it, but he couldn't convince me because I recoil against new ideas, especially of that kind. In proof he said we inspire only practical workers because we are practical workers ourselves; we are not theoreticians, not writers, journalists, and we inspire people of a like type who bring with them the same limitations. The normal processes of the party, in his opinion, the way it is moving now with this system and this method, is not going to produce theoretical, politically qualified people. What is his scheme? A scheme to create a hothouse wherein you will gather together a number of young people, presumably of college education, and sit them down and train them and teach them to become leaders of the movement.

I have seen him try to embody this scheme. What you see in the party is a kind of silent competition between me and Comrade Cassidy in the business of building up a writing staff of the paper. All legitimate. Every time he gets hold of a young college student who comes over to us, he sees a potential writer and leader of the movement and he preoccupies himself with that question. I have a different conception. I want every young intellectual thrown in the water, to do the rough and dirty work of the movement. I want him to get all ideas out of his head to become a leader, even in a branch, until he has shown what stuff he is made of. Let him study and grub in the meantime and then we will see. But I realize we need writers.

I have the theory that it is easier to make a journalist out of a Bolshevik than it is to make a Bolshevik out of a journalist. So I start from the other end and I look around for those workers in the party who show the most talent and promise and deliberately try to make writers out of them. How do you think George Breitman became an editor of the paper? Do you think that was an [unconscious] process? You have to accuse me of this. I was the one who conceived the idea that this fellow, who had been doing . . . I thought it was time to give him his chance to round out his experience and give him a job on the press in preference to taking some college boy who hadn't any background in the class struggle—modestly as an associate and eventually to become editor.

I propounded the theory that Comrade Dobbs, whom everybody seems to regard as I do, as a coming leader of our movement, who shows certain qualities that a leader must have, not only education—he has a certain necessary minimum of that—but experience and character, devotion and backbone enough to stand up and fight. He showed that to Dan Tobin and I imagine he will show that to anyone else. He and others here. Bert. I don't know whether you have given any serious attention to the analysis of the character of the people that you are so lightly dismissing. I have a different appreciation of them and I think I know more about them. And you caught a couple of Tartars in some of the people I named if you think they are anybody's stooges or people who can be denigrated or thrust aside.

Well, I came to the conclusion that Dobbs should go to work on *The Militant*. Why? Because I am thinking all the time of how to develop leaders so that they have a rounded and complete experience. I don't want him to become just an organizational worker, tied down to details all his life so that he does not have a chance to become involved with theoretical questions. So that is the origin of Dobbs going on *The Militant*. [. . .] You think he can't write on political questions? All I tell you is to wait and see and you will get an education on that point too, as on a lot of people you so lightly cast aside.

I give a little assistance to comrades to the extent that I can, not only with ideas, not only helping them determine what line to take in an editorial, to the extent of even helping them try to criticize their letters even, their punctuation, or any technical side of it. Because I think that is my duty. What is the use of my being the national secretary of the party if I can't give young comrades the benefit of everything I know in every department? That is one way to learn. Then try to criticize what is written.

I am willing to let Felix try his experiment at the other end. Eventually he will turn up something there. But I venture to say there will be a more solid body of Bolsheviks on my side than on yours because after these people have learned to write, they have got to learn what a revolutionist is, and that is not so easy. They can't get it out of a hothouse.

I don't want you to think that I am speaking definitively. What I want to [express] here is a method, that is all. I don't mean at all a self-defense. I am of the opinion that one of the things necessary in order to develop the best [leaders] is a rounded experience. That is why I won't let any comrade settle down too long in one place, because you reach a point where you learn all that can be taught in one town and then, if you don't move, you don't grow. Comrade Charles, for example, was very nicely situated out in Los Angeles, working, and was a leader of the party there and doing useful and highly valuable work, and comfortably situated—he and his wife who is also an active party member. And California is a mild climate. But I came to the conclusion that Charlie had been sitting there too long; he had become an L.A. provincial. [It was time for him to] come to New York. Dynamite him out of there; and at the same time we want to take Murry Weiss out of there. And then take Ted Grant out of there and bring him East, put him to work in a new environment with new experiences. We eventually did all those things.

You know the great things that Charlie did here. . . . [And Lillian Curtiss is now] business manager of Pioneer Publishers, which in a manner of speaking is doing OK. We not only got the immediate benefit of their services, but they got the enormous benefit of experience in the Political Committee, and comrades who have any ability to learn cannot fail to profit by it. And I propose to keep finagling along these lines to help any comrade with any capacity. So you may say, in a sense, if I have got a cult of personal domination of the party, I am building up my own destroyers insofar as I am. [. . .]

Now, I don't know about Comrade Cassidy here. The things he raises are on a rather narrow frame. He didn't pose the question the way Morrison did, on a more or less systematic line. His remarks are on a narrow basis about some personal difficulties and so forth of mine. So I won't make such a long answer to him, except to say that he is wrong if he says that I have any hostility to a comrade presenting a counterresolution. Not at all. The only objection that I have to your resolution is to the contents of it.

And what attitude am I supposed to take on a resolution which I think is not only worse than the other resolution, but is wrong?

I don't want Cassidy to make the magazine a playhouse of speculation and a playhouse for everthing under the sun. That magazine has got to be a weapon of the party to carry out the line of the party and only within very strictly guarded limitations is it going to indulge in speculations, etc. I tried to get Morrow to speak about some breach in our personal relations and so did Morrison—Morrison said they had a quarrel. I don't have any personal quarrels. I don't want to have any personal quarrels. I outgrew that. You can't benefit one bit by them. Especially among colleagues. My theory of the estrangement between Cassidy and me is different—my criticism is that Cassidy is not an independent and objective thinker. Cassidy is subjective. He doesn't seem to be able to approach people and problems to get the best results and the best answer. I don't think that is the explanation that you gave. I think the explanation is on the other side. Cassidy knew all about my limitations and faults way before and just made the [best] of it as all the other comrades will try to do. I haven't the same regard for Cassidy as I did before, and not just for hasty impressions, but for definite reasons.

I want Cassidy to do some writing because I, like everybody else, appreciate his literary gifts. He was editing both the weekly [newspaper] and monthly magazine. I initiated the proposal that after the trial he should be relieved of his editorship of *The Militant,* and edit only the magazine so that he would have time to do more theoretical research and study, etc. And so, you see, if I don't have time to do much writing myself—and that is a fault I will admit—I am at least interested in filling up this gap.

But I wanted Cassidy to take a definite assignment. I said we have to finish up [dealing with] Sidney Hook, etc. It has not been done. It can only be done by someone thoroughly schooled in this question. Which, of course, I am not. I am only a layman on questions of Marxist philosophy and not equipped by education to do that task as much as I want to. I know what needs to be done, but I am not qualified to do it. I thought Cassidy was the one to do it. I asked him to write a series of articles against this whole gang, tracing their [abandonment of socialism] and entry into the camp of American imperialism. Do a thoroughgoing job and then print it in a pamphlet or a small book. That is what I asked and that is what I thought we had the agreement on. Cassidy didn't produce. And you will never be the same Felix to me unless you do that or give me adequate reasons why not. The only reason would be that someone else is doing it. No one is.

[Morrow: "I thought that other things were more important."]

All right. But that doesn't suit me. All the more so because—and here is where you come to the question of communist integrity drawn to a fine point—you think you are worried about communist integrity, but I believe I am even more worried about it. I believe it is necessary for the leaders of our movement to give a clean accounting of their past, to come clean, and the fact that Cassidy was raised in the New York school of philosophy. He has not, in my opinion, given a sufficient accounting of that.[105] You may say it is a suspicion on my part. Then dispel it for me. It is an intuition. Then dispel this by not turning your guns on Warde but turn them on Hook and Eastman and Company from the point of view of Marxism, and I will be highly pleased. And the fact that you don't do it I think is indefensible. If we asked Grace Carlson to write a series of articles against the Catholic Pope and she said she couldn't do it. . . .[106]

I don't think Cassidy's interventions in the organization field in New York have been fruitful or profitable for the party. I am against that. I think they have been totally false, and he has been treated with the greatest restraint in order to give him an opportunity to correct himself. He didn't understand the [December 1942] city convention. He has completely misunderstood the purpose of the city convention. [I am not interested] in crossing the last *t* or dotting the last *i* in a dispute with a comrade. If I speak in a milder, more restrained form with other comrades—and I learned it primarily from Trotsky—it makes the possibility of agreement and retreat more easy.

Now, I think there is a certain kernel of merit in the accusation made against me by Comrade Morrison to the effect that I am cautious, too cautious. I believe there is an element at least of justification for that. Now, on the other hand, I think Morrison needs a great deal more caution and restraint as a party leader, and I will try to give, in my opinion, the psychological factors which condition each of us in the separate directions. I think I am more party-minded than Morrison in the sense that I identify myself more completely with the party—I think all the time about what will be the effect on the party of what I do, because I know I can't do anything that doesn't affect the party. I have to be a little more careful than I would be perhaps if I were completely footloose or fancy-free. I don't dare to write speculative articles—

and by God I am not completely devoid of ideas. Ideas pop into my head, and sometimes as bad as Cassidy's, I dare say. But I don't dare to write a speculative article which might prove to be completely unfounded and badly motivated—not because Cannon will be made a fool of, but the party will be made a fool of.

When we approach a question for decision I am worried always about the consequences of that decision. If we make a mistake the party will suffer. That inspires in me a certain caution and perhaps too great a caution—I am willing to make that concession. But I am not so sure that Comrade Morrison, before the eyes of the public, is as [cautious] as I am. When he writes an article I think he thinks too much in terms of, well, that is my opinion, why shouldn't I express it and get it out of my system?

If I were on such terms of collaboration [as to make it possible] I would take those articles of his and blue-pencil them merciless-ly. Such a relation does not exist. I think he creates confusion, sometimes without realizing it. [. . .]

I am perfectly willing to try to do better, to be a little more receptive to anybody that has got new ideas, if Morrison, on his part, will try to be more restrained. Maybe we can make a compromise along that line. Of course I have trouble because all these new ideas have been wrong as far as I have been able to see them yet. A good way to cure my overcaution would be to come up with something good; come up with a couple of good ideas and maybe we will get somewhere.

I was very sorry to see the whole course of Comrade Cassidy here today and the last few days. He doesn't show any signs of getting over his greatest difficulty [in trying] to be a Bolshevik leader—that is, his subjectivity, his concern with himself. You have got to be objectively critical. You have got to be an independent thinker, and when you permit yourself to do things or think things from a wholly or partly subjective consideration, then, I just say, I can't trust you as a party leader. You are likely to make the greatest mistakes. . . .

Your [Cassidy's] resolution is not the same as Morrison's. I don't see any reason why you hooked your resolution onto Morrison's amendments because some of Comrade Morrison's amendments were more in our direction. Some of them. I don't see why you identified yourself with Morrison on the organization question here. So far as I know, you have never yet shown the evidences of doubt on the Leninist organizational methods that Morrison has. I personally have had that impression of him and not of you. And my feeling is that you should have spoken separately from him. And, similarly, on these political questions. You should have answered the amendments of Morrison that cut out many of your basic points.

You would have stood higher I think in the conference if you had disregarded this tendency to make a bloc with whomever you could. You show this tendency in politics generally. You begin with subjective motives and this can only lead you on the road to hell. I came into the city convention with a bible to tell you what the truth is—I came in there to try to save your soul. Because if you fool around continuously, whether you know it or not, in the New York organization, you are going to wind up with a clique on your hands, without any principled foundations for it. I hope you will correct yourself on this, but I haven't as much confidence as I used to have. I hope you won't take this—what I say now—as a blow against you because you feel it hurts your prestige. I am trying my best to tell you you have got to find a different approach to questions or you are going to lose what prestige you have left in the leading circles of our party.

Cassidy's prestige increased up until the trial. I think at the trial for the first time Cassidy was being accepted by the party leadership with prestige that was due one of the central leaders of the party. But in the period since then he has succeeded in pretty well dispersing it as far as the leading staff is concerned, and you have done it because . . . you won't learn different, and you interpret attempts to correct you as oppression or something.

Wright delivered, expounded, a very interesting thesis here the other night, and I want to add, if I may, a third point to it. Wright said there are two ways to learn: the easy way and the hard way. I want to tell you there is a third way—those that can learn neither the easy nor the hard way—that is Cassidy. That is Cassidy up to now. . . .

Do you think Trotsky formed his judgment of Shachtman in the last faction fight? Trotsky actually put a cross over Shachtman's name in 1933, in the early part of it, after Shachtman played around with the Spanish comrades, Nin and others, and played around with the crucial fights in the French league and then changed his position without sufficient motivation and bounced around Europe and did a lot of damage. Trotsky wrote one of the most devastating letters I have ever seen him write to a comrade—addressed to A. Glotzer—and this was at a time when Trotsky was supervising a reconciliation of the factions, and in connection with his proposals in which he was very fair and generous to the factions. He didn't want any of the comrades hurt or persecuted, and he put restraint on me, and he wrote to Glotzer—"so that everything would be clear between us. I am going to tell you this—that I have had many disputes with Weisbord. They were very sharp and we were apparently going in opposite directions, but I want to tell you that I preferred disputes with Weisbord over disputes with Shachtman because Weisbord means it earnestly and Shachtman plays with ideas." I don't know how you can get a better characterization of Shachtman to this day than that—he played with ideas and that is fatal for a revolutionary leader.[107]

The kind of party that Comrade Morrison demands has never existed and never will exist. Not on this earth. And I think it is idle to speculate about that, comrades, or to think what we would do if we had it. We have got to take what we have got and do the best we can with that.

Comrade Morrison mentions the fact here as the motivation . . . that I attacked him in the course of the discussions and that I attacked Oscar Williams [Schoenfeld]—clubbed him on the head. I don't know what they are talking about. They can say anything they want to to me and I can't answer them. That is the only thing that I can construe from that. I had least of all any intention of attacking Oscar. I tried to give Oscar a warning. After his second speech I could only repeat what I said before, amplify it. You didn't talk here like a young Bolshevik. You got yourself involved subjectively with Cassidy and his little machinations and disorientations and you don't realize you are off the track. You have to stop and give yourself an accounting, approach things more seriously. You have been sitting for several years in the Political Committee and I learned for the first time yesterday that you think there is something bad there. I didn't know that before. And your contribution on the city convention. If time permitted I could show you that the only tragedy of that thing was that you didn't learn what really happened there, and if you didn't learn it then you are going to suffer in the party, not by any persecution I will take against you, but you will lose the prestige and authority you have in the party, if you continue to conduct yourself that way.

It is astonishing to me how people can know the experience of the past and not take it to heart and not even listen when they are reminded that they are going on the wrong track. I want to tell you that I honestly hope that you will quit fooling around, and above all, quit fooling around with the orientation of Cassidy, or you will only go down.

Now, to get back to the system of leadership. It has been debated before, but don't forget not only has it been debated before, but it has to be tested out, not only here but elsewhere with the different methods. Our method and the method of the petty-bourgeois opposition, which is the ultimate extension of an opposition to our line, have been tested out not only in the field of politics, but in the field of organization. Of course the two go together, but not always mechanically. We could have a perfectly correct program and that kind of organization as we used to have. . . . Eventually of course the two can't go together.

What kind of a madhouse do you think the Shachtman organization is now after three years of independent thinking and collective leadership and unlimited discussion and the denigration of centralism? You know that it is a party that is in a hopeless blind alley and can't find a way out of it from the point of view of its organization construction, besides its political deviation—the two go together.

I have in mind not them so much as the tragic and painful experiences of building the Fourth International throughout Europe. What the experience has shown on the question of selecting the cadres and building the organization. I would like to qualify what was said before, I think by Dunne, about us having the best party in the sense of the strongest of any in the Fourth International. I would like to qualify that—up until the war, as I don't know what the comrades have done there under persecution and terror. My reference is to the period of legality in France.

France had the same legality as we had, much riper political conditions, etc., but they fooled around so much with this question of organization, with the lack of discipline, caution, restraint, lack of understanding how valuable it is to keep cadres together, needless splits and foolish unifications, and generally, a light-minded dilettante attitude toward the organization question, with the result that our French comrades had to face the war practically without leadership. What leadership they have is more or less what they have been able to consolidate under the fascist terror. My experience in France is unforgettable. And in England. And what I have seen negatively has convinced me just as much as the positive experience that the only way to build a party is our way, and from that you can't budge me. And that is not dogmatic. That is a conviction based upon the tangible, upon the evidence before our eyes, in contrast to the evidence we have seen in other directions.

Now I am coming to the close. Close to it. As to what the differences come down to after the discussion: If it is a question of the system and the method as I have expounded it here, not of errors in the methods or personal faults, then I say we are not going to agree. I will not put personal faults under this heading. Our method is right. We have got to continue that method, that concept, not only defensively but affirmatively. We have got to educate the membership and the rank and file more as to what we understand by our organization methods.

Now, can our dispute as it has been put forward here go to the party? No, it cannot. Because you don't dare go before the party with an argument about the merits of the individual members and their faults. The rank and file will not permit it. They want to know and have been trained and educated in principled politics. You have got to put your [political] line on the table.

We don't want to have a dispute about their merits here. And as a matter of fact, it is impossible to take it that way. If you start it that way, it will have to get a political content. Look at what happened to Abern. Abern was an orthodox Trotskyist. He only wanted one thing. He didn't want Cannon. But every time there was an opposition, the logic of his position always drew him over into the lineups with an opposing faction. Now, of course, I don't for one moment say that that is any kind of design of Morrison's. But as Stein pointed out, you can't start this kind of discussion without envisioning it developing. You just can't call a meeting of the rank and file and tell them a story, say you were at fault, and then tell them to forget it. No, they will begin talking about it. And then the first thing you know, the fat's in the fire. They begin to take sides or to think the committee isn't as good as it should be. It is only if this kind of a dispute on the organization field and personalities is linked with some seriously motivated political differences, not the ones we had here—free from any ambiguity as to what each side means; free from the necessity of saying on each side, that is what is implied—only then can you take it to the party. [. . .]

You shouldn't even think of taking these things to the rank and file of the party. They have to be settled and discussed in the leadership of the party—at least tried; at least another attempt has to be made.

I grant this difference of opinion on Morrison's part. Understanding this clearly, on what basis is collaboration possible? I will give my opinon. It is possible, and will be greatly facilitated, if Comrade Morrison will have more respect for the institution of the National Committee and of the Political Committee. Besides personnel—more respect for the authority of this body as the body that decides and to which one must subordinate himself, and that is so far above any individual that you don't dare take it lightly. That is the way we feel about it and we bitterly resent any other attitude. I have the impression, have had for a long time, that Morrison doesn't share our rigid hierarchical conceptions.

I will mention a single incident. [My example as a] source of great friction in the difference of attitude is Morrison's attitude toward Comrade Loris's invitation to the plenum.[108] When it transpired that we had called the plenum, summoned comrades from 3,000 miles away for Friday morning, and then we are told that Comrade Loris could not be here—and he lives nearby—until Saturday afternoon [Morrison] interpreted [our refusal to postpone the plenum] as a very stupid disregard for an individual comrade. My reaction was different. My reaction was one of no less indignation at the very thought of such a proposal.

When the National Committee is set to meet Friday morning, it is not the committee that adjusts itself, it is the individual, whether in Seattle or nearby New Jersey. It is symbolic. But you see I approach the thing from the exact opposite end: that it is the committee that is dominant over the individual, and he must learn how to subordinate himself to it. [. . .]

The highest body you can hope to aspire to sit in outside the Executive Committee of the Fourth International is this body right here. The best men—the most independent, capable, loyal—you can possibly hope to meet, are in the national leadership of your party. And if you don't respect them, you don't respect the party, and you have a very poor perspective. I personally couldn't tolerate the attitude of Morrison in the past on two grounds: First, as regards me I am so constituted that I can't take any man's insults. I never did in all my life. I can't tolerate that anybody [insult me] without picking it up and throwing it back at him, and in my younger days I used to throw them back. That is one thing. But the most serious was the attitude he showed toward the younger generation. They are going to develop as the next generation of leaders, who will probably have to carry the

American revolution on their shoulders. [But he] didn't hesitate to intimate that they are fools, idiots, etc. This became a regular performance in the PC of the party. I didn't stay away all summer in upstate New York [for no reason]. I needed a vacation from that atmosphere. I didn't dare trust myself to go into another meeting of the PC because I don't think it is a place for personal quarrels. Personal quarrels in general are utterly profitless. But Comrade Morrison, when he says I precipitated this by an attack on him here in the plenum, is right only in this extent: I came to the plenum determined that if Comrade Morrison repeated his action in the PC here, I would call him to order right away and let the plenum know what the score was.

[I] didn't say anything until Morrison interrupted my speech with this sneer at me as though I were a fool who didn't even know the ABCs of Marxism, and later on, his other interjections, etc. To that extent I took the initiative of precipitating it [in response to] the conduct he has shown there. He misinterpreted me a whole lot when he said that is the system, "They are going to teach me a lesson." Well, if you mean teach you a lesson by attacking or hitting you because you have an independent position, you do us a great injustice. To teach you a lesson in communist morals and manners? Yes. I think that is worth fighting about, the idea that it is impermissible in a communist gathering to hurl insults or denigrate comrades and poison the atmosphere, make false accusations against them.

Comrade Wright showed me in some of the old minutes of the old Central Committee or conferences of the Bolshevik party, stenograms that were just simply revelations of what the Bolshevik party was under Lenin before it became Stalinized and brutalized. . . . That had a great influence in shaping my attitude toward the former factional opponents. [That is why] I was so friendly to Weber and Stein and Wright and others with whom we had the sharpest fights. One has got to learn to train himself to be a Bolshevik, to rise above subjectivity and desires and act in a manner worthy of our movement. And cut out boorishness and insults. I don't say they are all on Morrison's side at all. I think there are some comrades on our side that need a lesson.

If we can learn on these points I think the discussion will have been profitable and will have made the way possible for collaboration until we see how things develop. As I said, I will try to be more receptive, more patient, in discussing questions. You try to be a little more restrained and maybe we can work something out because, after all, we have to. We have to bear in mind all the time that the question that we don't have Trotsky any more was put a little one-sidedly. We don't have Trotsky any more or anyone of his stature. The other side is that we have to lead the party without him. That is the terrible thought that flashed in my mind the day the Old Man died. And it is vain to lament and to compare what we would be with Trotsky and without Trotsky because you can't count it and change it because we are only what we are and criticism and discontent will not make us different men because the difference between us and Trotsky is not a difference of a quantitative nature; it is qualitative.

Trotsky worked on the plane of a genius. You can't even speculate and dream of another Trotsky. Very likely Trotsky himself had no such hopes, because when he wrote in the discussion with the petty-bourgeois opposition, he said—he was discussing the dialectic—he said the next epoch will undoubtedly produce great revolutionists of action, but hardly another Marx— hardly another Trotsky, I think he meant.

If somebody approaching the caliber of the young Trotsky develops in the course of the revolution, that will be a great gain. I believe it is more realistic, instead of hoping that out of the European revolution we will find another Trotsky, that we will have to help the European comrades in more ways than one, not just by resolutions from afar, but by personal intervention, by direct participation. Trotsky was an initiator, an innovator. And, as Wright correctly quoted, from my memorial speech when the Old Man died, "We are men of common clay." Our deficiencies are great and glaring, but you can't solve that by some kind of scheme. You can't make men over; you can only improve them a little bit. That is what we can try to do—improve and learn—and forget about any one individual and remember that our strength is in our combination. That is what makes up for obvious [deficiencies] of me and of others.

Our strength is our combination; our solidarity on the fundamental program that Trotsky taught us, and our policy of selecting and helping people to emerge from the ranks to strengthen the leadership and our division of labor is a conscious system all up and down the line in organizing and disposing of the abilities of individual people. This is the cadre that you have got to do it with, Comrade Morrison. It is not a handpicked group.

It is not arbitrarily selected. It is truly the representative of the party. You can't find another one, not now. The task before us is how to improve and strengthen this one and to work together, and if the plenum, the comrades from out of town, have some criticism either of me or you, we have to heed that criticism because that is the only way in which you can raise. . . .

We of the Political Committee, having said our say, have got to yield to the sentiment and the mood of the comrades, whether expressed in direct resolutions or merely in an attitude. I know that the mood of the plenum is that we don't want any unnecessary fight or personal quarrels. I will promise you that, and I assure you that for my part I will do all I can within the limits I have outlined here to reestablish a spirit of collaboration.

SPEECH ON THE WAY TO PRISON[109]

December 26, 1943

This speech to a banquet at Irving Plaza, New York City, was first published in the January 8, 1944, Militant.

This last opportunity to speak to you for a period, comrades, is also the first opportunity I have had to thank you all for the gifts that were presented to me and Rose on the occasion of the fifteenth anniversary of our movement. We were both given gold watches by the comrades of Local New York. While I will not be able to take the watch with me to Sandstone penitentiary, I will nevertheless be able to take something even more valuable than the watch or any other material gift. That is the memory of your kindness and your friendship.

It is always the most important thing in a new situation to understand what it is, to know exactly what has happened and why. Trotsky taught us that, among so many other things. He frequently repeated his favorite motto, from Spinoza: "Neither to weep nor to laugh, but to understand."

The new situation is very clear to us, and I think our understanding is accurate. As the United States began to gear all its machinery for entry into the new imperialist war, it became necessary again to fool the people. Here, as throughout the world, a tremendous, worldwide mechanism of deception, falsification, and misrepresentation was turned loose on the people. It was once said that in every war the first casualty is the truth, and surely the truth was the first casualty of this war. The world is flooded, inundated by lies. We are living, you might say, in the epoch of the lie. Natalia Trotsky, in a letter she wrote to us not long ago, said that the lie has entered like a geologic layer into the spiritual life of the people of the world; but even geologic layers are not indestructible. The coming social revolution will blow the stratum of lies to bits, as a volcano blows up a geologic stratum.

In this time, when the people of the world, and the people of America among them, needed one thing more than anything else—to know the truth—they were fed on lies. All those in public life, all the political parties; all the preachers, priests, and rabbis; all the intellectuals who had promised to instruct and educate and inform the youth—they all betrayed the people of America; they sold them out and went over to the camp of the liars and deceivers. Our party alone did not betray, did not sell out. We Trotskyists told the truth. That is the reason, and the only reason, we are on our way to prison. We obeyed the first commandment in the decalogue of Trotskyism, which reads: "Thou shalt not lie."

We are not criminals, as you know, and as all of the others know. We are not going to prison for any fault or injury committed against unoffending people. We didn't kill, we didn't steal, and we didn't lie. On the contrary, we have been just and truthful. All the criminals are on the other side. And all the liars are on the other side, beginning with the judge and prosecutor in Minneapolis and ending with the highest court in the land. That is where the criminals are. I say that those nine black-gowned justices of the Supreme Court in Washington are just as criminal as any of them. They are on a level with Roosevelt and Biddle, who started the prosecution, and the lesser figures who carried it through. The august court did not pass judgment upon us. They played the ignominious role of Pontius Pilate, who washed his hands.

The Supreme Court of the United States, many of whom were once members of the American Civil Liberties Union—democrats, if you please, and liberals who frowned upon the morality of the Bolsheviks and the Marxists—showed us what their morality consists of. They were not concerned if honest people had been condemned. They were not concerned if the treasured Bill of Rights had been trampled into the mire. They didn't see the act. They turned away. They washed their hands.

I say they are all liars and conspirators. They are all on the side of the rich and the privileged, and their actions, from beginning to end, have been entirely consistent with this position. Everything, from the time when Roosevelt gave Biddle instructions to start the prosecutions against us, up to the trial, up to the verdict and the condemnation, up to the sentencing in the federal court of Judge Joyce, up to the Pontius Pilate action of the Supreme Court of the United States—everything is consistent, everything is in order in the camp of the liars, the friends of the rich and privileged.

But how do matters stand with us? Are we consistent too? Yes, indeed. Everything is in order on our side. We neither laugh nor weep; we understand. We have understood from the beginning what might be the consequences of our undertaking. All people pay for their ideas what they think the ideas are worth. If some men are not prepared to pay with the sacrifice of one day's liberty or the missing of one meal or a little inconvenience for the sake of their ideas, they are only saying thereby that they set no serious value upon them. But we think our ideas are the most important thing in this world, that they represent the whole future of mankind. That is why, if we have to pay even a high price for the sake of those ideas, we pay it without whimpering. We are Trotskyists, you remember, and that means we are political people of a different breed.

The Trotskyist party is not like the other parties. It is a different kind of a party, different not in degree, but in kind, in quality. Other parties and other politicians set limits to what they will do. But the Trotskyists set no limit on what they will do for their ideas and, in the last analysis, they set no limits on the price they are prepared to pay for them. The others play for pennies, but the Trotskyist stakes his head. Therein is the difference. Therein is the chasm that separates the vanguard of the coming proletarian revolution from all politicians and parties who merely dabble with the idea.

I am not one of those who take lightly the iniquity that has been perpetrated against us. It is a severe and cruel punishment. We who love freedom and live for the idea of freedom are condemned to lose it for ourselves. We will not be free to come and go as we please. Our days and nights, through the long months leading up to the end of our sentence, will be regulated, and all our movements will be circumscribed by others. That will not be easy for rebels to bear. We will be forced into inactivity. What can be more cruel to a revolutionary activist than to be deprived of the opportunity to take part in the movement which means life to him—the very breath of life?

And then, also, it is no light matter that we have to be separated from our families, and they from us. True, we don't cry, and, as Rose said so magnificently in her speech here tonight, our women don't mope. But, nevertheless, we are human too. If we are struck a blow, we hurt; and if we are stabbed, we bleed. Separation from those whose lives are bound to us in an intimate personal way is no less cruel a punishment for us than it would be for others. Perhaps it is even more cruel because our personal intimate associations are bound up with a complete community of ideas and activity in every element of life. Such associations are perhaps a little closer, even a little dearer, if you will, than those of people who don't value ideas very much and who, consequently, don't attract to themselves personal associations such as ours.

But even if it hurts a little more, we can stand it better than the others because we are doing it on behalf of a cause that is more important than our personal lives. It is the cause that lifts us up and gives us strength. Socialism is greater than a mother and dearer than a wife. Knowing that, and knowing that our separation is forced upon us because of our devotion to the higher cause, is what makes it possible to bear and to withstand.

We haven't been taken by surprise. We have not been suddenly pulled up short and required to make a decision whether we are prepared to pay this price. Our decision was made in advance. We knew to begin with that to tell the truth, to take up the cause of the poor and the persecuted against the rich and the mighty, to tell the truth in the face of all the liars in the world—we knew that course entailed risks. I knew that more than thirty years ago when I entered the socialist movement as a youth.

Socialism lifted me out of the drab surroundings and meager life of the poor town of Rosedale, Kansas, and showed me the vision of a new world. I thought it was good. I thought it worth fighting for. I was ready, more than thirty years ago, to fight for it at all hazards.

Nothing has ever changed my sense of proportion and of values in that respect. Neither persecution, nor poverty, nor hardship, nor the long days of internal struggles and factional quarrels that sear the souls of men in the political movement—none of that was able to change me or break me, because I never forgot what I started out to fight for. I kept undimmed my vision of the socialist future of mankind. Having that attitude, as all of the eighteen do, we can put so-called sacrifices in their proper setting and attribute to them their right place with a due sense of proportion.

Ben Hanford, one of the best loved of all the early socialist agitators in this country, once objected to a comrade's statement that he had made great sacrifices for the movement. He said he had received from the socialist movement something far greater and far better than he had ever been able to contribute to it. He had only been able to give time, effort and material means, but the socialist movement had given him a cause that was bigger than self. Therefore, he had a warrant for living in a world of poverty, hardship, discrimination, and injustice. "So please don't speak of my sacrifices," said Ben Hanford. "Socialism made a man of me, and I can never repay the movement for that."

We have not been idle in our time of comparative freedom. We have labored and we have created something that we can leave behind, very sure that it will not fall apart. A movement that is built upon ideas is a power that is hard to destroy. Indeed, it cannot be destroyed.

You remember the tragic time three years ago last August, when Trotsky fell victim to the assassin. Many people speculated that now, with the great genius-leader dead, the movement he had created would be scattered to the four winds and soon disappear. We knew it was not so, because the ideas Trotsky left behind were a mighty cement to keep the ranks together. The party didn't fall into disintegration. Far from it, the party continued to live and to grow. That will be the case now, too.

We go to prison confident that we are leaving behind us capable men and women who are qualified to take our places in the leadership of the party. They have not been selected in a hurry. When the decision of the Supreme Court was announced, we did not need an emergency meeting and a hurried search for comrades to take our places in the leading positions. That had already been decided by the Fifteenth Anniversary Plenum of our party. But even the plenum decision was only a formality. In reality, the substitute leadership had been decided by the fifteen years of work and struggle in which certain individual comrades had been sifted out. They had shown their caliber. They had come forward, and by common consent they were designated to step into the places vacated by the eighteen.

Our party is built on correct ideas and therefore is indestructible. But, in addition to that, I believe there is in this party of ours an intangible power which reinforces the power of its ideas. That is the spirit of the party—its comradeship, its solidarity. You know the word *comrade* has been so long abused and so badly defiled by self-seekers and pretenders that honest people sometimes shrink from using the word any more. But in the movement that has been created under the inspiration of Trotsky, with his example always before us, the word *comrade* has acquired a new, fresh meaning that animates the members of our movement not only in their political work in the class struggle, but also in all their daily lives and associations with each other. It is not anymore, not with us, a formal and conventional word, but a bond of unity and solidarity. Our comrades are devoted to each other and trust each other. That is an intangible source of power that will yield great results in the days to come.

The grandest figure in the whole history of America was John Brown. In John Brown of Osawatomie, the word and the deed were always in harmony with each other, never in contradiction, never in conflict. When the old warrior went to Harpers Ferry to "interfere," as he said, against the abomination of chattel slavery, he took a small group of young men with him, among them some of his own sons. They went to Harpers Ferry where they perished because, like Luther, they could do no other. They felt required to do it. When Watson Brown, the son of the old man, lay dying in the firehouse, bleeding from his wounds, with his head resting on an old pair of overalls, the great governor of the slave state of Virginia came in to see him. He said to Watson Brown, "Young man, what brought you here?" Watson Brown answered him in two words: "Duty, Sir!"

I believe that is the case with us. I believe that we have been under the same compulsion as John Brown's young men were. We were obliged to tell the truth. We saw the abomination of the imperialist war and we were under compulsion to tell the people the truth about it. We saw the vision of a socialist society and were under compulsion to fight for it at all costs and despite all hazards. We have done our duty. And that, to me, on the eve of departure for Sandstone, is the important thing. That is why we go to the next stage of the struggle with a sure self-confidence and self-assurance.

We are historically minded. We know that in the great scale of history our personal fate is a trifle, our lives are a trifle. But the socialist goal of our struggle—that is no trifle. To serve that goal, as we have served it, that is enough. Let the consequences be what they may. Whether we participate in the final victory of the struggle of mankind for its socialist future, or whether it has to be built on a foundation of our bones, it will still be good for us that we took part in it, and we will have our justification and our reward.

No liars and conspirators, no Supreme Court and no prison, can take that satisfaction away from us. We were obliged to do what we did. As a consequence of our truth-telling and our struggle, we are now obliged to go to prison. We go there, however, not as criminals, but because duty takes us there.

GLOSSARY

Abern, Martin (1898-1949)—A founding member of American CP and later of Trotskyist movement. Member of first NC of CLA. Split from SWP in 1940 with Shachtman-Burnham group.

Adams—Pseudonym of Henry Schultz.

Adler, Al—An SWP leader in Detroit, active in the auto union. Elected to the NC in 1941. Left SWP in 1953 with Bert Cochran.

American Labor Party (New York State)—Formed in 1936 by David Dubinsky of International Ladies' Garment Workers Union and Sidney Hillman of Amalgamated Clothing Workers to win labor votes for Roosevelt in New York and to support Republican-Fusion coalition of Mayor LaGuardia in New York City. Split in 1944 into ALP and Liberal Party. Supported Progressive Party in 1948. Dissolved in 1956.

American Workers Party (AWP)—Formed in December 1933 by Conference for Progressive Labor Action led by A.J. Muste. Fused with CLA in December 1934 to form Workers Party of the United States.

Barkley, Alben (1877-1956)—Democratic senator from Kentucky (1927-49). Majority leader in Senate (1937-47). Vice-president under Truman (1949-53).

Barr—Pseudonym of Farrell Dobbs.

Bennett—Pseudonym of Lydia Beidel.

Beidel, Lydia—Joined CLA in 1933. Elected to SWP NC in 1941. Business manager of *The Militant* (1941-42). A leader of Chicago branch, she supported Goldman-Morrow faction and resigned from SWP in May 1946 with Goldman to join Shachtman's WP.

Biddle, Francis (1886-1968)—U.S. solicitor general (1940-41). Roosevelt's attorney general (1941-45). Initiated prosecution in 1941 Minneapolis trial and denial of second-class mailing rights to *The Militant* in 1942-44. Later a leader of Americans for Democratic Action.

Blum, Leon (1872-1950)—Head of French Socialist Party in 1930s and premier of first People's Front government in 1936.

Bolsheviks—Majority faction formed in Russian Social Democratic

Labor Party at Second Congress in 1903. Led by Lenin. Became separate party in 1912. Organized October Revolution of 1917 that established first workers' state. Changed name to Communist Party.

Braverman, Harry—Elected to SWP NC in 1941. Wrote for SWP press under name Harry Frankel. Left SWP with Bert Cochran in 1953. At present director of Monthly Review Press.

Breitman, George (1916-   )—Joined Workers Party in 1935. Member of SWP NC from 1939. Editor of *The Militant* (1941-43). Editor of books by Trotsky and by Malcolm X.

Bridges, Harry (1900-   )—Then as now leader of International Longshoremen's and Warehousemen's Union (ILWU). Closely followed line of CP in 1930s and 1940s.

Browder, Earl (1891-1973)—Joined American SP in 1907. Edited weekly *Workers World* with Cannon in Kansas City in 1919. In CP, a supporter of William Z. Foster in factional disputes of 1920s. Elected CP general-secretary in 1930 on Stalin's directive after expulsion of Trotskyists and Lovestoneites. Deposed by Stalin in 1945 and expelled from CP in 1946.

Brown, John (1800-1859)—American abolitionist. Fought armed proslavery gang at Osawatomie, Kansas, in 1856. Led raid on government arsenal at Harpers Ferry, Virginia, in 1859 as part of plan for slave rebellion. Hanged after trial for treason by proslavery court.

Bulletin of the Opposition (Biulleten Oppozitsii)—Russian-language organ of Left Opposition, published from 1929 under Trotsky's editorship until his death. Ceased publication in 1941.

Burch, Arthur—Member of SWP NC in 1940s and 1950s. Branch organizer in Detroit and Newark. Later withdrew from politics.

Burnham, James (1905-   )—Professor of philosophy at New York University. Member of AWP National Committee. Elected to NC of Workers Party in 1934. Renounced defense of Soviet Union after Stalin-Hitler pact in August 1939 and split from SWP in April 1940. Broke with Shachtman in May, moving to far right. At present an editor of William Buckley's *National Review*.

Carlson, Grace (1906-   )—Joined WP in 1936. Member of SWP NC from 1941. Convicted and imprisoned in Minneapolis case. Ran for vice-president on first SWP presidential ticket in 1948. Resigned from SWP in June 1952 to return to Catholic Church.

Cassidy—Pseudonym of Felix Morrow.

C. Charles—Pseudonym of Charles Curtiss.

Ch'en Tu-hsiu (1879-1942)—Founder of Chinese Communist Party in 1921 and its principal leader until 1927. After defeat of Chinese revolution in 1927 came out in support of Trotskyist Left Opposition. Expelled from CCP in 1929 and helped found Chinese Trotskyist organization. Served five years in prison in Nanking in 1930s. Broke with Trotskyism in 1941.

Churchill, Winston (1874-1965)—Conservative Party prime minister of Great Britain (1940-45 and 1951-55). Advocate of armed intervention against Soviet Union after Russian Revolution; principal representative of British imperialism in World War II; architect of post-World War II cold war.

Civil Rights Defense Committee (CRDC)—Organization that rallied public support for defendants in Minneapolis case.

Clarke, George (1913-1964)—Joined CLA in 1929. Elected to NC of Workers Party in 1934. A merchant seaman in 1940s. Was campaign manager of SWP's 1948 presidential campaign. Later edited *Fourth International* and was SWP representative in Europe. Left SWP in 1953 with Bert Cochran. Killed in an automobile accident.

Clemenceau, Georges (1841-1929)—Leader of French bourgeois Radical Party. Premier (1906-09 and 1917-19). Chief inspirer of Versailles Treaty.

Cochran, Bert—Joined CLA in 1934. Elected to SWP NC in 1938. Union organizer for Mechanics Educational Society in Toledo, Ohio. Later a staff member of UAW. Left SWP in 1953. Author of biographies of Adlai Stevenson and Harry Truman. At present a resident at Columbia University's Institute on Communist Affairs.

Collins—Pseudonym of George Clarke.

Communist League of America (Opposition) (CLA)—Founded in Chicago in May 1929 by Trotskyists expelled from CP in October 1928. CLA fused with AWP in December 1934 to form Workers Party of the United States.

Cooper, Lou—Member of New York Local of SWP. Supported Goldman-Morrow faction. Left party in 1946.

Coughlin, Father Charles E.—Catholic priest and profascist demagogue in 1930s.

Curtiss, Charles (1908-   )—Member of CLA from earliest period in New York and Los Angeles. Elected to the NC of the WP in 1936. Worked with Trotsky in Mexico (1938-39) as representative of the International Secretariat of Fourth International to the Mexican section. Became acting national secretary of SWP during 1941 Minneapolis trial but was drafted into army before defendants went to prison. Left SWP in 1951 and joined Socialist Party.

Darlan, Admiral Jean Louis (1881-1942)—Commander in chief of French navy in 1939. Supported pro-Nazi Vichy government after fall of France. Surrendered to Allies in Algiers in November 1942. Made chief of state of French Africa under Eisenhower. Assassinated.

Davies, Joseph E. (1876-1958)—U.S. ambassador to Soviet Union (1936-38).

DeBoer, Harry (1907-   )—Leader of Minneapolis Teamsters Union from 1934. One of eighteen defendants convicted in Minneapolis trial.

Debs, Eugene Victor (1855-1926)—Leader of Pullman strike, Chicago (1894). Founder of Socialist Party (1901) and its four-time presidential candidate in 1904, 1908, 1912, and 1920. Most popular socialist leader of pre-World War I period. Imprisoned for his antiwar views (1918-21).

Dobbs, Farrell (1907-   )—Leader of Minneapolis drivers' strikes of 1934. Joined CLA in March 1934 and elected to NC of Workers Party in December. Became SWP national labor secretary in 1939. One of eighteen political prisoners in Minneapolis case. Served as SWP national secretary (1953-72). Four-time presidential candidate of SWP (1948-60). Completing a four-volume history of role of Trotskyists in Minneapolis Teamsters movement.

Dubinsky, David (1892-   )—Social Democratic president of International Ladies' Garment Workers Union (1932-66). Took ILGWU into CIO in 1936, withdrew in 1938, rejoined AFL in 1940. A leader of American Labor Party, which he split in 1944 to help found New York Liberal Party.

Dunne, Grant (1894-1941)—One of three Dunne brothers active in leadership of Minneapolis Trotskyist and labor movements. Prominent in 1934 strikes, he was later a leader of Federal Workers Section (WPA) of Local 544 and an organizer for Local 544-CIO. One of original twenty-nine indicted in Minneapolis case, and in poor health, he committed suicide before trial began.

Dunne, Miles (1896-1958)—With his brothers Grant and Vincent, a founding member of Trotskyist movement and a leader of Minneapolis teamsters' strikes of 1934. Editor of *Northwest Organizer*. President of Local 544-CIO. Indicted but acquitted in Minneapolis trial.

Dunne, Vincent Raymond (1890-1970)—Founding member of CLA and member of its first NC. A central leader of 1934 Minneapolis strikes. One of eighteen convicted in Minneapolis trial. An active leader of SWP until his death. In 1943 he served as acting national labor secretary in New York.

Eastman, Max (1883-1969)—Editor of *The Masses* before World War I. Supporter of CP in early 1920s and of Left Opposition from 1923. Translated several of Trotsky's books. Rejected dialectical materialism. Repudiated socialism at end of 1930s and became an anticommunist.

Field, B.J.—Member of CLA in New York. Expelled in 1932 for violating branch discipline. Readmitted at request of Trotsky. Expelled again in 1934 for violating party discipline in New York hotel workers' strike. Founded League for a Revolutionary Workers Party which survived into war years.

First International—The International Workingmen's Association, founded by Marx and Engels in 1864. Headquarters moved to U.S. after defeat of Paris Commune in 1871. Dissolved in 1876.

Fourth International—The World Party of Socialist Revolution founded by Leon Trotsky in 1938. It held an emergency world conference in New York in May 1940.

Fourth International magazine—Name given to SWP's theoretical magazine beginning with May 1940 issue after Shachtman had appropriated mailing rights for *New International*, the party's magazine from 1934. *Fourth International* changed name to *International Socialist Review* in 1956.

Franco, Francisco (1892-   )—Leader of fascist forces in Spanish Civil War (1936-39). Dictator of Spain after 1939. Neutral toward Britain and U.S. in World War II, he gave military aid to Hitler against Soviet Union.

Frank, E.R.—Pseudonym of Bert Cochran.

Frank, Pierre (1905-   )—A founding leader of French section of International Left Opposition. Sentenced to prison by French government at outbreak of war. Escaped to England, where he was interned by British government. Elected to International Secretariat of Fourth International at first postwar congress.

Franklin—Pseudonym of Albert Goldman.

Furth, Pauline—SWP member and leader of fish cannery workers in San Diego, California, during World War II. Left SWP in early 1950s.

Fuzzy—Nickname of Pauline Furth.

Garrison, William Lloyd (1805-1879)—American abolitionist. Founder of the *Liberator* (1831), famous antislavery journal. President of American Anti-Slavery Society (1843-65).

Gitlow, Benjamin (1891-1965)—CP vice-presidential candidate in 1924 and 1928. Member of Political Committee of CP and of Executive Committee of Communist International. Expelled from CP in 1929 with Lovestone. Broke with Lovestone in 1933. Became renegade from communism and published an anticommunist memoir, *I Confess* (1940).

Glotzer, Albert (1908-   )—A founding member of CLA and member of its first NC. A supporter of Abern throughout 1930s, he split from SWP with Shachtman in 1940.

Goldman, Albert (1897-1960)—Joined CLA in 1933. Left in 1934 to join SP. Became NC member of SWP in 1938. Served as Trotsky's U.S. attorney. Was chief defense counsel as well as defendant in 1941 Minneapolis trial. Formed faction with Felix Morrow while in prison. Left SWP in May 1946 to join Shachtman's Workers Party.

Gompers, Samuel (1850-1924)—President of AFL (1886-1924). Supported World War I and was appointed by President Wilson to Council of National Defense (1917).

Gordon, Sam—Member of CLA from 1929. Became NC member of WP in 1934. Worked in leadership of Fourth International during period it was in New York in World War II (in this work he used name J.B. Stuart).

GPU—Stalin's secret police. Also known at various times as NKVD, MVD, and KGB. Was used in worldwide intelligence and assassination operations on behalf of Stalinist bureaucracy.

Grant, Ted (1903-   )—Joined AWP in 1933 and became NC member of WP after merger with CLA in 1934. Active in union movement in Ohio in 1930s. Was SWP New York Local organizer in early 1940s. Withdrew from political activity in mid-1950s.

Green, William (1873-1952)—President of AFL (1924-52).

Hanford, Ben (1861-1910)—Leader of New York Typographical Workers Union. Member of Socialist Labor Party until 1899. Among founders of Socialist Party in 1901. Eugene V. Debs's vice-presidential running mate on SP ticket in 1904 and 1908. Creator of character "Jimmy Higgins" as prototype of unselfish rank-and-file party activist.

Hansen, Joseph (1910-   )—Joined CLA in 1934. Secretary to Leon Trotsky (1937-40). Elected to NC at SWP's April 1940 convention. Following assassination of Trotsky, served in merchant marine during war. In 1950s was editor of *International Socialist Review* and *The Militant*. Since 1963, editor of *Intercontinental Press* (begun under name *World Outlook*).

Harte, Robert Sheldon (1915-1940)—Member of the SWP in New York. Became one of Trotsky's guard-secretaries at Coyoacan in April 1940. Murdered by Stalinist assassins after the May 24 machine-gun assault on Trotsky's home.

Haywood, William D. (1869-1928)—Leader of Western Federation of Miners. A founder of Industrial Workers of World (1905). Tried on charge of murdering former governor of Idaho (1907). Mass defense movement led to acquittal. Arrested for opposing World War I (1917); convicted (1918). Went into exile in Soviet Union (1921).

Held, Walter (d. 1941)—German Trotskyist who moved to Norway after Hitler came to power in 1933. Served as Trotsky's secretary in Norway (1935-36). Traveling to U.S. in 1941, secured permit for passage through USSR. Seized on Soviet train by GPU and executed.

Henderson—Pseudonym of Joseph Hansen.

Hillman, Sidney (1887-1946)—President of Amalgamated Clothing Workers (1915-46). Vice-president of CIO. A founder of American Labor Party in New York (1936). Roosevelt's chief labor lieutenant during World War II.

Hindenburg, Paul von (1847-1934)—German chief of staff in World War I. Conservative president of Germany (1925-34). Appointed Hitler as chancellor (1933).

Hook, Sidney (1902-   )—Student of John Dewey at Columbia University. Close to CP in early 1930s. Was a leader of AWP but did not take part in WP after 1934 fusion. Became right-wing Social Democrat. Supported cold war and polemicized against Marxism, particularly in field of philosophy.

Hull, Cordell (1871-1955)—U.S. secretary of state (1933-44).

Jones—Pseudonym of V.R. Dunne.

Jouhaux, Leon (1879-1954)—Leader of French General Confederation of Labor (CGT), 1909-40 and 1945-47. A right-wing Social Democrat, he supported French government in World War I and de Gaulle forces in World War II.

Karsner, Rose (1889-1968)—Member of pre-World War I SP left wing. Founding member of CP. Cannon's companion from 1924. A founder and leader of American Trotskyist movement from 1928 until her death.

Kautsky, Karl (1854-1938)—Leader of German Social Democracy and a founder of Second International (1889). Editor of *Die Neue Zeit*, German Social Democratic theoretical journal (1883-1917). Best known Marxist theoretician before 1914. Took a pacifist position during World War I but abstained from Zimmerwald movement. Opposed Bolshevik revolution in 1917.

Keller—Pseudonym of Art Preis.

Kerensky, Alexander (1881-1970)—Member of a faction of Russian Social Revolutionary Party. Became prime minister of bourgeois Provisional Government created by February 1917 revolution. Overthrown by Bolsheviks in October 1917.

Konikow, Antoinette (1869-1946)—Born in Orenburg, Russia. Member of Plekhanov's Emancipation of Labor group, Russia's first Marxist organization, from 1886. Attended founding congress of Second International (1889). Emigrated to Boston (1893). Member of Socialist Labor Party. Founding member of SP (1901). Leader of left wing and a founder of CP in 1919. Physician and advocate of birth control. Author of *Voluntary Motherhood* (1923). Expelled from CP in Boston for Trotskyism (1928). Joined with Cannon, Shachtman, and Abern when they were expelled later that year. Made honorary member of NC at founding convention of SWP in 1938.

Kuomintang (KMT)—Nationalist Party, founded in China by Sun Yat-sen. Led after his death (1925) by Chiang Kai-shek. Chief instrument of bourgeois rule in China from 1925 to 1949. Remains ruling party in Taiwan.

Labor Action—Newspaper of Shachtman's Workers Party after split from SWP in April 1940. Not to be confused with newspaper of same name edited by Cannon in San Francisco (1936-37), which was paper of SP left wing.

Labor's Non-Partisan League—Political arm of CIO, organized in 1936 to win votes for Roosevelt. Controlled by John L. Lewis in 1940, when he supported Republicans. After this became political lobbying department of United Mine Workers.

LaGuardia, Fiorello (1882-1947)—Republican member of U.S. House of Representatives from New York (1917-21 and 1923-33). Three-time mayor of New York City (1934-45), elected by anti-Tammany Hall bloc of Republicans and labor unions. Endorsed by ALP for second and third terms.

Lang, Frederick J.—Pseudonym of Frank Lovell.

Lesoil, Leon (1892-1942)—A founder of Belgian CP, member of its Central Committee in 1923. A founder of Belgian Trotskyist movement in 1927. Leader of Charleroi miners in 1930s. Arrested by Nazis in 1941. Died in concentration camp.

Levi, Paul (1883-1930)—Follower of Rosa Luxemburg. Leader of German CP (1919-21). Expelled after opposing March putsch action in

1921. Rejoined Social Democrats, where he led a left wing. Committed suicide.

Lewis, John L. (1880-1969)—President of United Mine Workers (1920-69). Principal founder and leader of CIO from 1935 until he resigned presidency in 1940 after Roosevelt's reelection. Withdrew from CIO in 1942. Led miners' strike in 1943.

Lewitt, Morris—Joined CLA in 1930. Became member of NC of WP in 1934. Under name Morris Stein served as acting national secretary of SWP while eighteen Minneapolis defendants were in prison and in postwar period as national organizational secretary. Withdrew from political activity in early 1960s.

London Bureau—Officially, the International Bureau of Revolutionary Socialist Parties. Established in 1935, with organizational roots going back to 1932. Loose federation of centrist parties opposed to Second and Third Internationals but unwilling to join in founding of Fourth International. Included among its adherents the SAP (Socialist Workers Party) of Germany, Independent Labour Party of Great Britain, Spanish POUM (Workers Party of Marxist Unification), French PSOP (Workers and Peasants Socialist Party), and in U.S. the Independent Labor League (Lovestoneites).

Loris, Marc—Pseudonym of Jean van Heijenoort.

Lovell, Frank (1913-   )—Joined WP in 1935. Active in California in Sailor's Union of the Pacific. Elected to NC at 1942 SWP convention. Lived in New York during the war, shipping as a merchant seaman. Since late 1960s has been national trade union director of SWP and labor columnist for *The Militant.*

Lovestone, Jay (1898-   )—Leader of a faction of American CP in 1920s. Expelled in 1929. Founded Communist Party (Opposition), renamed Independent Labor League. Disbanded in 1940. Later became chief advisor on foreign policy to AFL-CIO President George Meany and a supporter of cold war.

Lundeberg, Harry (1901-1957)—Head of Sailors' Union of the Pacific from mid-1930s and of Seafarers International Union, AFL, from its chartering in 1938. Leader of "antipolitical," syndicalist tendency in labor movement in opposition to Stalinists and progovernment forces. Supported government in World War II but maintained more militant union policy than Stalinists who advocated no-strike pledge.

Luxemburg, Rosa (1870-1919)—A founder of Polish Social Democratic Party in 1893. From 1897 also a participant in leadership of German Social Democracy, where she championed revolutionary Marxist program against growing reformism of Eduard Bernstein. Jailed in 1915 for opposition to war, she helped found Spartacus League, which later became German Communist Party. Took part in Spartacus uprising in Berlin (1919). Arrested and murdered with complicity of Social Democratic government.

Mangan, Sherry (1904-1961)—American writer and journalist. Joined

Trotskyist movement in 1934. Active in France during German occupation until expelled by Pétain regime. Served on European Secretariat of Fourth International during last years of war and then on International Secretariat.

Marlen, George—Pseudonym of George Spiro.

Marlenites—See George Spiro.

Martin—Pseudonym of James P. Cannon.

Martin, Homer (1902-1968)—After career as Protestant minister and Olympic athlete, became autoworker in early 1930s. First president of UAW (1936-39). Led small group of UAW locals in break from CIO to rejoin AFL (1939). Left labor movement, later becoming antilabor attorney for an employers' organization.

Mazey, Ernest—An SWP leader in Detroit. Active in UAW. Elected to SWP NC in 1944. Left the SWP with Bert Cochran in 1953. Later became leader of American Civil Liberties Union in Michigan.

McGee—Pseudonym of Grace Carlson.

Meichler, Jean (1896-1942)—A founder of *La Vérité*, first French Trotskyist newspaper (1929). Executed by Nazis as a hostage in France.

Mensheviks—Minority faction at Second Congress of Russian Social Democratic Labor Party (1903). After 1912 became separate party. Supported bourgeois Provisional Government created by February 1917 revolution and opposed Bolshevik seizure of power in October 1917. Remained part of reformist Second International.

Merritt—Pseudonym of Murry Weiss.

The Militant—Newspaper of American Trotskyists starting with their expulsion from CP. First issue appeared November 15, 1928. With December 15, 1934, issue name changed to *New Militant* as result of fusion with AWP. Ceased publication in June 1936 when Trotskyists entered SP. In August 1937, after expulsion of Trotskyists from SP, *Socialist Appeal*, an internal SP paper, became public paper of Trotskyists. Name changed back to *The Militant* February 1, 1941, as gesture of continuity after forced disaffiliation of SWP from Fourth International under Voorhis Act. With December 13, 1941, issue ceased to be official paper of SWP and became property of Militant Publishing Association.

Minnesota Farmer-Labor Party—Organized in 1920s with trade union support. Controlled governorship from 1931 to 1939 when defeated by Republican Harold Stassen. In 1944 party merged with national Democratic Party, whose candidates it had previously supported in presidential elections. Thereafter called Democratic Farmer-Labor Party.

Morrison—Pseudonym of Albert Goldman.

Morrow, Felix (1906-   )—Joined CLA in 1933. Elected to NC of SWP in 1938. Editor of *Socialist Appeal* and *The Militant* from Shachtman split in 1940 to early 1942. Editor of *Fourth International* (1942-43). One of eighteen prisoners in Minneapolis case. In prison, formed faction with Albert Goldman and was expelled at November 1946

SWP convention for unauthorized collaboration with Shachtman's Workers Party. Dropped out of politics shortly afterward.

Munis, Grandizo—A leader of Spanish Trotskyists during Civil War. Escaped to Mexico several months after Franco's victory in 1939. Defended ultraleft and sectarian positions that led him to break with Fourth International in 1947. Later returned to Spain and was imprisoned in 1950s.

Murray, Philip (1886-1952)—Vice-president of United Mine Workers under John L. Lewis (1920-42). Succeeded Lewis as president of CIO in 1940.

Muste, A.J. (1885-1967)—Protestant minister and pacifist. Founded Conference for Progressive Labor Action (1929), which in 1933 organized American Workers Party. Fused with CLA in December 1934 to form Workers Party. Broke with Marxism in summer of 1936 to return to church. In 1960s played leading role in movement against Vietnam war.

Nancy—Pseudonym of Natalia Sedova.

New International—Theoretical magazine of American Trotskyists. Began publication in July 1934. Ceased for a year and a half (summer 1936 to the end of 1937) during the entry into SP. Resumed publication, 1938-1940. When Shachtman and Burnham split from SWP in April 1940 they took post office mailing rights of *New International*. Name was changed to *Fourth International* (1940-56). In 1956 name was changed to *International Socialist Review*.

New Leader—A Social Democratic magazine published in New York.

Nin, Andrés (1892-1937)—A founder of Spanish Communist Party and secretary of Red International of Labor Unions. Supported Left Opposition and was expelled from CP in 1927. Participated in formation of International Left Opposition. Broke with Trotsky in 1935 to merge with Workers and Peasants Bloc of Joaquín Maurín to form POUM (Workers Party of Marxist Unification). Arrested by the Stalinists in Barcelona in June 1937 and murdered.

Noske, Gustav (1868-1946)—Social Democratic minister of defense in Germany in 1919. Suppressed Spartacus uprising and was implicated in murder of Rosa Luxemburg and Karl Liebknecht.

Novack, George (1905-   )—Joined CLA in 1933. Secretary of American Committee for the Defense of Leon Trotsky, formed early in 1937, which was instrumental in bringing together Dewey Commission of Inquiry into the Moscow Trials. After indictments in Minneapolis case in 1941, was secretary of the CRDC, which organized legal defense. Elected to SWP NC in 1941. Well-known socialist scholar and author of many books on Marxist philosophy and history.

NRA (National Recovery Administration)—Set up under National Industrial Recovery Act of 1933. Was a major New Deal measure against the depression. Set price floors to protect marginal businesses from being undersold. Set minimum wages and hours and recognized right of collective bargaining. Aimed at reestablishing stable market conditions to stimulate business output.

Oehler, Hugo—CP trade unionist in Kansas City in 1920s. Joined CLA in 1930. Elected to NC in 1931. Opposed entry into SP and was expelled from WP in October 1935. Founded Revolutionary Workers League which survived into 1950s.

Palmer, A. Mitchell (1872-1936)—Democratic U.S. attorney general (1919-21). Ordered nationwide raids against CP and other radical tendencies in January 1920 in which hundreds were arrested and many foreign-born radicals were deported without trial to Soviet Union.

Pétain, Henri Philippe (1856-1951)—Marshal of French army from 1918. Headed pro-Nazi government at Vichy (1940-44) after fall of Paris to Germans. Convicted of treason in 1945 and sentenced to death; later commuted to life imprisonment.

Phelan, Terence—Pseudonym of Sherry Mangan.

Postal, Kelly (1897-1958)—A leader of Minneapolis drivers' union. Secretary-treasurer of Local 544 (1939-41). Indicted in 1941 Minneapolis case but acquitted. Indicted on charge of embezzlement for transferring Local 544 funds from AFL to CIO when membership voted to change affiliation. Served ten months of a one-to-five-year sentence (1943-44).

Preis, Art (1911-1964)—Joined AWP in 1933. Leader of 1934 Toledo Auto-Lite strike. Elected to SWP NC at April 1940 convention. Labor editor of *The Militant* from 1940s until his death.

Reuther, Walter (1907-1970)—A leader of Detroit autoworkers in mid-1930s. Sided with right-wing Hillman faction in CIO in split with John L. Lewis in 1940. Became president of UAW (1946) and of CIO (1952). Participated in merger of AFL and CIO in 1955 but withdrew UAW in 1968.

Rodney—Pseudonym of V.R. Dunne.

Rourke, Walter—One of Trotsky's guard-secretaries in Mexico. He remained at Coyoacan after Trotsky's assassination as a guard and aide for Natalia Sedova.

Sacco, Nicola (1891-1927) and **Bartolomeo Vanzetti** (1888-1927)—Central figures of famous American labor trial. Italian emigrants and anarchists, arrested in April 1920 on trumped-up charges of robbery and murder in Braintree, Massachusetts. Convicted in 1921, their case was appealed and aroused worldwide support and protests. Executed in August 1927.

Scheidemann, Philipp (1865-1939)—Leader of right wing of German Social Democracy. Entered cabinet of Prince Max of Baden in October 1918 and presided with Friedrich Ebert in crushing of German November 1918 revolution. Led Social Democracy in Reichstag until party was suppressed by Nazis in 1933.

Schoenfeld, Oscar (1916-   )—Joined SWP in New York. Received suspended sentence for activity in 1939 Minneapolis WPA strike.

Convicted in 1941 Minneapolis trial. Elected to SWP NC in 1941. Resigned from party in April 1946 to join Shachtman's Workers Party.

Schultz, Henry (1902-1969)—Joined the CLA in Minneapolis in early 1930s. Participated in 1934 strikes. Organizer for electrical workers. Served as guard at Coyoacan in spring 1940. Elected to SWP NC at April 1940 convention. Railroad worker after 1941. Developed differences with SWP and left party in mid-1960s.

Second International—Founded in 1889 as loose association of Social Democratic and labor parties. Included revolutionists and reformists. Strongest section was German Social Democracy. In 1914 most sections supported their own capitalist governments in World War I and the International collapsed. Revived in 1923 as reformist opponent of Third (Communist) International founded in 1919.

Shachtman, Max (1903-1972)—Member of Central Executive Committee of American CP. Expelled with Cannon and Abern in 1928 for Trotskyism. A central leader of the Trotskyist movement until April 1940 when he, Abern, and James Burnham split from SWP to form Workers Party. In 1958 dissolved his organization into SP.

Shliapnikov, Alexander G. (1883-193?)—An Old Bolshevik, member of Central Committee from 1915. First commissar of labor in Soviet government. Leader of Workers' Opposition, a syndicalist tendency in CPSU that opposed the New Economic Policy. Killed by Stalin in purges of 1930s.

Silver Shirts of America—Fascist organization founded in 1932 by William Dudley Pelley and used in antiunion and antiradical vigilante activities throughout 1930s.

Smith—Pseudonym of Farrell Dobbs.

Smith, Howard W. (1883-   )—Democratic member of U.S. House of Representatives from Virginia (1931-67). Author of Alien Registration Act of 1940, known as Smith Act, which sought to outlaw advocacy of socialist revolution.

Social Democrats—Name used by most Marxian socialists affiliated to Second International from its founding in 1889. Synonymous with revolutionary socialism until outbreak of World War I. After Russian Revolution it became a term signifying procapitalist reformism.

Socialist Appeal—Founded by Albert Goldman in Chicago in February 1935 as an internal newsletter of SP left wing. Supported by Trotskyists after their entry into SP in 1936. Moved to New York in August 1937 after expulsion of Trotskyists. Became official newspaper of SWP after party's founding in January 1938. Name changed to *The Militant* in February 1941.

Socialist Labor Party (SLP)—Formed in 1877 when American followers of Ferdinand Lassalle took control of earlier Working Men's Party. Came under leadership of Marxist Daniel De Leon in 1890 who led it until his death in 1914. Deteriorated into moribund sect after founding of Debsian Socialist Party in 1901.

Socialist Party (SP)—Founded in 1901 by Eugene V. Debs. Became mass movement in decade prior to World War I. Left wing supported Russian Revolution of 1917 and split from SP in 1919 to form Communist Party, taking two-thirds of membership. Trotskyists entered SP (1936-37). Declined to small sect after 1937. Split in 1972 into Social Democrats, USA, and Democratic Socialist Organizing Committee.

Socialist Workers Party (SWP)—Trotskyist party founded in Chicago, December 31, 1937-January 3, 1938, by expelled branches of SP.

Socialist Workers Party of Germany—SAP (from its German initials) formed in October 1931 by left-wing expelled members of German Social Democratic Party. In 1933 agreed to work with Left Opposition in forming Fourth International but soon changed its line and remained affiliated to London Bureau.

Social Revolutionaries—Russian populist party. Along with Mensheviks, dominated soviets (workers councils) from February 1917 revolution to September. Right wing of SRs was led by Kerensky. Left wing supported October Revolution and joined Bolsheviks in a common government. Soon moved into opposition, organized terroristic attacks on the Bolsheviks, and was suppressed.

Spiro, George—Known under name George Marlen. Joined CLA in 1933 but left with Oehler in November 1935 in opposition to entry into SP. Broke with Oehler in 1936 and formed Leninist League (1937-46) and later Workers League for a Revolutionary Party (1946-50). Marlenites over time rejected first Stalin, then Trotsky, then Lenin, and finally Marx and Engels.

Stein, Abe—Member of New York Local of SWP during war. Supported Goldman and Morrow in postwar dispute in party. Resigned from SWP with Oscar Schoenfeld in April 1946, one month ahead of Goldman, to join Shachtman's Workers Party.

Stein, Morris—Pseudonym of Morris Lewitt.

Third International—(Also known as Communist International and the Comintern.) Founded by Lenin and Trotsky in 1919 as instrument of world revolution. Transformed into agency of Soviet diplomacy by Stalin in late 1920s. Dissolved in April 1943 as goodwill gesture to Stalin's democratic imperialist allies in World War II.

Thomas, Norman (1884-1968)—Leader of Socialist Party from late 1920s. Six-time presidential candidate on SP ticket between 1928 and 1948.

Tobin, Daniel J. (1875-1955)—President of International Brotherhood of Teamsters (1907-52). Also chairman of Democratic Party's National Labor Committee. Asked Roosevelt to use federal government to defeat his opponents in Minneapolis Teamsters movement, resulting in 1941 indictments under Smith Act against leaders of Minneapolis truck drivers and SWP.

Trainor, Larry (1905-1975)—Joined CLA in 1933. Elected to NC at SWP founding convention in 1938. During war was organizer in Buffalo and Seattle. Organizer of Boston SWP branch in 1950s and 1960s.

Tresca, Carlo (1878-1943)—Well-known Italian-American anarchist, labor leader, and journalist. Served on Dewey Commission of Inquiry into the Moscow Trials. Assassinated in New York.

Turner—Pseudonym of Larry Trainor.

Umansky, Constantine Alexandrovich (1902-1945)—Stalinist diplomat. Soviet ambassador to Washington (1939-41).

van Heijenoort, Jean—French Trotskyist from late 1920s. Was Trotsky's secretary in four countries from 1932 to 1939. During World War II was part of leadership of Fourth International in New York. Supported Goldman and Morrow in dispute with SWP majority in 1945-46 and left Fourth International in 1946. He became a professor of philosophy.

Vanzetti, Bartolomeo—See Sacco.

Vanzler, Joseph (1902-1956)—Joined CLA in 1933. Elected to SWP NC in 1939. Best known under his pen name, John G. Wright, as a translator of Trotsky's works and for many articles on the Soviet Union and on theoretical questions. Remained on SWP writing staff in New York until his death.

Vereecken, Georges—Member of Belgian section of Trotskyist movement in 1930s. Split from section in 1935 out of sectarian opposition to entry into Social Democracy. Rejoined later only to split again in 1938, before founding congress of Fourth International.

Warde, William F.—Pseudonym of George Novack.

Weber, Jack—Joined CLA in early 1930s. Elected to NC of WP in 1934. In 1935-36 supported Abern in bloc with Muste against entry into SP. Broke with Abern in 1936 and sided with Cannon. Left SWP at end of war.

Weisbord, Albert (1900-   )—Expelled from CP in 1929. Founded Communist League of Struggle in 1931, small sectarian group which proclaimed adherence to International Left Opposition. His group was not admitted to membership. He later broke with Marxism and became an organizer for AFL.

Weiss, Murry (1915-   )—Joined CLA in 1932. Elected to SWP NC at 1939 convention. New York organizer for a period in 1939 during Burnham-Shachtman fight, then organizer in Youngstown in early 1940. Leader of Los Angeles branch of SWP through rest of war years. Editor of *The Militant* (1954-56) and of *International Socialist Review* (1959-63).

Weiss, Myra Tanner (1917-   )—Joined WP in 1935. Active in agricultural workers organizing drive in California in late 1930s. Los Angeles SWP branch organizer from 1940. Elected to SWP NC in 1944. Served three times as party's vice-presidential candidate (1952, 1956, and 1960). Withdrew from SWP in late 1960s.

Willkie, Wendell (1892-1944)—Republican nominee for president of U.S. in 1940 elections.

Williams, Oscar—Pseudonym of Oscar Schoenfeld.

Workers Party of the United States—Formed by fusion of

American Workers Party and Communist League of America in December 1934. Dissolved on entrance of Trotskyists into SP in 1936. Also: **Workers Party** formed by Burnham, Shachtman, and Abern after their split form SWP in 1940. Renamed Independent Socialist League (1949). In 1958 it dissolved into SP.

WPA (Works Progress Administration, later redesignated Work Projects Administration)—Established by Roosevelt as public works program to provide federal jobs for unemployed.

Wright, John G. —Pseudonym of Joseph Vanzler.

Zinoviev, Gregory (1883-1936)—Member of Russian Social Democratic Labor Party from 1901. Supported Lenin in split with Mensheviks (1903). After Lenin's death (1924) blocked with Kamenev and Stalin to exclude Trotsky from leadership. Joined Trotsky in Joint Opposition to Stalin (1926-27). Capitulated to Stalin in 1927. Defendant in 1936 Moscow trial. Executed.

NOTES

1. On August 22, 1939, the Soviet Union signed a nonaggression treaty with Nazi Germany, the **Stalin-Hitler pact**. This freed Hitler's hands for the invasion of Poland on September 1, 1939, which marked the beginning of World War II. On September 5, James Burnham submitted a document to the Political Committee of the Socialist Workers Party renouncing defense of the Soviet Union.

2. The **Franco-Soviet nonaggression pact** was announced in Moscow on May 2, 1935. The official communiqué stated that "Mr. Stalin understands and fully approves of the policy of national defense made by France in order to keep its armed strength at the level of security."

3. Cannon is referring to his article "The Struggle for a Proletarian Party," his summation of the fight with Burnham and Shachtman, finished on April 1, 1940, and published in the SWP's internal bulletin. This was later collected with other of Cannon's writings from the 1939-40 fight and published as a book under the same title by Pioneer Publishers in 1943.

4. The movement of **scientific socialism** or Marxism dates from the publication of the *Communist Manifesto* by Karl Marx and Frederick Engels in 1848. Marx's doctrine was elaborated in opposition to various unscientific, petty-bourgeois varieties of socialism advocated by figures such as Robert Owen, Francois Fourier, and Pierre Joseph Proudhon.

5. The **Oehlerites** were an ultraleft sectarian tendency in the American Trotskyist movement formed by Hugo Oehler in October 1934. They rejected Trotsky's proposal of that time for the French Trotskyists to enter the French Socialist Party and were against any extension of this tactic to the United States. They were expelled for acts of indiscipline in October 1935.

6. At the outbreak of World War I in August 1914 the leaders of most of the mass **Social Democratic parties** of Europe, the Marxist movement of its day, capitulated to their capitalist governments and offered them support in the war. Lenin and Trotsky were among those Marxists who denounced the action of the Social Democratic leaders as a betrayal and

called for the formation of a new international working-class organization.

7. **Anarcho-syndicalism** is a tendency in the workers' movement that combines the ideas of anarchism with an orientation toward the trade unions. It rejects both electoral activity and the formation of political parties. It envisions a transition from capitalism to a society without a central government, to be managed by the trade or industrial unions.

8. The reformist socialist parties in Russia after the February 1917 revolution accused Lenin and Trotsky of being paid agents of Germany on the grounds of their opposition to continuing Russian participation in World War I. This became a pretext for an attempt to suppress the Bolsheviks in July 1917 by the Kerensky government during which Trotsky was arrested and Lenin driven into hiding in Finland.

9. After the Moscow trials of the late 1930s in which Stalin had framed up and executed virtually the entire leadership of the Russian Communist Party that had been assembled by Lenin, he sought the death of Leon Trotsky in exile in Mexico. At 4:00 A.M. on the morning of May 24, 1940, a large band of armed men dressed in stolen military and police uniforms broke into Trotsky's house in Coyoacan, a suburb of Mexico City. Led by the Stalinist artist David Alfaro Siqueiros, they machine-gunned Trotsky's bedroom. Trotsky and his wife Natalia Sedova escaped death by taking refuge in an alcove of the darkened room. One of Trotsky's guards, Robert Sheldon Harte of New York, was kidnapped by the Stalinists and murdered. A delegation of SWP leaders went to Mexico shortly after the attack to assess the situation, make plans for reinforcing the guard and fortifying the house, and have a series of political discussions with Trotsky.

10. These **discussions with Trotsky** were held June 12-15, 1940. The SWP members who participated were Cannon, Farrell Dobbs, Sam Gordon, and Antoinette Konikow as well as Trotsky's American secretaries and guards, Joseph Hansen, Charles Cornell and Harold Robins. A rough stenographic transcript of the discussions was published in a June 1940 SWP National Committee bulletin. It is reprinted in *Writings of Leon Trotsky (1939-40)* (Pathfinder Press, 1973).

11. In the late afternoon of August 20, 1940, a Stalinist assassin using the name "Frank Jacson" and posing as a sympathizer of the Fourth International gained access to Trotsky's study on the pretext of inviting Trotsky's criticism of an article he was writing. Alone with Trotsky, he delivered a fatal blow to the head with an ice axe. Mortally wounded, Trotsky wrestled with his assailant who was subdued by Trotsky's guards. Trotsky was taken to a hospital in Mexico City where he died at 7:30 P.M. on August 21.

12. Trotsky's **seven secretaries** killed by the Stalinists were: **Mikhailo Glazman**, the head of Trotsky's secretariat in Russia during the civil war. Hounded by the Stalinists, he committed suicide in 1924. **Georgi V. Butov** was Trotsky's coworker in charge of the Revolutionary

Military Council's secretariat during the civil war. He was arrested for refusing to sign false charges against Trotsky, went on a hunger strike, and died in prison in 1928. **Jakob Blumkin** (1899-1929) had been a Left Social Revolutionary who became a Communist and a GPU official. He edited part of Trotsky's book *How the Revolution Armed Itself.* He was the first Russian supporter of the Left Opposition to visit Trotsky in exile in Turkey. Bringing back a message from Trotsky to the Opposition, he was betrayed to the GPU and shot. **N. Sermuks** was the chief of the military train that was Trotsky's mobile headquarters during the civil war, and a member for several years of Trotsky's secretarial staff. He was expelled with Trotsky from the Communist Party and tried to follow him into banishment at Alma Ata but was arrested, deported, and disappeared in the purges of the 1930s. **I. Poznansky**, another of Trotsky's secretaries, had been in charge of the Red Cavalry during the civil war. He too was arrested and never seen again when he tried to join Trotsky at Alma Ata. **Erwin Wolf**, a Czech, served as Trotsky's secretary in Norway. He was kidnapped and killed by the GPU in Spain in 1937. **Rudolf Klement** (1910-1938) was Trotsky's secretary in exile in Turkey and France. In charge of the committee preparing the founding conference of the Fourth International in 1938, he was murdered by the GPU in Paris shortly before the conference opened. **Robert Sheldon Harte**, kidnapped during the May 24, 1940, machine-gun assault at Coyoacan and later murdered, was the eighth of Trotsky's secretary-guards to die at the hands of the Stalinists.

By his first marriage, to Alexandra Sokolovskaya, Trotsky had two daughters. **Nina Nevelson** died of tuberculosis in June 1928 after her husband had been arrested and deported and she had been reduced to desperate poverty. Her sister **Zinaida Volkova** succeeded in joining the Trotsky family in exile in Turkey in January 1931. She brought with her a son, Vsievolod Volkov, but was forced to leave behind her imprisoned husband and a young daughter. She later moved to Berlin, where she committed suicide in January 1933. Natalia Sedova bore Trotsky two children, Leon and Sergei, who used their mother's last name. **Leon Sedov** was a leader of the Opposition in Paris, where he worked on the Russian-language *Bulletin of the Opposition.* Named along with Trotsky as a defendant in absentia in the Moscow trials, his name stood high on Stalin's death list. Suffering from appendicitis, he entered a Russian hospital in Paris in February 1938. He died under mysterious circumstances following the operation. **Sergei Sedov** was not involved in politics. He studied science at a Soviet university, but was arrested in 1935 and died in a Stalinist concentration camp.

13. This was written by Trotsky during his exile at Alma Ata in answer to the draft program by Stalin and Bukharin submitted to the Sixth World Congress of the Communist International in 1928. It is available in Trotsky's book *The Third International After Lenin* (Pathfinder Press, 1970).

14. Trotsky's **open letter** was written on April 23, 1940, and is published in *Writings 1939-40*.

15. Although Japan had been a signer of the anti-Comintern pact with Germany in 1936 and had invaded China in 1937, it did not formally join the Rome-Berlin military Axis until September 27, 1940.

16. The formal title of this document is the "Manifesto of the Fourth International on the Imperialist War and the Proletarian Revolution." Written by Trotsky, it was adopted by the Emergency Conference of the Fourth International, held May 1940 in New York. It was published in the *Socialist Appeal* of June 29, 1940, and is reprinted in *Writings 1939-40*.

17. Prior to the Stalin-Hitler pact of August 1939 the American CP had had an openly pro-Roosevelt line in keeping with the class-collaborationist People's Front policy adopted by the Comintern in 1935. After the bloc with Hitler the CP avoided criticism of German fascism but at the same time embarked on a "left" course in American domestic politics. Although it became discredited by its new attitude toward Hitler, it made some gains by its apparently more militant stance in trade union matters and in regard to the Roosevelt administration.

18. This was during the June 1940 discussions, reprinted in *Writings 1939-40*.

19. The **German-American Bund** was an American Nazi organization active in the 1930s and early 1940s. The **Coughlinites** were followers of Father Charles E. Coughlin, a Catholic priest in Detroit who was a profascist radio commentator. In February 1939 the SWP called a protest meeting outside Madison Square Garden in New York where the Bund and the Coughlinites had scheduled a rally. More than 50,000 workers turned out to the antifascist demonstration. In August 1939 the Coughlinites had called a march in New York to end with a rally in Union Square. The SWP called a counterdemonstration and the fascist march was canceled.

20. In January 1939 the United Auto Workers split into two factions, one led by Homer Martin, which called a convention in Detroit, and one led by Walter Reuther and the Stalinists, which called a convention in Cleveland. Burnham, who was acting national secretary of the SWP while Cannon was working in France for the Fourth International, proposed to support the Martin forces even though they were headed for a break from the CIO and reintegration into the AFL. His policy was rejected by the party's auto fraction which advocated support to the CIO gathering in Cleveland.

21. Two weeks after the German invasion of Poland, after German troops had encircled Warsaw, Russian troops invaded the country from the east on September 17, 1939. This led to the partition of Poland between Nazi Germany and the Soviet Union. Moscow then demanded territorial concessions from Finland. When these were refused, the Soviet Union bombed Helsinki on November 30, 1939, and sent an invasion force against the Finnish Mannerheim Line. After a series of initial defeats at

the hands of the Finnish army, the Russians staged a massive assault that broke through the defenses. An armistice on Russian terms was signed on March 13, 1940.

22. The Comintern and the American CP abandoned their radical stance the day after the German invasion of the USSR in June 1941. Thereafter they sought alliances with liberal bourgeois politicians in the imperialist democracies and subordinated all class-struggle issues to the campaign to produce for the war effort. In the United States the CP openly supported Roosevelt and advocated a no-strike pledge in industry for the duration of the war.

23. Cannon is quoting here from memory. Trotsky's exact words were: "Yes—in a certain sense—we are proletarian socialist revolutionary militarists. Possibly we should not use it at first. Wait until we are called militarists by Thomas or someone like that, and then make a polemical reply. Thomas has called us militarists. Yes, we can be called militarists in a certain sense. Then we can use it with this explanation" (*Writings 1939-40*, p. 257).

24. The letter Cannon is referring to, dated July 9, 1940, is reprinted in *Writings 1939-40* under the title "On Conscription." The precise wording of the paragraph Cannon quotes from memory is: "I don't see any reason why we should renounce the slogan of a people's referendum on the war. It is a very good slogan to unmask the futility of *their* democracy in such a vital question as the war."

25. In May 1940 Dale Edwards had transferred from New York to Houston, Texas, to aid in the building of the SWP branch there. Disagreements soon arose between Edwards and the National Office over the methods to be used in this work. At the September 9, 1940, meeting of the SWP Political Committee (PC) it was decided to recall Edwards to New York. On September 23 the branch organizer in Houston addressed a letter to the September 27-29 Plenum-Conference to be held in Chicago protesting the decision. The NC in Chicago heard reports from Cannon and Dobbs on the Texas situation and the September 23 letter was read. The NC voted unanimously to uphold the decision of the PC.

26. The **transitional program**, the full title of which is *The Death Agony of Capitalism and the Tasks of the Fourth International*, was written by Trotsky as the basic programmatic document for the founding conference of the Fourth International in 1938. It is reprinted in the book *The Transitional Program for Socialist Revolution* (Pathfinder Press, 1974).

27. Cannon is referring to **Will Herberg**, then a leader of the Lovestone organization who excelled in his denunciations of Trotskyism. Herberg later became a Zionist and author of books on religious sociology.

28. In the summer of 1939 Roosevelt ordered massive layoffs in the Works Progress Administration, the New Deal public works program established to provide jobs for the unemployed. At the same time, hours were lengthened and pay was cut. Some 500,000 of the 2.5 million workers

affected went out in a spontaneous nationwide strike in July. The largest and most effective strike of the WPA workers took place in Minneapolis under the leadership of the Federal Workers Section of Teamsters Local 544. A police attack on massed pickets on July 14 left one worker dead and seventeen wounded. This was followed by grand jury indictments against more than 150 strikers for "conspiracy" to deprive people of employment under the WPA. Three trials held in Minneapolis in October and November resulted in thirty-two convictions. The three longest sentences were handed down against Max Geldman, Ed Palmquist, and Leslie Wachter, who each served one year in the federal penitentiary.

29. This quotation is from Trotsky's unfinished article "Bonapartism, Fascism, and War," dictated shortly before his death. It is reprinted in *Writings 1939-40*.

30. In October 1940 Congress adopted a law sponsored by Representative Jerry Voorhis, a liberal Democrat from California, aimed at outlawing the international cooperation of socialist and working-class parties and groups. The Voorhis Act, still in effect, requires the registration with the U.S. government of any organization "subject to foreign control." This is defined as any group that "is affiliated directly or indirectly with, a foreign government . . . or a political party in a foreign country, or an international political organization." Any organization so defined is required to turn over to the government a list of the names and addresses of all of its members and financial contributors. This list is then to be published by the government, making such people subject to reprisals for their political views by employers or right-wing groups. Failure to comply with the provisions of the law is punishable by up to five years imprisonment and a fine of $10,000.

At its founding convention in January 1938 the SWP was recognized as the American section of the Fourth International and this international affiliation was written into the party constitution, as well as into the party's Declaration of Principles.

Cannon's proposals in this letter were discussed by the delegates to the Fourth (Special) National Convention of the SWP held in New York December 21, 1940. The following motion was passed by the convention on the question of international relations:

"Whereas, federal legislation (the Voorhis Act, etc.) has been adopted by Congress which imposes burdensome requirements on political organizations affiliated to international bodies, including the formal periodic registration of lists of individual members; and

"Whereas, such regulations could be of service only to the enemies of the workers, the Fourth (Special) National Convention of the Socialist Workers Party hereby resolves:

"1. To formally discontinue its affiliation to the Fourth International as of this date.

"2. To continue its struggle for socialism as a completely autonomous party.

"3. While complying with the provisions of the aforesaid legislation, we affirm our opposition to this and any similar measures designed to disrupt the international solidarity of the workers. We assure our cothinkers in other lands that nothing in this decision of compliance with arbitrary discriminatory legislation alters in any way our ardent sympathy with their own struggles for socialism."

The convention voted to amend the party constitution to remove references to international affiliation and to suspend the Declaration of Principles, authorizing the National Committee to prepare a draft of a new one at a future date.

31. This letter shows Cannon's realism in intervening into a complex union situation when the relationship of forces dictated a difficult tactical retreat. His advice—that if forced to choose, leaders of the Minneapolis Teamsters should give up their democratic right to public party membership rather than abandon their union positions—is in sharp contrast to the stance of sectarians who would make this a question of principle. Cannon was at this time in Los Angeles for several weeks. In February 1941 a "Committee of 100" was organized in Minneapolis to mount a red-baiting attack on the leadership of Local 544. On March 21, Daniel J. Tobin, president of the International Brotherhood of Teamsters, intervened on the side of the red-baiters, demanding a conference with Local 544's leaders in Chicago on April 8 to hear the charges against them and to consider placing the local under receivership. The local leadership received solid support from an April 4 meeting of shop stewards referred to by Cannon in his letter. As a result Tobin backed off at the Chicago meeting, postponing until June his attempt to remove the Trotskyists from Local 544.

32. During the first week of June 1941 Tobin summoned a committee of Local 544 leaders to Washington to answer charges of "radicalism" filed against them by the Teamsters International Executive Board. There Tobin asked the local to accept the appointment of a receiver with dictatorial powers. The local rejected this proposal. At a membership meeting of almost 4,000 in Minneapolis on June 9 the union voted to disaffiliate from the AFL and join the CIO under the name Motor Transport and Allied Workers Industrial Union, Local 544-CIO. Tobin immediately wired Roosevelt for help.

Roosevelt responded by ordering FBI raids on the offices of the Twin Cities SWP and of Local 544-CIO. On July 15, 1941, twenty-nine persons were indicted by a federal grand jury in St. Paul under the notorious Smith "Gag" Act on charges of "seditious conspiracy." Those indicted were all prominent leaders of the Minneapolis labor movement or national and local leaders of the SWP.

The twenty-nine, as reported by *The Militant* of July 19, 1941, were:

"James P. Cannon, national secretary, Socialist Workers Party; Farrell Dobbs, national labor secretary, SWP; Felix Morrow, editor, *The Militant*; Albert Goldman, attorney for the SWP; Miles B. Dunne, president, Local

544-CIO; Kelly Postal, secretary-treasurer, Local 544-CIO; Rose Seiler, business agent, Minneapolis Office Workers Union (AFL); V.R. Dunne, organizer, Local 544-CIO; Grace Carlson, Minnesota state organizer, SWP; George Frosig, vice-president, Local 544-CIO; Alfred Russell, former organizer, Teamsters Local 544, Omaha, Nebraska; Oscar Coover, Minneapolis secretary, SWP; Grant Dunne, organizer, Local 544-CIO; Dorothy Schultz, Twin City secretary, Workers Defense League; Carlos Hudson, editor, Local 544-CIO weekly; Walter Hagstrom, organizer, Local 544-CIO; Ray Rainbolt, organizer, Local 544-CIO; Harry DeBoer, organizer, Local 544-CIO; Carl Kuehn, secretary, Federal Workers Section (WPA workers), Local 544; Edward Palmquist, chairman, Federal Workers Section, 544; Harold Swanson, active in Minneapolis labor movement; Oscar Schoenfeld, 1939 WPA strike participant; Clarence Hamel, organizer, Local 544-CIO; Nick Wagner, organizer, Local 544; Roy Orgon, Minneapolis truck driver; Max Geldman, 1939 WPA strike participant; Jake Cooper, Minneapolis truck driver; Emil Hansen, organizer, Local 544-CIO; Carl Skoglund, former president, Local 544-CIO."

33. The **Palmer Raids** were so called after Democratic Attorney General A. Mitchell Palmer. The post-World War I repression culminated in a series of nationwide raids and mass arrests of radicals of all tendencies early in January 1920. Thousands were jailed and hundreds of foreign-born radicals were deported. Civil liberties and due process of law were completely disregarded by federal and local authorities. The newly formed Communist movement was driven into *de facto* illegality and had to begin underground organizations. The repression and the officially induced hysteria against "reds" continued until the Republican administration of Warren G. Harding took office in 1921, when it slowed down and gradually tapered off.

Roosevelt became an ally of Stalin immediately following the German invasion of the Soviet Union in June 1941. Thereafter the American CP abandoned its critical stance toward Roosevelt. In the Minneapolis trial the CP, whose opinion could be taken to represent that of Roosevelt's ally in Moscow, demanded the conviction and imprisonment of the American Trotskyists.

34. The little town of **Verdun** was the center of the principal French fortifications against Germany in World War I. The longest and bloodiest battle of the war was fought there, beginning on February 21, 1916. Two million soldiers were engaged there and of these a million died.

35. In 1937 Stalin ordered a massive **purge of the Red Army**. In May Marshal Tukhachevsky, the actual commander-in-chief, was arrested and executed without trial along with most of the experienced generals. This was followed by the arrest or execution of 25,000 officers, one-third of the total.

36. Cannon is referring to **Sherry Mangan**, an American Trotskyist, who worked as a professional journalist and translator. Mangan

participated in the French Trotskyist underground during World War II until his expulsion from France by the Pétain government. Mangan's articles in *Fourth International* appeared under the pen name Terence Phelan. These were "The End of French Democracy" in the March 1941 issue and "How Paris Fell" in June 1941.

37. **William D. ("Big Bill") Haywood**, secretary-treasurer of the Industrial Workers of the World, was arrested in 1917 on charges of opposing U.S. participation in World War I. He was convicted in 1918 in Chicago in a mass trial of 101 IWW members. He received the stiffest sentence—twenty years. In 1921 while free on appeal he jumped bail and went to the Soviet Union, where he died in 1928.

38. The **Haymarket martyrs** were members of an anarchist organization in Chicago. On May 3, 1886, during the struggle for the eight-hour workday, police killed six pickets participating in a strike at the McCormick reaper plant in Chicago. The following night anarchist trade unionists called a peaceful protest meeting in Haymarket Square. As it adjourned the crowd was attacked by armed police. In the scuffle an unknown person threw a bomb at the police. The police opened fire on the crowd. Seven police and four workers were killed. Immediate arrests were ordered of known radicals and labor leaders.

In the trial that followed no pretense was made of trying to link the defendants to the actions in Haymarket Square. They were convicted for their anarchist ideas. August Spies, Albert Parsons, Adolph Fischer, and George Engel were hanged on November 11, 1887. Louis Lingg committed suicide the day before his scheduled execution. Oscar Neebe, Samuel Fielden, and Michael Schwab were imprisoned until 1893, when they were pardoned by Illinois Governor John P. Altgeld.

Nicola Sacco (1891-1927) and **Bartolomeo Vanzetti** (1888-1927) were members of a small anarchist organization in Massachusetts. They were arrested and framed up on charges of robbery and murder of the paymaster in a shoe-factory payroll robbery in Braintree, Massachusetts, in April 1920. They were tried and convicted in 1921. Their case was appealed and aroused worldwide support. Cannon was secretary of the International Labor Defense, the CP defense organization, which supported the Sacco-Vanzetti case. They lost their appeal and were executed on August 22, 1927.

39. Cannon refers to the "attempt to imprison twenty-eight people." The original indictment had named twenty-nine. One week before this speech, on October 4, 1941, Grant Dunne committed suicide. He had been in failing health for some time and chose not to undergo the ordeal of trial and imprisonment.

40. The **Civil Rights Defense Committee (CRDC)** undertook the legal defense of those indicted in the Minneapolis labor trial and raised money to publicize their case. It won the support of a wide spectrum of labor and intellectual figures. Its officers were James T. Farrell, chairman; John Dos Passos, vice-chairman; and George Novack,

secretary. Its National Committee included such people as Warren K. Billings, John Dewey, W.E.B. Du Bois, Waldo Frank, Mark DeWolfe Howe, Dr. Antoinette Konikow, Mary McCarthy, A.J. Muste, Adam Clayton Powell, Philip Rahv, Meyer Schapiro, Edmund Wilson, and A.L. Wirin.

41. The underground **Communist Party convention of 1923 in Bridgeman, Michigan,** was famous because it was raided by the police. Forewarned, most of the delegates managed to escape but sixteen were arrested. Charles Ruthenberg was sentenced to five years; William Z. Foster was acquitted; the rest of the Bridgeman defendants never came to trial, although their cases were not dropped until 1933.

42. The October 11, 1941, issue of the CP's newspaper, the *Daily Worker*, announced the **withdrawal of the CP's candidate for mayor of New York,** Israel Amter. Amter's campaign had been decided on before Hitler's invasion of the Soviet Union. With the CP's new prowar stance it openly endorsed Mayor Fiorello LaGuardia for a third term, declaring that a victory for LaGuardia would be "a demonstration of national unity behind the policies of President Roosevelt." LaGuardia, who was running with the endorsement of the Republican Party and the American Labor Party, rejected the CP's backing, commenting in a public statement: "I have not sought, I do not seek, and I do not want the support of the Communist Party."

43. **The Chicago mass trial of leaders of the Industrial Workers of the World** in 1918 was part of a government conspiracy to destroy this militant syndicalist labor organization. On September 5, 1917, simultaneous police raids were staged on all known headquarters of the IWW, in which records and literature were seized. Indictments were handed down on September 28 against 166 IWW members in Chicago, and similar indictments were leveled in Sacramento, Wichita, Omaha, San Diego, and other cities. The Chicago trial, which began in April 1918, lasted five months. Charged with "criminal conspiracy," the defendants were found guilty not of overt illegal acts but of holding political views deemed subversive by the court. Convictions were handed down against 101 of the defendants and they were sentenced to terms of up to twenty years. The sentences in this one trial totaled 878 years in prison plus fines of more than $2.5 million. Most of the prisoners served terms of four to five years, being finally released in a general postwar amnesty. It was after this trial that Bill Haywood jumped bail and sought refuge in the Soviet Union.

44. **Lessons of October** was written by Trotsky in 1924, after the death of Lenin, as an introduction to a volume of his collected works for the year 1917. The passage Cannon refers to occurs in the last paragraph. It reads:

"Much has been spoken and written lately on the necessity of 'Bolshevizing' the Comintern. This is a task that cannot be disputed or delayed; it is made particularly urgent after the cruel lessons of Bulgaria and Germany a year ago. Bolshevism is not a doctrine (i.e., not merely a doctrine) but a system of revolutionary training for the proletarian upheaval. What is the Bolshevization of Communist parties? It is giving them such a training, and effecting such a selection of the leading staff as would prevent them from 'drifting' when the hour for their October strikes. 'That is the whole of Hegel, and the wisdom of books, and the meaning of all philosophy. . . .'"

Lessons of October is reprinted in Trotsky's *Challenge of the Left Opposition, 1923-25* (Pathfinder Press, 1975).

45. Entitled "Our Aims and Tactics in the Trade Unions," this speech was first published in the magazine section of the August 2, 1924, *Daily Worker*. It was reprinted in the November 1941 *Fourth International*.

46. **Sidney Hillman,** president of the Amalgamated Clothing Workers, and **John L. Lewis,** president of the United Mine Workers, led opposing factions within the CIO. Both had supported Roosevelt in 1936, but Lewis, displeased with Roosevelt's policies toward organized labor, reverted to his previous Republicanism and supported Wendell Willkie in the 1940 elections. While confining labor's political activity to the capitalist two-party system, Lewis opposed subordination of ordinary trade union rights to the demands of the war. Hillman, on the contrary, served as one of the two codirectors of the Office of Production Management and helped Roosevelt design the National Defense Mediation Board, whose aim was to impose compulsory arbitration in place of strikes.

A sharp clash between Hillman and Lewis took place in June 1941 over the strike of aircraft workers at the North American Aviation plant at Inglewood, California. Roosevelt ordered U.S. troops to break the strike and Hillman supported his action. At a national meeting of CIO representatives in Washington on July 7, Lewis denounced Hillman as a "traitor" who was "standing at Roosevelt's elbow when he signed the order to send troops to stab labor in the back . . ."

A few weeks before Cannon's speech, on September 14, some 53,000 miners went out on strike, demanding a closed shop in the mines. They had returned to work under a thirty-day restraining order from the NDMB at the time of Cannon's speech, but the strike was renewed shortly afterward and by mid-November resulted in a victory for the miners.

47. **Priorities unemployment** was a phenomenon created by the granting of special preference to war industries at the expense of other sectors of the economy, a policy that began before formal U.S. entry into the war. A Super-Priorities Board (SPB) was established in Washington to decide the allocation of government contracts and the use of natural resources and raw materials. Its members included Sidney Hillman, Harry Hopkins, William S. Knudsen, Henry Wallace, and James V. Forrestal. By late 1941 despite the general increase in employment as a result of war spending some 2 million workers faced layoffs as a result of cutbacks imposed by the SPB. Consumer goods were especially hard hit with the biggest cutbacks coming in automobile production.

48. **Harry Bridges,** the leader of the West Coast International

Longshoremen's and Warehousemen's Union (ILWU), was strongly influenced by the Communist Party in the thirties and forties. On several occasions right-wing prosecutions were initiated against him in an effort to deport him to his native Australia. After defeating such an attempt in 1939, he was faced in 1940 with special legislation authorizing his deportation. This was later ruled unconstitutional by the Supreme Court.

Following the Stalin-Hitler pact, **Earl Browder,** then head of the CP, was tried on trumped-up charges of unlawful use of his passport and sentenced to four years in prison, which he began to serve in March 1941. After the German invasion of the Soviet Union in June the CP became prowar and in May 1942 Roosevelt commuted Browder's sentence and he was released.

49. The editors have been unable to identify the person mentioned here as **Serge Evrikoff.** Cannon may have known of him under a pseudonym or an error in transcription may have garbled the name. It is possible that Cannon is referring here to Efraim Sklyansky, who was Trotsky's deputy in the Council of Defense during the Russian civil war, where he worked closely with Lenin. Sklyansky visited the United States in 1925, where he was killed in a boating accident.

50. On December 7, 1941, Japanese planes bombed the American naval base at Pearl Harbor, Hawaii. Congress passed a formal declaration of war the following day. The defendants in the Minneapolis case had gone on trial on October 27. After a month-long trial, eighteen of the twenty-eight were convicted of "seditious conspiracy" under the Smith Act for advocacy of socialist views. All were acquitted of the charge of violating an 1861 law prohibiting overt acts against the government, an admission that the case involved only expression of opinion.

The eighteen were sentenced in Minneapolis on December 8, 1941, the same day that war was declared. Twelve were given sixteen-month sentences; six received prison terms of one year.

With the declaration of war the Espionage Act of 1917, used in the mass prosecution of the IWW in that year, came back into force. As soon as the defendants had returned to New York a special meeting of the Political Committee was called to discuss the party's public response to the declaration of war.

51. The **discussion with Trotsky** Cannon refers to took place on March 23, 1938. A transcript of it under the title "A Summary of Transitional Demands" appears in the second edition of the Trotsky collection *The Transitional Program for Socialist Revolution* (Pathfinder Press, 1974).

52. The March 1936 convention of the Workers Party, the Trotskyist organization at that time, voted to approve a proposal by Cannon and Max Shachtman that the party dissolve in order to enter the Socialist Party of Norman Thomas. An open split had appeared in December 1935 between the right and left wings of the SP and the right wing was in the process of leaving the party. The SP had begun to recruit hundreds of

militant young students and workers who could be expected to be interested in Trotskyist ideas but who had established organizational loyalties to the SP that could not be breached from outside the organization.

The perspective of entry was opposed by the **sectarian faction within the Workers Party led by Hugo Oehler.** In particular Oehler objected to the harsh conditions for entry proposed by Norman Thomas, which prohibited a public Trotskyist newspaper, despite the fact that other groupings within the SP were permitted their own press. Cannon and Shachtman argued that since the WP was not yet a mass party it was incorrect to make the preservation of the form of an independent party or its press an inviolable principle. The entry lasted for a year and ended with the expulsion of the Trotskyists from the SP in the summer of 1937. Throughout this experience the Trotskyists had doubled in size and they took with them a majority of the Young People's Socialist League, the youth organization of the SP.

53. Cannon has in mind here two separate publications, the **Spartacus letters** and the **Junius pamphlet.** Both were issued illegally by the revolutionary wing of the German Social Democracy during World War I in opposition to their party's shameful capitulation to the imperialist war policies of the Kaiser. The Spartacus letters were issued throughout the war, at first in mimeographed form and later printed. They were distributed by an underground network of supporters of the revolutionary movement which became the Spartacus League in November 1918 and was the nucleus of the German Communist Party founded a month later. The leaders of this movement and the principal authors of the letters were Karl Liebknecht, Clara Zetkin, and Rosa Luxemburg. Luxemburg was imprisoned for a year beginning in February 1915 for her antiwar position. While in prison she wrote many of the Spartacus letters and in April 1915 completed the Junius pamphlet, which takes its name from the pseudonym under which it first appeared. The Junius pamphlet is a long document refuting the arguments advanced by the reformist leadership of the German Social Democracy for supporting the war. The text can be found in *Rosa Luxemburg Speaks* (Pathfinder Press, 1970).

54. The minutes of the Political Committee meeting of December 16, 1941, report a point on the agenda headed "magazine policy." At the following meeting, on December 22, Cannon presented the "Statement on the U.S. Entry into World War II" published here. The correspondence that follows, in January and February 1942, indicates that these discussions decided to make a distinction between the weekly agitational newspaper and the monthly theoretical magazine and to risk the magazine's mailing rights in the event of a prosecution while maintaining for the time being the editorial restraint in *The Militant* decided on at the December 10 special meeting of the PC.

55. Early in January 1942 Cannon went to Los Angeles, remaining there until shortly before the plenum of the National Committee held in

New York February 28-March 1. In the first paragraph of Cannon's letter of January 20 to Barr (Farrell Dobbs) he refers to criticism by Munis. Grandizo Munis was at that time a member of the Fourth International who had fought against Franco in the civil war in Spain. In 1942 he was in exile in Mexico. The gist of his criticism was that Cannon and Goldman had failed to advocate revolutionary violence against the bourgeois state as an avowed aim of the socialist movement. His article and Cannon's reply to it are available in an expanded edition of *Socialism on Trial,* the transcript of Cannon's testimony in the Minneapolis trial (Pathfinder Press, 1973).

The letter from Natalia Sedova to Grace Carlson mentioned by Cannon, dated January 6, 1942, aired some of the same criticisms made by Munis. At one point she argued, "In place of conducting an offensive against the jury and the bourgeois judges, we took a defensive position."

56. **Blanquism,** after Louis-August Blanqui (1805-1881), is the theory of armed insurrection by small groups of selected and trained conspirators, as opposed to the Marxist concept of mass action.

57. The **letter of January 24** was from Franklin (Goldman). It read in full:

"At the last club meeting four members expressed dissatisfaction with the policy that we have been following in the newspaper. They are Warde [George Novack], G.C. [George Clarke], [Morris] Stein and young Harry [Braverman].

"The discussion was prolonged and somewhat heated. In view of the discussion I thought it best to write a statement explaining our position. I am sending you a copy of the statement and would like to have your opinion first on the statement itself, and second on the advisability of sending it out to the club executive members [the National Committee] to arm them with the same arguments in case of any dissatisfaction."

58. Cannon is referring to the group of twelve people mentioned in his October 11, 1941, report to the SWP Plenum-Conference in Chicago as having been recruited from the Shachtmanite Workers Party in Los Angeles.

59. Albert Goldman's closing speech to the jury in the Minneapolis case was published in March 1942 as a pamphlet under the title *In Defense of Socialism* with an introduction by Felix Morrow. The phrase about "idol worshippers" does not appear in Morrow's introduction and was evidently deleted before the pamphlet went to press.

60. Cannon had received a copy of Natalia Sedova's letter to Grace Carlson of January 6.

61. **Trotsky's letter** is reprinted in *Writings 1939-40* under the title "How to Defend Ourselves."

62. **"War and the Fourth International"** (published June 10, 1934) is reprinted in *Writings 1933-34* (Pathfinder Press, 1972). **"Learn to Think"** (May 22, 1938) appears in the second edition of *Writings 1937-38.* **Georges Vereecken** was the leader of a sectarian tendency in the

Belgian section of the Fourth International. He opposed the tactic of entry into Social Democratic parties in the mid-1930s. Trotsky wrote a number of articles dealing with Vereecken's positions. A typical example is "Sectarianism, Centrism and the Fourth International" (October 22, 1935) which can be found in *Writings 1935-36.*

63. Morris L. Ernst (1888–) was for many years general counsel for the American Civil Liberties Union in New York. Cannon's files contain Ernst's letter accompanying his original loan to Cannon, dated May 3, 1929. At that time Ernst wrote, "If you don't think you can meet the exact dates that you anticipate for repayment, I hope you will not act like so many other people and get sore at me in the future. I lost more good friends and acquaintances by lending money than by any other process in life." Ernst was a personal friend of Roosevelt and in 1934 tried unsuccessfully to persuade Roosevelt to admit Trotsky to the United States.

64. A mass membership meeting of Teamsters Local 544 had voted on June 9, 1941, to disaffiliate from the AFL Teamsters union and join the CIO. Tobin contested the transfer and went to court to impound the union funds. Kelly Postal, who had succeeded Farrell Dobbs as secretary-treasurer of the local, carried out the democratically arrived at decisions of the membership and established a bank account for the union as a CIO affiliate. For this he was indicted for "embezzlement." It was never charged that he had personally appropriated any union funds, merely that he had acted for the union membership in refusing to turn over the funds to Tobin's agents. He was tried and convicted on April 24, 1942. After exhausting the appeal procedure he went to prison in June 1943 to serve a one-to-five year sentence. He was paroled on May 30, 1944, after serving eleven months.

65. From the beginning of 1940 a number of members of the San Diego SWP branch had been working in the fish canneries. There were at that time five canning plants in the city; the largest was organized by the Cannery Workers Union, CIO, which was then under Stalinist leadership. The other four were organized in a single local under the Seafarers International Union, AFL. The Trotskyists were working in the plants in the SIU local, which had a membership of 1,400.

In the course of their work, several Trotskyists were elected to the executive board of the San Diego SIU local and Pauline Furth, known to her friends by the nickname Fuzzy, was elected secretary-treasurer of the local. On July 27, 1942, Lester Balinger, a member of the local executive board, filed charges against Furth which read as follows:

"I hereby charge Pauline Furth with having political views that owing to the high office that she holds she should be removed from said office." Balinger specifically objected to the SWP's antiwar stand and cited the convictions in the Minneapolis trial as ground for his red-baiting attack. A trial before the full membership was scheduled for August 10. In preparation for this, Pauline Furth drafted a statement which was sent to the SWP National Office in New York along with an explanatory letter from Murry Weiss, a leader of the party in Los Angeles.

Cannon's reference to "Henry" is to Harry Lundeberg, the head of the SIU.

66. At a meeting of the executive board on August 3, prior to the trial, all members supported Furth with the exception of Balinger. At the trial itself some 350 union members, overwhelmingly Chicano, attended. Balinger presented his case, arguing that the SWP was "un-American" and should be excluded from the union for opposing President Roosevelt in time of war. He cited the Minneapolis case as an example of the "illegal" character of the SWP. Furth spoke, first in English and then in Spanish, to the meeting, defending her democratic right to hold socialist views. Balinger was the only one voting for his motion to remove her from office.

In her report to Cannon she raised a related matter that led to an SWP Control Commission investigation in San Diego. The party had recently recruited one Joe Howard, a business agent in the Fisherman's Union, which was linked to the SIU. Howard had revealed internal party discussions of the union situation to Lundeberg and asked for Lundeberg's intervention in the situation. He had also maintained friendly relations with Balinger, passing information to him that was used in the accusations made against Furth, and he had publicly agreed to a suggestion by Balinger that he (Howard) would accept the post of secretary-treasurer if Furth were forced out. A few weeks later, when the employers in two of the fish canneries began circulating a petition among the workers calling on the company to bar Furth from the premises on the grounds of her "un-American" affiliations, Howard advised several workers to sign it (it received less than thirty signatures among 1,400 workers).

67. The **Control Commission** met with Joe Howard during the last week of August. He admitted all the charges. The commission concluded that he was inexperienced in party matters and that he should be given an opportunity to redeem himself. He was offered a six-month probation period during which he would withdraw from his union post and accept reassignment elsewhere by the party. He refused these conditions and was expelled.

In December new elections were held in the fish cannery local and Furth won reelection by a unanimous vote.

68. Cannon's information from China was not correct. **Ch'en Tu-hsiu,** the founder of the Chinese CP and the Chinese Trotskyist movement, developed differences with Trotskyism while in prison. After his release in 1937 he proposed to give uncritical support to the resistance against Japanese imperialism and objected to public criticism of the Kuomintang in wartime. In 1941 he came out for support to the Allies against fascism and renounced defense of the Soviet Union. He was opposed and defeated in the Chinese Trotskyist movement by Peng Shu-tse. Ch'en broke with

Trotskyism after the defeat of his positions at the August 1941 national convention of the Communist League of China. He died in June 1942.

69. The conventions of the Socialist Workers Party following this one have been numbered from the founding of the Trotskyist movement in 1928, not from the founding of the SWP a decade later. Thus while here Cannon refers to the Fifth Convention of the SWP, the next convention, held in November 1944, is counted as the eleventh.

70. Grandizo Munis's criticism of the conduct of the defense in the Minneapolis trial and Cannon's reply were published in an internal bulletin in June 1942 and shortly afterward issued as a pamphlet under the title *Defense Policy in the Minneapolis Trial.* This has since been incorporated in Cannon's book *Socialism on Trial.*

71. The **resolutions of the founding congress of the Fourth International** and the **1940 manifesto of the Emergency Conference** are reprinted in *Documents of the Fourth International: The Formative Years (1933-40)* (Pathfinder Press, 1973). The **1940 manifesto on the fall of France,** the **1941 manifesto on defense of the USSR,** and the **1941 manifesto on China** will appear in a forthcoming second volume of the *Documents of the Fourth International.* The **1940 SWP convention resolution on the Soviet Union** was published in the April 20, 1940, *Socialist Appeal.* The **SWP resolution on proletarian military policy** is included in the collection *Revolutionary Strategy and the Fight Against the Vietnam War* (Education for Socialists Bulletin, SWP, 1975). The SWP's **1941 manifesto on the Soviet-Nazi war** was printed in the June 28, 1941, *Militant.* **Grace Carlson's election statement** was published in the March 7, 1942, *Militant.*

72. The **Indian National Congress,** or the Congress Party, was founded in 1885. In the 1920s under the leadership of Mohandas Gandhi it became a mass movement demanding an end to India's status as a British colony. This was agreed to in principle by Britain in 1947 and formal independence was granted in January 1950. The Congress became the dominant bourgeois party in India after independence, first under Jawaharlal Nehru and later under his daughter, Indira Gandhi.

73. **Trotsky's open letter to the workers of India** (July 25, 1939) is reprinted under the title "India Faced with Imperialist War" in *Writings 1939-40.*

74. In the Detroit branch in 1942 **E. Henry (Ernest Mazey)** was one of the members critical of the party's policy of caution in the unions and in favor of a more aggressive and public activity inside them. Mazey was elected to the NC at the 1944 convention.

75. Mike Bartell, who was a member of the **Workers Party group** that came over to the SWP in Los Angeles, was elected to the NC at the 1944 convention.

76. The **Los Angeles organizer** at this time was Myra Tanner Weiss. She was elected to the NC at the 1944 convention.

77. Cannon and the Political Committee were interested in the

possibility of buying radio time for a series of short socialist lectures. Cannon's proposal was to raise money in a special fund for a series sponsored by *The Militant* in which he would discuss events in the news from the socialist standpoint. During the war, radio censorship was very strict and the political content of such speeches would have to be severely restricted in comparison to what could be published in *The Militant*. The PC had before it the text of a proposed speech by Cannon on the undemocratic character of the poll tax in Southern states. Goldman and Morrow objected that the speech was unacceptable because it did not explicitly call for socialism. The transcript is incomplete, containing only Cannon's remarks and a short statement by Goldman. The radio station—WPAT—in the end refused to sell time to the SWP and the series was not given.

78. In 1932 a sizable group of left-wing miners in Illinois broke from the United Mine Workers Union to form the **Progressive Miners Union.** The editor of the PMU newspaper was a Trotskyist, Gerry Allard. On January 29, 1933, the PMU held a conference in Gillespie, Illinois, to consider the formation of a new national federation of labor in opposition to the AFL—this was before the formation of the CIO. Cannon was one of the invited speakers. He argued that the Progressive Miners had the potential to become a strong local union but did not have the contacts or forces to project becoming the center of a national labor federation. The "hue and cry" against this speech in the CLA was led by Shachtman and Abern.

79. The first discussion of the possibility of buying radio time took place at the November 2, 1942, meeting of the Political Committee, where a motion was passed establishing a committee to investigate the costs.

80. This report to the New York Central Branch was originally supposed to discuss plans for the radio series sponsored by *The Militant*. Shortly before the meeting it was learned that the post office had impounded the November 7 and 14 issues of the paper without notification. This was the beginning of a year-and-a-half struggle for the right to distribute *The Militant* through the mails, an essential requirement for a national newspaper. On December 28, 1942, Attorney General Biddle sent a letter to the postmaster general offering support from the Justice Department for a ruling by the post office revoking *The Militant*'s second-class mailing rights under the Espionage Act of 1917. On January 21, 1943, at a hearing in Washington, post office attorney William C. O'Brien declared, "We are not concerned here with questions of truth or falsity. It does not make any difference if everything *The Militant* said is true."

On March 3, Postmaster General Frank C. Walker, who was also chairman of the Democratic Party National Committee, announced cancellation of the paper's second-class mailing rights. At that time four issues had been destroyed by the post office and others held up for long periods of time.

For the next year *The Militant* was mailed by third- and fourth-class mail, which was slower and more expensive. The post office continued its practice of arbitrary delay and destruction of selected issues of the paper. The supporters of the paper campaigned in the labor movement for an end to the ban. With the exception of the Communist Party, which publicly supported the suppression, most tendencies and many trade unions protested the government's action. On March 7, 1944, *The Militant*'s second-class mailing rights were restored and on March 17 the post office agreed to cease its other restrictions on the circulation of the paper.

81. The **July days** of 1917 began with mass spontaneous demonstrations by Russian workers in Petrograd. The Bolshevik party considered it premature to launch an insurrection and sought to restrain the antigovernment workers. Nevertheless the Kerensky government falsely accused the Bolsheviks of plotting a coup and ordered their suppression.

82. George Breitman was the SWP candidate for U.S. Senator in the 1942 New Jersey elections. As part of the election campaign the socialist campaign committee bought time on radio station WPAT, where Breitman spoke on October 17 and 24 and Cannon spoke October 31. Cannon's speech is reprinted in his book *Speeches for Socialism* (Pathfinder, 1971).

83. **Jean Louis Darlan** was admiral of the French fleet under the profascist Vichy regime of Marshal Pétain. In November 1942 he surrendered Algiers to the Allied invasion forces and was in return made chief of state in French Africa under the Allies. At the time of the Allied invasion in November, Roosevelt sent a letter of assurance to dictator **Franco** of Spain, which held colonies in North Africa. Fascist Spain claimed to be neutral in World War II, but Franco had sent Spanish troops to fight alongside the Nazis in the invasion of the Soviet Union. Roosevelt in his November 1942 letter to Franco declared: "I hope you will accept my full assurance that these moves are in no shape, manner, or form directed against the government or people of Spain or Spanish territory, metropolitan or overseas."

84. **Joseph E. Davies** was U.S. ambassador to the Soviet Union from 1936 to 1938. In 1941, after Hitler's invasion of the USSR, he published the book *Mission to Moscow* purportedly recounting his experiences but in fact serving as a propaganda tract aimed at prettifying the Stalin regime in light of the new alliance between Washington and Moscow. In particular he vouched for the authenticity of the notorious Moscow frame-up trials. Warner Brothers made a film of the book starring Walter Huston which was released with much fanfare in April 1943.

85. The **Spanish Trotskyists** advocated a military bloc with the bourgeois Loyalist government against the fascist insurrection of Francisco Franco in July 1936. They participated in the organization of antifascist workers' militias, particularly in Catalonia. A majority of the Spanish Trotskyist movement had broken from the International Left

Opposition and from Trotsky in September 1935 to form the Workers Party of Marxist Unification (known as the POUM after its Spanish initials). The Trotskyists in Spain after the creation of the POUM were represented by the Bolshevik-Leninist Section which published the newspaper *La Voz leninista*.

86. In his *Struggle for a Proletarian Party* Cannon discusses the role of **Martin Abern**, one of the three founding leaders of the American Trotskyist movement. Abern drew around himself a group of people united solely on their opposition to the "regime" of the party and on no other political basis. The Trotskyists had taken the majority of the Young People's Socialist League, or "Yipsels," with them out of the Socialist Party. But this inexperienced middle-class student group was largely won over to Burnham, Shachtman, and Abern in the 1939-40 dispute and left the Trotskyist movement along with the petty-bourgeois opposition.

87. Carlo Tresca, former leader of the IWW, a close associate of Sacco and Vanzetti, and editor of the New York Italian anarchist newspaper *Il Martello* (The hammer), had long been a friend of Cannon's and they had collaborated together on many civil liberties and labor defense cases. He was assassinated on a New York street corner a few weeks after this letter, on January 11, 1943. It has never been conclusively established whether the murder was committed by Italian gangsters as a favor to Mussolini or by agents of Stalin's GPU in reprisal for Tresca's uncompromising criticism of the repression of workers' rights in the Soviet Union. Among his last letters was Tresca's undated reply to Cannon's note. It read:

"My Dear Jim,

"It was very kind of you to give me an expression of sympathy at a time when I really needed it. Thanks so much, my old pal! Best wishes to you all in the fight for the right to print what is more than fit to print.

"Happy New Year to you, to all.

> "Affectionately yours,
> "Carlo"

88. In addition to the section on Abern in *Struggle for a Proletarian Party*, two articles by Joseph Hansen on Abernism were published in the SWP internal bulletin in 1939 and 1940. They are reprinted in a pamphlet entitled *The Abern Clique* published in the Education for Socialists series put out by the National Education Department of the SWP.

89. The incipient factional situation in the New York Local of the SWP was discussed in the Political Committee at two meetings. At a PC meeting on December 21, it was agreed that Cannon would make an oral report to a general New York membership meeting. In the PC Cannon stated his opinion that the factional opposition to the New York Local leadership had been promoted by a member of the NC, Felix Morrow, but that in the absence of clear-cut political differences he would refrain from mentioning Morrow by name in his report to the ranks.

90. Almost from the moment that the Trotskyist movement was formed

in 1928, sharp differences emerged between Cannon on one side and Shachtman and Abern on the other. Many of the issues were organizational with no clear political content. Shachtman accused Cannon of organizational inefficiency and conservatism and viewed Cannon's search for contacts in the labor movement as nonpolitical and opportunist. Cannon opposed many of Shachtman's organizational proposals as beyond the means of the group and hence irresponsible. He regarded Shachtman as tied to a petty-bourgeois layer in the New York section of the CLA that was incapable of finding its way to real workers and that tried to substitute literary propaganda activity for a genuine communist perspective. The organization came to the point of split in 1933, when Trotsky intervened through a series of letters to effect an organizational compromise until the differences should take on a more political form. Two of these letters are contained in *Writings 1932-33* ("The Situation in the American League," March 7, 1933, and "More on the American Dispute," April 17, 1933). Cannon and Shachtman dissolved their respective factions at this time and worked together until 1939 when Shachtman came out in support of Burnham's revisions of Marxism.

91. On May 15, 1943, the Presidium of the Executive Committee of the Communist International passed a motion for its own dissolution. The official statement did not once mention socialism and the word "Communist" appeared only in the title of the organization. It stated that the purposes for which the Comintern had been formed in 1919 had been accomplished, enumerating these as the need to form "real working-class parties," to defend workers' economic rights, to struggle against fascism and war, and to support the Soviet Union. It called on all supporters of the Comintern "to concentrate their energies on whole-hearted support of an active participation in the war of liberation of the peoples and states of the anti-Hitlerite coalition."

92. The **Paris Commune** was the first workers' government in history. Established on March 28, 1871, after the defeat of the French army in the Franco-Prussian War, it was drowned in blood by the Versailles regime during the week of May 21-28, 1871. Between 20,000 and 30,000 Communards were executed by the bourgeois army after the defeat of the Commune.

93. Cannon was wrong on the name used here. The Left Opposition (Bolshevik-Leninists) did establish itself as an international tendency in 1930, but under the name International Left Opposition. It was only in 1933, after the German CP's shameful capitulation to Hitler had convinced the Trotskyists that a new international would have to be built, that the ILO changed its name to the International Communist League.

94. **Lenin's manifesto on the war**, signed by the Central Committee of the Russian Social Democratic Labor Party, was first published November 1, 1914. It appears in Volume 21 of the English edition of Lenin's *Collected Works* published in Moscow under the title "The War and Russian Social-Democracy."

Zimmerwald and Kienthal, both villages in Switzerland, were the scenes of two antiwar conferences during World War I. The Zimmerwald Conference, in September 1915, brought together thirty-eight delegates from left-wing Social Democratic parties or groups, including Lenin and Trotsky. It issued the famous Zimmerwald Manifesto, written by Trotsky, opposing the imperialist war. The Kienthal Conference took place in April 1916.

95. This speech was given by Cannon during the section of the plenum devoted to the selection of a substitute leadership to take over the administration of the SWP in the event that the appeals of the eighteen defendants convicted in the Minneapolis case should not be upheld. In the course of this discussion both Goldman and Morrow were sharply critical of the "regime" in the party, prefiguring the differences that would lead them after the war to a break with Trotskyism.

96. In the discussion of the Political Committee's draft resolution on international developments in the light of the overthrow of Mussolini in July 1943 after the Allied invasion of Italy, Morrow had submitted extensive amendments, constituting virtually a different document, generally more pessimistic about the prospects for revolution in Europe than the majority resolution. Goldman submitted a smaller number of amendments that sought to bridge the differences, granting at one point that the Italian partisan movement might develop sufficient scope to sweep beyond the confines envisaged for it by the Allied conquerors and the Badoglio regime. The documents of this plenum, including Morrow's minority report and both his and Goldman's amendments to the international resolution, were published in the SWP internal bulletin in 1944.

97. The Akron and Philadelphia branches had written to the National Office in the spring of 1942 requesting information on the right of criticism in the branches. Cannon's replies appear earlier in this book under the heading "Criticism and Discussion of Current Party Policy."

98. **Joseph Hansen's discussion** of "independent thinkers" appears in his December 1, 1939, article "Organizational Methods and Political Principles," included in the pamphlet *The Abern Clique*.

99. **Cannon's letter**, dated October 26, 1939, was addressed to Joseph Hansen, then Trotsky's secretary. It appears on page 96 of *The Struggle for a Proletarian Party*.

100. At the 1903 conference in exile of the Russian Social Democratic Labor Party where the split took place between the Bolsheviks (majority) and the Mensheviks (minority), Trotsky opposed Lenin, criticizing his allegedly authoritarian regime. Trotsky maintained an independent position between the two factions, although on most political questions he stood closer to the Bolsheviks. He joined the Bolsheviks in August 1917, four months after his return to Russia, and was immediately placed on the Central Committee.

101. In **March 1921** the German CP called for an armed insurrection

to seize power. This disastrous putsch was motivated not by an estimation that a mass revolutionary situation existed but by the erroneous "theory of the offensive" put forward by Bukharin who was then in his ultraleft period. The action was sharply criticized at the Third Comintern Congress by Lenin and Trotsky who counterposed to the "theory of the offensive" the slogan "To the masses!"

Paul Levi, a cothinker of Rosa Luxemburg, became head of the German CP after her assassination. He opposed the March 1921 action, but was outvoted by the Central Committee. Lenin at first supported Levi, who was expelled for violations of party discipline after March. In a letter to the Jena Conference of the German CP, which met in late August 1921, Lenin wrote, "I defended and had to defend Levi insofar as I saw before me opponents who merely shouted about 'Menshevism' and 'Centrism' and refused to see the mistakes of the March action and the need to explain and correct them." ("A Letter to the German Communists," August 14, 1921, in Lenin's *Collected Works*, Moscow edition, volume 32, page 517.)

Lenin became convinced that Levi's opposition to the March action stemmed from opportunist rather than revolutionary considerations. This led Lenin to support Levi's expulsion for violation of party discipline.

102. Cannon was wrong here. Three books by SWP members preceded his. These were *Behind the Moscow Trial* by Max Shachtman (1936); *Revolution and Counterrevolution in Spain* by Felix Morrow (1938); and *Maritime* by Frederick J. Lang (Frank Lovell) (1943).

103. **"The War and Bureaucratic Conservatism"** was the document presenting the organizational platform of the Burnham-Shachtman-Abern minority. It is included as an appendix to Cannon's book, and the opening essay, "The Struggle for a Proletarian Party," is a point-by-point refutation of it.

104. **Van A. Bittner** had been a top official of the United Mine Workers and a chief lieutenant of John L. Lewis from the 1920s. Lewis had publicly broken with Roosevelt in January 1940, but in October he announced his alternative as a vote for Willkie. He added that he would resign as CIO president if Roosevelt were reelected, which he did at the November 1940 CIO convention, two weeks after the election. Bittner went over to the Roosevelt camp at this time.

105. Felix Morrow had studied philosophy under John Dewey at Columbia University and did not accept dialectical materialism, the philosophical method of Marxism. He had been asked by the Political Committee to write the introduction to *In Defense of Marxism* (1942), Trotsky's writings on the 1939-40 fight with Burnham and Shachtman in which Burnham's rejection of dialectics was an important issue. When Morrow refused to include a section in the introduction on Burnham's philosophical method the assignment was withdrawn and the introduction that was published in the book was written by George Novack and Joseph Hansen.

106. Grace Carlson had been an active supporter of the Catholic Church before joining the Trotskyist movement in 1936. In 1952, in the midst of the McCarthyite witch-hunt, she broke with socialism and returned to the church. Cannon writes about her defection in his article "How We Won Grace Carlson and How We Lost Her" in his *Notebook of an Agitator.*

107. Shachtman was the CLA delegate to the April 1930 meeting in Paris where the International Left Opposition was established. Thereafter he became the League's representative to the International Secretariat of the ILO. While in Europe in 1931 and again in 1932 he came into conflict with Trotsky by supporting minorities in the French and German sections and soliciting the support of Andrés Nin of the Spanish section for this course. Numerous letters by Trotsky on Shachtman's activities in Europe can be found in the *Writings* for 1930-31, 1932, and 1932-33. The letter to Glotzer that Cannon mentions has not been located, though a copy may exist in the closed section of the Trotsky Archives at Harvard University which will be made public in 1980.

108. **Marc Loris** was a pseudonym used by Jean van Heijenoort, one of Trotsky's secretaries, who came to New York in November 1939 and took on responsibilities in the International Secretariat of the Fourth International which had been transferred to New York after the outbreak of war in Europe. Goldman placed a motion on the floor of the plenum to delay for one day the report on the international situation for Loris's convenience. The motion was defeated. Loris supported Goldman and Morrow in the dispute that was to break out in the SWP after the war.

109. The Supreme Court refused to hear an appeal of the Minneapolis convictions and on November 23 the defendants received a notice to surrender within thirty days. On New Year's Eve, December 31, 1943, the eighteen began their sentences in federal penitentiaries. Cannon, Cooper, Coover, DeBoer, Dobbs, Dunne, Geldman, Goldman, Hamel, Emil Hansen, Hudson, Morrow, Palmquist, and Skoglund served their time at Sandstone penitentiary in Minnesota; Grace Carlson was imprisoned at Alderson, West Virginia; and Kuehn, Russell, and Schoenfeld were incarcerated in Danbury, Connecticut.

INDEX

Entries from the glossary included in this index are identified by the letter "g" after the page number. Entries from the notes are identified by the letter "n."

Abern, Martin, 19, 372-74, 384, 397g, 429n, 431n, 432n; and cliquism, 309, 324
Adams. See Schultz, Henry
Adler, Al, 188, 397g
Aesopian language, 283-84
Amalgamated Clothing Workers Union, 313, 422n
American Labor Party (ALP, New York), 306, 312-13, 316-17, 397g, 421n
American Workers Party (AWP), 308-09, 314, 397g
Anarcho-syndicalism, 44, 174, 413n
Antimilitarism, 99

Balinger, Lester, 426-27n
Barkley, Alben, 158-59, 397g
Barr. See Dobbs
Bartell, Mike, 428n
Beidel, Lydia, 271, 356, 358, 397g
Biddle, Francis, 390, 397g; and FBI harassment of SWP, 147, 292-93; and indictment of SWP leaders, 165, 170-71; instigates post office harassment of The Militant, 25, 429n; professes support for civil liberties, 296
Billings, Warren K., 421n
Birchman, Robert L., 102
Bittner, Van A., 374, 434n

Blanqui, Louis-August, 211, 425n
Blum, Leon, 77, 397g
Blumkin, Jakob, 414n
Bolshevik-Leninist Party of India, 264
Bolshevik-Leninist Section (Spain), 431n
Bolshevik party, 247-48, 281, 344, 386, 397g, 430n; underground experience of, 172-73; legal press of, 281-84. See also Lenin; Trotsky
Bolsheviks and the World War (Gankin and Fisher), 217, 248
Braverman, Harry (pseud. Harry Frankel), 398g, 425n
Breitman, George, 367-68, 398g, as candidate for U.S. Senate, 173, 289, 430n; as editor of The Militant, 282, 376; and National Committee, 269
Bridges, Harry, 20, 188, 398g, 422-23n
British Labour Party, 316
Browder, Earl, 20, 89, 94, 188, 336, 398g, 423n; Trotsky proposes electoral support of, 85-86, 363
Brown, John, 394, 398g
Brown, Watson, 394
Bukharin, Nikolai, 434n
Bulletin of the Opposition (Biulle-